VICO AND CONTEMPORARY THOUGHT

EDITED BY

GIORGIO TAGLIACOZZO
MICHAEL MOONEY
DONALD PHILLIP VERENE

and
for the first time in English translation
Vico's essay
ON THE HEROIC MIND

VICO
AND
CONTEMPORARY
THOUGHT

HUMANITIES PRESS

ATLANTIC HIGHLANDS, N.J.

Reprinted from *Social Research,* an international quarterly of the Social Sciences, Volume 43, Numbers 3 & 4, 1976.

Published in book form 1979 in the United States of America by Humanities Press Inc. with permission of the editors of the journal and the Graduate Faculty of The New School for Social Research.

Cataloging in Publication Data

Conference on Vico and Contemporary Thought, New York, 1976.
Vico and Contemporary Thought.

"Reprinted from Social research, Autumn 1976 and Winter 1976."
Consists of papers originally presented at the conference held in New York City, Jan. 27-31, 1976; sponsored by the Institute for Vico Studies, in association with the Casa Italiana of Columbia University and the Graduate Faculty of the New School for Social Research.
 1. Psychology—Congresses. 2. Sociology—Congresses. 3. Vico, Giovanni Battista, 1668-1743 —Congresses. I. Tagliacozzo, Giorgio. II. Mooney, Michael. III. Verene, Donald Phillip, 1937— IV. Institute for Vico Studies. V. Columbia University, Casa Italiana. VI. New York (City). New School for Social Research. Graduate Faculty of Political and Social Science. VII. Social research. VIII. Title.
BF41.066 1976 150 78-15669
ISBN 0-391-00911-7

Printed in the United States of America

VICO AND CONTEMPORARY THOUGHT—1

Table of Contents

Introductory Remarks

BY GIORGIO TAGLIACOZZO

It is for me not merely an honor, but a source of deep personal satisfaction, to be able to welcome you to this conference on Vico and contemporary thought. For it is a conference of an unusual and perhaps unprecedented type. Why this is so, and why the meeting has such significance, I shall try to make clear in a moment. But first I should explain how this meeting came about and how it relates to the Institute for Vico Studies.

Institute and Centro

The Institute for Vico Studies was founded in 1974. Its founding was an outgrowth of my long-standing fascination with Vico and of my growing conviction that among seminal thinkers in the history of Western thought he has a special significance for today. The Institute has for its purpose to further not only the study of Vico but also the development of new ideas and perspectives in the spirit of his thought. As part of this purpose, it aims to be an agency through which scholars both within and beyond the United States can be brought together either because of their interest in Vico himself or because their own thought embodies ideas analogous to those of Vico.

In this sense, the Institute is a counterpart of the *Centro di Studi Vichiani* in Naples, whose representative, Professor Gustavo Costa, we are pleased to have with us for this meeting. As the *Centro* in Naples is the guiding force for editing Vico's texts and studying the historical context of his thought, so it is the aim of our Institute to promote the study of Vico for contemporary scholarly endeavors. Hence it is fitting, I believe, that Vico, the philosopher of humanness and the creator of a "science of humanity," should also find a home outside his native land, and that this home should be New York. New York is in many ways the cultural capital of the world, the crossroad of cultural differences and competing ideologies, the embodiment of cosmopolitanism. This conference, then, as the first of the formal endeavors of the Institute, brings Vico to New York in a special way and initiates what I hope will be an ongoing effort to assess the importance of his thought for contemporary work in the humanities and social sciences.

It also seems fitting that two of New York's great centers of learning should sponsor the two parts of this conference: the Casa Italiana of Columbia University, long eminent as an American center of Italian humanistic studies, is the sponsor of the humanities portion of our meeting; and the Graduate Faculty of the New School for Social Research, known widely for its tradition of hospitality to foreign scholars and its openness to new ideas of all origins, is the sponsor of the social science portion. I wish to thank these distinguished institutions for their splendid cooperation in helping to organize this meeting and to express my personal hope that the Institute may continue its collaboration with them.

A Pioneer of Things to Come

In several ways this conference is an unprecedented event. It is the first meeting of such a nature and scope to be held on Vico's thought on the American continent. Indeed, it is one of the very few meetings of size to be held anywhere on his thought. No previous conference has brought together so many scholars from so many fields of knowledge to examine Vico's ideas. The very breadth of disciplines represented here is indicative of the universal character of his thought and suggests that it may well have the power to integrate many areas of contemporary investigation. For few figures in the history of thought could such a claim be made. The question may be raised, in fact, whether any other single thinker could, in our day and age, attract representatives of so many disciplines and provide a basis for their interaction.

What accounts for this power of attraction? The simplest answer is that Vico was a man of wide interests and broad learning —one of the last great polymaths before the knowledge explosion and subsequent specialization of the late eighteenth and the nineteenth centuries. Another is that he was a scholar of limited but significant influence—a half-forgotten giant of the Enlightenment. More likely, and certainly more frequently heard, is that he was a powerful forerunner—a precursor of great ideas and modes of thought that would arise only in the nineteenth century or in our own.

Now, there is doubtlessly truth in all these claims, and I expect that we will find each supported in many fascinating ways in the course of this meeting. As we set about our work, however, I wish to offer a suggestion—call it a warning, if you like—about the way in which we should speak of Vico and to advance a somewhat immodest thesis as to his significance for contemporary scholarship. My concerns can be stated in three propositions: (1) that Vico should only with great caution, and perhaps not at all, be called a "forerunner" of later thinkers and their ideas; (2) that the "true" Vico has been practically without influence until the present; and (3) that Vico's importance is rather that of a pioneer of things to come, of what the humanities and social sciences in our age and the next can and should accomplish. Let me explain.

Although there are obvious parallels between certain of Vico's ideas and those worked out in the disciplines of our day, it is misleading—and possibly unfair—to speak of Vico in such instances as a *forerunner,* as though his achievement was to have expressed in *proto*form ideas that acquired full stature in a later day. Many resemblances, first of all, are purely coincidental. But even those ideas that are properly related are most frequently terms of a false comparison: for what in later thinkers are products of a professional specialty, the accomplishment of a lifetime devoted to a single problem—I am thinking, for example, of the linguistics of Wilhelm von Humboldt or the developmental psychology of Jean Piaget—such ideas in Vico are but corollaries of a seamless philosophical system, mere spokes extending from a philosophical "hub" related to many other spokes and to the wheel as a whole. In being hailed as a forerunner, therefore, Vico is in fact *disadvantaged*—and doubly so. Not only is he faulted, by implication, for not having developed an idea more fully than he did, but the very novelty of a suggestion is frequently missed because it is dislodged from his total vision and treated in isolation from other equally essential ideas. Is it not possible that the aggregate of his ideas—his total vision—is more important than any or all of his discoveries taken separately? Similarly, is it not possible that the fully developed ideas of later authors, however brilliant, are caught up in some philosophical limbo, denied a greater glory because they are deprived of a philosophical fullness that Vico's thought enjoys?

The question becomes more insistent when we reflect that Vico left no intellectual progeny, inspired no truly Vichian school. Indeed, a number of highly original thinkers in the last century and our own—most notably Croce—have claimed him as an ancestor. But we now recognize that most of those who have sought to appropriate his thought have actually disemboweled it, so as to invoke his authority to support their side in an ideological battle. On the other hand, we are beginning to assemble evidence that, to a degree greater than we had suspected, his contemporaries throughout the Continent and in England were influenced, though usually indirectly, by many of his ideas. It was all to no avail, however. Borrowed piecemeal from his works and passed about like playthings from author to author, the ideas were frequently misunderstood and almost always misapplied. One is reminded of the children's game "Telephone," in which a message is whispered from child to child only to reach the last ear in the most grotesque of forms.

The Value of the Imagination

Our situation, then, is this: We know, and continue to discover, how much Vico used and transformed ancient traditions of thought reaching back even to the pre-Socratics. We know, and continue to discover, how much more influential, directly and indirectly, his thought was in the England, France, and Germany of his day than we had previously realized. We know of, and continue to discover, striking resemblances—true or apparent— between his ideas and countless developments in various disciplines of our day. The time has come, I believe, for us to ask whether the thought of Vico as a whole—as an integral philosophical system with its sundry corollaries—has relevance for what we are doing today.

Let me be blunt: However impressive the many ideas our age has brought forth on the nature and development of man and society, are they not in the end a chaos of rootless, isolated, incomplete, at times conflicting pieces, needing correction, direction, and a basic philosophical unity? Until not long ago—deep in our own century, in fact—the problem of philosophical coherence seemed solved: a tradition of thought arising with Descartes and Locke, continuing in new dress during the Enlightenment, and leading in our day to logical positivism and much of linguistic analysis, appeared to have settled the question of the human mind and its powers and to have marked off a course— the only course, in fact—for the progress of knowledge. In our own day, however, due in large measure to a number of advances made independently in various humanistic and social-scientific disciplines, this approach to the human spirit and its endeavors has been seriously challenged. However indispensable it may be

for the illumination of the logical faculties of man, it is unable
to satisfy our renewed concern for understanding particularly the
noncognitive—the imagination, the will, the sensuous, the creative, the aesthetic. We feel the need today to see such forms of
human spirituality not simply as support systems for our cognitive activity but as elements as fundamental to our nature as
reason itself and as equally constitutive of our social and cultural
life. We know that Cartesianism and its many variants cannot
afford the integration we require; and yet we are without a
synthesis.

Is it possible that the thought of Giambattista Vico, taken as
an integral whole, can furnish a new start for the humanities and
the social sciences by providing a philosophically sound framework in which to order their many advances of the last one hundred years? This is a bold suggestion, I know, but one I consider
defensible. By asserting the value of the imagination, Vico begins
with an insight into the noncognitive faculties of man. The multiple activities which imagination generates are not taken to be
secondary or protoforms of the rational. On Vico's terms, the
mind can be understood in all its complexity and can be seen as
the basis for a truly genetic understanding of the human world.
Vico can account for the unity of knowledge and culture because
he returns to the origins of the human world and finds in its
original state the principles that unify the mind and its life. There
are, of course, a host of contemporary thinkers concerned to understand mind, society, and culture in such categories of wholeness and development and to this extent they share Vico's perspective: one cannot read the works of such figures as Freud,
Husserl, Cassirer, Piaget, or Lévi-Strauss without noticing how
many ideas forged in response to contemporary problems in various fields of inquiry have affinities with those formulated by Vico
in his *New Science*. Almost instinctively one thinks of such
thinkers as extensions of the various spokes within Vico's wheel.

But this same image makes clear to us a choice we must make:
either we can continue marveling at the separate spokes and carry

on with our praise of Vico as a great precursor; or we can come to see the spokes as scattered and dispersed, as unassembled parts of a hubless wheel, and begin to consider Vico as the pioneer of a bold and still viable, if not fully accomplished, integrating vision of man and his culture. A precursor can be acknowledged, then forgotten. An influence can be thanked, then passed by. But a pioneer must be continually reckoned with as the holder of an original vision. His thought is a veritable fountainhead, a source to which one must return again and again and contend with anew. My hope, of course, is that we will choose to think of Vico in this latter way and that in doing so we will in some small way begin to revitalize humanistic and social-scientific studies. I consider this hope anything but groundless, for the need so widely felt today to recast much of social thinking in humanistic terms and the need of humanistic thought for a comprehensive theory of man are, to my mind, variations on themes already present in the *New Science*. It is this work, of course, first published by Vico in 1725, that our conference specifically celebrates.

This is the hope that has motivated me in bringing us together. I expressed this hope in the applications I made to our funding agencies—the National Endowment for the Humanities, the Rockefeller Foundation, the American Council of Learned Societies. It is an indication at least of their common realization of a need for some unity in our knowledge, if not necessarily of their confidence in Vico's ability to provide it, that they should have so readily given their support. In each case it has been a form of support that has gone beyond the level of mere funding to the more subtle reaches of personal encouragement and genuine excitement. While I can now express my own thanks to the officers of these invaluable agencies, a far richer gratitude, I know, will be embodied in the stimulating presentations at this meeting and in the train of events which the conference should set in motion.

I have one final thing to say that lies close to my heart. When Charles of Bourbon arrived in Naples as its new king in 1734, it was Vico's task as Professor of Eloquence to offer the University's formal greetings. At the close of his remarks he spoke of how honored he was by the occasion, for some thirty years before he had paid similar tribute to Charles's father, Philip V of Spain, when he visited the city as king.[1] If I cannot pretend to Vico's eloquence, I can pretend to his privilege. For as I look this evening first to the podium and then to my audience, I am made aware of my honor to greet, not two generations of royalty, but two generations of scholars, gathered at one time and in one place to explore the thought of Vico. To the first generation I say with Vico, *"O scientissimi doctores!"* and to the second, again with Vico, *"O pulcherrimae spei adolescentes!"* And to both of you, and to all our guests, I say, *"Benvenuti!"*

---

[1] Giambattista Vico, *Scritti vari e pagine sparse,* edited by Fausto Nicolini (Bari: Laterza, 1940), pp. 179–180.

What Has Vico to Say to Philosophers of Today?

BY MAX H. FISCH

W HAT has Vico to say to philosophers of today? It would be presumptuous of me to offer a short answer this evening to a question that will receive several longer answers tomorrow. Moreover, what Vico has to say to philosophers is in large part what he is already saying to anthropologists, sociologists, psychologists, linguists, and educationists, so that it is not only tomorrow's sessions but the entire conference that is to answer my question. My function this evening is only to introduce the question, to explicate or unfold it, to urge you to carry it with you throughout the conference, and to invite your thoughtful and critical atten tion to the answers the conference will propose or suggest.

As you will have assumed, my title is short and colloquial for something too complicated to be put into nine words. I mean in the first place what philosophers would be likely now to understand Vico as saying to them if their attention were drawn to his writings, or to extensive quotations from them in the writings of his best recent interpreters. And since it is the *New Science* whose 250th anniversary we are celebrating, I mean primarily what he has to say to them in that work, in one or another of its three editions. I do not assume that they would in all or even in most cases find what he says convincing, but only that they would find much of it important and relevant to some of their present concerns, and think it worth their while to come to terms with it.

What Vico in this sense has to say to a given individual philosopher today depends on what that philosopher is now ready to hear him say, and that depends on what the live questions now are for that philosopher, and that in turn depends in large part on the unique route of occasions that has brought that philosopher to Vico.

Though my concern is rather with philosophers in general at present, I begin by offering an example from the past of how one philosopher was brought to Vico by such a unique route of occasions, and what he then understood Vico to be saying to him.

Fifty years ago our philosopher was casting about for a topic for a doctoral dissertation. He had been brought up to think that in order to do philosophy intelligently one needed to be well grounded in the history of philosophy from the Greeks onward, and also in the history of the other chief elements in our intellectual tradition. He took these to be Jewish, Christian, and Islamic religious thought from the Old and New Testaments onward; the physical and biological sciences, including medicine; and Roman law. He was already well grounded in the history of philosophy and of religious thought. He had some acquaintance with the history of science and expected that to be a lifelong concern. But he was still ignorant of Roman law, and foresaw no future occasion or opportunity for studying it. So he began looking for a dissertation topic that would take him in that direction. There was some discussion at that time of the influence of Greek rhetoric and of Greek philosophy, and especially of Stoicism, upon Roman law. There seemed to be ample room for a more thorough study of the influence of Stoicism than had yet been made, so he settled on that. The dissertation took him two years longer than he had expected, but he received his degree in 1930.[1]

For several years thereafter he worked away at the revision of

[1] Max H. Fisch, *Stoicism and Roman Law*, unpublished Ph.D. thesis, Cornell University, 1930.

his thesis for publication. Its chief weaknesses, he thought, were due to the inadequacy of his grasp of Roman law. So he was continually searching both for detailed studies of it and for general interpretations of more than common originality and depth. Eventually he came upon Vico's *Universal Law* and *New Science*. He was soon sure he had reached the end of the line. Further searching would turn up nothing deeper or more original. But the *Universal Law* was in difficult Latin and the *New Science* in equally difficult Italian. There were no English translations, and those into other languages were of little help. The one thing that was clear almost from the beginning was that if Vico was right the dissertation had been misconceived and should be completely abandoned. Instead of deriving Roman law in part from Greek philosophy, Vico derived Greek philosophy from Greek law; or, more exactly, he derived the logic, metaphysics, and ethics of Socrates, Plato, and Aristotle from the disputations of the Athenian marketplace, assembly, and courts: first, popular government, he said; then laws; then philosophy.[2] Roman law, like Greek law, was an indigenous growth, and the borrowings our philosopher had made so much of, if real at all, were late and insubstantial.

From the easier Latin of Vico's earlier writings, however, it appeared that, like our philosopher, he had started out as an unconscious diffusionist and that he had only gradually become the multilinear evolutionist of the *New Science*. How had the transition come about? The best plan would be to master first Vico's last and greatest achievement, the *New Science*, and work back from that. And the surest way to mastery would be to make

---

[2] Giambattista Vico, *Scienza nuova*, 3rd ed. (1744), par. 1043 as numbered in Fausto Nicolini's editions and in *The New Science of Giambattista Vico* (hereinafter *NS*), translated by Thomas G. Bergin and Max H. Fisch (Ithaca: Cornell University Press, 1968). Max H. Fisch, "Vico on Roman Law," in Milton R. Konvitz and Arthur E. Murphy, eds., *Essays in Political Theory: Presented to George H. Sabine* (Ithaca: Cornell University Press, 1948), pp. 62–88, at 84–86. A somewhat similar view of the relation between law and pragmatism is suggested in Max H. Fisch, "Justice Holmes, the Prediction Theory of Law, and Pragmatism," *Journal of Philosophy* 39 (1942): 85–97, at 94 and in n. 22.

one's own translation, as carefully as if for publication. So, on sabbatical in Italy in 1939, our philosopher consulted the leading Vico scholars, Nicolini and Croce. They knew of no English translation in preparation and encouraged our philosopher to undertake it. He enlisted the collaboration of a friend who was a professor of Romance languages. That friend joined him in Naples and they began their translation on Capri in June, 1939. They showed their results to Nicolini and Croce and were encouraged to proceed.

In sum, what Vico began by saying to that philosopher was: "You are an unconscious diffusionist. So was I at first. You think that diffusion proceeds even from high philosophy. So did I at first. I now hold to the hypothesis of multiple independent origins and multilinear evolution, with philosophy developing late in every line. Let me tell you why." [3]

Though every philosopher who comes to Vico at all comes by a route of occasions as unique as this, the single example must suffice, and I turn now to some more general features of the philosophic scene today that make it probable that more philosophers than at any time in the past will be asking themselves what Vico has to say to them.

In English-speaking countries, the dominant philosophical movement of the last generation or two has been the one variously called "ordinary language philosophy," "analytic philosophy," "linguistic analysis," and "Oxford analysis." Its basic assumption is that, as Charles Peirce put it a little over a century ago, "all thought is in signs." [4] Thinking is not something that we do without words or other signs and then express in words or other signs to communicate it to another person or to ourselves at a later

[3] Further details in Max H. Fisch, "The Philosophy of History: A Dialogue," *Philosophy (Tetsugaku)* 36 (1959): 149–170, reprinted in Richard Tursman, ed., *Studies in Philosophy and in the History of Science: Essays in Honor of Max Fisch* (Lawrence, Kans.: Coronado Press, 1970), pp. 193–206.

[4] C. S. Peirce, "Questions Concerning Certain Faculties Claimed for Man," *Journal of Speculative Philosophy* 2 (1868): 103–114, at 111–112; *Collected Papers of Charles Sanders Peirce*, edited by Charles Hartshorne, Paul Weiss, and Arthur Burks, 8 vols. (Cambridge: Harvard University Press, 1931–38), 5: pars. 250–253.

time. Language is not merely *a* medium for the communication of thought but is *the* medium of thought itself. So in analyzing the way we use words and other signs, we are analyzing not an optional mode of transmission of thought but thought itself.

Analytic philosophy no longer dominates the philosophic scene as it did, but it is still flourishing. And now philosophy is being driven to concern itself with language in another and different way by the rapid expansion both of linguistics and of semiotics, the general theory of signs. And philosophers can scarcely concentrate for long on the study of language without more of them having their attention drawn to Vico, one of the greatest philosophers of language, in some respects perhaps the greatest.

At this point I imagine Vico saying to us: "I applaud your attention to language, but why do you present-day philosophers give it so little study as a developing social institution, and why do you give so little study to other institutions and to the fashioning of a critic of institutions in general?" [5]

Neither analytic philosophy nor any of the other recent movements has held the history of philosophy in high esteem. The living philosopher of greatest repute is supposed to have said: "There are two reasons why a person is attracted to philosophy: one is because he is interested in *philosophy*—and the other is because he is interested in the *history* of philosophy." [6] We seem in fact to have lived through and to be emerging from a period in the middle of the twentieth century in which to devote oneself to the history of philosophy was to confess oneself not quite a philosopher, and even to take an excursion into the history of philosophy was to take time out from philosophy itself, and to run the risk of becoming a dropout from philosophy. If indeed

[5] Max H. Fisch, "The Critic of Institutions," *Proceedings and Addresses of the American Philosophical Association* 29 (1956): 42–56, reprinted in Tursman, *Studies in Philosophy*, pp. 182–192, and in Charles J. Bontempo and S. Jack Odell, eds., *The Owl of Minerva: Philosophers on Philosophy* (New York: McGraw-Hill, 1975), pp. 135–151.

[6] Frederick Suppe, ed., *The Structure of Scientific Theories* (Urbana: University of Illinois Press, 1974), p. 310, n. 10.

that period has passed, or is beginning to pass, one obstacle to philosophers hearing what Vico has to say to them will have ceased or greatly diminished.

Taking the history of philosophy seriously again may bring us to Vico not only as one of the philosophers it treats of, but to Vico as one of the philosophers who treat of it. Not that Vico ever wrote a history of philosophy, but that it comes within the scope of his new science. Which reminds me that in the oral phrase "Vico's new science" there is an ambiguity which is not wholly removed in the phrase as written or printed. The oral phrase may refer to Vico's book in one or more of its three editions, or it may refer to the science of which the book treats and of which Vico supposed himself to be the founder. The science is not contained but only begun in the book. To take the present example, the science would embrace the history of philosophy, but the book contains no such history. It does, however, contain what Vico calls a short specimen—"una particella"—of "the history of philosophy narrated philosophically." [7] And it was precisely that short specimen that convinced the philosopher with whom I began that his own thesis on Stoicism and Roman law was misconceived.

Most histories of philosophy have in themselves, as histories, no philosophic character, and are valuable, if at all, only as reference tools. Their unphilosophical character helps to explain the low esteem in which leading philosophers of the recent past have held the history of philosophy. But a philosopher disposed now to take the history of philosophy seriously, and desiring to produce a history of philosophy narrated philosophically, may hear Vico telling him how to do it.

Even when the history of philosophy was held in least esteem, the philosophy of history was considered a proper field of inquiry. More exactly, that phrase was used to designate two different but related fields of inquiry, now commonly referred to as the analytic and the speculative philosophy of history. Vico was understood

7 *NS*, par. 1043.

to have contributed to both these fields, but rather more to the speculative than to the analytic. But Leon Pompa's recent book on Vico shows that he was a deliberate and intentional contributor to the analytic philosophy of history, perhaps the first great such contributor, and perhaps the greatest. Now the analytic philosophy of history has recently focused on the problem of historical explanation, and more particularly on the covering law model of historical explanation. Though Pompa does not use this language, the main argument of his book might be briefly paraphrased as follows: What has been taken as Vico's contribution to the speculative philosophy of history was really the archetypal example of the covering law model of historical explanation in the analytic philosophy of history. (Parenthetically, I remark that Pompa is careful to show that Vico, in spite of his "had, has, and will have to be," was not a metaphysical determinist.)[8]

The most flourishing branch of philosophy is epistemology or theory of knowledge, and the most flourishing branch of that branch is philosophy of science. It must, among other things, try to tell us what science is and how scientific knowledge differs from prescientific or nonscientific knowledge. There are many sciences, and new ones are still starting up from time to time. A new science must somehow make good its claim to be science, and that helps keep alive the question what science is. But perhaps there was never a new science so self-conscious as Vico's about its claim to be science. It might therefore be expected that a philosopher of science, wishing in the first place to test his definition of what science is by trying it out on particular sciences, and in the second place to test the claims of not-yet-established sciences to be science, would turn to Vico's science as at least one of his test cases. I do not recall that any author of a general treatise on the philosophy of science has ever done this. If any have thought of doing so, they may have been deterred

8 Leon Pompa, *Vico: A Study of the New Science* (New York: Cambridge University Press, 1975).

by the difficulty of making out from Vico's book just what science it is that he claims to be founding. But now that Pompa's book is out and the reviews are beginning to appear, it may be that philosophers of science will begin to hear Vico saying: "Here is *my* science. Try *it*."

If we ask Vico what science it is that he is founding, he will say "that of the common nature of nations" or of "the principles of humanity." But it soon appears that the terms "nature," "nations," and "principles" all have genetic or in a broad sense historical meanings.[9] And there are other indications that we shall not be far wrong if, as a first approximation, we understand Vico as saying that his new science is the science of history.

Perhaps the reason he does not explicitly say this is that it would have had the air of flagrant paradox. For from antiquity through the Middle Ages and into the Renaissance, not only was history not a science but it was the exact opposite of science. To be sure, like science, it aims at knowledge, but, whereas scientific knowledge is knowledge of the universal and eternal, historical knowledge is knowledge of the local and temporal—of particulars in their times and places.

So, although there were great historians as far back as there were great philosophers and great scientists, and although classifications of the sciences and curricula of higher education go back nearly as far, history does not appear in those classifications or in those curricula. Selected writings of great historians were read, to be sure, but they were read as prose literature, in courses taught by rhetoricians, not by historians.

Otherwise than as pure literature, the highest that history could aspire to in the company of the sciences was to be an auxiliary to the moral sciences, and even then not to the sciences as such but to instruction in them, by supplying apt examples by which their principles might be memorably illustrated. History at its best was moral science taught by examples rather than by principles.

9 *NS*, p. xx, par. A3.

So if we understand Vico to be promoting history as such to the company of the sciences and to the curriculum of higher education, we are ascribing to him the most revolutionary proposal in the entire history of classifications of the sciences and of higher education.[10]

But of course we shall not understand him as claiming that history has been a science all along, and demanding that it be recognized as what it has always been. He is claiming rather that, although history has not hitherto been a science, it can be made one, and that he has shown how this is to be done, and is well along in the doing of it.

On the other hand, Vico is not asking the established sciences to open the door just wide enough to let history in, as it were on probation, as the humblest of the sciences because the youngest. He is rather saying that if the business of a science is not only to ascertain facts of a certain kind but to render those facts intelligible, and if it does this not only by subsuming them under universal and eternal principles but by determining their causes, and if the ultimate object of historical inquiry is not the actions of particular individuals on particular occasions but the historical development of the cultural world, the world of human institutions, and so of man himself, then, since we have ourselves made that world, it is in principle more intelligible than the objects of any other science. And therefore, so far as the new science of history succeeds in its task, its place among the sciences will not be that of the least but that of the most scientific.

I do not understand, however, that Vico claims that he himself

---

[10] Though there are histories of historical writing, and though there are studies of particular espisodes in the history of historical research and teaching, there is no comprehensive history of history in relation to classifications of the sciences on the one hand and to curricula of higher education on the other. The brief sketch in the preceding and following paragraphs will need revision when such a history appears. For the Neapolitan scientific background of Vico's new science, see Max H. Fisch, "The Academy of the Investigators," in Edgar A. Underwood, ed., *Science, Medicine, and History: Essays on the Evolution of Scientific Thought and Medical Practice, Written in Honour of Charles Singer*, 2 vols. (London: Oxford University Press, 1953), 1: 521–563.

or any other individual scientist of the new science, by virtue of sharing the humanity of the makers of the human world, already comprehends that world, or will at any assignable future time have fully comprehended it. His claim is rather, I think, that it can in principle be comprehended by the community of historians in a way in which the astronomical world, for example, cannot be comprehended by the community of astronomers.

Since every science is science of some kind, he who claims to have founded a new science may fairly be asked if it belongs to one or another of the recognized kinds. The classifications of the sciences current in Vico's time were still variations on Aristotle's. The particular variation that Vico seems to assume divides the sciences first into theoretical and practical and then divides the practical into active and factive—that is, of doing and of making. Vico has no hesitation in assigning his new science to the practical rather than to the theoretical branch, both because what it studies is of human doing or making and because the end at which it aims is not knowing for the sake of knowing but knowing for the sake of doing better what we are already doing. As to whether it belongs to the active or the factive branch of practical science, he is less clear. In either case, a practical science has relatively theoretical and relatively practical parts, and what Vico has given us in his book, in any of the three editions, belongs almost wholly to the more theoretical part; and even the third edition leaves the more practical part to be almost wholly supplied by others.[11]

Suppose finally that we imagine Vico asking you and me: "What has become of my new science in the 232 years since my death?"—and imagine him adding, "the science, I mean, not the book."

We might reply: "The science as you conceived it has never gained integral acceptance either as science or as a department of higher education. It was too much for us. But the more theo-

11 Max H. Fisch, "Vico's *Pratica*," in Giorgio Tagliacozzo and Donald P. Verene, eds., *Giambattista Vico's Science of Humanity* (Baltimore: The Johns Hopkins University Press, 1976), pp. 423–430.

retical part has been broken up into manageable subparts, such as anthropology, sociology, psychology, linguistics, and most recently semiotics; and these have one by one achieved scientific standing and been added to the curriculum. History itself, after two millennia of waiting, was added to the curriculum but not to the sciences, and without having become the science you meant to found; yet not without having undergone some changes in that direction. Just what those changes were, and how they came about, in response to what felt needs, we have as yet no comprehensive account to tell us. But we are slowly learning, episode by episode, and some of the chief investigators of those changes are among us at this conference."

Vico might then ask: "And what of the more practical part of the new science, which I left to be supplied?"

And we might reply: "It has been supplied only in the form of applied this and applied that, and these are nowhere brought together." And it might occur to us to add: "Even history has been broken up and distributed. More of it is studied and taught outside of departments of history than in them—the history of anthropology, for example, in departments of anthropology, and so with the rest."

And Vico's last word might be: "You may in time persuade me that all this fragmentation was somehow necessary, and even that it has borne rich fruit that could not otherwise have been brought forth. But I should like to persuade you that it is high time for some of the philosophers among you to return from analysis to synthesis, and to join with likeminded scientists in founding once again a new science of humanity."

Vico's Philosophy of Imagination

BY DONALD PHILLIP VERENE

CONTEMPORARY epistemology, which has its origins in Descartes and Locke, has built its account of knowledge through reflection on the logical, scientific, and commonsensical operations of the mind. The activities of the human spirit that derive from its powers of imagination and social memory have not found a place in this sphere of philosophical inquiry. Those activities which German thinkers began to assemble under the term *Geisteswissenschaften* in the midnineteenth century and which they opposed to the *Naturwissenschaften,* a conception which goes back in German thought as far as Adelung, Herder, and Hegel, and one which is more recently found in Dilthey and Cassirer, have not become subject matters for the mainstream of theory of knowledge. The philosophy of science and the sciences has become a definite field of philosophical inquiry; a counterpart to this, a philosophy of the humanities, has not developed.

I wish to examine the sense in which Vico's *New Science* provides a basis for understanding those powers of the mind upon which the humanities, the *Geisteswissenschaften,* depend. The *New Science,* I will maintain, gives form to powers of the human spirit that differ in kind from those that generate the methodology of the natural and observational sciences.[1] The *New Science*

---

[1] I wish to acknowledge the debt this paper owes to my reading of three essays on Vico by Sir Isaiah Berlin: "The Philosophical Ideas of Giambattista Vico," in

provides the ground for understanding the humanistic project of self-knowledge—that activity in which the self comes to "objective" knowledge of itself, its own nature, through understanding the nature of its world. This requires not a logic of the object itself, or a logic whereby the knower comes to know the object as an other—a known. It requires a logic of imagination, a logic of the image and the creation and manipulation of images.

I wish to organize my account around three ideas: those of (1) the origin, (2) recollection, and (3) the myth. The relationship between these ideas can initially be seen in the following way. Vico's *New Science* is a science of origins. In it Vico shows us the form of the human mind wherein it seeks a knowledge of the origin of itself. The manner in which a knowledge of origins is possible is that of recollection or reminiscence, namely, the act of recalling those things that are past. Such an act of recollection is not history but a mode of knowing that history itself presupposes. The discovery of the origin through recollective activity depends upon the discovery of the myth; as Vico states early in the *New Science*, "the first science to be learned should be mythology." [2] Vico's conception of myth, a conception

---

Art and Ideas in Eighteenth-Century Italy (Rome: Edizioni di storia e letteratura, 1960); "A Note on Vico's Concept of Knowledge," in Giorgio Tagliacozzo and Hayden V. White, eds., *Giambattista Vico: An International Symposium* (Baltimore: Johns Hopkins Press, 1969); and "The Divorce Between the Sciences and the Humanities" (The Second Tykociner Memorial Lecture, University of Illinois, 1974). Although my view of the difference in kind between the sciences and the humanities and the importance of the *New Science* for the understanding of humanistic thought had taken shape before reading the third of these essays, it has been greatly stimulated by it.

[2] Par. 51. By the *New Science* I mean in all instances what is commonly called the *Scienza nuova seconda* as edited by Fausto Nicolini in the Laterza edition. All quotations are from *The New Science of Giambattista Vico* (hereinafter *NS*), translated by Thomas G. Bergin and Max H. Fisch (Ithaca: Cornell University Press, 1968). Cassirer, in the fourth volume of his study of the *Erkenntnisproblem*, states: "Giambattista Vico may be called the real discoverer of the myth." He adds that the other figure to be connected with this discovery is Herder. See Ernst Cassirer, *The Problem of Knowledge: Philosophy, Science, and History since Hegel*, translated by William Woglom and Charles W. Hendel (New Haven: Yale University Press, 1950), p. 296.

reached and maintained through recollection, is the basis for
his theory of poetic wisdom or poetic *sapienza,* which is his general term for those modes of formative activity that constitute
primordial humanity.

Imaginative Universals

With this sketch of the interrelationship between these ideas
in mind, I wish to explore more fully what I hold to be the
philosophical center of the *New Science.* At the center of Vico's
theory of poetic wisdom is his theory of "imaginative universals"
(generi or *universali fantastici).*[3] Vico's notion of the imaginative
universal is the notion of a logic of metaphor, and more specifically it is a logic of identity, of immediate identities between
things.[4] The shape which the imaginative universal takes in

---

[3] The view of the logic of imaginative universals described here appears at greater
length in my essay "Vico's Science of Imaginative Universals and the Philosophy of
Symbolic Forms," in Giorgio Tagliacozzo and Donald P. Verene, eds., *Giambattista
Vico's Science of Humanity* (Baltimore: The Johns Hopkins University Press, 1976),
pp. 302–311. In the *New Science* the central passages for the interpretation of
Vico's conception of imaginative universals are: pars. 34, 204–210 (axioms 47–49),
and 400–403 (section on "Poetic Logic").

[4] By a logic of identity as it is present in poetic wisdom I do not mean simply
ways of asserting the principle that A is A, nor, for example, a < a, the principle
in the calculus of classes that every class is included in itself. The principle of
identity, conceived simply as A is A, is not sufficient as a principle for logical judgment, a problem that goes back as far as the Cynic Antisthenes in the fourth
century B.C., since the identity of the subject must allow for the property of its
predicate. Vico's descriptions of imaginative universals explain the movements and
structure of identities as present in metaphorical speech which precede the relationships of class logic. Cohen and Nagel, in discussing the logic of fictions, state
the point as: "Metaphors may thus be viewed as expressing the vague and confused
but primal perception of identity, which subsequent processes of discrimination
transform into a conscious and expressed analogy between different things, and
which further reflection transforms into the clear assertion of an identity or common element (or relation) which the two different things possess" (Morris R. Cohen
and Ernest Nagel, *An Introduction to Logic and Scientific Method* [New York:
Harcourt, Brace, 1934], p. 369). With the exception of calling the perception of
identity in metaphors "vague and confused," which they in fact are from the point
of view of nonmetaphorical mentality, Cohen's and Nagel's threefold distinction

the language of the first men is that of the poetic character. These characters, which are the central figures of fables, Vico says, were "images for the most part of animate substances, of gods or heroes." [5] Every metaphor, Vico says, "is a fable in brief." [6] Vico distinguishes between two types of poetic characters or imaginative universals which correspond to the first two of his three ages of human culture— the age of gods and the age of heroes, the ages which constitute poetic wisdom. In the age of gods, that in which men thought and acted in terms of gods, these poetic characters were the formation of natural phenomena or social institutions that spring directly from physiological functions.[7] In the age of heroes what is most often represented is some quality of character, such as the formation of valor as the figure of Achilles.[8]

---

is remarkably close to Vico's. Cf. Vico's description of the Egyptians' imaginative identification of their inventions with Thrice-great Hermes as based on their inability to form the genus "civil sage," and moreover their inability to conceive of civil wisdom (NS, par. 209).

[5] NS, par. 34.

[6] NS, par. 404.

[7] E.g., in regard to poetic characters of natural phenomena: "This is the way in which the theological poets apprehended Jove, Cybele or Berecynthia, and Neptune, for example, and, at first mutely pointing, explained them as substances of the sky, the earth, and the sea, which they imagined to be animate divinities and were therefore true to their senses in believing them to be gods" (NS, par. 402). E.g., in regard to social institutions: "The goddess Juno imposes great labors on the Theban, that is the Greek Hercules. (For every ancient gentile nation had a Hercules as its founder.) This signifies that piety and marriage form the school wherein are learned the first rudiments of all the great virtues. And Hercules, with the favor of Jove under whose auspices he was begotten, surmounts all the difficulties" (NS, par. 514). Thus it is through the union of Jove and Juno (even though a stormy one) that the institution of marriage comes about, and through the original labor of Hercules that the institution of labor is structured. Such activities are also the origin of social virtue, or what among other thinkers would be called Sittlichkeit.

[8] NS, par. 403. Given empirical individuals gain their reality through their immediate identity with the poetic character of the hero, who is the true presence of a particular quality. Vico states this in one passage as: "So that, if we consider the matter well, poetic truth is metaphysical truth, and physical truth which is not in conformity with it should be considered false. Thence springs this important consideration in poetic theory: the true war chief, for example, is the

What the first men were able to do was to stand apart from the perceptual flux of their senses and to give form to it, to arrange it into elements having certain characters. Vico says that the first men were all body and thought in terms of bodies.[9] Jove, who is the primary poetic character for the first men, the character through which the power to form imaginative universals is first realized, is seen directly as thunder, and thunder is seen as his body.[10] This original act of *fantasia*, of imagination, is one

---

Godfrey that Torquato Tasso imagines; and all the chiefs who do not conform throughout to Godfrey are not true chiefs of war" (*NS*, par. 205). A version of this relationship between physical and metaphysical truth is present in Vico's "ideal eternal history," which I shall suggest in remarks which follow. Vico states the distinction between divine and heroic characters most clearly at *NS*, pars. 933–934.

[9] Vico speaks of three different senses in which primordial thought is bodily thought: (1) That language is originally used to give form to inanimate things by means of metaphors constructed from the body, such as eyes of potatoes, shoulders of hills, and teeth of rakes (e.g., *NS*, par. 405). This is quite like, although Vico's is a broader conception, the principle employed in ethnology and mythology that spatial and geographical distinctions are derived from the projections of the structures of the human body onto the world. Vico also means that: (2) The mind itself is originally immersed in the body and cannot be apprehended apart from it. Thus, "The human mind is naturally inclined by the senses to see itself externally in the body, and only with great difficulty does it come to understand itself by means of reflection" (*NS*, par. 236; see also pars. 331 and 1045). And (3) the thought of the first men was literally a bodily act of sensing. Vico says that Jove was a "truth of the senses for them" (*NS*, par. 508), and that human ideas began as divine ideas through the contemplation of the heavens with "bodily eyes" (*NS*, par. 391). Also the first acts of meaning are connected to mute acts of bodily gestures (*NS*, par. 401).

[10] I believe Vico would have liked the following words of the Tasaday, the primordial people of the Philippine rain forest discovered by the modern world in 1971, as reported by the journalist, John Nance. The Tasaday were asked:

" 'What is the worst thing in the forest?'

" 'The big word is the worst thing. We are afraid of it. Our ancestors also were afraid.'

"This was puzzling. Mai, who could readily convert metaphorical language into common terms, smiled and said, without asking them, that the 'big word' was thunder—the worst thing in the forest was thunder.

" 'What do you do when the big word comes?'

" 'We stay in our places and some of us put our hands on our ears.'

" 'Where does this big word come from?'

" 'We don't know . . . we don't know' " (John Nance, *The Gentle Tasaday* [New York and London: Harcourt Brace Jovanovich, 1975], p. 58).

of discovering that things have a meaning. When thunder is seen as Jove, it is no longer simply sensed; it is sensed as a spiritual entity. This spirituality is not something conceived; it is felt as fear.[11] Thunder is not apprehended as something representing or "standing for" Jove. Jove is not seen as being *like* thunder. It involves not a logic of similarity but of identity. Jove *is* the thunder, and the thunder is the bodily presence of Jove. For Vico, sensation is a form of "thinking." The thought of these first men is something Vico says we can barely approach. His discovery of imaginative universals, which he calls the "master key" of his science, Vico says, cost him twenty years of his mature life.[12]

The *fantasia* of the first men, the power of thinking and acting through the senses, is the ability to bring things into being; it involves the creation of identities in perceptual immediacy. The problem of grounding modern mentality in a point of origin, in a point of the origin of mentality itself, is one of establishing an identity between this mentality and the point of origin. This identity is not one of giving form to immediate perceptual flux but one which involves the process of recollection.[13] This process

---

Of Jove's body Vico says: "It is impossible that bodies should be minds, yet it was believed that the thundering sky was Jove" (*NS*, par. 383). One is hardly surprised when several pages on in Nance's reportage the local interpreters and the Tasaday discuss the nature of the moon (about which there is some confusion) and the sun in terms of their having bodies.

[11] Although Vico's formulation is different, his view of bodily thinking is based on the same epistemological insight that Cassirer calls "expression" or the *Ausdrucksfunktion* of consciousness (Ernst Cassirer, *The Philosophy of Symbolic Forms*, translated by Ralph Manheim, 3 vols. [New Haven: Yale University Press, 1953–57], 3: pt. 1). They share the common awareness that sensation or perception is not to be understood as the passive acquisition of content by the mind but is itself an activity of formation, and that it is to be philosophically grasped as an actual phenomenon in cultural life.

[12] *NS*, pars. 34, 338.

[13] By the notion of identity as connected with recollection I mean that notion of self-involvement which Hegel expresses in logical terms in his conception of the *spekulative Satz* in the *Phenomenology of Spirit*, in which the identity of subject and predicate is seen to be the result of a process of rhythm between them. Speculative thought approaches the judgment in terms of a movement in which the locus of its unity is placed first in its subject, then moved to the universality of its predicate, and then this movement is transposed back upon the subject (G. W. F.

of seeking an origin is not one of simple chronological tracing, nor is it one of metaphysical reasoning to the principle of a ground. It is a process in which the origin is approached as if it were something present to the senses. Recollection aims at having its object as something "quasi-perceptual," as a phenomenon. The grasping of this origin involves the mind attempting to enter actually into the original exercise of its powers.

To recollect is to order things in terms of their origin, to obtain a totalization of all the fragments of the activity of the human spirit through a progressive ordering of things between the origin point, once found, and the form of the present mentality from which the ordering takes place. This process cannot be fully typified by the notion of *reflection*. Reflection is essentially a logical term. Even if it is taken in a transcendental sense of self-conscious reflection of the mind upon itself, it falls short because it does not necessarily involve the notion of a time that moves from a primordial point of origin to the present.[14] What must

---

Hegel, *Phänomenologie des Geistes,* edited by Johannes Hoffmeister [Hamburg: Felix Meiner, 1952], pp. 51–54; cf. above n. 4). In referring to this I do not mean to subscribe to the traditional Hegelian notion of *Aufhebung*—that consciousness moves forward by a smooth mechanism of continuous self-recapitulation. The sense of recollection or *Er-Innerung* of which Hegel speaks in the closing pages of the *Phänomenologie (ibid.,* pp. 563–564), and which is the power of mind upon which the ability to form speculative judgments rests, is the same as that which I wish to connect with the *New Science.* A fresh look at the relationships of Hegel's *Phenomenology* and Vico's *New Science* is much needed in the philosophical history of ideas.

14 Leon Pompa employs the term *reflection* to characterize the type of knowledge in the *New Science:* "The concept of *reflection* is therefore the crux of Vico's later theory of knowledge. Vico is claiming that by self-conscious reflection upon our own ways of seeing our world and our own attitudes to it, we can come to understand what are the natural propensities which cause these" (*Vico: A Study of the New Science* [New York: Cambridge University Press, 1975], p. 166). When Professor Pompa's meaning of reflection is considered fully in the discussion of the final two chapters of his excellent study, it comes, I believe, quite close in the principles of its definition to what I mean by the term *recollection.* The central point of difference, and I believe a very important one, is that his view is not grounded in Vico's notion of *fantasia.* Professor Pompa does not explore the sense of *fantasia* present in the origin of human mentality, upon which the *New Science* rests; nor does he explore the sense in which *fantasia* raised to a different level is involved in the "reflective" activity of the *New Science* itself.

be sought is a sense of self-identity that extends through time from the origin to the present. It is also not simply *memory*, since what is involved is not merely the act of recalling the past. The past must be brought back to mind in a progressively causal order, so that the connections between beginning, middle, and end can be seen.[15] The process of recollection is one in which *fantasia* discovers itself as the original form of the human spirit, and *fantasia* discovers its own origin in the immediate identities of the imaginative universal.

Ideal Eternal History

Fantasia exists in the *New Science* in two senses: (1) there is the *fantasia* which Vico describes in his theory of poetic wisdom, the mentality of imaginative universals; and (2) there is the *fantasia* which functions as the medium through which the *New Science* itself gains its recollective understanding of the human world. The discovery of the first sense of *fantasia* is the discovery out of which the *fantasia* of the second sense constitutes itself. The discovery of the primary *fantasia* is the discovery of the myth and a theory of concept formation for mythical mentality. This mentality does not create universality in terms of recollection. The mentality of the first men is one that does not order the world

15 Sir Isaiah Berlin uses the term *memory* to characterize the faculty whereby we come to Vico's comprehension of the past: "memory, not analogy, seems closer to the required faculty of imaginative understanding—*fantasia*—whereby we reconstruct the human past" ("The Divorce Between the Sciences and the Humanities," p. 33). Berlin makes clear that he wishes to call more attention to the contrast between memory and analogy than in his writings which have preceded this one. I very much agree with this emphasis on memory as having the primary connection with *fantasia*. Against my insistence on recollection it keeps closely to Vico's use of memory or *memoria* and his connection of it with imagination or *fantasia* (a relationship which I will discuss shortly). A sense in which I think Berlin's account of *fantasia* and its relationship to knowledge differ from my own (at least as far as I know his view) is my interest in developing the systematical connections between *fantasia* as a logic of identity present in primordial mentality and the *fantasia* of the mentality of the *New Science* itself.

under the notion of time. To the extent that time can be said to be present for the first men, their logic of metaphorical identities, of poetic characters, and of fables is a denial of time.[16] Time is in a certain sense present, in that the age of the first men as an age is subject to time; it will pass away. The men of this age stand to time as children, and for Vico they are the children of the human race.[17] They live in a world of mimetic realities, timeless and wholly presentational.

The second sense of *fantasia* differs from the first in that it functions not in terms of a denial of time but in terms of an envisionment of time. It surmounts time by seeing time as a whole. At the center of this sense of *fantasia* is Vico's conception of ideal eternal history or *storia ideale eterna*. In describing this Vico says: "Men first feel necessity, then look for utility, next attend to comfort, still later amuse themselves with pleasure, thence grow dissolute in luxury, and finally go mad and waste their substance." [18] From the standpoint of ideal eternal history, time is seen as a drama in which there is an identity between origin and end. Time is seen as a form internal to the human world which puts the beginning against the end. The conceit of nations and of scholars of which Vico speaks lies in their failure to take seriously the fragmentation of the past from the present.[19] Their solution to the problem of the nature of society is one of simply seeing the past as the same as the present. These conceits rest on a failure of recollective *fantasia*. They are unable to visualize the drama of a mediated identity between an origin and an end.

The primary imaginative universal of the first men is Jove. It is from the initial act of forming the thunder as Jove that

---

[16] I have in mind here a point similar to Claude Lévi-Strauss's view when he terms both music and myth "instruments for the obliteration of time" (Claude Lévi-Strauss, *The Raw and the Cooked*, translated by John and Doreen Weightman [New York: Harper & Row, 1969], p. 16).

[17] *NS*, pars. 215–217, 498.

[18] *NS*, par. 241.

[19] *NS*, pars. 125, 127, 330.

human consciousness is born, and Vico says "every gentile nation had its Jove." [20]   All of the original powers of mind that are manifest in the various forms of poetic wisdom are present in this initial act.   It is this act that must be sought out and followed in its development if we are to grasp the origin point of any nation.   The imaginative universal of Jove is the basis for this primary *fantasia*.   As Jove is the primary universal of the original *fantasia*, so the ideal eternal history is the primary universal of recollective *fantasia* of the *New Science*.   The ideal eternal history is the recollective imaginative universal through which any nation and consequently the human world can be grasped as a whole.   As Vico says, the ideal eternal history is "traversed in time by every nation in its rise, development, maturity, decline, and fall." [21]   This notion, variously visualized, that the human world is a whole which develops from an origin that lies within itself, and that anything within it can be understood as having a beginning, middle, and end, is the initial act of consciousness that lies at the basis of the understanding necessary to the *Geisteswissenschaften*.[22]

What is involved in the notion of ideal eternal history is the notion of a self-identity, but one which exists through time.   This has its basis in Vico's discovery of the principle of *verum-factum*— that the true or *verum* is convertible with that which is made or constructed, the *factum*.[23]   The human world can come to know itself, because what it meets in recollection is itself apprehended under the aspect of time.   The human world is nothing other

[20] *NS*, par. 193.

[21] *NS*, par. 245.

[22] Each humanistic thinker must internalize (i.e., "make") this principle for himself; as Vico states: "he who meditates this Science narrates to himself this ideal eternal history so far as he himself makes it for himself by that proof 'it had, has, and will have to be'" (*NS*, par. 349).   Cf. Hegel's notion in the *Phenomenology* that each individual has the right to demand that this science provide him with a "ladder" that will allow him to attain the mentality of the science itself (*Phänomenologie des Geistes*, p. 25).

[23] *De antiquissima Italorum sapientia* in *Opere*, vol. 1, edited by Giovanni Gentile and Fausto Nicolini (Bari: Laterza, 1914), pp. 131–132.

than what has been founded and established through the activity
of the original *fantasia* acting in relation to the world of practical
action and objects of social life.   There is a sense in which the
human world cannot be as completely known as can the objects
of mathematical thought, Vico's paradigm for the convertibility
of the true and the made.   Although the human world and the
objects of mathematics are both something *made,* and their truth
cannot be separate from the act of the knower who creates them,
the science of the human world, unlike the science of numbers
or geometry, operates through time.[24]   The recollected identity
that exists between origin and end that is present in the image
of humanity as ideal eternal history is not an unmediated identity of calculation nor a truth of deduction; it is an identity
through time ordered in terms of the notion of progressive causes.
In logical terms what recollection establishes is a structure of phenomenal ground-consequent relationships through which the origin can be seen in relation to the end.

In a view which Vico presents in his early work, *De antiquissima
Italorum sapientia,* and which he reiterates in the *New Science,*
he states that: "Imagination is a genuine faculty." [25]   And he
identifies imagination or *fantasia* with memory or *memoria.*   He

[24] I have in mind the sense in which the intrepretation of the *New Science* which
I have developed here can account for a nonparallelism that exists between mathematical thought and the science of the human world in respect to Vico's formula
of the convertibility of the true, the *verum,* and the made, the *factum.* Vico notes
one sense in which geometry and ideal eternal history are not parallel in that
"institutions having to do with human affairs are more real than points, lines,
surfaces, and figures are" (*NS,* par. 349).   There is a sense, however, in which truth
in geometry is more directly convertible with the made than in history.   Since truths
in geometry are deductively made, they do not involve the mediation of time.   But
our knowledge of the human world as ideal eternal history involves a mediation
of the object through time.   There is a sense in which the axioms of the *New Science*
can never directly produce the object in the way that the axioms of geometry can.
Because the object of the human world can be determined only by temporal
mediation, it is never fully present for recollective *fantasia.*   The temporal medium
always threatens *scienza* with *coscienza,* to turn self-knowledge into empirical consciousness of the human world.   See also my remarks in the final paragraphs of
this paper.

[25] *De antiquissima Italorum sapientia,* p. 175.

says that memory has three different aspects: "memory when it remembers things, imagination when it alters or imitates them, and invention [*ingegno*] when it gives them a new turn or puts them into proper arrangement and relationship." [26] For this reason Mnemosyne is the mother of the Muses, whose daughters govern the arts of civilization, or humanistic knowledge. Since the first men thought through their bodies, these three activities were accomplished through the senses. We can barely imagine what it would be like to think through the body, and to sense the world as an order of bodies, with meaning not being separable from bodies. Sensation as a mode of mind wherein the mind presents the world immediately to itself can take three directionalities: as sensation immediately remembered, as a mimetic thought or image,[27] and as a synthesis or rearrangement of immediately present elements. It is memory in its threefold sense, or the power realized by the first men to preserve through the sensuous formation of the world, through the image, what is otherwise merely immediate and transitory. In this way the first men escape the life of momentariness, of the protohumans before the apprehension of Jove in his thunderous body. Mnemosyne is the mother of the Muses because she is the art of preserving and forming what is otherwise without form and momentary.[28]

Mnemosyne is present in the *New Science* as such, in its *fantasia*, not as a project of sensation but as a project of temporal recapture. It is a project of cultural memory which has its analogue not in the imitative or mimetic thought of childhood but in the self-conscious recollections of adult life out of which the humane and spiritual personality is born. It is not a project of abstract or

---

[26] *NS*, par. 819; *De antiquissima Italorum sapientia*, pp. 177–179.

[27] By mimetic thought I mean a primordial mode of presentational thought, in which the object itself is brought into being for the knower, not a mode of thought in which an external reality is copied or reflected. It is this type of presentational thought which Vico intends when he speaks of "imitation" (e.g., *NS*, pars. 215–216) as a first mode of thought and of myth as *vera narratio* (e.g., *NS*, par. 401). It is that state of mind of metaphorical identities which Plato, one of Vico's "four authors," placed at the beginning of the divided line, *eikasia*.

[28] *NS*, pars. 508, 819.

"intelligible universals" *(generi intelligibili),* which are typical of Vico's third age, the age of men, and which are a mode of thought more fitting with the natural sciences—the *Naturwissenschaften.*[29] Intelligible universals are the result of the dimming of the powers of *fantasia* to the point that what is before the mind is preserved without the power of the image and apart from immediate sensation. Through the intelligible universal the world is disembodied. Intelligible universals are always the future of the original *fantasia* of divine and heroic universals, but it is also its death. The age of men is the certain outcome of the poetic ages.

A Phenomenology of the Human Spirit

As Jove is the archetypal imaginative universal of *mythic fantasia* or *poetic fantasia,* so the ideal eternal history is the archetypal "imaginative universal" of *recollective fantasia.* As every culture has its beginning in its Jove, so every culture as recollected, as known as something made, a *factum,* has its ideal eternal history. The act of understanding humanity, or a given culture, or the human individual itself in this way is the basis for humane knowledge. It is the notion of a phenomenology of the human spirit,[30] of a type of understanding in which an origin is systematically and recollectively apprehended as the basis of understanding the present state. The notion of "classics"

---

[29] Vico's conception of intelligible universals would not be adequate for a theory of concept formation for relational concepts as found in modern science (for example, those discussed in Cassirer's *Substance and Function,* translated by William C. Swabey and Marie C. Swabey [New York: Dover Publications, 1953], chap. 1). Vico's formulation of the intelligible universal is too closely tied to the Aristotelian theory of the generic concept to account for the mathematically functional relations of modern science. In a broader sense, however, the age of intelligible universals is the age of scientific mentality and its accompanying social and life forms.

[30] Cf. Berlin: "What is novel is Vico's notion of what later came to be called the phenomenology of the human spirit" ("The Philosophical Ideas of Giambattista Vico," p. 203). Berlin is the discoverer of the fact that the *New Science* contains a new conception of knowledge and that it involves a "sense of knowing which is basic to all humane studies" ("A Note on Vico's Concept of Knowledge," p. 375).

which is so central to humanistic pursuit is a notion of the origin as the touchstone of any understanding. The notion of "history" as having a structure, a meaning, is dependent on the notion of ideal eternal history. The notions of the "primitive" and the "child" are also dependent on such phenomenological imagination. The notion of "value," when not thought in the rarefied air of ethical argumentation but grasped as something in cultural life, rests upon our sense of identifying and recollecting what is continually being lost.[31] The notion of ideal eternal history and the concept of origin it involves is the heart of humanistic knowledge. Its various fields involve the multiple ways in which this idea can be refracted throughout the contents of the human world.

From the standpoint of recollective *fantasia,* the intelligible universals of the natural and observational sciences represent the logic of barbarity. Such scientific mentality, unlike Vico's but like Descartes',[32] represents no interest in the mother of the Muses—Mnemosyne. The history of science, which is a project of humanistic understanding, not science, finds its place in the *New Science.* What is important in the mentality of science proper is always the enterprise-at-hand, the manipulation of the present conditions against an infinite, progressive future. Like the barbarian, the scientific mentality has no past except the

---

[31] The origin of value for Vico can be traced to the Muse, born from a thunderbolt of Jove, and said by Homer to be "knowledge of good and evil." Vico considers the first Muse to be Urania, who in her earliest activity "contemplated the heavens to take the auguries." Thus distinctions of value begin as distinctions of divination associated with the body of Jove, the sky (*NS,* pars. 381, 391, 508).

[32] Descartes makes clear that he considers attention to fables and history not only an impediment to the pursuit of truth but a danger to the conduct of life. "Thus it happens," Descartes says, "that those who regulate their behavior by the examples they find in books are apt to fall into the extravagances of the knights of romances, and undertake projects which it is beyond their ability to complete or hope for things beyond their destiny" (*Discourse on Method,* translated by Lawrence J. Lafleur [New York: The Library of Liberal Arts, 1960], pt. 1). Should it have been possible for Descartes to have read it, he surely would have found the *New Science* just such knight-errantry. I have discussed the relationship of Descartes to contemporary mentality in my essay, "Vico's Science of Imaginative Universals and the Philosophy of Symbolic Forms."

immediate past of scientific discovery against which new scientific discovery is always forged. New scientific knowledge is forever trying to overcome its own past on behalf of a truth of the object, a *coscienza*. The barbarian has no interest in memory; his interest continually lies in the possibilities of immediate power over the world. Vico's theory of barbarity does not lie only in his conception of the life of the first men but in his understanding of the life of the last men, the men of the third age of a culture, the age of dimmed *fantasia*. It is an age in which the mentality of intelligible universals has dimmed all social life and thought to the manipulation of the present and Vico's "dissolute luxury" of its spoils.[33]

Humanistic understanding must always have at its center the notion of the myth. In its movement toward the recollection of origin, it discovers always again the myth, the original power of image-making or mimesis, the science of which, as Vico says, is the first that must be learned. The humanity upon which all the humanities depend is mythology. In the myth, the traditional enemy of intelligible science, is the original power of the image upon which the capabilities of humanistic *fantasia* rest. Any theory of knowledge, and any theory of the humanities, must be founded on a theory of mythical consciousness. "Doctrines," Vico says, "must take their beginning from that of the matters of which they treat." [34] This is true both in the sense of beginning at the beginning and in the sense of recapturing that energy of the human spirit necessary to philosophical and humanistic understanding.

Heralds of Dissolution

There is a final point that must be raised in the completion

---

[33] In the conclusion of the *New Science* Vico states: "rust will consume the misbegotten subtleties of malicious wits that have turned them into beasts made more inhuman by the barbarism of reflection [*riflessione*] than the first men had been made by the barbarism of sense" (par. 1106).

[34] *NS*, par. 314.

of this sketch of Vico's *fantasia*. I have maintained that the *fantasia* that is taken up by the humanities, and the masterwork of the very form of knowledge they embody, the *New Science*, is a force that runs counter to the mind's interest in intelligible universals that exists in the age of men. Within Vico's conception of the ideal eternal history is not only the notion that time has a structure, a beginning, a middle, and an end, but that there are radical discontinuities in the human world which stem from the fact that there are genuine origins and ends. The view I have been describing implies that there are many sequences of ideal eternal history that follow each other and exist side by side in various temporal positions. In a given sequence of the human spirit from the standpoint of the ideal eternal history, the end point is as genuine a phenomenon as is the beginning. There is thus a day side and a night side to the act wherein a given culture at the point of the age of men attempts to preserve itself by a return to a knowledge of origin, to the attainment of self-identity through the activity of recollective *fantasia*. This impetus toward recollective understanding must be considered as much a part of the oncoming night of dissolute luxury in which men "finally go mad and waste their substance" as is the drive toward intelligible universals.

When the powers of *fantasia* are employed to achieve the totalization of the fragments of the human spirit through a grasp of its origin and genesis, the quest for identity is never complete. It yields a selfhood that is mediated through time. However, the version of itself that the human spirit discovers in the myth, in the *fantasia* of the origin, is a "timeless ordering." What it meets is the power of the image itself. Thus what it discovers is that the completion of its longing for identity can only be found in the "true speech" of the myth, in the immediate identities between things of which only mimetic speech is capable, something that can never be had through recollection. *Fantasia* has thus two heads: it is what is needed in order for men in the age of men to become human, to know who they are, to have an identity, an origin; and it is the awakening of the longing for the true *fantasia* of that origin, for the immediacy of life that knows only the memory of the senses. Intelligibility and recollection are both in their own ways the heralds of dissolution.

To conclude, the view I have attempted to suggest is that Vico's *New Science* involves two senses of *fantasia* or imagination, one which Vico describes, that of *mythic* or *poetic fantasia,* and one which Vico uses to create the knowledge upon which the *New Science* rests, that of *recollective fantasia.* This second form of *fantasia* is that upon which humanistic knowledge depends. *Fantasia* in both its senses involves types of knowledge that are substantially unexamined in theory of knowledge.

Comment on Professor Verene's Paper

Let me begin by saying that I found Professor Verene's paper most interesting and, in its essentials, convincing. He stresses, rightly in my opinion, what is of central importance in Vico's thought, namely, Vico's conviction of an inadequacy in the theories of knowledge both of the rationalism and of the empiricism of his day, both that which stems from Descartes and that which derives from Locke, which have dominated philosophy ever since; namely, their inadequacy as accounts of what is involved in the entire field of the humanities— history, criticism, ethics, aesthetics, law or the study of man, especially as a social being. Professor Verene, in my view, correctly identifies Vico's method as involving his doctrine of the imagination—*fantasia*— as a basic human faculty, active both in understanding and in the creation of what is understood. Furthermore, he brings out the fact that, for Vico, to understand or interpret is to grasp the genesis, through time, of whatever is involved in human understanding and action at any given moment, and that such genesis is a continuous process, causally determined, though not as causality is understood by Hume or Kant. Finally, Professor Verene seems to me right, and indeed original, in distinguishing two senses of Vico's use of *fantasia:* on the one hand, that whereby our primitive ancestors, the *grossi bestioni,* conceived their world timelessly, that is, the world of primitive myth and ritual, and also its successor, the world of heroes, metaphor and epic poetry; and, on the other, the *fantasia* whereby we, living in the age of men, are enabled, though with much mental difficulty and, indeed, agony, to locate these strange worlds in time, to understand them historically, and, by understanding them, to understand ourselves. All that Professor Verene says on this is true and important, even though it leaves at least one central question about Vico's theory of knowledge unanswered.

But before I come to this, I should like to say that one point made by Professor Verene does somewhat puzzle me: in speaking of *recollective fantasia,* by which, in his words, "the human world can come to know itself," he says—I use his words again—"what recollection establishes is a structure of phenomenal ground-consequent relationships in which the origin can be seen in relation to the end." Now, whatever may be meant by *recollection*—on which our collective knowledge of ourselves through our progess in time may rest—"ground-consequent relationships" seems an odd phrase to apply to Vico's notion. The relation of ground to consequent is a logical one, one of strict entailment, and belongs to logical or mathematical or metaphysical reasoning as used by Aristotle, or the Stoics, or the Schoolmen, or Descartes, or Leibniz; this is surely very different from, let us say, the genetic connection of thundering, terror-inspiring Jove with the origin of the family, or of the connection of the revolts of plebeians against their masters with the origins of written law, legal argument, prose, criticism, democracy, which is part of Vico's account of social development. The imaginative reconstruction of this succession of phases surely does *not* involve the use of the ground-consequent nexus as it is used in, say, geometry or rationalist metaphysics—"cultural memory," as Professor Verene felicitously calls it, does not operate by deductive rules. Vico's notion of development is not the logically inexorable exfoliation of some teleologically developing essence, as Aristotle or Leibniz or Hegel conceived it, but a providential sequence, powered, if I may so put it, by the dynamism of desires, passions, needs, which feed the creative imagination and generate images, myths, ritual, systems of belief, symbolic forms, social orders, languages, entire cultures—create them and undermine them and supersede them. The *storia ideale eterna* is a pattern, yes, but is it a ground-consequent pattern? I may well have misunderstood Professor Verene, but I should be grateful for light on this.

The second equally marginal point about which I do not feel clear is the relationship between what Professor Verene calls "recollective *fantasia*," which he rightly maintains is at the heart of Vico's entire system, and what he describes as "the oncoming night of dissolute luxury," in which men "finally go mad and waste their substance"—what Vico calls the "second barbarism of reflection," which characterizes the disintegration of a society before its final collapse. It is not clear to me in what way such "recollection" necessarily, in Vico's view, disintegrates social bonds—does *all* self-consciousness do this? This theory seems to be similar to Schiller's doctrine in his famous essay on sentimental and naive poetry; is it also Vico's? Is the practice of history according to the precepts of the *New Science* one of the causes, or at least a symptom, of inevitable decadence? "Intelligibility and recollection," says Professor Verene, "are both in their own ways the heralds of dissolution." Is the naive myth-making of barbarism indispensable to the cohesion of human groups? Does Professor Verene see some affinity between Nietzsche's doctrine that it is critical self-consciousness—Socrates—that is the fatal solvent of social solidarity, strength, creativity—between this and Vico's philosophy of history? Despite Vico's strain of Platonism? Does Vico regard his own work—his own doctrine of the development of historical self-consciousness—as subversion of the social bonds he approves? On this, too, I should like to be enlightened.

Finally, let me come to the central problem of Vico's theory of knowledge. How does what Professor Verene calls the second sense of *fantasia*, or imagination, that which provides the knowledge on which the *New Science* rests—Professor Verene's "recollective *fantasia*"—how does it work? How do we "enter," "descend into," the minds of those savage fathers or heroes—our ancestors? How do we reconstruct those wildly unfamiliar worlds where "thinking" is "through the body," without some grasp of which we cannot understand history, society, ourselves? On this everything in the *New Science* turns. How does recollective *fantasia* work? Is it individual or collective? Does it work by *analogy* between us and others—between our sophisticated selves and the primitive savages who are declared to be so very different from us? But that way lie the dangers of anachronism, against which Vico utters dire warnings, as Mr. Pompa, in his published works, has done well to remind us. Or do we resurrect these remote cultures by using that faculty by which we remember our own childhood, growth, the successive phases of our own changing experience? Yet the parallel between individuals and societies, microcosm and macrocosm, ontogenesis and phylogenesis, even if it has suggested fruitful ideas to modern psychologists and anthropologists—is it more than a vivid smile, is it a scientific hypothesis? Such a notion as racial or cultural memory seems to rest on no more than a dubious personification of societies: Plato's notion of the *polis* as the individual soul writ large is not perhaps one of his happiest inspirations, and is, fortunately, not part of Vico's design. What, if any, is the relation of Vico's "descent" into the cave of the monster Polyphemus or, indeed, into the brighter world of Ulysses? What is its relation to Herder's *Einfühling*—empathy—or the concepts of later German and Italian thinkers who distinguished historical and critical understanding—*Verstechen*—from scientific knowledge? How, according to Vico, do we establish that the sense that we make of what he calls the huge surviving fragments of the past—of buildings, customs, texts or recorded ritual—that such sense is based on, and indeed involved in, a *correct* reconstruction of such remains? How can we be sure that we are right? How do we choose between rival interpretations of history and coherent fictions? How can we be sufficiently sure of the meaning of the symbolic expressions of diverse cultures to be able to perceive the *sensus communis* of all gentile nations? Vico, so far as I can see, nowhere clearly tells us. Vico's achievement in raising this, the central problem in all subsequent attempts to explain the nature of historical understanding, is perhaps his greatest claim to immortality. His own effort to solve it does not, even now, seem to me to have been discussed adequately. If Professor Verene could tell us how he conceives of this—the working of recollective *fantasia*—he would put us even more deeply in his debt that he has done already.

SIR ISAIAH BERLIN

Response by the Author

Sir Isaiah has raised three questions for my paper which are most stimulating and for which I am most grateful. It is not possible here to give full answers to each of them, particularly the third, but I should like to sketch the general outlines of how I think they might be answered. I should like to clarify first my use of "ground-consequent" relation, which has caused some trouble. I prefaced the sentence in which I used this by saying "in logical terms," and I had in mind not this notion as it comes out of Aristotle, the Stoics, the Schoolmen, Descartes, Leibniz, et al., but the notion of ground-consequent relation as it comes primarily out of philosophical idealism. I would understand the principle of ground-consequent to be a principle applied to change—the notion of a common principle of structure or *ground* which exists in relation to a plurality of successive states or *consequents*. Thus any given stage of consciousness, culture, or social life can be seen as having a common structure (as it is viewed from the perspective of ground) which develops in terms of successive states (as it is viewed from the perspective of consequent). In like manner the entire process of consciousness or human culture can be seen according to this principle as having a structure or ground (e.g., Vico's ideal eternal history considered as such) and as having particular stages (e.g., Vico's three ages). This principle is only the statement in logical terms of the notion of there being a systematic whole through time. The relationship of ground-consequent is one of the double perspective through which a whole can be viewed and is not intended to entail a process of understanding by deductive rules. I do not mean it to be a relationship between a transcendent, infinite ground and its finite accidents such as might be had in a substance metaphysics or ontology. If this were so, then Sir Isaiah would be right in identifying it with the position of Descartes, Leibniz, et al. My remark concerning ground-consequent relationship was intended only to express in logical terms the conception of an immanent relationship a whole has to itself through time.

Sir Isaiah's second point concerns the sense in which I consider Vico's project of recollective *fantasia* itself to contribute to the disintegration of the society which Vico wishes to understand. This is a most interesting point and one about which I was able to say something in the final pages of my paper. Perhaps I can here suggest something further. I do not believe that Vico's philosophy of history involves a point similar to Nietzsche's doctrine that self-reflection is fatal to social solidarity and social strength. Vico's *New Science,* which I have conceived as a project of recollective *fantasia,* is a type of thought that takes place within the age of men, and it is also the thought by which the age of men is to be understood. On Vico's philosophy of history there are real ends as well as real beginnings in history. As the age of men is always the age which marks one of those real ending points, so Vico's recollective thought must be conceived as a part of the end and not something transcendent of it.

Although I do not see Vico's recollective *fantasia* as transcendent of the age of men, I see it as positive rather than negative in its effect. It is not positive in the sense of showing us a way to overcome the barbarism of intelligible universals and the "oncoming night of dissolute luxury." It is not a means for doing away with the ideal eternal history itself and passing somehow into some stage beyond. It is positive in the sense that there are better and worse ways to exist within the third age of culture. The third age, as Vico says, is one in which men "go mad and waste their substance." Recollective *fantasia* is a power of the mind for coping with "madness." It does not prevent the dissolution (such a view would dissolve Vico's project into simply a scientific or technologically oriented project); it is a way of coming to terms with necessity, the necessity of dissolution. In this sense it is the possibility of giving expression to the dignity and ingenuity of thought and human spirit in the face of the necessity of dissolution that time works on a given culture in its enactment of its pattern of ideal eternal history. It can be seen as like that orientation that can occur in the individual toward the naturalness and necessity of death, to which there is no technological or scientific answer. As Vico is fond of calling attention to the similarity of the first age of humanity and that of childhood, so the third age is like the aging of the individual toward his end, whose humanness can be manifest in the collecting of the workings of time through recollection.

Sir Isaiah's third question, which he says concerns the central problem of Vico's theory of knowledge, involves how what I have called "recollective *fantasia*" works. Sir Isaiah asks how we are to descend to the minds of the first humanity. This involves my extending the central thesis of my paper further than I have. What I have attempted to do in formulating my notion of recollective *fantasia* is to uncover something of the power of the mind that is required for "cultural memory." I am concerned to show that this activity functions neither on the basis of analogy nor on the basis of memory. It is not memory since it is not simply the act of "calling back to mind" or remembering. It involves systematic recall. It is also not the function of analogy constructed off of one's childhood, about which Sir Isaiah asks. Although Vico says that there is a special structural relationship between the individual as child and the first men ("the children of the human race"), I do not think that one can be said to reach the structure of culture as ideal eternal history by an analogy off the individual's remembrance of his childhood. The same power of the mind, the power of recollective *fantasia,* is required by both tasks and is presupposed by them. I think further that, as with Plato's notion of the *polis* as the individual soul writ large, the activity of such recollective understanding is best taken from the side of the larger, or culture, to the side of the smaller, or individual. This method allows us to align our understanding with the ethnological understanding of humanity, which shows that the human appears first in communal form, out of which the individual human being is developed. The history of the self begins with the community, not the reverse; the being of the individual emerges from the being of human culture.

What I am most interested in understanding through the notion of recollective *fantasia* is what might be called the *epistemology of origination*. Vico shows us a conception of theory of knowledge which is focused on how things come into being. Since Descartes and Locke, epistemology has been directed either toward the problem of how connections can be asserted between things, especially causal connections, or toward how we can establish that what we think ourselves to know about a thing is indeed knowledge. Both of these directions of investigation into knowledge have little concern with the origination of the things known. The problem of knowledge begins with the things in one way or another already present. The problem of knowledge is conceived as the problem of understanding the relations between things or the assessment of our knowledge of their existence. Vico directs our attention to how a thing comes to be a thing at all. The notion of Jove as the primary example of an imaginative universal is the notion of a kind of knowledge whereby things themselves can be understood to come to be. It is the notion of an epistemology that does not presuppose the existence of things but explores the origins of things. I think that the notions of *Einfühlung* and *Verstehen*, to which Sir Isaiah makes reference, are present in this conception of the epistemology of origination, but they are present in it as a secondary moment. They must be understood not as insight into the nature of things which are already present and "there" in the human world, but as ways of developing meaning once what is originally only momentary has been given form through the imaginative universal.

The original momentariness and pure flux of "thereness" of experience is what is given form through the power of the mind to create imaginative universals. Thus I think that the metaphor is what is fundamental, not analogy. What I have tried to suggest is that the metaphor (when not conceived as a collapsed analogy) is the fundamental power upon which all knowledge depends. It constitutes the power to create identity where only flux is present. Through the imaginative universal objects and meaning emerge where previously there were none. From the perspective of the recollective *fantasia,* ideal eternal history functions as the primary imaginative universal; it is the "Jove" of conscious recollection. Through it time itself is brought into being where previously there was only sequence, flux, and change. Acts of mythic *fantasia* of the first men or of recollective *fantasia* of the last are not acts of empathetic insight based on analogical powers of the subject in relation to the object. Such acts already presuppose the power of the mind to form identities within what is merely momentary and diversely "there."

These are very difficult problems, and I am not prepared to say any final words on them. I think, however, that the solution to them lies in the notion of the metaphor which lies within Vico's most original notion—the imaginative universal. It is the notion which Vico himself so clearly called the "master key" to the *New Science.*

DONALD PHILLIP VERENE

Human Nature and the Concept of a Human Science

BY LEON POMPA

In this paper I want briefly to outline, and then discuss, what I take to be the two main philosophical claims involved in Vico's conception of a human science.[1] The first of these is that our knowledge of the world of human phenomena can be as rigorous and scientific as our knowledge of the world of natural phenomena. The second is that, because it is a *human* science, it involves an appeal to antecedent, experiential knowledge of what it is to be human, which renders its products more intelligible than those of any purely natural science. It has often been assumed that these claims are incompatible and, hence, that they represent a confusion in Vico's thought. I shall argue, on the contrary, that they are not incompatible and that the realization that they are not represents one of Vico's most important contributions to philosophy.

It is worth noting that the history of Vichian scholarship itself reflects the assumption that these claims are incompatible. According to one line of interpretation, adopted initially by some of Vico's nineteenth-century Italian commentators, Vico's main insight lay in the suggestion that our knowledge of human affairs could be rendered scientific. Since, however, this was thought to be incompatible with any reliance upon antecedent knowledge, Vico's references to the latter were disregarded, thus giving rise

[1] Vico did not himself call his science a human science. One has, however, only to refer to the list of topics summarized in Book IV of the third *Scienza nuova* to realize that he intended to include all human phenomena susceptible to scientific treatment. For this reason I shall refer to it in what follows as a human science rather than use the more cumbersome phrase "science of human phenomena."

to the positivist interpretation of his doctrines. According to the line of interpretation favored by the Idealist interpreters, however, Vico's main insight lay in his recognition of the role of some sort of antecedent knowledge in the construction of our knowledge of human affairs.[2] Thus they located Vico's mistake in his suggestion that man could be the object of an empirical science. The assumption which has guided both interpretations has been that the concept of an empirical science precluded any reliance upon antecedent knowledge. The differences between them have depended upon which of the allegedly incompatible claims has been thought to represent Vico's "real" view and which some sort of dispensable aberration. For the rest of this paper I shall try to show how the assumption common to these radically divergent interpretations has obscured a correct understanding and assessment of what Vico has to say.

The New Science as Science

I shall begin by stating briefly my reasons for believing that Vico intended to present a science and what he took a science to be. One might, of course, appeal to the historical fact that he entitled his work, in its three published editions, a *science,* and that throughout them and his *Autobiography* he refers to it constantly as such. Of itself, however, this does not establish much, since the word "science" has been used by a variety of different thinkers in a variety of more and less rigorous senses. It remains to be shown, therefore, that Vico intended to produce a science in a rigorous sense of the word.

First, then, there is the fact that he believed that a science must rest on adequate philosophical foundations, and that his own work did precisely this. I can mention here only two points

---

[2] They did not, of course, interpret these as an appeal to antecedent, *experiential* knowledge, as I propose to suggest, but to an *a priori* deduction of the main principles of human history.

relevant to this claim. In Elements v–xv of the second and third *Scienza nuova,* he offers summaries of the main aspects of his conception of man as a social and historical being. These, he says, both "give us the foundations of the true" and "will serve for considering this world of nations in its eternal idea, by that property of every science, noted by Aristotle, that science has to do with what is universal and eternal."[3] Again, he argues that former historians have not succeeded in giving their work any claim to truth because they have failed to rest it upon a correct philosophical conception of man. Conversely he criticizes previous philosophers for their failure to relate their conceptions of man to any historical research. Had either not failed in these respects, he asserts, they would have anticipated his own science.[4] Thus the suggestion is that his science involves applying the concepts of universality and necessity, appropriate to the Aristotelian conception of a science, to the empirical subject matter with which the historian is concerned.

Second, Vico says explicitly that he is using the method which served Francis Bacon so well in the natural sciences. But he is extending its use beyond Bacon's by "carrying it over from the institutions of nature . . . to the civil institutions of mankind."[5] Exactly what Vico took Bacon's methods to be is problematic, but he seems to have thought that it involved use of systematic, verifiable theory.[6]

Finally, and perhaps most importantly, there are his descriptions of the fruits of his work: "the decisive sort of proof in our Science is this: that the course of the institutions of the nation had to be, must now be, and will have to be such as our Science demonstrates."[7] Vico outlines the structure of this pattern in

---

[3] *Scienza nuova,* 3rd ed. (1744), par. 163. All quotations are taken from *The New Science of Giambattista Vico* (hereinafter *NS*), translated by Thomas G. Bergin and Max H. Fisch (Ithaca: Cornell University Press, 1968).

[4] *NS,* pars. 138–140.

[5] *NS,* pars. 163, 359.

[6] I have discussed this more fully in my book, *Vico: A Study of the New Science* (New York: Cambridge University Press, 1975), pp. 87–103.

[7] *NS,* par. 348.

the "ideal eternal history," which, he says, "is traversed in time by the history of every nation in its rise, development, maturity, decline and fall." [8] Furthermore, he asserts, anyone "who meditates this science narrates to himself this ideal eternal history so far as he himself makes it for himself by that proof: 'it had to be, it has to be, and will have to be.' " [9] In short, the suggestion is that there is a necessity in human affairs which is rendered evident by Vico's science.

The Role of Antecedent Knowledge

I shall now turn briefly to the question of the role of antecedent experiential knowledge in a human science. Vico's conception of this can be understood by attending to three related points: that his science depends upon a certain kind of human *making;* that our knowledge of this making involves recourse to our knowledge of certain modifications of the human mind; and that we achieve the latter by a process of self-reflection. Since it is my contention that Vico fully understood what he was doing in connecting his work *qua human* science with an appeal to antecedent, experiential knowledge, it is necessary to note that he makes these points while drawing a crucial epistemological distinction between the concept of a natural science and that of a human science. Previous philosophers have erred, he complains, in concerning themselves solely with study of the natural world, which, since God has made it, He alone knows, and in neglecting the human world, which, since men had made it, men could come to know. [10]

Vico's formulation of this critical principle is not as unambiguous as one might hope, and it is necessary first to decide what kind of making is in question here. It would seem that there

---

[8] *NS,* par. 349.
[9] *Ibid.*
[10] *NS,* par. 331.

are two possible senses in which men make their history. First, as historical agents they make the activities, institutions, laws, deeds, the *res gestae* themselves, which form the content of that world. Second, as historians they make historiographical accounts of the past.[11]   In the case of the natural sciences it is clear that the scientist is involved in a kind of making which is similar to that involved in making historiographical accounts, insofar as he creates the concepts, theories, and methods of science. What he does not make are the natural phenomena themselves which form the subject matter of his science. The first point Vico is making, therefore, is that the natural world cannot be known because God creates its contents, whereas the human world can be known because man creates its contents.

The second, connected claim is that men can know the world which has been made by men because the principles involved in its creation can be rediscovered within the human mind, that is, "within the modifications of the mind of him who meditates . . . [this science]."[12]

The modifications which Vico himself mentions break down into two kinds. First, there is a series of beliefs which forms a basis for what he claims are the basic institutions of society: religion, marriage, and burial of the dead.[13] Second, there is a series of phases of human mental development in which men are successively imaginative and nonrational beings, semirational but excessively literal-minded beings, and, finally, rational beings, capable of understanding themselves and their world.[14]   This

11 These two senses of "making" are related, of course, to the well known distinction between the two senses of the word "history," that is, as between the historical events themselves and historians' accounts of these events.

12 *NS*, par. 374. Elsewhere Vico descibes this process of meditating his science as a process of "narrating" to oneself and "making" for oneself. See *NS*, par. 349.

13 *NS*, pars. 332–333. In the paragraphs immediately following these Vico argues that these institutions are basic in the sense that, were they not to exist, human nature, being what it in fact is, could not attain its full development. They are basic, therefore, in providing the context necessary for the development of human nature.

14 *NS*, pars. 218–219, 916–918. The world which rational man is capable of

sequence is, moreover, necessary in that each state in it must, in certain circumstances, arise from its predecessor and give rise to its successor. Access to these modifications alone, Vico claims, enables us to understand the necessity in human affairs and in human history. Thus the knowledge made available by Vico's science rests upon antecedent knowledge of these modifications.[15]

Before commenting upon what this means, it is necessary briefly to mention Vico's third point: that we acquire knowledge of these modifications by exercising our capacity for self-reflection. It is not within the compass of this paper to discuss the nature of this capacity itself. What must be emphasized, however, is that what its exercise makes available to us is an understanding of the causes and processes by which, and only by which, human nature, as it exists in us and insofar as we can understand it, develops. It is not just that we understand how human nature can and must develop, but that we understand that to have developed in that way, and as a result of those conditions and causes, is part of what it is to be human, and, hence, that it is part of what it is for anything else, such as a nation, to be human.[16]

There are two points to note about this process before its full significance for Vico's conception of a human science can be made clear. First, it is not essentially a rational process. Man does not develop reason, and hence the capacity to understand himself, by the exercise of reason. He develops it initially through the exercise of certain other psychological capacities, such as those of willing and wanting, and of imagining in accordance with certain principles of the association of ideas, and then by the painful process of testing the ideas thus created by his confrontation with

---

understanding is not of course the natural world, knowledge of which is God's prerogative, but the human world, which man himself creates. Thus this understanding is a form of self-knowledge.

[15] For the nearest Vico comes to saying this in quite these words, see *NS*, pars. 348–349, where he states that the necessity involved in the "ideal eternal history" rests upon principles available to us as modifications of our own human mind.

[16] Vico states the general principle underlying this claim in Elements xiv and xv, *NS*, pars. 147–148.

reality. We develop reason, the capacity to think logically, profitably, and accurately, through our contact with reality and our capacity to feed the fruits of this contact back into our mode of mental operation. This explains Vico's frequent recourse to our understanding of ourselves as children in illuminating man's early history. For the same principles which cause children to imagine nonexistent spirits cause early man to anthropomorphize his whole world, and the principles which underlie the erosion of these beliefs are the same in both cases. For Vico, therefore, activities of the imagination and the will are just as intelligible as purely rational processes. Our understanding of any of them depends upon our capacity to reflect upon them insofar as we ourselves can exercise, or have exercised, them.

Second, Vico's appeal to antecedent knowledge in a human science is not an appeal to knowledge of the purely formal properties of human nature. It is an appeal to knowledge of the *content,* be it genetic or social, of human nature. Thus it is not enough that the concept of human development should be operative in a human science. It is necessary that we should have knowledge of the process through which anything which is to count as a human development should go, and in what conditions such a process can, and should, occur. And since it would seem to be a question of fact whether or not such conditions and processes obtain in the world, it would seem that the antecedent knowledge upon which Vico's concept of a human science rests is antecedent, factual knowledge.

The Concept of Being Human

I want to begin my examination of this conception of a human science by considering the objection I mentioned at the start of this paper, that is, that it involves two incompatible claims. For, it might be suggested, insofar as Vico, in approaching any subject matter, is making certain factual knowledge about that subject matter a condition of treating it as he does, his claims cannot be open to empirical testing, hence his conclusions cannot represent a species of scientific knowledge. For what Vico is doing is building certain antecedent *factual* knowledge into his science as a sort of *metaphysical* substratum. And this alone would be enough to render the enterprise nonscientific.

The assumption behind this objection is that an explanation of something can be scientific only if every factual principle involved in it is open, in theory at least, to empirical testing. Of course, it would not be part of the objection that everything involved in a scientific explanation ought in fact to be tested. For it is an important methodological point that where, in the attempt to explain something, a clash arises between two or more principles usually accepted as part of the science relevant to that thing, we ought to accept as true those principles which occupy a more basic position in the structure of the science and jettison those which are less basic. So it is not as if the natural scientist has a completely free hand when he approaches the explanation of some phenomenon, as if, in difficult cases, he can call in question all the basic laws and theories of his science. He operates under definite methodological restrictions. Nevertheless, in the last analysis, even if only *in extremis,* any of the principles of such a science, no matter how fundamental, can be questioned and, if necessary, jettisoned. So, ultimately, the objection would hold, antecedent knowledge of certain matters of fact is incompatible with the claim of a body of propositions to be a science.

If we ask, however, what follows from this, I think it will be evident wherein lies the strength of Vico's position. .For, given that we are prepared to accept that no antecedent knowledge whatsoever is permissible in a science, then in principle anything whatsoever can figure in scientific laws and theories, no matter how difficult to understand we might find the correlations and entities involved. But if we are going to allow that something is a science only if it conforms to this condition, then in principle there is no reason why we should not have to accept, in the case of some human science, that phenomena which we find quite incredible may be the causes of human behavior and invoked to explain the latter.

But this, in fact, is something we are reluctant to do. Social scientists, for example, when they look for explanations of human behavior, antecedently discount numerous logical possibilities by their selection of which correlations to search for, and this prior selection turns upon their conception of what it is to be a human being and what sorts of explanations are admissible as parts of a social science. It is not, of course, that they deny *a priori* that there may be correlations between, for example, certain features of the chromosome structure of a given group of people and their views on private property. But rather that, were there such a connection, it wouldn't be intelligible in the same way as, let us say, a connection between people's feelings of frustration or non-frustration under certain conditions of social mobility and their views on private property. It would lack the kind of intelligibility that social scientists look for in their explanations. Thus a certain conception of the kind of explanation appropriate to a human science underlies the practice of social scientists.

Now it could be argued that nothing in this goes to support the view I have ascribed to Vico. For, of necessity, any intellectual discipline with pretensions to being scientific works with a system of concepts which establishes and limits the range of its subject matter. But this system of concepts can be defined conventionally. Thus in the social sciences, in history and so on—that is, in all those branches of knowledge which purport to be about *man*—there is no need to base these definitions upon some alleged antecedent knowledge we have of certain basic human characteristics. It is enough if some conventional definitions are offered or implied such that they can provide the practitioner with an unambiguous vocabulary for the pursuit of his researches. Of course, it would hardly be suggested that these definitions need contain mention of no properties by which we could relate the social scientist's or the historian's "man" to what we all recognize as man.

But this could be done by mention of certain observational properties—for example, biological properties—and in such a way as not to set antecedent limits to the kind of explanation which might be found appropriate.

To see how implausible this is, however, we need only ask ourselves how widely we would be prepared to construe the limits of these explanations and still believe that it was man we were investigating. Let us take, for example, the two sets of "modifications" Vico wants to build into his conception of man—the genetic, psychological development of human nature leading to the growth of reason, and the three necessary social principles. With regard to the genetic principles, it would be easy enough to conceive of beings who did not conform to them—for example, beings in whom rationality sprang to life full-blown without need of the teaching and education which reflection on our own experience shows to be necessary. It would be easy enough to conceive of such a being, but could we seriously consider him to be a man, or a nation of such beings to be a nation of men? If we had to write the history of such a being, how could we understand his acquisition of reason if we could not illuminate it by analogy with something we know about ourselves? It might, of course, be held that we do not require to understand his *acquisition* of reason to be able to think of him as man. All that would be required is that we can understand what it is that he has, and what he can do, when he possesses reason. But, as Vico fully realized, this is certainly not enough. The historical process whereby we acquire reason as a development from nonrational capacities is as much a part of what we take ourselves to be as are the things we can do when we possess it. Neglect of this point, incidentally, goes some way toward explaining why many philosophers who feel instinctively that computers, even perhaps fairly advanced computers, are not men have found it difficult to offer an adequate philosophical defense of this position.

And the same, surely, is true with regard to Vico's three necessary social relationships. How could we really understand as a human being somebody who did all the things that we know we do as a consequence of involvement in certain kinds of social situations, or exposure to certain kinds of social teaching, conditioning, and pressures, without having to be involved in all this? Nor, indeed, is it enough that, to think of somebody as a human being, we have to be able to think of him as susceptible to certain kinds of conditioning. He has also to be susceptible to it by virtue of the very same factual properties as render ourselves susceptible to it. Thus we can conceive of somebody who might be conditioned to learn or acquire a foreign language by being subjected to sequences of nonsense syllables. But could we really say we could understand how he acquired it as we can of somebody who learns it by our own techniques, which depend upon an understanding of all sorts of experiential truths about the way in which our minds work and the conditions in which we learn best? Could we, indeed, in these circumstances, understand what would be meant by saying that he had *learned* the language at all?

It must be stressed again that it is not a question of not being able to conceive such a being. It is, rather, how we could think of him as a man, or his history as human history, if we were not prepared to take such facts for granted. It does not follow, of course, that we *ought* to think of him as a man, and we may, indeed, finally have to conclude that we ought not to think of him in this way. But it remains the case that as long as we can think of him as a man we are committed to taking for granted such facts about him.

Vico's claim is thus that the concept of a human science depends upon our own conception of what it is to be human. It may be that this enters the science by way of definition, but if so it must be by the construction of definitions incorporating those factual properties which are basic to the whole concept of being human, properties which we can know about only by living through, and being able to reflect upon, the situations and means whereby we acquire our own human nature. A natural science, on the other hand, involves no such knowledge. Definitions and theories are, indeed, required, but these need satisfy only the purely formal and logical conditions required by the concept of a science. They need not satisfy the further conditions required by the concept of being human. A natural science thus operates under fewer restrictions than a human science, but it pays for this greater freedom by lacking the kind of intelligibility that is proper to anything we can truly recognize as human.

Comment on Professor Pompa's Paper

It is already apparent that Leon Pompa's book, *Vico: A Study of the New Science,* will be a landmark in Vichian scholarship. He rightly remarked in his preface that "in the two centuries since it appeared the *Scienza nuova* has not been the subject of any analytic commentary or monograph whatsoever." His book was preceded by a long article, "Vico's Science," in *History and Theory* 10 (1971): 49–83, and it has been followed by another, "Vico and the Presuppositions of Historical Knowledge," in Giorgio Tagliacozzo and Donald P. Verene, eds., *Giambattista Vico's Science of Humanity* (Baltimore: The Johns Hopkins University Press, 1976), pp. 125–140, and now by the paper we have before us. Doubtless there will be others to come. It will take us a decade or more to assimilate the book, and our misunderstandings and questions will provoke restatements, elucidations, more detailed elaborations, and supplementary arguments.

There is no single, simple, easy way to assimilate all at once what Pompa is trying to tell us about the *New Science*. Nevertheless, we shall all be trying various ways of putting his main argument to ourselves, each of them only an entry into it, not an overview of it. My own paper in the present conference is in large part a response to his book, and it contains some of the particular entries I have tried myself; for example, that from "the philosophy of history."

I am not aware of being in disagreement with Pompa on any point that seems to me to be essential to his argument. But I shall offer here some incidental queries and comments, on the chance that one or another of them will betray a misunderstanding which he may then try to remove.

The title and the opening paragraphs seem to assume that there might be more human sciences than one; perhaps even that Vico's "new science" is but one of an indefinite plurality of human sciences. Vico does describe several "principal aspects" of the new science. But does he concede that one or more of these might be detached and developed independently, or that there might be a human science that had from the start been independent of it? And are the presuppositions of the new science simply those of any human science there may be?

In the initial statement of "the two main philosophical claims involved in Vico's conception of a human science," the terms "phenomena" and "products" strike me as unVichian. (Vico does use the phrase "two horrendous human phenomena" in speaking of Messalina and Nero.) Fortunately, Pompa has told us what he means by "human phenomena" in the second of his previous papers, at the top of p. 128. We should not know from the present paper.

With regard to "antecedent, experiential knowledge of what it is to be human," this might be taken to mean knowledge derived from our having ourselves been born and passed through infancy, childhood, and adolescence on the way to maturity. I suggest that more of it is derived from living with human individuals in all stages of development from infancy to old age, and from the institutions in, under, and through which that living is done. (Is it relevant to remark that genetic psychology persuades us that there is a large admixture of error in that antecedent experiential knowledge?)

In general, Pompa likes to avoid the technicalities of Vico's time and substitute technicalities of our own. So far as I recall, he never mentions the transcendentals and never uses the phrase *verum factum*. For the latter he uses such phrases as "the causal theory of truth" or "the creative theory of knowledge." He is quite aware that, although Vico of course uses the nontechnical distinction between true and false, his technical distinction is that between true and certain, and that these are in the first place characters of the things we apprehend rather than of our apprehension of them, or of our statements about them. He is aware also that *scienza*, science or knowledge, as a technical term, is contrasted not with ignorance or error but with *coscienza*, consciousness. Yet Pompa sometimes uses "true," "truth," "science," etc., as if he had forgotten these technicalities, or did not wish to trouble his readers with them.

Even if Pompa's argument comes to be generally accepted by Vico scholars, most of Vico's readers will doubtless continue to value the *New Science* as an inexhaustible treasure trove of precious insights, quotable sayings, adumbrations of later discoveries, thought-provoking claims, and will not concern themselves with such questions as whether these insights are presuppositions or deliverances of one or more sciences, whether they all hang together, and, if so, how.

MAX H. FISCH

Response by the Author

Professor Fisch's welcome comments give me the opportunity to clarify certain points in my paper in answer to the questions he raises. I shall take these in his own order.

First, despite my choice of words, it is not my intention to suggest that there might be more than one human science. Rather, what I had in mind in this paper was that Vico is proposing a minimal set of conditions that must be satisfied by anything that could intelligibly be called a human science. That is to say, he is stating the minimal presuppositions we must make in thinking about something if we are to think of that thing as human. He is certainly, therefore, claiming that there could not be more than one such set of conditions. Of course, it is an arguable matter, as Professor Fisch implies later, whether he has located the correct set of conditions, and if it were to turn out that he had not, then we should have to say that Vico's own science was not a human science and that some other body of knowledge, which did satisfy them, was such a science.

These comments apply primarily to Vico's overall science, that whose proper object is the "common nature of nations." It is true, however, that Vico distinguishes a number of different aspects of his science, and Professor Fisch raises the question whether these could be detached and developed as sciences independently of it. Although it seems clear that Vico can, indeed does, allow that there may be certain difficulties that are peculiar to these different aspects, he can scarcely allow, nor, I think, does he suggest, that these could ever count as human sciences, whatever else they be, if they were pursued independently of the conditions claimed to be necessary to all human sciences. Moreover, since the latter conditions pervade these different aspects equally, connecting them in the complex of activities which constitute human affairs, it is difficult to see how these aspects can be properly grasped except in their connections with one another. This seems clearly enough to be Vico's own view insofar as he himself points to a series of logical and causal relationships in which these aspects stand to one another, while also insisting that they are infused with the unity of the human spirit.

It does not follow from any of this, however, that once this science has been established there is no further point in empirical research and that history can be written once and for all. For the conclusions of such a science are always established in the light of evidence, and as the latter varies, both in quantity and quality, so may the former, both in their solidity and in the range of human activity which they encompass. Thus Vico may allow that the conclusions of such a science be extensively revisable, provided always that the presuppositions involved in their establishment be such as to allow us to grasp what is human in them. If, as I have argued in this paper, some of these presuppositions are of a factual nature, then the range of such revisions will not be such as to cover every possible fact whatsoever, but these factual presuppositions are of a high level of generality and still leave empirical research its proper and indispensable role in the establishment of the conclusions of the science.

I welcome Professor Fisch's remarks about the meaning of the expression "antecedent, experiential knowledge of what it is to be human." In using this expression, I did not mean to suggest that it was sufficient for the requisite antecedent knowledge that we should ourselves have passed through the sequence from infancy to childhood to maturity. It is, however, necessary. It is necessary because such a sequence is part of the reality of the human world. Equally, however, it is not sufficient precisely because it is only a part. Professor Fisch is correct in suggesting that we require in addition knowledge of the "institutions in, under, and through which such living is done," for this is what is implied in Vico's claim that man is necessarily social. The essential point here is that without this context of institutions our potential for being human would simply fail to be realized. It would fail because a large part of our common human nature consists in the structuring of our activities by concepts and beliefs which have an internal reference to such institutions and which therefore could not obtain without a context of such institutions. But though we require knowledge of such institutions, it is important to realize that we require knowledge also of the characteristic way in which humans are affected by them. To be brought up "in, under, and through" them is not, for example, merely to be brought up in their presence, as the failure of domestic animals to become human demonstrates. It involves the human capacity to learn to think in, and to regulate one's conduct by, terms which involve the concepts of these institutions. And to be able to understand this process, it is not merely necessary to have gone through it oneself, it is necessary also to be able to reflect upon the whole context in which, and by which, our potentialities are realized, in order to understand how we come to be human. Hence the importance of the concept of self-reflection for Vico.

On only one point would I wish to express some disagreement with Professor Fisch's remarks. This concerns his ultimate suggestion, if this is the suggestion, that it is perhaps not so important, after all, whether Vico has produced a systematic science, as he claimed to have done. I certainly would not want to deny that for future generations Vico's works may provide an inexhaustible source of stimulating thoughts. Nevertheless, the interpretation of the latter is an important matter on a number of counts. And the doctrines of the *New Science* interconnect in such a way that, even were one not interested in the concept of the enterprise as a whole in itself, it would be very difficult to interpret many of Vico's more particular insights in a satisfactory way without seeing how they relate to one another in the overall enterprise. The idea of the "ideal eternal history," for example, is one of the most striking in Vico, but I cannot see how we can understand what the "ideal eternal history" is unless we can decide what is its relation to empirical fact, to providence, to the common mental language, and, indeed, to the nature common to all nations. Thus even if one's interests lie in other matters than that of the possibility of a systematic, human science, there are large areas of Vico's thought which cannot be interpreted with any sense of persuasion without taking them, as Vico presents them, as aspects of a putative science and hence grappling with the problem which, in my view, is central to the interpretation of Vico's thought.

LEON POMPA

Vico's Theory of Science

BY ERNAN McMULLIN

In this paper, I propose to inquire into the notion of science that underlies Vico's *Scienza nuova*. It would be fairly generally agreed today that the account of the origins of social institutions given in that work did, in fact, in some sense constitute a new science. But in what sense *was* it a science? In particular, did it incorporate new ideas on the theory of science itself, on the nature of proof, for instance, or of explanation? Did the methodology implicit in it differ in any important respects from that of the great natural scientists of the generation before Vico?

The Rhetorician as Scientist

There is, however, one potential challenge that must be disposed of right at the beginning. After all, Vico was a professor of rhetoric, a learned philologist, a historian of jurisprudence. He was not familiar with the science of Galileo or Newton. Though he had read Bacon and Descartes, he showed very little concern for the niceties of the complex tradition in theory of science stretching back from them to Aristotle. He rejected the Cartesian application of geometrical method to physics, true. But he has little to say of his own methods, and what he does say is often enigmatic.

Is it not possible, then, that our attempt to discern an implicit theory of science in Vico's work is misplaced? Is it not characteristic of our age to impose on early writers "scientific" intentions that in reality would have been alien to them? Is this not

another symptom of "positivism," that dread disease of the judgment against which many commentators on Vico find it necessary to warn their readers? Ought not Vico be taken as a rhetorician, a poet, and his work in consequence as a fiction, to be judged
primarily on aesthetic criteria? Angus Fletcher asserts that the
style of the *Scienza nuova* is the "natural drunkenness," the
"Dionysian whirl," of a rhetorical tradition which has only at
most a semblance of science.[1] It persuades us (he suggests) not
as science does, but as Plato's *Symposium* or as Neapolitan opera
does. It combines disparate elements for reasons that are at bottom rhetorical rather than scientific; it is ultimately intended as
allegory, not as scientific theory.

Though there can be no denying that Vico taught rhetoric
and was formed in the traditions of jurisprudence rather than
those of philosophy, to judge his great work by the canons of
rhetoric only would seem to betray both its intention and its
achievement. It *is* important, of course, to notice the role he
gives to metaphor, to the poetic modes of thought in the "age
of heroes"; it is enlightening to follow with Hayden White the
generic similarities between transitions in societies and the tropological transformations of speech from metaphor, to metonymy,
to synecdoche, to irony.[2] But one must always return to the intention of the work, stated in so many ways within it, to discover
the "universal and eternal principles (such as every science must
have) on which all nations were founded and still preserve themselves." [3] He supposes himself to be following the "best ascertained method of philosophizing, that of Francis Bacon" in his
manner of interweaving fact and idea; his axioms can claim to

[1] In a paper on "What Vico Suggests to the Aesthetician of Our Time" read at
the conference at which this essay was originally presented.

[2] Hayden V. White, "The Tropics of History: The Deep Structure of the *New
Science*," in Giorgio Tagliacozzo and Donald P. Verene, eds., *Giambattista Vico's
Science of Humanity* (Baltimore: The Johns Hopkins University Press, 1976), pp.
65–85.

[3] *The New Science of Giambattista Vico* (hereinafter *NS*), translated by Thomas
G. Bergin and Max H. Fisch (Ithaca: Cornell University Press, 1968), par. 333.

provide "foundations of the true" that are "universal and eternal" in nature and hence sufficient to constitute science in Aristotle's sense of that term.[4]

More important than explicit statements of this sort is the connective structure of the work itself. There are "axioms" which are asserted to be "necessary"; numerous consequences are said to "follow" from these. There are "hypotheses" which are said to need justification. There are frequent readings of fables or etymologies in the light of the general principles of the "ideal history of the nations," which are asserted as definitive, while other readings are held to be refuted. Vico indeed constantly supposes himself to have "refuted" a variety of predecessors. Their assertions about early man, their interpretations of Roman law, and so forth, are shown to be "false." Bodin's account of the successive forms of civil constitution, for example, is declared to be lacking in "scientific foundation":

> We might here content ourselves with having refuted him completely by the natural succession of political forms which we have established by such numberless proofs, particularly in this [fourth] book. But it pleases us to add, *ad exuberantiam,* a refutation based on the impossibilities and absurdities of his own position.[5]

What he seeks is quite evidently the true. It is also the universal. His ideal eternal history is proposed as a general account of "the eternal laws which are instanced by the deeds of all nations." [6]   When, as frequently happens, they do not apply, he goes to elaborate lengths to show just why an exception might have been expected in this particular case. Or he will insist that, despite appearances, it really is not an exception. Assyria, for instance, could not have begun as a monarchy: "in virtue of the uniform course run by all the nations," that monarchy *must* have been preceded by a democratic regime despite the entire lack of any documentary evidence for this.[7] His schema allows

4 *NS*, par. 163.
5 *NS*, par. 1009.
6 *NS*, par. 1096.
7 *NS*, par. 737.

him to interpret hundreds of items drawn from records of all kinds—historical, legal, religious, literary—and he is altogether confident about the reliability of the historical reconstructions he bases on these interpretations.

The ideal eternal history is for him no allegory; it rests on a theory sufficiently precise and sufficiently powerful to enable him "purely by understanding" to fill in the "beginnings of universal history" even where records are totally lacking.[8] This is the claim to a *science,* in the strongest possible sense. We must not be misled by the giants and witches who wander through his pages; we must not conclude that he could not possibly have intended his readers to take his work literally. Allegorical elements can, of course, be found in his pages, notably in the preface where he explains the details of the florid frontispiece he had had designed for the book. Yet even in this preface, he will proudly assert that he is about to break away from the "monstrous opinions" of his predecessors. He is proposing a new account of the origins of language, one which will be "fully proved" in the course of his book, and which rests on a "demonstrated necessity of nature" of the first gentile peoples. The discovery that these peoples were "poets who spoke in poetic characters" is indeed "the master key of this Science," one which has cost "the persistent research of almost all our literary life." [9] This is the language of a man who really believes he *has* discovered something new about how language came to be, and he is expressing it as best he can in a language that is itself often metaphoric but whose manifest aim is to reveal the truth about the past.

The first men "were all robust sense and vigorous imagination." [10] Unimpeded by the possession of adequate class concepts, they "created things according to their own ideas." [11] In their

---

[8] *NS,* par. 738.
[9] *NS,* par. 34.
[10] *NS,* par. 375.
[11] *NS,* par. 376.

fables, they projected imaginative universals, "Achilles," for example, connoting the valor common to all strong men.[12]   These "first poets attributed to bodies the being of animate substances, with capacities measured by their own—namely, sense and passion."[13]   Of course, *we* know that they were wrong in this ascription.   Their poetry was "born of their ignorance of causes, for ignorance, the mother of wonder, made everything wonderful to men who were ignorant of everything."[14]   What made it poetry was not just the feeling and imagination that suffused it, nor the leaps of metaphor that made it possible, but the objective impossibility (unknown to the "poets" themselves) that underlay it.   It is, in fact, an "eternal property" of poetry that its material should be "the credible impossibility": the poet by his art makes the impossible appear credible.   It was, from *our* vantage point, "a deficiency of human reasoning" that gave rise to this first poetry, for it was impossible—as *we* know—that "bodies should be minds, yet it was believed that the thundering sky was Jove."[15]

The contrast between science and poetry is here quite sharp. The first men were poets, not scientists, because their metaphorical extensions of language were not tested by reason and were in the outcome often unjustified.   The *Scienza Nuova*, on the other hand, announces "a new critical art that has hitherto been lacking," one which will allow philosophy to "reduce philology to the form of a science" with the aid of decisive proofs and indubitable principles.[16]   This science will employ a "poetic logic" to decipher the myths and other linguistic remains that come down to us from early man, but it will not itself be constructed after the fashion of the poetry it takes as the object of its study.   As a science, it will be reflective, analytic, methodologically self-conscious; in other words, it will be typical of the

[12] *NS*, par. 403.
[13] *NS*, par. 404.
[14] *NS*, par. 375.
[15] *NS*, par. 383.
[16] *NS*, pars. 7, 348–349.

rational products of the age of men, with perhaps one reservation to be discussed below.[17]

In an earlier work, *De nostri temporis studiorum ratione*,[18] Vico characterizes poetry in a somewhat different way. Poets, he reminds his readers, "keep their eyes focused on an ideal truth, which is a universal idea." Indeed, they may be said to be

> no less eager in the pursuit of truth than philosophers. The poet teaches by delighting what the philosopher teaches austerely. . . . He may depart from the daily semblances of truth, in order to be able to frame a loftier semblance of reality. He departs from inconstant, unpredictable nature in order to pursue a more constant, more abiding reality. He creates imaginary figments which, in a way, are more real than physical reality itself.[19]

Is it possible that it is this "truth" of poetry that Vico is pursuing in the *Scienza nuova?*

The answer must once again be: No. The context of the *ratio studiorum* should be recalled. He is criticizing the emphasis on deductive geometric method in the curriculum of the day. In its place, this method can be quite effective. But applied to physics and other nonmathematical fields, it is a "faulty and captious way of reasoning," [20] and this for two reasons. First, it depends on the availability of certainly known axioms. But these are obtainable only in fields where we ourselves create the forms that are being explicated: in mathematics and the human sciences. Not, however, in physics, where the forms are created by God and where men have no independent access to them. Second, the geometrical method is ruinous to eloquence, to the arts of

[17] Max Fisch, "Introduction," *NS*, p. xli.

[18] Published in 1709. As the phrase was used in Vico's time, the *ratio studiorum* of a college could mean simply its curriculum, i.e., the division of studies actually proposed to its students. Or it could mean the educational theory *underlying* the curriculum. More often, perhaps, it was used to cover both of these. The phrase is still in use at Jesuit colleges today as a convenient way of referring to "curriculum and its theory."

[19] Giambattista Vico, *On the Study Methods of Our Time*, translated by Elio Gianturco (Indianapolis: Bobbs-Merrill, 1965), pp. 42–43.

[20] *Ibid.*, p. 22.

expression. To move forward in small rule-guided steps, as axiomatic geometry proceeds,

> is apt to smother the student's specifically philosophical faculty, i.e. his capacity to perceive the analogies existing between matters lying far apart and, apparently, most dissimilar. It is this capacity which constitutes the source and principle of all ingenious, acute, and brilliant forms of expression. . . . Metaphor, the greatest and brightest ornament of forceful, distinguished speech, undoubtedly plays the first role in acute, figurative expression.[21]

There are two points to note here. Vico is talking about eloquence of expression, and notes the importance of metaphor to it. Teachers and writers in *any* field, even scientific fields like physics, should remember that metaphor engages the imagination and forces the hearer to search through analogies to catch what is being said. He rejoices in the advantage that the Italian tongue gives him: it "forces the attention of listeners by means of metaphorical expressions, and prompts it to move back and forth between ideas which are far apart." [22] Metaphor is an essential part of pedagogy, because it strengthens imagination and thus indirectly "nurtures the reasoning powers" too.[23] More, it helps in persuasion, and the aim of the scientific treatise, no less than the orator's speech, is to persuade. One would expect, then, to find—as one does—a free use of metaphor in the pages of the *Scienza Nuova*. But this ought not lead us to treat the work as itself allegorical or "poetic" in the narrower sense in which he separates "poetry" from other parts of the curriculum in his *ratio studiorum*. Philosophy has to worry about the *validity* of argument and not just the imaginative process by which the argument is constructed or the modes of expression by which it is conveyed.[24]

Vico is, however, making a further point about metaphor. The capacity for metaphor is the specifically *philosophical* faculty, it

---

21 *Ibid.*, p. 24.
22 *Ibid.*, p. 41.
23 *Ibid.*, p. 14.
24 *Ibid.*

appears. The philosopher has to discern relations between "matters lying far apart and apparently most dissimilar." It is no simple matter of abstraction; the class concepts do not lie to hand, as the Aristotelian tradition had too easily supposed. Does this mean that the philosopher's assertions are themselves metaphorical? To serve as principles for the new science, they will have to be true and universal, capable of establishing with certainty the numerous consequences to be derived from them. Is this consistent with their metaphoric status?

Vico does not pursue this issue, alas. Nor does he attempt (we shall return to this point below) an answer to the other question that occurs to the modern reader: How are these metaphors to be evaluated? What is to serve as justification for metaphorical assertion in science? It would, indeed, have been difficult for him to push these issues further than he did. One reason for this was the classic conception of science as "the universal and eternal" which not only he, but most of his contemporaries, still entertained. Though natural philosophers had been making reluctant use of hypothetical models in their explanations of physical phenomena from Descartes' time onward, the implications this shift held for the theory of science had not as yet been clearly realized.

Vico had no analyses of models-use in the natural sciences to go on in his pioneering attempts to formulate the role of metaphor in the sciences of man. If he had, he might conceivably not have drawn so sharp a line between the natural and social sciences. For the creative use of metaphor in the human sciences, enabling concepts to be stretched to form new patterns of connection, might not then have seemed so different from its use in constructing the models of the physicist. But this is to get ahead of the story. Enough has, perhaps, been said to allow us at least to conclude that the presumption on which our essay is based, namely, that Vico intended his work to be taken seriously as science, is a valid one.

Vico's Notion of Science

Asking about Vico's *notion* (rather than his *theory*) of science is a way of asking what sort of knowledge he believed "science" to be. What kind of assertion does a "scientific" statement make? We have already intimated that he shared in the classic view inherited from the Greek tradition: science is a set of universal principles which are asserted with certainty and finality. The "eternity" and "necessity" on which Aristotle insisted in the *Posterior Analytics* still appeared to Vico, as to most of his contemporaries, to be the only respectable goal for philosophers to aim at in their attempts to construct a proper science.

This can be seen from the entire structure of the *Scienza nuova* as well as from the language employed in it. The terminology of "axioms, definitions, and postulates that this science takes as elements from which to deduce the principles on which it is based and the method by which it proceeds" [25] was the familiar one of the Aristotelian and the later Cartesian traditions. His scrutiny of the institutions in which all men agree provides him, he asserts, with "the universal and eternal principles such as every science must have." [26] And the methodology which makes this possible derives from "a truth beyond all question," the *verum/factum* principle (we know with certainty only what we make). [27] Phrases like "indubitable principle," "logical proof," "follows with necessity," "establish," "demonstration," are dotted through his pages.

The *Scienza nuova* reveals an ideal eternal history traversed in time by nations in their rise and fall. The common nature of the nations can be fully and definitively grasped by us, since the nations themselves are the products of mind. On the other hand, the physicist can never make a defensible claim to science in this strong sense. The material world is not his creation; he can

---

[25] *NS*, par. 41.
[26] *NS*, par. 332.
[27] *NS*, par. 331.

never fully penetrate it. His truths are "not really truths but wear the semblance of probability." [28] He must content himself with verisimilitude, a limitation that ought to be (Vico adds) a salutary curb to human presumption and pride. The new mechanics of such as Galileo and Newton could not lay claim to "science" in the classic sense, then, but the new science of man could—and did!

What makes this assessment doubly piquant for us is that the physicists themselves were at this time just beginning to realize that "science" in the older sense might be beyond their grasp. Such "science" cannot be yielded either by the generalizations of the inductivist or the hypotheses of such as Descartes. Yet even though the dependence of science upon induction and hypothesis had been obvious from the beginning of the seventeenth century at least, it was only with the greatest reluctance that physicists gradually faced the realization that a science of the "eternal and necessary" was not within their power. Even Newton hesitated on this; the axioms of his mechanics could still be construed as definitive, as "science" in the best Aristotelian sense. Chemistry he could leave in the status of hypothesis. But mechanics seemed to be able to transcend the status of inductive generalization. Others, like Huygens and Locke, were not so optimistic, and the view that perhaps the best to which a "science" of nature could aspire was the status of the probable or the gradually improving approximation slowly began to gain acceptance. What held it back, of course, was the enormous authority of Newtonian mechanics. It was, indeed, only in our own century that the classic conception of science was finally abandoned, as Newtonian mechanics yielded to the reshaping hands of Einstein.

It is tantalizing to see Vico come so close to the truth in his assessment of the "scientific" status of physics (admittedly without much more than intuition to bear him out) and yet miss the mark in his own chosen domain. Yet perhaps this is not a fair

---

[28] Vico, *On the Study Methods of Our Time*, p. 23.

way to put it. It was altogether understandable that Vico should have retained the older notion of science to characterize his own work. The *verum/factum* principle made this notion a plausible ideal for the systematic reflective analysis of human institutions, Vico's "new science," as well as for the "old science" of mathematics. Had it not been for the force of this principle, and for the undoubted authority the classic conception of science still retained, especially in the scholastic tradition familiar to Vico, he might well have been the first theorist of a new sort of "science," one where metaphor (or model) would play a central role, where scientific concepts themselves would be seen to be developing, where theory would be regarded as never definitive but always open to reformulation in the light of new challenge. There was much in his work to incline him to such a view: his sensitivity to the importance of probable reasonings of the *ars topica*,[29] his grasp of explanation through origins, his conviction that human culture and human knowledge grow through transformation. But the time was not yet ripe for such a radical abandonment of long-held convictions about the reach of mind. On the contrary, the *Scienza nuova* seemed to its author to offer the first real hope that these convictions could be realized in any domain other than that of mathematics.

So much, then, for Vico's notion of science. But what *theory* of science underlay it? Vico saw justification or proof to be the characteristic mark of science. What was his theory of proof? He wrote no *Discourse on Method*; indeed, his remarks on method are sparse and scattered. To answer this question about his theory of science, we shall have to turn to the *Scienza Nuova* and ask what methods he actually follows there. In particular, what notion of *justification* underlies the work? In all the complex tangle of "axiom" and "consequence," it ought to be possible to discern the ways in which evidence is characteristically offered for what is being asserted. What we are seeking, then, is not an explicit account but the "theory" that lies implicit in the struc-

29 *Ibid.*, pp. 14–20.

ture of the work when it is considered as science, that is, as warranted assertion.

In the course of the seventeenth century, there was endless debate as to what mode of inference was proper to science. On what sort of logic ought properly "scientific" claims rest? Vico would not have been aware of the complexities of this discussion, which went on mainly among those interested in the new science of mechanics. But it may be of some interest, before we discuss his own response to this question, to review the variety of answers that had already been given it.

The Seventeenth-Century Debate

Three of these answers, in particular, will concern us. The first is that of Aristotle himself. He argued that two sorts of warrant are needed in the construction of a science. First is the skilled intuition by means of which the principles of a science are secured. Second is the rule-governed deductive process by means of which one moves from principle to theorem, from syllogistic premise to conclusion. Axiomatic geometry gave him the model for this intuitive-deductive account. Once one comes to understand such concepts as *line* and *point* (and this involves at least as much experience as is required to allow one to come to use these concepts correctly), one can grasp the truth of the axioms immediately. But how is this sort of intuition to operate in fields like biology and physics? How are the necessary connections of essence and attribute to be known? Can the axioms be known with assurance prior to the deductions that might be made from them? If they cannot, they lack the status of necessary truths, because deductions made from them could at best confirm them only as good hypotheses.

This was the question that lay so heavily over the Cartesian enterprise. Descartes began by accepting the Aristotelian axiomatic account; the first truths are supposed to be self-warranting, and their warrant is then transferred by means of deduction to the more specific truths. Effects must be understood by understanding the causes first. One cannot work with assurance from effects back to causes because of the logical possibility of a multiplicity of alternative causes that could produce the same results. But what if the causes be outside the immediate range of experience? And such hypothetical causes Descartes was forced to introduce when faced with the complexity and variety of physiology, meteorology, even optics.

In the *Discourse*, Descartes concedes that hypothetical reasoning must be utilized in some parts of science. But he feels he has to apologize to the reader for this, and appears to hope that all hypotheses save the correct one can, in principle, be excluded by persistent testing. Others, like Kepler and Boyle, saw perhaps more clearly that a new sort of warrant is involved here: the hypothesis is validated by the number and variety of verified consequences derivable from it rather than by any intuitive plausibility it may possess.

Bacon, on the other hand, stressed the importance of induction from particulars to the general. The purpose of induction, he says, is "to find such a nature as is always present or absent with the given nature." He relies heavily on the method of exclusion: one must proceed by negatives until "exclusion has been exhausted," at which point one has "a Form affirmative, solid, and true and well-defined." [30] This is a new method, he insists, since it results not in probable generalizations but in principles known with certainty:

> In establishing axioms, another form of induction must be devised than has hitherto been employed; and it must be used for proving and discovering not only first principles . . . but also the lesser axioms, and the middle and indeed all. For the induction which proceeds by simple enumeration is childish; its conclusions are precarious and exposed to peril from a contradictory instance. . . . But the induction which is to be available for the discovery and the demonstration of sciences and arts, must analyze nature by proper rejections and exclusions; and then after a sufficient number of negatives, come to a conclusion on the affirmative instances:

30 Francis Bacon, *Novum Organum*, Book II, aphorisms 15, 16.

which has not yet been done or even attempted, save only by
Plato.[31]

Of course, this begs a good many questions, both epistemological
and ontological, as a glance at the only worked-out example he
provides (the form of heat) quickly shows. The reader is left with
the impression, nonetheless, that there exists in principle some
sort of systematic way of working from particular empirical instances to axioms asserted (i.e., "natures" discovered) with certainty.
Bacon is combining under the single title "induction" several
different modes of inference that later writers would prefer to hold
distinct. This is of importance to us because of the influence that
Bacon's logic ("the best ascertained method of philosophizing" [32])
had upon Vico.

The seventeenth-century theorists of science never quite succeeded, therefore, in disentangling the relations between the various types of inference employed in the science of the day. In particular, as we have already seen, it was not clearly realized that although inductive and hypothetical modes of inference could work
together, neither could be combined with properly axiomatic reasoning. If an axiom really *were* an axiom in the Aristotelian sense,
that is, if its necessity could be directly perceived, it could not receive further confirmation from inductive or hypothetical argument. It would make no sense to speak of "confirming" something already known with certainty. Only if the status of the
axiom were hypothetical or postulatory would this have a point.
But in this case, the reasoning would not be axiomatic in the
classic sense, and the axioms themselves could not be regarded as
necessary truths.

In order to avoid ambiguity in what follows, let us stipulate clear
meanings for the terms we shall employ. Three types of warrant
will particularly concern us:

(1) *Axiomatic*: where the axiom is directly certified on the basis
of an immediate intuitive grasp. This is the sort of warrant that

---

[31] *Ibid.*, Book I, aphorism 105.
[32] *NS*, par. 163.

Aristotle calls *epagōgē* (sometimes translated as "induction" but more properly called "intuition" or "insight"), and that Descartes in the *Regulae* believes he can attain through a grasp of the relations between clear and distinct ideas.

(2) *Inductive*: where the assertion rests upon the perception of similarity in a group of particulars. When a scientist draws a curve through a number of experimentally fixed points on a graph, and on the basis of this curve formulates an algebraic relationship between the variables involved, the warrant for the resulting "law" is the set of individual experiments represented by the points. Or when a social scientist formulates a generalization about the behavior of people in crowds, his "law" will depend for its warrant upon the individual observations from which it has been derived.

(3) *Retroductive*: where the assertion is a hypothetical one, and where its warrant lies in the number and variety of verified consequences drawn from it. When the consequences are deductively derived, this is called the hypothetico-deductive (HD) method. Peirce's term "retroductive" will be employed here in a more general sense to include weaker relationships than the deductive one between hypothesis and consequent. The warrant moves backward from consequence to hypothesis instead of forward from axiom to theorem as in the first case above. In a retroductive proof, we accept the hypothesis, not because of its intuitive cogency, not because it is a generalization from instances of the "same" sort, but because a variety of the inferences drawn from it, when tested, have proved to be correct. The hypothesis remains provisional, except in the case (relatively rare in science) where all alternative hypotheses can be systematically eliminated. Retroductive assessment is a very complex affair,[33] but it is relatively simple to determine whether a particular assessment *is* in fact retroductive or not.

These three types of reasoning are in principle distinct, though

---

[33] For a detailed treatment of it, see Ernan McMullin, "The Fertility of Theory and the Unit for Assessment in Science," *Boston Studies in the Philosophy of Science* 39 (1976): 681–718.

they can be employed together. In the remainder of this essay, we shall investigate the logical structure of the *Scienza Nuova* to determine the sort of warrant on which it rests. Vico has something to say about this himself, but we have to take his words cautiously, both because his use of methodological terms is not precise and because he is sometimes mistaken about the method he is actually following.

The Role of Induction

There can be no denying that Vico has given his work an axiomatic form. Book One is entitled "The Establishment of Principles," and it contains chapters on "Elements," "Principles," and "Method." The section on "Elements" begins: "We now propose the following axioms, both philosophical and philological, including a few reasonable and proper postulates and some clarified definitions." [34] He goes on to give 114 "axioms," many of them accompanied by "corollaries" which are said to be "proved" by the axiom or the immediately preceding set of axioms. The analogy with Euclid is evident. The axioms are usually asserted without explicit supporting discussion and with a great deal of assurance. Sometimes they are put forward tentatively: "Let that be granted which is not repugnant in nature and which we shall later find to be true in fact . . . ." [35] And again: "Let it be granted as a postulate not repugnant to reason that after the flood men lived first on the mountains, somewhat later came down to the plains, and finally after long ages dared to approach the shores of the sea." [36] Yet a few lines later this "postulate" with the two following "axioms" (one a reference to a passage where Plato says that after certain great floods men dwelt in caves in the mountains, and the other an "ancient tradition" that Tyre was first founded inland) are held

---

[34] *NS*, par. 119.
[35] *NS*, par. 248.
[36] *NS*, par. 295.

to be sufficient to "show us that the inland nations were founded first."[37] This last assertion is described as an "axiom," and it is said to be "confirmed" by the fact that the first monarchy, that of the Chaldeans, was an inland one.

These "axioms" are obviously quite diverse in their types of warrant. And the "showing" he refers to is remote from anything like coercive deductive demonstration. An axiom whose warrant is less obvious is often called a "postulate," especially if it has not been prepared for by other axioms. But the "postulate" above is used, just as are other axioms, to reconstruct assertions about the patterns of development through which nations must pass. The success of this reconstruction is sometimes said to "confirm" the postulate or axiom, suggesting a retroductive type of warrant.

Some of the axioms are explicitly stated to have inductive warrant:

> Only by extreme necessities of life are men led to abandon their own lands, which are naturally dear to those native to them. Nor do they leave them temporarily, except from greed to get rich by trade, or from anxiety to keep what they have acquired. This axiom is the principle of the migrations of peoples. It is an induction from the heroic maritime colonies, the inundations of the barbarians . . . the latest known Roman colonies, and the colonies of Europeans in the Indies.[38]

And something like induction appears to underlie the axioms in which he notices current features in the eternal history of the nations: every gentile nation had its Jove and its Hercules, he claims.[39]

Leon Pompa warns us, however, about taking such assertions to be genuinely inductive. He argues that "one of Vico's central points is that [general] facts and laws are mutually supporting."[40]

[37] NS, par. 298.
[38] NS, pars. 299–300.
[39] NS, pars. 193, 196.
[40] Leon Pompa, "Vico's Science," History and Theory 10 (1971): 49–83; see p. 75. I found this essay and his subsequent book, Vico: A Study of the New Science (New York: Cambridge University Press, 1975), most helpful when preparing this paper.

"Philology" does not become a science until philosophic reasoning is applied to it; the *certum* of the historical narrative needs supplementation by the *verum* of the general principles. Pompa takes Vico to be saying that the historical facts he is utilizing cannot be assumed to *be* facts prior to the application of interpretive theories. If this is so, an induction over these potential facts cannot be proposed as the warrant for the very system of theories that later constitute them *as* facts. The point is similar to one made in recent philosophy of science: the "facts" on which science is supposed to rest are, it is argued, necessarily "theory-laden." Indeed, they are sometimes "laden" with the very theories the facts themselves are subsequently brought forward to support. Where Feyerabend views this circularity as a potentially vicious one, Pompa takes it to be a strength for each that history and sociology should be, in the way he takes Vico's work to suggest, "complementary aspects of the same epistemological enterprise." [41]

Vico's classification of alleged historical facts as facts that fall under a particular axiom in one sense does, of course, "presuppose" the axiom. For instance, before he could investigate inductively whether every gentile nation did indeed have its Hercules, he would have to know how to identify a Hercules figure in a nation's mythology. This would involve a reference to his theory of the origins of religion, within which it is shown that each nation ought to have a hero figure, born of the principal god, and so forth. But this reference to theory does not, it would seem, require one to suppose the adequacy of the theory *as* a theory. It only defines a set of categories that enable us to know where to look for a Hercules figure. Thus induction is still possible.

Vico notes with satisfaction that Varro, "the most learned of antiquarians," succeeded in identifying no less than forty Hercules figures in the myths of different nations.[42] That this carries some inductive weight for him is clear from the inference he

41 Pompa, "Vico's Science," p. 80.
42 *NS,* par. 196.

draws: the fact that so many nations have Hercules figures in their mythologies shows us that these nations "could not grow without valor." [43] He excludes the possibility that the presence of the Hercules figure could be due to diffusion or to coincidence. These nations "were forest-bred and shut off from any knowledge of one another." In those circumstances, he feels justified in appealing, as he often does, to what he regards as one of his cardinal prin ciples: "uniform ideas originating among entire peoples unknown to each other must have a common ground of truth." [44] This principle is necessarily an inductive one: when one finds the same idea in numerous historical instances, it can be asserted to have a public ground of truth. The force of the idea comes in the first instance from its being found the same in many cases, not from the role it plays in the overall explanatory theory.

What is more, he associates this principle with the view that there is a "common sense of the human race" which enables men "to define what is certain in the natural law of the *gentes.*" We can arrive at this certainty "by recognizing the underlying agreements which despite variations of detail obtain among all of them in re spect of this law." [45] We must, therefore, look for these agree ments (an inductive task) in order to arrive at a knowledge of the natural law of the nations. Furthermore, from this in turn will issue a "mental dictionary," needed in order to assign origins to our diverse languages; this is a "mental language common to all nations, which uniformly grasps the substance of things feasible in human social life." [46] It is by means of this "dictionary" that the task of the *Scienza nuova* of articulating the ideal eternal his tory is to be carried out. [47] It is not wholly clear whether this dic tionary is to be set up by noting the occurrence of certain ideas across all the languages studied (an inductive task) or whether the feasibility of creating such a dictionary is inferred in advance "from

[43] *NS*, par. 198.
[44] *NS*, par. 144.
[45] *NS*, par. 145.
[46] *NS*, par. 161.
[47] *NS*, par. 145.

the nature of human institutions" and then confirmed by an inductive search that turns up, for instance, "proverbs or maxims of vulgar wisdom, in which substantially the same meanings find as many diverse expressions as there are nations ancient and modern." [48] There can, however, scarcely be any question in regard to the inductivist thrust of principles such as these. Whether Vico actually carries them through in any detail, or relies on them for major insights, is another matter.

What Pompa principally wishes to exclude is an "abstractionist" reading of Vico which would have him derive the explanatory categories of his science from an induction across myth, language, and law, an induction which would merely note similarities and make of the "ideal eternal history" an empirical regularity observed to obtain across the known histories of the nations. This is certainly *not*, it is true, how the ideal eternal history was arrived at. But one has to be wary about pushing this too far. In particular, Vico's perspicuous manner of relating philosophy and "philology" (theoretical reasoning and the specific histories of institutions that depend on human choice, such as law, language, and myth) ought not lead us to attribute to him the "theory-ladenness-of-fact" thesis of contemporary philosophy in all its amplitude. He did not develop the crucial *verum/certum* principle [49] in any detail. And the "mental language" axioms ought to give us pause.

Vico *did* search through masses of ancient literature. He *did* find regular recurrences of theme and idea. But it is correct to say that he went at the search with an already fairly well articulated theory in mind, one which told him where to look and what to look for. And he did imply, in a way perhaps no one before him had, that this was how it had to be done, that the inductive search had to be guided by the imaginative categories of the theorist and the axiomatic structures of the theorist filled in and anchored by the results of the inductive search.

[48] *NS*, par. 161.
[49] *NS*, par. 7.

Retroductive Warrant?

There is something of a paradox here, however, and it is quite central to the entire question of Vico's theory of science. If the philosopher could *really* discover the true on his own, what could the "philologist" contribute to him? Why should the *verum* of the philosopher have to be supplemented by the *certum* of the historian? Is this to be read as testing a theory against the facts? If so, it sounds as though Vico is proposing something like retroduction, as we have defined it. He notes that philosophers who have speculated about social history have so far "failed by half in not giving certainty to their reasonings by appeal to the authority of the philologists." [50] What failure, what incompleteness, is he pointing to? Is it no more than a lack of concrete application, since his term, *certum,* has to do with the particular and the concrete (as well as having overtones of the Platonic notion of "true belief" and the Aristotelian "knowledge of the fact")? It would seem to be more than this. The fairly frequent mention of confirmation suggests that evidential support is needed by the axioms in order to qualify as science in the full sense.

Part of the problem here comes from the identification of the *true* and the *made*: "History cannot be more certain than when he who creates the things also narrates them." [51] The criteria of the philosopher and the geometer are those of the *maker*; they are matters of proportion and coherence. They are not yet anchored in the empirical regularities of history. For although history is the work of men, it is a different set of men who come to write it, and yet another who make a science of it. The work of discerning its laws, and of deciding when these laws apply in particular contexts, is thus a complex mediated affair where warrant may have to be sought in a variety of directions.

Is the warrant of the *Scienza nuova* a retroductive one, as it might be for a modern chemical theory, for example? The answer

50 *NS*, par. 140.
51 *NS*, par. 349.

comes in three stages. First, it is certainly not *purely* retroductive. The axioms (some of them, at least) carry weight in their own right, as we shall see in detail in the next section. Their acceptability is not entirely a matter of verified consequences; they are not usually evaluated by testing inferences drawn from them against the specifics of the historian. Second, it *is* partly retroductive. The axioms, as we have seen, are sometimes said to be "confirmed" by specific consequences; his analysis of the manner in which the transition from barbarism occurs in a nation he goes on to "confirm by the example of the French nation." [52] At the end of Book Four, he opens a chapter entitled "Final Proofs to Confirm the Course of Nations" as follows:

> There are other instances of the congruity of effects with the causes assigned to them in the principles of this Science, which confirm the natural course of the lives of nations. We have already mentioned most of them in scattered passages without any order. Here we shall bring them together. . . .[53]

A long list follows; it is proposed as a "confirmation" of the principles from which the work had begun. The reader's confidence in these principles grows, Vico says, when he notes that the causes they assign are sufficient to explain a myriad of detailed features of the historical development of social institutions in specific nations (e.g., the types of punishment meted out).

Some, at least, of the axioms have an intrinsic (axiomatic) warrant giving them weight, though not apparently conclusive weight, prior to any inspection of consequences. The axioms as a whole are, however, capable, it would appear, of retroductive confirmation. How does this retroduction operate? It would be tempting to describe it as hypothetico-deductive, and indeed many commentators have so labeled it. However, this will not do. Though Vico uses deductivist language constantly, the inferences he makes are not really deductive most of the time. When he says "from

---

[52] *NS*, par. 159.
[53] *NS*, par. 1020.

this axiom it follows . . .," or "this axiom proves . . .," the inference is usually far from a straight-line deductive one.

Axiom 58, for instance, says that "mutes utter formless sounds by singing, and stammerers by singing teach their tongue to pronounce." [54] And Axiom 59 goes: "Men vent great passions by breaking into song." [55]   Vico immediately adds:

> From Axioms 58 and 59 it follows that the founders of the gentile nations, having wandered about in the state of dumb beasts and being therefore sluggish, were inexpressive save under the impulse of violent passions, and formed their first languages by singing. [56]

The sense in which this striking assertion "follows" from the two axioms is certainly not a deductive one.   Even if one were to call on the various other axioms where the powers and disabilities of the first men are described, one would still not be able to deduce that they formed their first languages by singing. At best, one could only describe this as a plausible suggestion, an analogical extension of the axioms.   Given what is said elsewhere of the first men, and the relationships postulated between speech, emotion, and song, a *plausible* answer to the question: how did speech originate? would be to say that it originated in song.   Of course, someone who accepted the antecedents here might very well deny the likelihood of this particular suggestion. He might say, for instance, that since the basic needs of primitive man were food and security, speech would be much more likely to originate as a set of signals connected with the hunt or with defense.   This too is compatible with the principles of the New Science; to decide between the two, one would have to argue in terms of coherence, noting perhaps the poetic character of the first men and the consequent likelihood that their first utterance would be song rather than signal.

Instances of this sort could be multiplied, but perhaps this one will suffice to make the point that the logical connections in

---

[54] *NS*, par. 228.
[55] *NS*, par. 229.
[56] *NS*, par. 230.

Vico's argument are much looser than the terminology of axiom and consequence would lead one to expect. This is important from the point of view of confirmation. HD confirmation can occur only where there is a strict deduction (or at the very least a statistical deduction) from the hypothesis. Even if we invoke suppressed premises from elsewhere in the system, the system as a whole will be confirmed in an HD manner only if the consequence can be derived in a strictly deductive way. And this is relatively rare in the *Scienza Nuova*.

Yet one still wants to say that there is *some* sort of retroductive, effect-to-cause warrant operating in the work. Could it be called "hypothetico-suggestive"? The axioms suggest tentative analogies, possible consequences in the realm of the *certum*; when these are verified, the axioms are confirmed. This is a very weak form of retroduction, for not only is the logical move from consequent to antecedent problematic, so also is the move from antecedent to consequent. There are thus so many possible sources of logical failure that one might wonder whether such an "argument" could serve as a mode of confirmation at all. And yet one has only to read Book Two to see that it somehow does. The rich detail of Roman legal and social history yields all sorts of instances that can be linked, admittedly only in analogical and tentative ways, with the original axioms. Yet the persuasive impact on the reader is considerable.

We recall that Vico believes the "specifically philosophical faculty" to be the capacity "to perceive the analogies existing between matters far apart." In the *Scienza nuova*, this capacity is exercised to the full, both by author and reader. The persuasion is one of metaphor rather than of inference. Here is where the affinity between science and poetry is most evident. Each relies upon metaphor for producing its effect. The metaphors will be tested quite differently in the two cases, of course. And the sort of "truth" that each seeks is different. But there is enough resemblance to allow us to speak of a "poetic" sort of retroduction, perhaps, in Vico's work as long as this does not lead to the sort of underestimation of the ultimately scientific character of the work that we criticized at the beginning of this paper.

There is, finally, one other way in which Vico himself describes the relation between axiom and consequent in his work. Having concluded the long list of axioms, he opens the section on "Principles" as follows: "Now, in order to make trial whether the propositions hitherto enumerated as elements of this science can give form to the materials prepared in the Chronological Table at the beginning. . . ." [57] Here he takes the relation between philosophy and "philology" to be that between form and matter. Each on its own is incomplete; together they form a substantial unity. The reality of each derives from its contribution to the composite. It is an attractive metaphor, but it reminds us of the issue we have left until last: do the principles of the *Scienza Nuova* have an intrinsic warrant independently of the consequences derived from them, and if so, of what kind? What are the credentials, if any, of philosophy/sociology to be regarded as the *verum* prior to any matching against the *certum* of philology/social history?

Intuitive Warrant

Vico is quite specific as to how some of the axioms, at least, are to be directly warranted: "The world of civil society has been made by men, and its principles are therefore to be discovered within the modifications of our own human mind." [58] Philosophers, he says, ought to have

> begun with metaphysics, which seeks its proofs not in the external world but within the modifications of the mind of him who meditates it. For since this world of nations has certainly been made by men, it is within these modifications that its principles should have been sought. [59]

[57] *NS*, par. 330.
[58] *NS*, par. 331.
[59] *NS*, par. 374.

These cryptic phrases have elicited more discussion from Vico scholars than perhaps any others. They cannot be taken at their face value: he is *not* saying that we can directly empathize with primitive men and in that way recreate the sequence of his development: "It is beyond our power to enter into the vast imagination of those first men whose minds were not in the least abstract . . . We can scarcely understand, still less imagine, how those first men thought." [60]   The difficulties in penetrating this barrier are so great that it cost him "the research of a good twenty years. We had to descend from these human and refined natures of ours to those quite wild and savage natures, which we cannot at all imagine and can comprehend only with great effort." [61]   But how is this to be done?   Vico warns us about one way it is *not* to be done.   It is the inveterate weakness of scholars, he says, that when they "can form no idea of distant and unknown things, they judge them by what is familiar and at hand." [62]   How does he, then, avoid the "conceit of scholars" himself?   He has to determine some basic features of human living that link us to those first men and that are not postulated just because of a failure of imagination on our part.   Men act according to need and utility.   The particular needs and utilities change.   But not to act according to perceived need and utility would make one something other than man. Though human nature alters as institutions alter, there is nonetheless an invariant which binds the human race into one.   All men exercise a prereflective judgment in respect to personal need and utility.[63]

We can thus be certain that the first men acted to fill their desires.   What might these have been?   In that wild and desolate state, man "desires something to save him."   This leads him to a primitive form of belief in God and to the practices of religion. The need for food leads to agriculture, to settled families, to the

60 *NS*, par. 378.
61 *NS*, par. 338.
62 *NS*, par. 122.
63 *NS*, pars. 141–142.

institution of marriage. The needs of the family lead to the establishment of settlements and ultimately cities. And so on. What commends this sort of account is "its naturalness and simplicity," as Vico puts it when he suggests a more detailed account of the origin of cities. Elsewhere he advises us: "He who meditates this science narrates to himself this ideal eternal history so far as he himself makes it for himself by that proof: 'it had to be, it has to be, and will have to be.' " [64] Such a science rests on our estimates of psychological likelihood, in the context of social roles at least partly understood by us. [65]

One special (and it must be said, especially dubious) device to enable us to reconstruct the world of early man is given Vico by his "proof" that the first men were akin to children. This allows him to make use of some rather primitive child psychology as a bridge to the "eternal history of the nations." Even though we are forbidden to use ourselves as models, we can, it appears, use our children to understand early man: "In children, memory is most vigorous and imagination is therefore excessively vivid. . . . This axiom is the principle of the poetic images that the world formed in its first childhood." [66]

The faculty that Vico is calling upon is an intuitive ability on our part, based on the richness of our own human experience, to enter into human situations, no matter how alien, and grasp them in categories appropriate to them. It is akin to Weber's *Verstehen,* as has often been observed. [67] There are some obvious problems about how it functions, but these we shall have to leave aside in order to focus on two points only. The first is that this faculty can operate in two rather different ways. We can enter into the conscious world of desires and utilities of beings remote from us in time. But in addition, we can see how the

[64] *NS,* par. 349.

[65] Pompa, "Vico's Science," p. 58.

[66] *NS,* pars. 211–212.

[67] Isaiah Berlin discusses it in a particularly perceptive way in his *Vico and Herder: Two Studies in the History of Ideas* (New York: Viking Press, 1976), pp. 105–114.

outcome of purposive action can lead causally to other outcomes, perhaps unintended ones. This latter is akin to grasping a causal law, as Pompa points out. But there appears to be no reason why such laws might not be grasped in much the same direct way as the structures of conscious desire and utility. They both lie within the "modifications of mind" that a sensitive and experienced observer might claim to possess.

Vico frequently emphasizes that the major stages in human development are brought about in ways that are not directly intended by those involved; the movement to a good which is "always superior to that which men have proposed to themselves" [68] is for him the strongest demonstration of the providential character of the ideal eternal history. It is, in fact, a "rational civil theology of divine providence" because it shows how "without human discernment or counsel and often against the designs of men, Providence has ordered this great city of the human race." [69] When, for example, primitive man, moved by the desire for family, took on a new style of living, he found himself ultimately committed to a wider set of utilities, that of the city, which he had not consciously foreseen.

It is important to notice that Vico does not take providence to be operating here in some sort of miraculous way. If it were miraculous or inscrutable, our faculty of "intuition" would have no entry into what happened in the great stages of human history. Providence operates through the regularities of the world which God has brought into being. These regularities are His doing, but we can grasp them because they *are* causal regularities of the world. What leads us to think of them as providential in the form in which they appear in the ideal eternal history is that, although they were not the product of human intention, they do serve long-range human utility. In a universe that is known in advance to be God's creation, this automatically makes them testimonies of providence. But it does *not* withdraw them from the

[68] *NS*, par. 343.
[69] *NS*, par. 342.

domain of our commonsense knowledge. We know well enough, for example, how family living leads to dependence on a wider community.

The direct knowledge that Vico calls on here is of two rather different sorts, then, depending on whether it is of human purposes or of the causal outcomes of human actions. But in both cases, it demands a knowledge-skill of an immediate sort. It provides what we have called an "axiomatic" or direct warrant for the principles that can claim it as foundation. Vico speaks of "modifications of mind," a "turning inward," in startlingly Cartesian figures of speech. But when we ask how these modifications of mind are brought about (for Vico they are not innate), we are forced to refer to the interpersonal experiences that shaped them, to a learning process that is in a broad sense inductive.[70]

The analogy between this sort of "intuition" and the *epagōgē* on which Aristotle's axioms were supposed to rest is manifest. Each is direct, unmediated by inference. Each demands a skill which has been shaped by experience of language-use or of living. Neither is, therefore, properly called *a priori*. Vico's major principles (those that claim an insight into the patterns of social history) rest on his projective capacity, and this is conditioned by

[70] It is worth noting that this issue recurs in recent debates among philosophers of history regarding Hempel's deductive-nomological model of historical explanation. The faculty of understanding that Vico postulates for the philosopher/historian has to perform two functions: to enter empathetically into the structures of human decision in order to explain them and to formulate simple causal regularities relating the outcomes of human action. The former is reminiscent of the views of Collingwood and Dray, the latter, that of Hempel. Hempel would insist that causal regularities formulated on the basis of commonsense "modifications of mind" can never furnish a basis for explanation in the fullest sense; only if the generalizations are formulated and supported as empirical (inductive) sociopsychological laws can they serve as a firm basis for explanation. Dray focuses on the former sort of insight, and argues that it cannot be reduced to (or strengthened by) inductive formulation. Vico's approach might seem to suggest a *rapprochement* between the Dray and Hempel views. He is clearly seeking to formulate ideal law-like patterns, as is Hempel; he is relying on an intuitive *Verstehen*, as is Dray. He believes, as we have seen, that his *verum/certum* principle allows him to combine the two. But to pursue this further would lead us too far afield.

his prior experience. These major principles are not themselves inductive in character, however, because they are not generalized from a knowledge of the precise individual situations described in the principle.

Vico's axiomatic warrant works rather better than does that of Aristotle. Our direct intuitive skills are more successful with the structures of human action than they are with Aristotle's cosmo-logical categories. And the qualities of human action are easier to penetrate and define than are the primary qualities of seven-teenth-century mechanics, which seemed so simple but ultimately proved so slippery. But of course, *Verstehen* has its limitations too, and these are especially obvious in the *Scienza nuova*.

Conclusion

It is a mistake to assume that Vico's theory of science must con-form to one and only one type of warrant. It clearly depends on all three. Certain axioms are capable of standing on their own, with an axiomatic warrant of a direct intuitive sort. But even these are capable of being strengthened by means of retroductive success or by the role they play in the larger system. What is dis-tinctive about the *Scienza nuova* is the way in which the three types of warrant are interwoven, and the awareness Vico shows of the importance of combining the axiomatic and the retroduc-tive types of warrant in a special way in the context of the social sciences. Each *can* function on its own: one *could* try to validate the axioms of the New Science by means of the consequences drawn from them. Or one could try to certify the axioms di-rectly by turning to the "modifications of mind." What Vico proposed was that true science could be obtained only by com-bining the two approaches, that the defects of each would be made up by the other. He did not clearly see just what those defects were. And he was rather too casual in his use both of re-troductive and of axiomatic warrant: the analogies underlying his retroduction are a trifle too exuberant, and the projections of his intuition are a good deal too bold. But the "systemic" view of scientific warrant, in which the meaning and justification of each concept and each assertion of the theory in some sense depends on that of the whole, is just as clearly presaged here as it is in the pages of Newton's *Principia*. These two works, appearing within a few short years of one another, from the pens of men totally dissimilar in temperament, in background, in direction of scientific concern, set the stage for a new and far more complex view of the meaning and justification appropriate to scientific theories. The *Scienza Nuova*, like the *Principia*, will remain a milestone in the long, unfinished story of man's attempt to chart the reaches of his own understanding.

Comment on Professor McMullin's Paper

Professor McMullin has proposed a set of questions and offered some answers of an extremely valuable kind for our understanding of the structure of certain aspects of the enterprise undertaken by Vico in his *Scienza nuova*. I find myself in such substantial agreement with so much of what he says, particularly in his conclusions, that, if it is the job of a commentator to express a radically different point of view, I fear I am going to fall down rather badly.

What I find particularly valuable in McMullin's paper is its recognition of the fact that the theory of science implicit in the *Scienza nuova* involves assertions requiring more than one kind of warrant. Where I am inclined to disagree with it is in its suggestion that these assertions require as many as three kinds of warrant, that is, axiomatic, inductive, and retroductive. My doubts center on the question whether there is any place for induction proper in the *Scienza nuova* and whether McMullin has interpreted Vico a bit too widely in treating the hypothetico-deductive form of warrant more as suggestive than deductive in character.

Readers of my own paper in this collection will note that in it I argue that Vico did not believe that all the assertions in his science were testable by formal methods. Some of them, constituting what I have called "antecedent experiential knowledge" and referred to by Vico as the "modifications of our own human mind," are meant both to stand on their own and, by their place in his science as a whole, to show what is peculiarly human about the things with which it deals. These, I suggest, approximate fairly closely to those propositions described by McMullin as having "an axiomatic warrant of a direct intuitive sort." With regard to these, however, I would like to suggest that there is an important feature not given enough stress in McMullin's account. They not only, as he says, stand on their own in a way none of the other assertions do, but they are also more basic than the others, for they represent what Vico invites us to treat as indispensable in human nature. Since McMullin's paper is more directly concerned with the notions of support and warrant, it is perhaps not surprising that he should have omitted this feature. Nevertheless, I think it is important to note that it is precisely the same propositions that are both epistemologically independent of the others in the *Scienza nuova* and that are basic to all its conclusions. For it is precisely in virtue of this fact that Vico's science differs from a natural science and takes on its unique character. Since a natural science is not a science about us *qua* human beings it operates under no obligation to produce statements of things which we can recognize as statements about ourselves *qua* human. Accordingly, it can demand that all propositions of a factual nature be open to empirical verification or disproof. A science of human things, on the other hand, is about us, and we must be able to recognize its statements as statements about characteristically human experience and conduct. It cannot, therefore, do other than accept, as a basic presupposition, all statements without which we would not be able to recognize its conclusions as statements about ourselves. Vico's appeal to our antecedent knowledge of these statments, statements of the modifications of the human mind, is his way of insisting on this fundamental point.

With regard to those statements which are testable in the *Scienza nuova*, I have two reservations about McMullin's account. The first concerns his suggestion that some of the statements are supported inductively. My basic objection to this view is that the inductive establishment of laws can proceed only on the basis of facts whose epistemological status is not in question, whereas in the *Scienza nuova* one of the things Vico is trying to do is show how we can understand and establish those facts about our past relevant to the development of our human nature. Apart from the axiomatic statements mentioned

earlier, Vico is neither able nor willing to take over facts not establish-
able within and by his science. This is the force of his much-quoted
remark that "for the purposes of this enquiry we must reckon as if
there were no books in the world." Thus in the case of the assertion
that every nation must have its Hercules, Vico must show that each
nation had its Hercules before he can draw any further conclusions.
Here we require more than just a set of categories that tell us how to
identify a Hercules. We need in addition to understand what a Her-
cules-figure really is, and we cannot do this without understanding how
such a figure relates to certain human utilities and necessities and to
certain fundamental modes of human thought and feeling. Thus the
facts from which inductions could be drawn would require the whole
framework, both conceptual and methodological, that Vico provides
for the establishment of historical truths.

In this connection it is worth mentioning that although Vico does at
times describe his method as inductive, he also describes it as the
method used by Francis Bacon, which he then goes not to characterize
as seeing in fact what has been contemplated in idea, that is, theorizing
and confirming. This is, to say the least, a highly unusual view of
induction and points rather to the hypothetico-deductive method.

For these reasons I am inclined to think that the principal, if not
sole, method of empirical confirmation open to Vico is the hypothetico-
deductive method and that Vico's use of the term "inductive" is meant
to indicate that his claims are susceptible of some degree of empirical
confirmation, though this is confirmation within the framework of his
science and not independently of it.

McMullin points out, in effect, that in this case very few, if any, of
Vico's arguments would survive in a course on deductive logic. And
this, of course, is true. But here, I submit, we have to remember both
the enormous difficulty of producing sound, well-supported hypothetico-deductive arguments in a field as complex as that to do with
human conduct and in a framework such as that provided by Vico, in
which genuinely historical properties are to be recognized and allowed
for, and the difficulties facing anybody such as Vico who is attempting
to show how the enterprise might be accomplished without anything
like enough evidence to fill in all the premises of his arguments. It is
more important, I believe, at this point to look not at the validity of
the arguments but at their intended form, and here, as McMullin
makes abundantly clear, all Vico's terminology would go to suggest
that he thought of them as deductive.

McMullin's final suggestion, that perhaps these arguments are hypothetico-suggestive rather than hypothetico-deductive, to some extent acknowledges the presence of this terminology. But, as he himself points out, it is difficult to see how these could be rigorous enough either to exclude statements not supported by Vico or to lend genuine support to the results he does arrive at. Since it is Vico's theory of science that is here under discussion, it would be more profitable to consider, not whether his allegedly deductive arguments are valid or not, but whether, in the areas with which he is concerned and within the axiomatic limitations laid down, it would be theoretically possible for there to be valid hypothetico-deductive arguments. For it looks as though this is what he thought himself committed to, and it is only if these are shown to be theoretically impossible in his preferred area that his enterprise would have to be reassessed.

LEON POMPA

Vico and the Verification of Historical Interpretation

BY LIONEL RUBINOFF

In the year 1739 David Hume published his monumental *Treatise of Human Nature,* which he described as an attempt to introduce the experimental method of reasoning into moral subjects. Since, according to Hume, all forms of human reasoning, including mathematics and natural philosophy, have a relation greater or less to human nature, the possibility of building a foundation for any of the sciences depends on the success with which we can explain the principles of human nature. And as the science of man is the only solid foundation for the other sciences, so the only solid foundation we can give to this science itself must be laid on experience and observation.[1]

But so faithful was Hume to the experimental method that he brought empiricism to the edge of bankruptcy. And so powerful was the spell of empiricism on the eighteenth-century mind that with its collapse went the hopes and dreams of the Enlightenment "faith of reason," a faith founded on the Baconian dictum that "knowledge is power"—a power through which mankind can finally enter into active partnership with divine providence, thus hastening the realization of man's utopian dreams. It was with this spirit of optimism that eighteenth-century philosophers undertook their voyage of discovery into the foundations

[1] David Hume, *A Treatise of Human Nature,* edited by L. A. Selby-Bigge (Oxford: The Clarendon Press, 1951), p. xx.

of human knowledge. And it is against this background of optimism that we must appreciate the pathos of Hume's well known *cri de coeur*, when in response to the skeptical implications of his own conclusions he declares:

> I am affrightened and confounded with that forelorn solitude, in which I am placed in my philosophy, and fancy myself some strange uncouth monster, who not being able to mingle and unite in society, has been expelled all human commerce, and left utterly abandoned and disconsolate. . . . When I look abroad, I foresee on every side, dispute, contradiction, anger, calumny and detraction. When I turn my eye inward, I find nothing but doubt and ignorance.[2]

Could Hogarth himself have painted a more vivid portrait of the despair and destitution with which the dream of reason, confronted by its own impotence, erupted into nightmare?

The first systematic attempt to confront the implications of Hume's philosophy was, of course, the critical philosophy of Immanuel Kant, whose herculean labors brought together into one magnificent system the diverse strands of rationalism, empiricism, humanism, and optimism. But notice that Kant's philosophy remains at its core faithful to the underlying presupposition of the Cartesian outlook, the presupposition, namely, that the being and reality of the phenomenal realm (which included the socio-historical world of human action) is derived ultimately from some transcendental, supersensible source, which, although it must be presupposed, yet cannot be comprehended.

Kant begins the celebrated *Critique of Pure Reason* of 1787 by declaring: "Human reason has this peculiar fate, that in one species of its knowledge it is burdened by questions which, as prescribed by the very nature of reason itself, it is not able to ignore, but which, as transcending all its powers, it is also not able to answer." [3] The dreams of reason remain but dreams. But while the *Critique* begins with a declaration of despair concern-

---

[2] *Ibid.*, p. 264.
[3] Immanuel Kant, *The Critique of Pure Reason*, translated by Norman Kemp Smith (London: Macmillan, 1953), p. 7.

ing the ambitions of reason, it concludes on a note of optimism. The very last sentence raises the question whether "it may not be possible to achieve before the end of the present century what many centuries have not been able to accomplish; namely, to secure for human reason complete satisfaction in regard to that with which it has all along so eagerly occupied itself, though hitherto in vain." [4]

What precisely Kant had in mind is not entirely clear, though one cannot resist the temptation to view the development of transcendental idealism through Fichte, Schelling, and Hegel as realizing to some extent the promise contained in Kant's prophetic remark. Be that as it may, the fact is that, unknown to Kant, the revolution that promised to overcome Cartesian doubt and Humean skepticism, with respect to the understanding of matters of fact and *res gestae,* was already underway even as the sage of Königsberg was working out the details of his first *Critique.* For with the publication in 1725 of the first edition of Giambattista Vico's *New Science,* the much needed synthesis of experience and reason was given its first formulation. Long before Kant was awakened from his dogmatic slumber by the somber reflections of David Hume, Vico had already shaken the foundations of European thought, although it was to take over a century before the full impact of this event was to be felt. With Vico modern thought passes beyond the limits of rationalism and empiricism toward the possibility of understanding more precisely than ever before the rationality of the world of historical and social action. More importantly, perhaps, Vico provides the foundations for an epistemology which accounts for the possibility of a rapprochement between theory and practice in a manner that has served as a paradigm for all future attempts. Consider the probable consequences for Western civilization had the great Immanuel Kant read the *New Science* before composing the *Critique of Pure Reason!*

[4] *Ibid.,* p. 669.

The Scope of the New Science

Vico's *New Science* expresses the idea that history and historical temporality is the product of human subjectivity rather than the moving image of an eternity beyond human comprehension. There is, of course, a sense in which the study of history is the study of eternity. It is, however, an eternity that is embodied rather than merely reflected in time and history. And because embodied, it is itself a product as well as a presupposition of history. In other words, to anticipate the well known doctrine of Hegel, it is a "concrete" as opposed to a merely "abstract" universal.

The core of Vico's thought consists of the doctrine *verum et factum convertuntur,* truth and fact are convertible; the condition of being able to know anything truly, as opposed to merely perceiving or having "certainty" of it, is that the knower himself should have made it:

> Create the truth that you wish to cognize; and I, in cognizing the truth that you have proposed to me, will "make" it in such a way that there will be no possibility of my doubting it, since I am the very one who has produced it.[5]

History cannot therefore be more certain than when the one who creates it also narrates it.[6]

From this doctrine it follows that, contrary to the Cartesian philosophy, history, which consists exclusively of *res gestae,* is especially adapted to be an object of human knowledge. And since history consists of events and institutions which "express" (in the sense of giving concrete embodiment to) the universal "modifications" of mind *qua* mind, the mind or self which only in isolation can be experienced with "certainty" becomes, through the study of history, an "object of *knowledge.*" History rather

---

[5] Cited by Elio Gianturco in his introduction to Vico's *On the Study Methods of Our Time* (Indianapolis: Bobbs-Merrill, 1965), p. xxxi.

[6] *The New Science of Giambattista Vico* (hereinafter *NS*), translated by Thomas G. Bergin and Max H. Fisch (Ithaca: Cornell University Press, 1968), pars. 331, 349.

than natural science is therefore the model for the development of a genuine *Geisteswissenschaft* which is at once a science of culture, a science of mind, and a science of wisdom.

Admittedly, the *verum et factum convertuntur* principle bears a strong resemblance to the earlier doctrine of Hobbes that "civil philosophy is demonstrable, because we make the commonwealth ourselves." [7] Vico's formulation, however, adds a dimension not present in Hobbes: the theory, namely, of the cyclic evolution of human institutions having their basis in the modifications of the human mind, and to be understood by means of a "metaphysic of the human mind" involving exegesis based on comparative mythology and genetic psychology. Whether Vico's genetic psychology stands the test of being compared with the accomplishments of Rousseau, Freud, Dewey, Jung, or Piaget is of course a matter for careful consideration. Whatever the outcome of such a comparison, Vico's genius is surely testified to by the very fact of his having divined that there is a genetic psychology, or metaphysics of the mind, that can be brought to bear on the study of the origins of history and society, while the historical study of the origins of society throws light on man's genetic psychology. Vico also realized, unlike Hobbes, that the state of nature out of which history and consciousness arise is, to borrow Hegel's term, *aufgehoben* by the very processes to which it necessarily gives rise. And it is primarily through reflection on their experiences that men create new institutions which in turn give rise to new experiences and new modes of reflection. Already in Vico, in other words, we find an embryonic version of Hegel's principle of the "cunning of reason" as expressed in the maxim, "the actual is the rational and the rational is the actual."

As in the case of Hobbes, Vico sought to do for the study of civil institutions what Bacon had done for the study of nature.[8] In fact, Vico's methodology is more Kantian than Baconian, rest-

---

[7] Thomas Hobbes, "Lessons of the Principles of Geometry," in *English Works*, edited by Sir William Molesworth, 11 vols. (London: J. Bohn, 1839–45), 7: 184.

[8] *NS*, par. 163.

ing as it does on a concept of mind that is totally absent in Bacon. For Bacon, knowledge is entirely the result of inductive reasoning, although it is a reasoning guided by questions that are posed by the inquiring mind. For Vico, however, "to know" *(scire)* is "to compose," "to collect" and bring together what is known. The activity of mind in the act of apprehending causes is thus logically tied to the determination of the causes apprehended. The mind knows causes by itself causing what is known to be knowable. It is in this sense that Vico's *New Science* embodies the Kantian principle that "reason has insight only into that which it produces after a plan of its own." [9]

The Vichian enterprise, then, while Baconian in origin, is in form and substance more likely to be understood as an exercise in the critique of historical reasoning, as exemplified in the modern period by philosophers like Wilhelm Dilthey and R. G. Collingwood. With Bacon, Vico asserts that the works of man, *res gestae,* cannot be deduced from abstract postulates. They can be interpreted only as they come from experience. And that interpretation proceeds, as Kant was later to point out, by "constraining nature (i.e., the object of our inquiry) to give answer to questions of reason's own determining." [10] For Vico, however, interpretation is not simply a matter of apprehending the facts by means of testimony, whether that testimony be given unsolicited or in response to questions of reason's own determining. The so-called facts can be apprehended only in the context of the inner world of human experience, or the "modifications" and eternal categories of the human mind.[11] As history *a parte objecti* is the product of creative reason, so it is by means of the same creative reason that history *a parte subjecti,* history as knowledge of fact or knowledge of causes, is made possible or caused.

Through the application of what he calls the method of philology and philosophy, which combines the knowledge of ideas with

---

9 Kant, *The Critique of Pure Reason,* p. 20.
10 *Ibid.*
11 *NS,* par. 349.

the knowledge of facts—that is to say, discerns in the facts the expressions of ideas which have their origins in the categories of mind *qua* mind—Vico sets out to construct the ideal eternal history which all the particular histories of the nations exemplify in their rise, development, maturity, decline, and fall.[12]   Since the course followed by each nation, insofar as it expresses the eternal idea, has been ordained by God, while the determination of the means whereby this ideal has been realized is left to the free will of man, Vico's "ideal eternal history" is both a rational civil theology of divine providence and a philosophical anthropology, a study of human freedom and of human nature in the making, the study of man making himself.   That Vico did not completely succeed in this enterprise is not nearly as important as the impetus he created, which sustained itself over two centuries and eventually gave birth to the various philosophies of historicity that have come to exercise such a profound influence on the course of modern thought.

Vico and the Revolt against Cartesianism

Vico's revolution in philosophy begins with a revolt against Cartesian rationalism.   For Descartes, the paradigm of all knowledge is mathematical knowledge achieved by means of the geometrical method.   Whatever cannot be assimilated to this paradigm remains in the shadow realm of mere opinion.   As defined by Descartes, the geometrical method excludes not only history and poetry but all forms of practical wisdom based on the experience of intersubjectivity.   As Croce puts it, for Descartes "the daylight of the mathematical method rendered useless the lamps which, while they guide us in the darkness, throw deceptive shadows." [13]   While Vico did not question the validity of mathe-

---

[12] *NS*, pars. 348–349.

[13] Benedetto Croce, *The Philosophy of Giambattista Vico*, translated by R. G. Collingwood (New York: Russell & Russell, 1964), p. 2.

matical knowledge as such, he did question the Cartesian dogma that no other kind of knowledge was possible. In order to demonstrate how knowledge other than mathematics is possible he engages in what I have already referred to as a critique of historical reasoning, an enterprise most usually associated with the names of Dilthey and Collingwood. The parallel between Vico and Dilthey is particularly interesting. Like Vico, Dilthey asserts the principle that "the spirit understands only what its has itself created." [14] And like Vico, Dilthey seeks the essence of human reality in the various expressions of mind—language, art, poetry, custom, and law—expressions which, while they undergo historical change, yet reveal a common reality. While for both philosophers the most critical problem becomes one of reconciling the goal of historical science, which is to reach verifiable knowledge, with the conditions of historicity under which both the quest for knowledge and the process of verification must be undertaken.

Vico thus attacks the Cartesian principle that the criterion of truth is the clear and distinct idea. He argues, on the one hand, that the Cartesian principle is only a subjective or psychological idea. The fact that I think my ideas clear and distinct only proves that I believe them, not that they are true. Or, as Hume was eventually to put it, Descartes' beliefs are nothing more than the vivacity of his perceptions. Descartes' *cogito* proves only that the certainty one has of one's own thinking and existing is indubitable. It is the certainty of being conscious, which is itself a mode of consciousness, the first stage in the evolution of reason. But it is not *scientia*, a truth based on knowledge of causes. What is needed, if we are to understand what it means to know, is a principle which sets forth the logical limits of knowing as such, as opposed to a principle such as Descartes' which sets out to evaluate every particular claim to knowledge. Indeed, before we can

---

[14] Wilhelm Dilthey, "Der Aufbau der geschichtlichen Welt in den Geisteswissenschaften," *Gesammelte Schriften*, 17 vols. (Stuttgart: B. G. Teubner, 1957–74), 7: 148 ("Nur was der Geist geschaffen hat, versteht er").

determine whether any particular claim is true we must first determine whether it is even logically possible for that claim to be true. And to do this requires a principle which establishes, in accordance with the Lockean approach, the necessary limits of human knowledge. Only then can skepticism be overcome.

Vico finds this principle, as we have already noted, in the doctrine *verum et factum convertuntur*. To Plato's principle that all knowledge is recognition of what is already known, Vico adds that all knowledge is recognition of what has been produced. From this principle it follows that while nature is intelligible only to God, mathematics, history, and poetry are intelligible to man. This does not mean that things are created by their being known but only that their having been created by the knower is a logical condition of their being known.

Vico elaborates this argument as follows. Just as the Christian asserts that God alone can fully know all things because he alone is their creator, so man declares himself to be the sole knower of his products. Vico, in other words, as Croce points out, adapts a principle already accepted with respect to the infinite power of God. Just as with God intellect and will are convertible and form one single unity, so in the case of man, created in the image of God, cognition and action in the form of making are convertible and identical.

Subjectivity and Self-Making

Central to Vico's position is an affirmation of the importance of human subjectivity. While the form of human history has its basis in the ideal eternal history, the details of the plan of history are wholly human inventions. Or to put it another way, while the plot of history is the creation of God, details of the story are left to the invention of man. Like God himself, man is a real creator, bringing into existence a synthesis of form and matter as he fashions institutions through which the needs of his complex nature find gradual satisfaction. Since the fabric of human society is created by man out of his own experiences, every detail of this fabric is therefore a human *factum*, eminently knowable to the human mind as such. Indeed Vico's approach to man's creative role in history resembles closely the approach of his contemporary, the eighteenth-century mystic and founder of Hasidism, the Baal Shem Tov. In the *Zevaat Ribesh* the Baal Shem Tov describes the meaning of man's being created in the image of God. The man of true piety, he writes, "takes unto himself the quality of fervor . . . for he is hallowed and become another man and is worthy to create and is become like the Holy One, blessed be He, when he created His world." [15]   As God made man and the world into which he was first placed, so man must remake and renew the world as well as himself.

In this doctrine Vico affirms, perhaps for the first time in the history of Western philosophy, a doctrine of human self-making. But, I would argue, it is a doctrine which places the act of self-making within a wider situation, a situation which defines *a priori* the limits within which human self-making can take place. These limits are prescribed by providence, and are defined by the fact that the institutions of society and the progress of knowledge proceed from the condition of sensation, through that of imagination, to that of reason; and the development of civilization in *every* nation proceeds according to the modifications of a common human nature, as expressed through the primary institutions of religion, marriage, and the burial of the dead. But the choice of means and the decision to act upon the knowledge reached through the study of history, to act so as to benefit humanity as well as oneself, to continue the process of creation for the sake of the well-being of mankind, *this* choice and *this* decision falls within the province of man's free will, which, like the *situation* in which man finds himself, is also a gift of the creator, to use as he

---

[15] "The Bahl-Shem Tov's Instruction on Intercourse with God," in Martin Buber, *Hasidism and Modern Man*, edited and translated by Maurice Friedman (New York: Harper & Row, 1966), p. 185.

chooses. In short, according to Vico, human being must be understood as something *more* than a mere product and yet as something *less* than a self-making. Man makes himself through the accepting or choosing of something already constituted, and yet also not constituted, because the accepting or choosing, together with the details of choice, is a matter of free will.[16]

What are the consequences for historical science of Vico's doctrine of human self-making, which affirms both the conditions of subjectivity and the objective or eternal conditions under which human self-making occurs? Since man is by nature a creature of sensation, imagination, and reason, such that at both the individual and collective levels his development proceeds in that order, the philosophy of history must begin where the subject matter begins.[17] The ideal eternal history thus begins with the dawn of consciousness, with life experienced and lived in the forests, with the first expressions of thought in the form of poetic wisdom; and it is only after we have traced the evolution of knowledge in this manner that we can expect to reach a vision of history from the perspective of the Academies, in which reason now flourishes fully developed.[18] As in the *actual* history of mankind, in which reason emerged through imagination, so in the *reconstruction* of history the rationale underlying its development must be apprehended in the context of an imaginative reliving of the processes whereby imagination has evolved into reason. Finally, Vico argues, all this is possible because mankind at present possesses still the fundamental structure of human nature as created by God. The mind of contemporary man, while essentially rational, is at the same time sensuous and imaginative; and indeed, every individual in his own personal history has traversed the route already taken by history. Here is the doctrine that "ontogeny recapitulates phylogeny and phylogeny recapitulates

---

16 Cf. Emil L. Fackenheim, *Metaphysics and Historicity* (Milwaukee: Marquette University Press, 1961).

17 *NS*, pars. 238, 338.

18 *NS*, par. 239.

ontogeny." Thus does Vico affirm, as a condition of the possibility of the verification of historical knowledge, the principle of the uniformity of human nature, according to which the mind of contemporary man continues to participate in the common experience of the race.

Human Nature and the Method of Historical Reconstruction

But Vico's formulation of this principle does not coincide with the typical Enlightenment version of it. For Vico, human nature is not conceived as an eternal unchanging substance to be apprehended either by simple introspection or by inductive reasoning. It is neither a conjectural hypothesis nor a hypothetical construct. It is rather a self-constituting identity which is directly apprehended in the context of experiencing and comprehending its various modes of expression—myth, language, literature, art, religion, law, philosophy, and the like—which have their basis in the *sensus communis*. And these modes are apprehended in the context of historical change. Vico's human nature, like the eternity embodied within it, is not an *abstract* universal that transcends its variable element but a *concrete* universal whose generic essence is identical with the variable element. For this reason there can be a genuine history of the institutions to which the modifications of mind give rise. Religion and art were not simply the first expressions of consciousness evolving toward reason. They are also perennial forms of expression, each one of which continues to develop and change under the influence of the other forms to which it has given rise and from which it has arisen. And within the development of each form there is room for innovation, novelty, and change. The history of institutions is not just an endless repetition or replication of forms, each one the same as the last. The history of institutions is a process in which nothing ever repeats itself in exactly the same way. History moves in spirals, not circles, and apparent repetitions are always differ-

entiated by having acquired something new. Thus wars and revolutions reappear from time to time in history, but every new war
and revolution is in some ways a new kind of war and a new kind
of revolution, owing to the lessons learned by human beings in
the past. This is the meaning of my claim that for Vico the ideal
eternal history is a concrete universal whose generic essence does
not transcend but is identical with its historically conditioned
variable element.

Vico's conceptualization of the historicity of the relation between human nature, common sense, and its expressions is the
revolutionary starting point for the scientific history of the eternal.
The method whereby Vico reaches knowledge of the ideal eternal
history is the twofold method of philology and philosophy. The
foundation of this science is the principle that "there must in the
nature of human institutions be a mental language common to
all nations, which uniformly grasps the substance of things feasible in human social life and expresses it with as many diverse
modifications as these same things have diverse aspects." [19] Philology makes available the facts as revealed by language, while
philosophy decodes the thought or idea implicit in the language.
The possibility of interpretation with respect to language so different from that of the historian is established through "introspection." Through introspective analysis, the historian discovers the categories or modifications of mind by means of which
men have created their world.

Introspection and Historical Interpretation

Vico's reliance upon introspection as the form of reflection
through which the historian has direct access to the causes of his
own mental development and social activity, and on the basis of
which he can achieve empathetic understanding of how men of
the past reacted to their world and developed their faculties, is

[19] *NS*, par. 161.

not without difficulties. But the logical problems associated with introspection are most evident in cases where introspection is alleged to occur in isolation from experience, as if it were possible for me to know my own mind in isolation from the behavior through which it expresses itself. It is not at all clear, however, that this is Vico's doctrine. I would suggest, to the contrary, that for Vico introspection is a process that occurs simultaneously with the critical reconstruction of past thought as expressed in historical behavior. For Vico, mind is what it does, and it is only by experiencing what mind *does* that we can come to understand what mind *is*.

It is thus only in the course of being confronted by actual expressions of the modifications of the human mind that I discover them in myself and am thus able to identify, reflect, and meditate upon what I have discovered. It is in this respect that philology is a condition of reaching "certainty" with respect to the facts so that philosophical reflection can then transform that certainty into "truth" and "knowledge." It is in the course of this transition that the "making" of the fact occurs. The fact presented becomes an occasion for a rediscovery of self such that the presented fact can be comprehended. Thus, for example, the poetic utterances of primitive man become the occasion upon which I discover within myself the anxiety of man confronted by a universe over which he has no control; from which experience arises the idea and institution of a "fearful divinity." It was out of this initial encounter with divinity that mankind first began to think and act humanly, first began to restrain its passions. The principle implicit here, according to Vico, is the notion that

> man fallen into despair of all the succors of nature, desires something superior to save him. But something superior in nature is God, and this is the light that God has shed on all men. Confirmation may be found in a common human custom: that libertines grown old, feeling their natural forces fail, turn naturally to religion.[20]

20 *NS*, pars. 339, 385.

The role of introspection operating in accordance with the *verum et factum convertuntur* principle may be illustrated by means of the following example. Consider for a moment what is involved in reconstructing the history and consciousness of the magical society characteristic of the mythopoeic age. In this process it is the historian who is responsible for imposing the category of magic upon the testimony of evidence. Such a category is possible only in a scientific society for whom the distinction between science and magic has become a conceptual possibility. Such a distinction is not possible for the society whose consciousness is being reconstructed. What presents itself as an object of knowledge for the historian, the "magical mind of mythopoeic man," is as much a creation of the historian's act of rethinking as it is a datum or given offering itself for understanding in the form of evidence. It is in this way that the historian "creates the truth that he wishes to cognize." The historian's object of knowledge is thus a curious synthesis of past and present, of testimony collected and organized by the creative imagination of the historian. The point to be made here is that the constitution of an object as an object of knowledge, through the synthesizing activities of the historian's imagination, is a logical and not a merely psychological process.

At the same time, however, it is only through the act of rethinking that the historian discovers within himself his own capacity for magical thinking, a "modification" through which he has actually traveled on his way from childhood to adulthood. And this capacity remains latent in the psychic makeup of the mature adult. By thus evoking, through the study of history, the potentialities of his own nature, which then become known through introspection, the historian virtually creates for himself a nature. *A parte subjecti,* insofar as the mind of the historian is concerned, *esse est scire.* Or, as Collingwood puts it, in a statement that expresses the essence of Vico's doctrine: "The historical process is a process in which man creates for himself this or that kind of human nature by recreating in his own thought the past to which he is heir" [21] and "as the human mind comes to understand itself better, it thereby comes to operate in new and different ways." [22]

Man the cognizer of history is thus the creator of history in a twofold sense. He is the creator first in the sense that the institutions of history grow from the modifications of mind. Thus, for example, the institutions of polymorphism, such as the totemic and tabu systems, grow from the mythopoeic imagination, which is essentially polytheistic. Since this imagination remains a permanent feature of mind, it is potentially capable of being recovered at any time. But since the act of recovery is an act of a mind that is itself the product of historical change, and thus different from the mind of the past, it cannot, in the act of recovery, avoid rethinking the past through the categories that define its new shape of existence. The mind of the past thus becomes *known,* in a sense in which it could not otherwise have known itself (though it could always be *certain* of itself), as *magical,* as a stage on the way to reason, and as causally related to the institutions to which it has given rise. This aspect of the past, as known, is also the creation of the mind that knows it. *A parte objecti,* so far as history is an object of knowledge, *esse est scire.*

Vico and the Paradigm of Historical Knowledge

It is in the context of these reflections that Vico developed his paradigm of historical knowledge. For Vico, as I understand his doctrines, the grounds of the possibility for ascertaining the "meaning" of history, as well as for verifying the objectivity of causal explanations, derives partly from his doctrine of fixed cycles and partly from the accumulated wisdom of common un-

[21] R. G. Collingwood, *The Idea of History* (Oxford: The Clarendon Press, 1946), p. 226: cf. also pp. 169, 171.

[22] *Ibid.,* p. 85. Cf. R. G. Collingwood, *Speculum Mentis* (Oxford: The Clarendon Press, 1924), pp. 207, 250; *An Autobiography* (Oxford: The Clarendon Press, 1939), pp. 114–115.

derstanding—an understanding that is made explicit through "introspection" that occurs either in the context of intersubjective experiences or else in the context of experience mediated through the study of history. But since Vico regarded mind as a product as well as a source of the historical process, the accumulated wisdom on the basis of which we "understand" is itself subject to historical change, and the unity of the "cycle" within which change occurs is more like the unity of an infinitely increasing spiral than the unity of a rotating circle. There is in Vico, as I have already pointed out, the embryo of the doctrine that "ontogeny recapitulates phylogeny and phylogeny recapitulates ontogeny." But if this recapitulation is subject to the conditions of historicity, then each generation must attempt all over again both to ascertain the "eternal" meaning of the past and to evaluate that meaning in the light of the "eternal truth," a truth which both makes itself and is other than what makes itself. Does this recognition of the historicity of meaning and truth cancel the possibility of objectivity in historical understanding and explanation for Vico as it threatens to do for philosophers like Dilthey and Collingwood?

This is a question with which all Vichians must wrestle. But every attempt to do so must face the risk of relapsing into the very positivism, or neo-Cartesianism, from which the doctrine of historicity is an attempt to escape. This is especially true in cases where the historian is faced with the interpretation of events for which there is no analogy in his own personal experience. Thus for example in his *The Presuppositions of Critical History*, F. H. Bradley deals with the problem of testimony for which there is no analogy in the historian's own experience by resorting to a positivist version of the principle of the uniformity of nature. Dilthey seems to have resorted to much the same solution in his writings of 1894–95. The transposition of the "I" into the "thou," to which Dilthey refers, seems to rest on a doctrine of psychological uniformity which would undermine the notion of the historicity of human nature that Dilthey makes central to his overall enterprise.

The question for Vico scholars is thus whether the paradigm of knowledge implied by the principle *verum et factum convertuntur* can be systematically exhibited without either relapsing into a positivism which makes the human mind exempt from the conditions of historicity or else disappearing into a relativism which cancels all possibility of objectivity in knowledge. In wrestling with this question for myself, I have been led to the conclusion that the answer depends on what importance, if any, is given to Vico's concluding remark in the *New Science* that "this science carries inseparably with it the study of piety, and . . . he who is not pious cannot be truly wise."

Vico's reliance on providence as the indirect force behind man's making of a history which is both a product of human creativity and yet an ideal eternal history may for some of Vico's critics be as unacceptable as was Berkeley's introduction of God to avoid the implication of solipsism. I would argue, however, that an understanding of Vico's doctrine of providence is indispensable to an understanding of his epistemology. As employed by Vico, providence must be understood as more than a presupposition of the principle of the uniformity of nature. It is also the source of a principle of teleology. The proposition "God exists" means, in other words, not only that there is a continuity at the basis of human nature but that this continuity is the continuity of a created being, which, because created, unfolds and develops according to a pattern which is as purposeful as it is functional. The proposition also reminds us that because he is created with free will, he is a "fallen creature" capable of corruption. Through piety mankind comprehends itself as fallible.

If this be the case, then Vico's statement at the conclusion of the *New Science* may contain a clue to the nature of the verification of historical interpretation. The understanding, interpretation, and verification of explanatory statements about historical phenomena is possible because not only have the phenomena under consideration been created by the mind that seeks to know them but mind itself is a creation of God and thus characterized by what might be called an essence. Because mind has an essence, whatever conduct is occasioned by it is subject to understanding in accordance with the principle of the uniformity of human nature. For Vico, then, the principle of the uniformity of human nature is logically tied to the conception of man's nature having been created by God. Hence Vico's concluding remark that "this science carries inseparably with it the study of piety." It is the piety of not only believing in the existence of God but of bearing witness to that belief through a life of dedicated and unending creativity.

A teleologically based science of human behavior views human conduct in terms of a series of logically connected categories which reveal the underlying essence of man conceived as Being, which in the case of Vico means a "created" being. And since man is created as an essentially historical being, his essence can only be realized and hence expressed in time; in which case it is only through the study of temporality, which must itself take place in time, that it can be known. Just as Kant resolves the dilemma created by Hume by distinguishing clearly between the psychology of belief on the one hand and its logical foundations on the other, so Vico's critique rests on a similar distinction. The fact of man having been created is for Vico a logical, not a psychological consideration. It establishes the uniformity of human nature not as the outcome of blind mechanistic forces but as the outcome of the exercise of God's will acting in accordance with His intellect. This means that, insofar as the history of human conduct is concerned, it is primarily through reflection on their experiences that men create new institutions which in turn give rise to new experiences and new modes of reflection. This is the logical and metaphysical doctrine of mind as both the product and the presupposition of its own self-making activities.

Vico's view of history thus seems to rest on a principle that begs comparison with the Leibnizian notion of "the principle of suffi-cient reason," the Hegelian notion of "the cunning of reason," and the Bergsonian notion of creative evolution as the outcome of an *élan vital*. It might even be argued that Vico's *New Science* marked the rebirth and restoration of the principle of teleology that had become one of the first casualties of the Renaissance. But in keeping with the spirit of Vico's own doctrine, the teleology of the *New Science* differentiates itself by having acquired some-thing new and without precedent.

Vico's teleology acknowledges the fact that social change often comes about as a result of "unintended consequences."

> It is true that men have themselves made the world of nations . . . but this world without doubt has issued from a mind often di-verse, at times quite contrary, and always superior to the particular ends that men had proposed to themselves; which narrow ends, made means to serve wider ends, it has always employed to pre-serve the human race upon this earth.[23]

As an example of how an unintended yet "purposeful" action comes about, Vico explains how in the early history of mankind the institutions of marriage and the family arose from the condi-tions of sensuality. "Men mean to gratify their bestial lust and abandon their off-spring, and they inaugurate the chastity of mar-riage from which the families arise." [24]   At this stage of primitive existence the intentions of men were to satisfy their bestial lusts, but as a result of having been frightened by thunder and light-ning during the act of fornication they found themselves faced with an unexpected and unintended situation to which a response was required. The response took the form of behavior out of which the institutions of marriage and the family arose. What else is this but evidence of "the cunning of reason" through which di-vine providence expresses itself?   It is in much the same way that Vico explains the origins of "the civil powers from which the

[23] *NS*, par. 1108.
[24] *NS*, pars. 504–509, 1108.

cities arose," [25] of the "laws which establish popular liberty," [26] of monarchy, and so on. In each of these cases the motives and passions of men are made means to serve wider ends. But this is not to be confused with a doctrine of fate. Thus Vico insists: "That which did all this was mind, for men did it with intelligence; it was not fate, for they did it by choice; not chance, for the results of their always so acting are perpetually the same." [27]

The structure of Vico's explanations throughout the *New Science* is both empathetic and causal. The possibility for both empathetic understanding and the perception of causal connections is accounted for by the principle of the uniformity of human nature. Because we understand what it means to be human, in the sense outlined above, we understand how it is possible for these sequences of events to have occurred. The accounts are both credible and meaningful. The causal explanation of these sequences of events is made possible by an examination of the evidence to which the ideal eternal history hypothesis is brought to bear as a principle of hermeneutics. Here is the combination of the methods of philology and philosophy. As W. H. Walsh has suggested, the examination of evidence involves inferences and deductions of the sort employed by a detective who relies on insight into his subject matter to make connections between facts rather than on the kind of reasoning engaged in by mathematicians, who confine themselves to what strictly follows according to logical rules, or the reasoning of natural scientists, who deduce consequences from covering laws.[28] Reasoning by means of insight appears to be what Vico is doing throughout the *New Science*. The implied logic of explanation is more akin to what

25 *NS*, par. 584.
26 *NS*, par. 598.
27 *NS*, par. 1108.
28 W. H. Walsh, "The Logical Status of Vico's Ideal Eternal History," in Giorgio Tagliacozzo and Donald P. Verene, eds., *Giambattista Vico's Science of Humanity* (Baltimore: The Johns Hopkins University Press, 1976), pp. 147–151. Cf. also Georg H. Von Wright, *Explanation and Understanding* (Ithaca: Cornell University Press, 1971), chap. 4.

might be called "a logic of situation" than a "covering law" logic. It may be compared not only with Collingwood's logic of question and answer but also, as Walsh has pointed out, with what G. H. Von Wright has called "the logic of quasi-causal explanation." The emphasis in a "logic of situation" is on explaining the actions of individuals or groups motivated by particular aims when confronted by unexpected situations requiring immediate adaptive responses. It is primarily a logic of imagination and innovation, and for this reason causal connections are discerned through insight rather than through the application of causal laws. The intelligibility of the sequence as explained is a function of the art of "colligating" and "interpolating" evidence in accordance with the ideal eternal history hypothesis, which expresses our insight or understanding of what it means to be human. The logical basis of understanding and explanation is the logical symmetry between the mind of the knower and the humanity that offers itself for understanding. Except on the basis of this logical symmetry, how would it be possible for the datum to become an object of knowledge at all? The principle that in the human studies knowledge presupposes knowledge is the principle that defines the limits of knowledge as such. The same logical symmetry must exist with respect to the relation between the structure of explanation, the *explicans,* and the structure of what is explained, the *explanandum.* Since man acts and produces the world of *res gestae* by means of a logic of imagination and innovation, which is inventive and intuitive, so the explanation must be inventive and intuitive. The rationale of human conduct can be exhibited systematically and rigorously without deriving it from covering laws.

Vico and the Rise of Scientific History

It is in the context of the preceding reconstruction of Vico's thought that his paradigm of historical knowledge is to be understood. What is both living and dead in Vico's philosophy of history may be identified by considering his claims against the background of some of the more serious criticism to be made of his doctrines. Of these I would single out for special attention the comments of R. G. Collingwood, who was one of the first English-speaking philosophers of any magnitude to discuss seriously Vico's contribution to the philosophy of history. In his well known historical review of the idea of history, Collingwood distinguishes between what he calls "scissors and paste history," "critical history," and "scientific history." In this account, Collingwood credits Vico with having played an important role in the development of the "idea" of history.[29] But he regards Vico as primarily an exponent of "critical" rather than "scientific" history. Indeed, Collingwood credits Vico with having made possible the transition from "scissors and paste" history, in which the historian accepts the authority of testimony without criticism, to "critical" history, in which testimony is now regarded as a source of "meaning" as well as "fact" and it is left to the historian to determine both what that meaning is and whether the testimony has credibility. The criteria by means of which the credibility of testimony can be established and the criteria by means of which the meaning or significance of the facts reported by that testimony can be discerned are logically distinct. Thus, for example, while I may be prepared to accept the credibility of Luther as a witness to the spiritual impoverishment and decadence of the Roman Catholic Church during the early sixteenth century, it is only on the basis of my understanding of human nature together with the psychology and sociology of the times in which Luther lived that I can come to appreciate the significance of Luther's revolt as an expression of the perennial yearning of mankind for creativity, freedom, and spiritual nourishment. With respect to the reconstruction of Luther's revolution, this means not only identifying the motives and reasons (i.e., causes) that led Luther to act as he did but evaluating these motives in terms of their authenticity and "truth value." Was he

29 Collingwood, The Idea of History, pp. 63–70.

"right" to do as he did? Was his revolution inspired by a vision, or did he simply invent a vision in order to justify a revolution? Did his actions result in a better and more genuine form of spirituality?

But this is not yet a causal explanation which answers the question, why did Martin Luther's revolt take the particular form it did at the particular time at which it occurred? To answer this question is the primary aim of "scientific" history, which seeks to give particular causal explanations that are factually or objectively true. Collingwood claims that Vico is not much interested in either constructing or questioning the truth or falsity of particular causal explanations. On the basis of his methodology, Vico is able to understand (in the sense of *verstehen*) the character or spirit of an age, regardless of how remote it might be from the historian's own age. But he does not, according to Collingwood, provide much help when it comes to determining whether a particular explanation of the causal variety *(erklären)* is true or false as an explanation. Thus while critical history may account for the verification of historical understanding insofar as the meaning of history is concerned, it was not until the development of "scientific" history that criteria were established for the verification of causal explanations. And Collingwood regards his own "logic of question and answer" as supplying the methodology for the latter. It is through the application of the logic of question and answer that historians are able to rethink the thought of the agent, "the very same thought, not another like it." [30]

But in addition to rethinking the thought of the agent, as a basis for providing a causal explanation of the action under consideration, the scientific historian, according to Collingwood, is required to criticize the reconstructed thought with a view to deciding whether it was true. Scientific history, according to Collingwood,

is not a passive surrender to the spell of another's mind; it is a labour of active and therefore critical thinking. The historian

30 Collingwood, *An Autobiography*, p. 111.

not only re-enacts past thought, he re-enacts it in the context of his own knowledge and therefore in re-enacting it, criticizes it, forms his own judgment of its values, corrects whatever errors he can discern in it. This criticism of the thought whose history he traces is not something secondary to tracing the history of it. It is an indispensable condition of the historical knowledge itself. Nothing could be a completer error concerning the history of thought than to suppose that the historian as such merely ascertains 'what so-and-so thought', leaving it to someone else to decide 'whether it was true'. All thinking is critical thinking, the thought which re-enacts past thoughts, therefore, criticizes them in re-enacting them.[31]

At the same time, to borrow Dilthey's well known example, it may only be through the study of Luther's mind that I am able to discover the possibility of living through religious experiences that are not likely to arise for me because of the nature of the times in which I live, "a religious process of such eruptive power, of such energy, in which the stake is life or death, that it lies beyond any possibility of personal experience for a man of our day." [32]

With scientific history, then, we are introduced to yet a fourth set of criteria. The first established the credibility of testimony, the second is concerned with "meaning," the third with truth in the sense of "objectivity," and the fourth with truth in what I shall call the "metaphysical" sense. It is with respect to the latter problem, the problem of metaphysical truth, that the philosophy of history, according to Collingwood, faces its greatest challenge. In fact the problem extends to all four sets of criteria. Since for Collingwood truth and reality, including the principles of historiography, are as much products of history as presuppositions, the question arises, how if the very *a priori* of history is itself a part of the historical process is it possible ever to realize the goals of scientific history?

But this is precisely the problem already faced by Vico. Collingwood is simply wrong to suggest that Vico's thought has not

[31] Collingwood, *The Idea of History*, pp. 215–216.
[32] Dilthey, *Gesammelte Schriften*, 7: 125.

passed beyond the stage of critical history. It may be that Vico did not completely solve the problems posed by scientific history as defined by Collingwood. But it seems grossly unfair to suggest that he is neither aware of nor concerned with these problems. Indeed, it could be argued, the question whether Vico's solution is more or less adequate than Collingwood's is a question that remains to be settled.

Conclusion

Whether and to what extent Vico's paradigm of knowledge can be made to account for the foundations of the *Geisteswissenschaften* depends then entirely on the concept of mind and human nature that underlies that paradigm. If the paradigm is to mean anything at all, it follows that the mind which is assigned responsibility for producing the world it then seeks to know and to understand must throughout the course of its development exhibit a continuity sufficient to account for the possibility of communicating across the differences that divide individuals, cultures, and societies from each other. These differences find expression in language, customs, myth, art, poetry, religion, and a host of other human institutions which express the *sensus communis*. Through the study of these various phenomena, men are confronted not simply with further instances of the operation of causal laws but with opportunities for rediscovering and recognizing the potentialities of their common nature. But the self-understanding that is made possible through the *Geisteswissenschaften* is also a form of self-making. If, as a creature of God, the potentialities of human nature remain "fixed" in order to provide for unity and for the possibility of communication among men and nations, then as creatures of history these same potentialities must be "open," capable of giving rise to variations, in order to account for the freedom and uniqueness of individuals. Thus, for example, while in poetry we recognize and respond to the universal expressions of "love," "passion," "pride," "grief," and "sorrow," each individual poem, and the experience thereof, adds a new and unpredictable increment to the reality of what is expressed. Novelty and innovation arise as essential modes of expression within the fixed cycle of change, and the study of history is therefore infused by an attitude of piety toward *change* as well as toward the external truth and reality that both transcend and yet come to be through the course of that change. Through the study of history, mankind learns to be human by reliving the stages through which humanity has traveled on its way to becoming that standpoint from which "the study of history" is itself undertaken. The study of history is thus one of the acts through which the mind makes itself. In which case, it would follow, as Vico's disciple Collingwood puts it, that the study of history is "to be regarded not simply as a luxury, or mere amusement of a mind at leisure from more pressing occupations," but as a prime duty, "whose discharge is essential to the maintenance not only of any particular form or type of reason, but of reason itself." [33]

Isaiah Berlin has raised the question whether Vico has provided any criteria for evaluating conflicting interpretations. How do we really know, he asks, that our explanations are not simply coherent fictions? The answer implied by my reconstruction of Vico's thought is that we can never know with absolute certainty whether even the most well attested interpretation is in the end a description of "what really happened." Indeed, the very demand for this kind of certainty is misleading. For Vico, truth is historical and hence variable. If historians differ in their interpretations, their differences may themselves reflect rather than hide the truth. Or, as Heidegger has more recently argued, it is only through the encounter with differences that truth as such can be revealed and uncovered. It thus follows that no single individual can expect to find truth for himself. The pursuit of truth becomes not an individual project but a community affair; perhaps the most fundamental of all community activities, the source of communion

[33] Collingwood, *The Idea of History*, pp. 227–228.

through which men celebrate their differences and convert them into a mosaic of scholarship and wisdom that becomes the basis of tradition and culture. And, as Goethe was later to put it, each generation must earn for itself this inheritance in order to possess it.[34] The manner in which tradition is earned is, of course, the study of history.

Viewed in this way, Vico's community of scholarship may be regarded as the rational and dialectical outcome of the state of anarchy out of which civilization arose. To impose upon such a society the Cartesian notion that truth can be "certified" through the application of a single method is a barbarism disguising itself as sophistication. Cartesianism implies an idolatry of method that falsely presents itself as the true piety: the worship of truth conceived as a single, unchanging substance to be apprehended only in the form of clear and distinct ideas. Vico's notion of truth as a creative process, to be apprehended through communion and *communitas*, is an affirmation of the true piety. In Vico's society the study of history is the altar upon which the offerings of art, religion, philosophy, and the other forms of culture combine to celebrate a divine presence expressing itself through differences. The wise man, the man of true piety, is he who meditates these differences with pious respect and Aristotelian wonder, and who bears witness through active participation in the divine process of creation. As God made man and the world into which he was first placed, so man must remake and renew the world as well as himself.

[34] *Faust,* Pt. I, lines 682 ff.

Vico and the Problem of Historical Reconstruction

BY B. A. HADDOCK

I am concerned here with Vico's formulation of the difficulties encountered by an historian trying to reconstruct the practices of a remote civilization. The aim of the historian is to piece together, from the fragmentary evidence available to him, a coherent conception of a world. His peculiar difficulty derives from the lack of a clear criterion of what constitutes success in this undertaking. Where exact disciplines can rely on logical symmetry, prediction, utility, or a combination of all three, history has only the *Zusammenhang* of a *Weltanschauung*. The character of a past *Weltanschauung* cannot be presumed before an inquiry; but the historian must nevertheless employ critical criteria in his interpretation of evidence.

Lost in ignorance, historians use their present world of practical ideas to interpret the past.[1] They assume that the past resembled the present in specific respects. All that is required to maintain history's unique epistemological status is that human engagements in the past should be intelligible (in principle) to present observers. Men can understand "the world of civil society" because it is a network of conventions and practices.[2] But it is not a prerequisite for their understanding that the practices of the past should be

---

[1] *The New Science of Giambattista Vico* (hereinafter *NS*), translated by Thomas G. Bergin and Max H. Fisch (Ithaca: Cornell University Press, 1968), par. 123.

[2] *NS*, par. 331.

identical with their own, only that men conducting their affairs in the past should have adopted conventions which they knew how to use and abuse. The specific rules that men employed to regulate their relations might have no substantive connection with those of the present. The "first human thinking" might be "quite wild and savage." [3]

Without a notion of rules, however, it is difficult to envisage what could be meant by "human thinking." Vico presupposes a formal continuity which enables men to reconstruct practices. He suggests that this reconstruction will be facilitated if they cease to read the past backwards (the "conceit of scholars" and the "conceit of nations"); [4] and that a necessary condition for understanding civil society is that "its principles" should "be found within the modifications of our own human mind." [5] Vico advances two claims here which have important consequences for philosophy of history. On the one hand, he maintains that the character of human actions distinguishes history from the natural sciences. On the other, he claims that the injunction to fashion historical explanations from the perspective of agents in no way entails anachronism. While it has become a commonplace to distinguish the *Geisteswissenschaften* from the *Naturwissenschaften*, such a separation has normally been bought at the price of objectivity. In what follows I want to consider the character of the distinction, and the sort of general statements which Vico supposes enable him to reconstruct past modes of thought without recourse to his own assumptions.

Ideas Are Contextual

In a celebrated essay, Collingwood sought to establish the autonomy of history from natural science by including within his-

[3] *NS*, par. 338.
[4] *NS*, pars. 125 ff.
[5] *NS*, par. 331.

tory only that which concerned rational action.[6] An action, as he conceived it, was the unity of thought and its embodiment in physical movements. While the irrational elements of human conduct, impulses and appetites, were properly the sphere of the natural sciences (such as psychology and physiology), there remained to the historian who knew his business a mode of understanding which could not be attained by mere observation. And this privileged access to past conduct was open to him precisely because *verum et factum convertuntur*. Men made history in the sense that they "enacted" intentions.

History, then, was not a succession of "mere events," connected only by constant conjunction, but a *Zusammenhang* of intentions. An historical inquiry would not be complete with the enumeration of the sorts of occasions on which events of a specific kind might be expected. An historian would want to know why *A* did *B*. His answer would state a logical, rather than contingent, connection between the thoughts in the mind of an agent and the actions he performed. The historian's task was to "reenact" the thought of the agent. Faced with a puzzling piece of evidence, he had to establish what a man in particular circumstances could logically be up to. His solution to the dilemma would be an inference from the documents at his disposal. And historical knowledge would be demonstrable because the historian could show at each stage of his argument how he was led to relate questions to answers as intentions to actions.

This view is not without merit. It has formed the basis for much of the criticism of the "covering law" model of historical explanation.[7] But, in important respects, it is unable to meet the critical requirements which Vico demands in his *New Science*. One of the weaknesses Vico identified in the historical thought of his time was that scholars judged the origins of humanity "on the

6 R. G. Collingwood, "Human Nature and Human History," *Proceedings of the British Academy* 22 (1936); reprinted in R. G. Collingwood, *The Idea of History* (Oxford: The Clarendon Press, 1946).

7 See especially William Dray, *Laws and Explanation in History* (London: Oxford Univerity Press, 1957).

basis of their own enlightened, cultivated, and magnificent times."[8] They assumed that the criteria of rationality of the early eighteenth century had prevailed in ancient history. But the thinking of the first men had been quite otherwise. Because they were unable to conceive the world in terms of rational concepts, it became a phantom of their imaginations. The rules and conventions which governed their conduct were fantastic rather than rational. Accordingly, it was "beyond our power to enter into the vast imagination of those first men, whose minds were not in the least abstract, refined, or spiritualized, because they were entirely immersed in the senses, buffeted by the passions, buried in the body."[9] To apply a logic of question and answer to these men would presuppose that one had already established what (in principle) could belong to their range of descriptions. Collingwood's methodology of history presupposes that thought is "an eternal object," unaffected by "the fact of its happening in time."[10] Vico's point, however, was that ideas are contextual. And it was by disregarding the historical character of ideas that the accounts of early societies proffered by "the three princes of the doctrine of the natural law of the gentes" were rendered anachronistic.[11]

Some of the difficulties of Collingwood's formulation are avoided by the tradition which concentrates on actions as expressions rather than enacted intentions. Meaning remains an organizing concept, but its use is not restricted to the reconstruction of an agent's intention in performing a certain action. In addition to the deliberate attempt to say or do something, it embraces the manifold gestures and facial expressions which, though they are not intended to signify anything, betray an attitude of mind. Here the way a thing is done is as important as the purpose for which it is done. Both belong to a common *Weltanschauung*. And, as a consequence, both can serve as evidence for the reconstruction of that *Weltanschauung*. This view is associated with Wilhelm Dilthey.

8 *NS*, par. 123.
9 *NS*, par. 378.
10 Collingwood, *The Idea of History*, p. 218.
11 *NS*, par. 329.

Its basic premise is that thoughts and actions express a world of ideas, even though agents themselves may not be able to articulate the character of that world.

The affinities with Vico's historical inquiries in the *New Science* are manifest. When Vico explores the character of poetic wisdom in its various modes, he is concerned with the ramifications of a common attitude of mind. The connections which obtain between metaphysics, morality, politics, economics, physics, cosmography, astronomy, chronology, and geography were neither "intended" nor conceived by agents. They derive from the fact that the life of a people is not fragmented, divided into categorially distinct compartments. The language they use to describe one group of activities extends into others. And implied in all their engagements is a *Weltanschauung* which it is the historian's business to reconstruct.[12]

There remains the difficulty, in Dilthey's formulation, of how expressions can be understood. His contention was that the historian could understand actions performed in the past because, like actions performed in the present, they could be subsumed under categories like purpose, volition, and feeling.[13] The historian, in other words, could reexperience the attitudes of historical agents because his experience as a partical agent had provided him with categories which might, by imaginative extension, be used to interpret evidence. But while purpose, volition, and feeling look like formal categories, the necessity to use empathy in

12 The affinity between Vico and Dilthey on this issue extends to Collingwood's notion of "absolute presuppositions." But from Collingwood's methodological recommendations it is difficult to see how he thought a history of absolute presuppositions could be written. Since they were not, by definition, intended, his logic of question and answer would seem inapplicable. He speaks of metaphysics as an historical science, concerned with "the question what absolute presuppositions were made on a certain occasion," but part of his point is surely that absolute presuppositions simply happen to have been unconsciously employed. They are not answers to questions but assumptions without which questions cannot be asked. See R. G. Collingwood, *An Essay on Metaphysics* (Oxford: The Clarendon Press, 1940), p. 49.

13 See Wilhelm Dilthey, *Gesammelte Schriften*, 12 vols. (Leipzig and Berlin: B. G. Teubner, 1921–65), 1: xviii.

their application to historical research means that the historian's experience serves as a limit to the range of meanings he can attribute to the documents before him.

Sir Isaiah Berlin has emphasized that we can understand human behavior as purposive only because we are ourselves purposive agents. We seek connections in our daily lives in terms of "the central succession of patterns that we call normal." [14] History, in this view, "is merely the mental projection into the past of this activity of selection and adjustment." [15] Berlin warns that the corollary of this conception is that the historian is liable to reconstruct the past according to his own assumptions. And he accepts that historical interpretation is possible only if we presuppose that human beings in the past were sufficiently like ourselves for our fundamental notions to be applicable to them. [16]

Vico, however, set himself the task of descending "from these human and refined natures of ours to those quite wild and savage natures, which we cannot at all imagine and can comprehend only with great effort." [17] He eschewed the use of imaginative extension because the substantive gulf which separated the historian from remote civilizations made anachronism inevitable. One simply could not "imagine" how primitive men conducted their affairs. They could be understood only through the critical methods elaborated in the *New Science.*

Formal Continuities

It remains to explore the formal continuities which had to obtain if the methods of criticism were to be applied to the conduct of people unlike ourselves in substantive respects. Scholars had used their own experience as a key to interpret the past. But this

[14] Sir Isaiah Berlin, "The Concept of Scientific History," in William H. Dray, ed., *Philosophical Analysis and History* (New York: Harper & Row, 1966), p. 41.
[15] *Ibid.*
[16] *Ibid.*, pp. 43–44.
[17] *NS*, par. 338.

procedure had led them to assert "improbabilities, absurdities, contradictions, and impossibilities" concerning "the principles of humanity." [18] The traditions I have associated with Collingwood and Dilthey sought connections with the past which avoided the cruder sorts of anachronism. But both fall afoul of the canons of Vico's criticism. In the first case, it is supposed that the criteria of rationality are sufficiently similar across the ages for the historian to "reenact" the thought of historical agents; in the second, it is supposed that our categories of meaning are applicable to other cultures. In each case, the question at issue is begged.

Vico takes the argument back a stage further. He examines the context of rules and conventions in which alone it makes sense to speak of rationality and meaning. These notions exist only in relation to what Wittgenstein called a "form of life." Vico's problem, then, is to reconstruct a form of life without presupposing the specific character which it must take. His solution is to concentrate on language as a phenomenon coeval with human society. "There must in the nature of human institutions be a mental language common to all nations, which uniformly grasps the substance of things feasible in human social life and expresses it with as many diverse modifications as these same things may have diverse aspects." [19] He does not have to specify what is "feasible in human social life" because he presupposes that, whatever the limits of human relations might be, there is a language adequate to the task of expression and communication. Rationality, modes of thought and feeling, have their place within a language. Practices, be they never "so remote from ourselves," can be understood if they can be translated into a language which we can understand. [20] Vico's three epochs are distinguished by the use of "three kinds of languages." [21] It is language that connects the various activities of a period with one another and provides the means by which those activities can be reconstructed as they were conceived by agents.

But the problem of interpretation does not end here. In order to understand the connections between aspects of a way of life, an historian has to rely on more than his ability to translate an utterance from one language into another. In this interpretive exercise he has to call on assumptions which he takes for granted in the course of his historical research. Philosophically these might constitute a very mixed bag. Vico speaks of the axioms of his *New Science* as "both philosophical and philological, including a few reasonable and proper postulates and some clarified definitions." [22] They do not constitute a system any more than the truisms of common sense constitute a system. They are not covering laws which warrant our explanations. They are simply recognition that we all bring general assumptions to history, coupled with an awareness that our assumptions are not those of early civilizations. Ideas, in short, have an historical and temporary currency. To suppose that our own are exempt from this condition would be to repeat the folly of social contract theory. But to acknowledge that this was the case would be to intimate that philosophy was second-order reflection on the presuppositions of a practice.

[22] *NS*, par. 119.

Vico and the Phenomenology of the Moral Sphere

BY ROBERT WELSH JORDAN

Vico's principle that to be true is the same as to be made led him, in the work we are celebrating, to conceive a comprehensive field of investigation for a new science. It is a science whose task is to comprehend the man-made world and the activities through which this world and its components are generated. Vico thus draws a distinction within the sphere of real entities. Those things which are not made by human beings cannot be known as they truly are. As they are in themselves and for God, purely natural entities, having been made by God alone, can be known by God alone. Considered as a description of actual entities, the formula for the hydrogen atom, for example, cannot be known to be true. It cannot be known to be true because no human being can experience the origin or creation of any such entity. The natural scientist cannot experience any of the things conceived in his science as they are conceived to be, and he cannot know that his concepts have any factual instances at all. On the other hand, the natural scientist's *concepts* do not belong to the sphere of purely natural entities. They are instead components of the historical, the man-made world. The science of physics and all of its component concepts are entities created by human beings. The scientist who constructs such a concept knows his concept as it is in itself, for it *is* his creation, and he has come to know it through his having constructed it. An historian who succeeded in reconstructing the science would know the concept in the same way as its creator knew it. The concept and the science of which it is a part are artifacts or institutions—that is, they are products of human activity.

Purposive human activity, its products and by-products, define sharply the scope of the subject matter for Vico's science. Its subject matter is sharply delineated and coincides with that of what Hume called "moral philosophy"—in contrast to "natural philosophy." Vico's way of delineating the subject matter of his science is directly in line with the conception developed by Alfred Schutz in his *Phenomenology of the Social World*.[1] Schutz's conception of the *Geisteswissenschaften* or moral sciences as sciences whose central aim is the comprehension of actions which are purposive and subjectively meaningful was developed through a criticism and revision of Max Weber's "interpretive sociology." The criticism and revision of Weber's position resulted very largely from a sound and original application of Husserl's phenomenological psychology to the analysis of action. Moreover, Schutz rejected as a misconception Weber's attempt to differentiate between mere behavior which is devoid of subjective meaning and action in the strict sense of the word. The latter is rationally directed response to stimulation and involves restraint of passion in order to direct the response toward a deliberately chosen individual end. Uncontrolled emotional responses and automatic reactions to habitual stimuli would tend to fall under the heading of mere subjectively meaningless behavior. Since Weber's interpretive sociology is to concern itself with action—that is, with subjectively meaningful behavior—Schutz's rejection of this distinction in favor of the view that all experiences are subjectively meaningful places him much closer to Vico's conception of the subject matter proper to the moral sciences.

In using the term "moral sciences" as an equivalent for the well known German *Geisteswissenschaften*, I am reintroducing—for

---

[1] Alfred Schutz, *The Phenomenology of the Social World*, translated by George Walsh and Frederick Lehnert (Evanston: Northwestern University Press, 1967).

the duration of this paper at least—the long-forgotten English original of which the German word is a translation. Just how forgotten the English term has become is indicated by the fact that Sir Isaiah Berlin in his essay on "The Philosophical Ideas of Giambattista Vico" actually reverses the historical relation between the German and English terms. The word *Geisteswissenschaft* is, he writes, "what J. S. Mill, probably mistranslating the word *Geist*, somewhere called 'Moral Science'. It was not a fortunate rendering and did not take." [2]   The somewhere to which Berlin refers is the chapter on "The Logic of the Moral Sciences" in Mill's *System of Logic.* The suggestion that Mill was casting about for a way to translate *Geisteswissenschaften* is strange in view of the fact that this word did not occur in German before it was used in 1849 by J. Schiel to render "moral sciences" in his translation of Mill's logic. [3]   Nor was Mill trying to coin a neologism for sciences dealing with whatever it is that German idealists and romantics were calling *Geist,* for the word "moral" had been used with much the same meaning that Mill gives it in such terms as "moral philosophy," "moral reasoning," "moral sciences" at least since Hume wrote his *Enquiries.* When used in this way by Hume and others as well as by Mill, the word "moral" refers to those things which are matters of or are conditioned by habit and custom. The phrase "the moral sphere" refers not just to the field of ethics but to the entire field of historical things which is the subject matter of Vico's new science as well as of the *verstehende Geisteswissenschaften* as conceived by Schutz. The subject matter of the moral sciences is indeed quite inseparable from the consciousness of values; this fact will be elaborated shortly. But ethics, considered as a theory of *correct* moral valuation, would, if possible at all, be but one branch of moral science. Even correct valuations can readily be regarded from a positive point of view simply as facts

[2] Isaiah Berlin, "The Philosophical Ideas of Giambattista Vico," in *Art and Ideas in Eighteenth-Century Italy* (Rome: Edizioni di storia e letteratura, 1960) p. 172.

[3] Johannes Hoffmeister, ed. *Wörterbuch der philosophischen Begriffe* (Hamburg Felix Meiner, 1955), p. 251.

The Subject Matter of the Moral Sciences

The moral sciences are to be contrasted not with amoral sciences but with natural sciences. Moral phenomena or historical phenomena are all of them phenomena that have been made by men. It is important to bear in mind here that in a certain sense the selfsame things investigated by the moral sciences are investigated, albeit from a quite different theoretical attitude, by various natural sciences. The point made with almost equal emphasis by Vico and Schutz along with other phenomenologists, as well as the entire Kantian tradition, including Dilthey, is that the natural sciences do not and cannot investigate these things *as* moral phenomena: their methods are not adapted to the investigation of human beings as historical or of actions as subjectively meaningful (Schutz) or of persons as rational (Kant) or of *Dasein* as being in the world (Heidegger) or of consciousness as intentional (Husserl). Among the philosophers just mentioned, Vico and the phenomenologists emphasize as well that we are able to know moral phenomena both because each of us makes and experiences his making such phenomena and because each of us is a moral being. Their insistence upon this point perhaps sets them off from the members of the Kantian tradition.

The things in the world around us, including ourselves and other human beings, are indeed physical things. As physical things, they are objects of sensory perception and behave in a regular fashion; they behave in a manner perfectly consistent with laws of nature, causal laws. Kant—at least so far as Kantians are concerned—provided us with a coherent account of how we come to experience these objects as unitary phenomena whose behavior follows typical patterns. But within this world, some things have dimensions of meaning which are not exhausted by their meaning as "natural" objects. In the world as a human environment, this is true by now of most, perhaps all, objects. There are in the human world things which, as Kant put it, cannot be accounted for solely in terms of natural causation.

All artifacts are things of this sort. Now all artifacts can be considered as objects of sense perception; they are natural objects which can be felt, seen, heard, tasted, and smelled. To perceive a pencil visually is to apperceive it as something that can also be felt, but to perceive it *as* a pencil involves other sorts of references as well.

Seeing it *as* a pencil involves a reference forward in time toward a use to which it can be put, toward a purpose for which the thing can be used. Seeing the pencil as a pencil involves comprehending the *value* which it has as a means toward achieving a specific sort of goal. Merely to see the thing is to *experience* its visual appearance, its color for example, so that seeing the thing would be evidence that there exists something of this shape and color. The shape and color are given originally through visual perceiving. But the thing's value for writing is not experienced in merely seeing it. The fact that it is useful or valuable for writing is given authentically or originally to me when I use it to write. My experience of writing is of course founded upon the tactual as well as visual perception of the pencil in motion and the marks it makes and on the visual, tactual, and kinesthetic perception of the specific bodily motions involved in writing. But this is not by any means all there is to writing. For writing is not normally an end in its own right but a part of a more inclusive act involving other values and having a specific place in the writer's life as a whole. All of this the writer experiences; he normally has an awareness, an understanding of it; and it all enters into the subjective meaning of his action.

Moreover, a full apprehension of the thing *as* a pencil would involve being referred *back* in time to a process of production through which materials have been transformed in order to produce just this sort of thing with this sort of utility as a cheap instrument for writing. This process of production was itself an action of the sort just mentioned; more precisely, it was a set of carefully planned collective actions each of which was of that general sort. But here each participant experiences originally

only a part of the productive process, and the process has its place
in an overall economy as well as in the lives of the direct participants. All of this is there to be understood with more or less distinctness by those who see pencils. It is not something that can
be simply seen by anyone who can see colors and shapes. The
ability to apperceive pencils in these ways is a matter of complex
experience and can be acquired only by someone with a definite
sort of personal history. In particular, the ability to apperceive
the pencil as the result of a productive process will be acquired
relatively late in the person's life unless for some reason he becomes familiar with pencil factories relatively early on.

Understanding both sorts of references—the reference forward
to its possible use and the reference back to its having been produced—is involved necessarily in, is essential to, the comprehension of anything at all as an artifact. Artifacts are objects which
have been shaped by persons acting more or less deliberately;
they are objects transformed by persons acting with specific purposes in mind. In this broad sense of the word, *all* aspects of a
culture are artifacts. All institutions in any culture whether they
be regarded as political, economic, social, or what have you are
artifacts in this sense. Moreover, the members of a culture are
each of them artifacts in this same sense. Each exists the way he
does only as a result of his "training." As Vico saw clearly, what
is called "enculturation" or "socialization" is a process which enables members of our biological species to become human persons, enables them to become participants in a culture and in a
history. Each has been transformed by his parents or others, who
acted, more or less deliberately, with purposes in mind and who
may be said to have valued whatever it was that they intended to
do to him.

The object of any moral science then is the comprehension of
the actions through which artifacts in our broad sense of the word
have been produced. This I believe was clearly understood by
Vico as well as by the Kantian tradition, Dilthey, Weber, and
phenomenologists in the tradition stemming from Husserl. Since

Dilthey, this conception of what the moral sciences are about has correctly been seen to link the moral sciences inseparably with psychology. For any clarification of the nature of their subject matter or of the methods they employ requires an adequate descriptive account of the nature of action as a mental process. The objections of Collingwood and his closer adherents to basing the moral sciences on psychological analysis appear to be directed chiefly against efforts such as those of John Stuart Mill—where psychology is conceived to be a positive, explanatory, and strictly empirical science. Such objections will, I hope, be removed if the relevant branch of psychology is itself conceived to be a moral science and purely descriptive in nature. This issue will be addressed more squarely in the concluding section of this paper.

Methodology in the Moral Sciences

Having presented a sketch, based on Alfred Schutz's work, for a phenomenological conception of the subject matter of the moral sciences, I wish now to provide a stark outline of some of Schutz's conclusions regarding methodology in the moral sciences and to indicate analogies with Vico. Here, too, his conclusions are best presented by way of his critique of Weber. When we are concerned with methods in the social sciences, the basic issue is: How is it possible to understand the so-called "data" by interpreting the actions of which they are signs—that is, the actions through which the "data" have presumably resulted. Briefly, and as Schutz thinks correctly, Weber's answer is that this understanding is achieved by constructing what he called ideal types. Whenever the moral scientist attempts to understand behavior, he does so by beginning with the completed act and the artifacts in which it has resulted. He attempts to determine the *type of action* which produced these. He then proceeds to deduce from the action type the *type of person* (personal ideal type) who executed the action. The point here is that the scientific understanding of action and persons is always an understanding of ideal types: action types on the one hand and personal types on the other. Understanding the person-type is founded on understanding the course-of-action-type. The interpreter must begin with his own perception of someone else's behavior or of its results. His aim will be to discover the motive for the sake of which the other person was acting. The motive as reconstructed will again be an ideal type; it will be the typical motive for performing the type of action which results in this type of artifact. The typical act will be conceived to have a single typical motive or goal. On the basis of the reconstructed action and motive, the person-type is then reconstructed. The actor must be the sort of person whose actual motive could have been of the reconstructed type.

All of this seems simple enough until one realizes how badly Weber himself misconstrued the procedure he was proposing and the nature of its results. Weber's misconstruction of his own procedure is crucial. It might account in large part for the hostile reception his brand of interpretive sociology so often encounters, and it points once again to the basic need in the moral sciences for an adequate descriptive psychology. If Schutz is right in his criticism, which was mentioned earlier in this paper, of Weber's distinction between behavior and action, then Weber would have misconceived that distinction through the lack of an adequate description of what he referred to as the intended or subjective meaning of action. Schutz maintained that Weber did not adequately explicate two quite different things, both of which he calls subjective or intended meaning, and this leads to a disastrous equivocation on the term.

(1) In the first place, subjective meaning is the meaning of the action the way the agent himself is aware of it.

(2) In the second place is (1) *as* understood and interpreted by the observer or moral scientist. The action *as* interpreted is the result of:

(a) an initial comprehension called "direct observational understanding [*aktuelles Verstehen*]" and

(b) a further explication or comprehension, through what is

called "explanatory understanding" of the action as initially comprehended. This further understanding is explanatory in that it is supposedly a comprehension of the intended meaning in terms of its motives.[4]

Weber, as Schutz interpreted him, simply assumed that (1) and (2) are *perfectly alike.* Thus Weber wrongly assumed that (1) can be observed. We observe either artifacts or bodily behavior; and, in doing so, we place what is observed within a wider context of meaning which we ourselves, the interpreters, supply from our accumulated knowledge and experience. The meaning (2) which the observed behavior has for us its observers is thus an *objective meaning* from the outset. This objective meaning is the meaning which the observed behavior has, for persons other than the agent, as *indicating* the existence of a subjective meaning. The initial phase of understanding apperceives (comprehends) what is being observed (e.g., bodily behavior, written words, or other culturally formed objects) as a field of expression for actions having a subjective meaning. The subjective meaning which is indicated is *not* itself given, is not directly observed. As Dilthey might have said, the action is lived through by the agent, not by the moral scientist; what the scientist is living through is the process of understanding the action.

If Schutz is right here, then his criticism of Weber would apparently apply to Collingwood as well. For Collingwood tells us of historical knowledge that

> Its object is . . . not a mere object, *something outside the mind which knows it;* it is an activity of thought, which can be known only insofar as the knowing mind reenacts it and knows itself as doing so. To the historian, the activities whose history he is studying are not spectacles to be watched, but experiences *to be lived through in his own mind;* they are objective, or known to him only because they are also subjective, or *activities of his own.*[5]

4 Schutz, *The Phenomenology of the Social World,* pp. 24–25.
5 R. G. Collingwood, "Human Nature and Human History," *Proceedings of the British Academy* 22 (1936): 16 and *The Idea of History* (London: Oxford University Press, 1956), p. 218; emphasis added.

It seems clear that the historian, at least when he interprets suc-
cessfully, is himself living through, experiencing, an action which
is *perfectly like* the past action he is investigating. This claim is
perhaps even stronger than the one implicitly made by Weber.
The claim overlooks the same fact. The intended meaning of
the action as it is lived by the agent himself "remains a limiting
concept even under optimum conditions of interpretation."[6] It
appears that neither Weber nor Collingwood recognized this fact.
The recognition is, however, crucial for a variety of reasons.

Without it, interpretive understanding appears to lay—and
does in fact lay—claim to a sort of knowledge which must per-
plex its adherents as well as its opponents.

The subjective meaning (1) of the action being explicated is
a limiting concept which the moral sciences strive to approximate
with maximum clarity. *The* subjective meaning of the action
which the moral scientist is explicating is something which the
scientist neither has nor ever will have *experienced* in an original
way. But this does not imply that subjective meaning is a regulative concept in a *strictly* Kantian sense, where what is conceived
in the concept is never given in experience.[7] As was emphasized
earlier in this paper, Vico clearly saw that the subject matter of
the moral sciences is familiar *in kind*. We do have absolute and
indisputable—that is, apodictic—evidence that there exist in fact
instances of the universals which our ideal types conceive. This
above all else distinguishes the moral sciences from any science
which might endeavor to describe natural objects as they are "in
themselves."

It also indicates that the psychology basic to the moral sciences
is of the sort which Husserl called eidetic. It is not an empirical
science at all. It is an a priori science. But it is an a priori science
whose factual relevance can be established conclusively. Eidetic
psychology is able to ascertain the factual relevance of its a priori

[6] Schutz, *The Phenomenology of the Social World*, p. 38.

[7] Edmund Husserl, *Ideas: General Introduction to Pure Phenomenology*, translated by W. R. Boyce Gibson (London: George Allen & Unwin, 1931), pars. 74, 83.

judgments. For, accessible to each eidetic moral scientist, there is apodictic evidence that the "ideal types" his science conceives are conceptions of universals *(eide)* which are indeed instantiated in experiences with which he is familiar or in experiences he can imagine as possible modifications of experiences with which he is familiar.

Thus—to present this basically Vichian insight in the garb of yet another phenomenologist—Heidegger tells us that interpretation is able to "create concepts belonging to the entity that is to be interpreted and to create them out of the entity itself, or it can on the other hand force the conceptuality belonging to this entity into concepts to which the entity in question is opposed." [8] And speaking this time specifically of cognition in the moral sciences, Heidegger says that

> The "circle" of interpretative understanding harbors a positive possibility for the *most original sort of cognition.* But this possibility is authentically realized only to the extent that interpretation has understood that its task is to guarantee that its subject matter is "scientific" by elaborating the purpose, prospect, and preconception of its interpretative activity out of the subject matter rather than letting them be determined [*vorgegeben*] by fancies and popular conceits. [9]

The objective validity of any interpretation in the moral sciences depends upon the extent to which it succeeds in interpreting its "data," instances of moral existence, in terms of the a priori structure of *all* moral existence. Objective validity is achieved to the extent that interpretative understanding "reveals the 'universal'—even in the unique." [10]

An eidetic psychology of moral phenomena would establish necessary material (as opposed to purely formal or "analytic") conditions for truth of judgments in any moral science. As Husserl conceives them, eidetic sciences are based on intuitive evi

8 Martin Heidegger, *Sein und Zeit* (Halle a. S.: Max Niemeyer, 1927), p. 150.

9 *Ibid.*, p. 153.

10 *Ibid.*, p. 395. The universals referred to here are what Heidegger otherwise calls "existentials."

dence, which here means clear imagination; they result in apodictic propositions concerning what is possible, impossible, or necessary. In Vico's terms, an eidetic moral science would show what
sort of "modifications" mental life is capable of; it can establish
the kinds of mental lives that can occur, the kinds of mental
processes that can or that must occur in them, and the kinds of
statements which may be, must be, and cannot be true of mental
processes of a specific kind or mental lives of a specific kind. Clear
imagination is a species of intuitive evidence, a species which provides evidence of eidetic or essential necessity. It can never establish *factual* necessity: it can provide evidence that *if* an event of
type *x* occurs, then it must have properties *a, b, c* and may have
properties *d, e, f* and cannot have properties *g, h, i*. But *eidetic*
intuition can provide no evidence that an *x* actually has occurred,
is occurring, or will occur. Evidence of actuality is provided by
empirical intuition—that is, perception and memory, experience.
Although eidetic intuition might yield evidence as to what type
of experience can count as evidence for a specified type of actual
occurrence, the discovery and evaluation of evidence for actual
occurrences of the type would fall entirely within the province
of empirical disciplines within the moral sciences.

Comment on Professor Jordan's Paper

In these remarks I would like to elaborate what I understand to be
the thrust of Professor Jordan's paper, and to introduce and relate
to his work a notion of lived experience, which is suggested to me by
his material throughout. Professor Jordan claims that the phenomena
investigated by the moral sciences imply fields of meaning quite different from the meaning found in material objects of mere sense perception. Thus there is in fact a divergence of focus in the methods
and the subject matter of the moral and natural sciences. The moral
sciences comprehend the subjective, conscious dimension of thoughts,

actions, and values by means of which the artifacts are produced. The attempt to understand this interior dimension of human existence and culture, at least since Dilthey, has linked the moral sciences with descriptive psychology. This attempt has also reinforced the claim of the moral sciences to an autonomous method. Professor Jordan also discusses the idea of a phenomenological moral science by outlining Alfred Schutz's critique of Max Weber, and by asking how it is possible to understand the data of the moral sciences by an interpretation of the actions through which the data have been produced. I shall also speak briefly about his reference to an eidetic psychology.

It was pointed out that Weber's aim in moral science explanation was the attempt to discover, understand, and typify an agent's motives for action. But Schutz has claimed that Weber confused the following two aspects of motive-action explanation as if they were one: (A) The subjective meaning, or the meaning of the action as the agent understands it; and (B) the subjective meaning of the action as it is interpreted by the moral scientist. Weber's assumption that A and B are identical is attended by his belief (1) that A is actually observable and (2) that A is interpreted from the context of meaning supplied by the moral scientist himself. The implication here is that an "objective" and imposed meaning is given to the agent from the outset.

Apparently the issue here is that the agent's subjective intention is not observed in its originary status, but is merely indicated. I believe that we can best understand this subjective intention and its place in moral science by relating it to what has been called by Dilthey "the lived experience" (*Erlebens*). This is that conscious state which is immediately lived through by the human subject and, as such, is epistemologically prior to an idealized or "objective" interpretation such as that discussed under B above. Complementing the lived experience is another concept which has come to be called the life world (*Lebenswelt*). I am convinced, incidentally, that both of these ideas were intuited by Vico in their modern sense. By the term "life world" I shall mean the world in which we actually live, the world intended by everyday awareness as the primary province of reality as it is actually lived. Our immediate consciousness of this world is the lived experience—that is, our awareness unmediated by presuppositions, constructive hypotheses, or arbitrary selectivity. Such experience is immediate in that the status of its content involves nothing more than its being lived. As such, a lived experience is understandable by another only potentially, by derivation, or by interpretation of human cultural expressions.

I believe that the above situation is what Schutz refers to in his claim that Weber mistakes the lived experience of the moral scientist's interpretation process for the lived experience of the agent to be understood. But we must note here that while it is inevitable that we cannot possess the identical lived experience of another, it does not follow that the moral scientist cannot, in principle, experience a content which has the same meaning as that of the agent's. The possibility of such a reliving of another's meaning is a necessary condition for culture. For without a meaningful reliving of another's experience, intersubjectivity of understanding would not exist. Schutz seems to recognize this fact when he tells us that "being with another" (*Mitsein*) is a primordial given in the human condition—that is, one of the existentials without which man would not be man. We might well ask if the explanatory role of eidetic psychology is anything but a reification and clarification of this fact.

At this point Vico's thought is relevant. One reason that the moral sciences have an explanatory priority is that the *verum est factum* formula establishes the very possibility of intersubjectivity. The culture and meaning "made" or constituted by the individual occurs in the lived experience. When the human being deliberately performs the subjective, symbolic operations that constitute a meaning, then it is possible for another to "do the same thing." When another "does the same thing," then he can self-consciously refer to his own states of immediate awareness—that is, a like meaning is potentially lived in each because a similarly constituted meaning is created by the like action or experience of each. For example, for two children to understand the meaning of mastering a bicycle there is entailed a being able to "do the same thing." The doing or making of a like thing provides a basis for a similar lived experience.

When professor Jordan refers to the eidetic psychology, I take it that this is a contemporary response to Vico's charge that the moral sciences must determine the "modifications of mental life." This psychology after Husserl's program would try to determine in an exact and generally valid manner what the universal structures (*eidoi*) of these modifications are. It would ask, for example, how such entities as motives, values, meanings, and volitions are actually constituted in the lived experience of man. Such an eidetic science would help insure that we do not mistake, as Weber apparently did, originary, lived states of experience in an agent for explanatory states of experience in the moral scientist. In other words, it attempts to determine Vico's modifications of mental life, or those universal constituents which make given experiences what they are and not something else. We may note, finally, that the need for such eidetic and originary science was first conceived by Vico during the lone vigil of his genius.

Howard Tuttle

Vico: The Problem of Interpretation

BY B. A. HADDOCK

Vico has a peculiar position in the history of thought. Largely ignored in his own lifetime, a figure outside the mainstream of the European intellectual tradition, he has yet been seen by the various schools of thought as a startlingly original anticipator of their own positions. Interpretations of Vico read like a compendium of European philosophy of the last three hundred years. We have been treated to idealist, empiricist, Marxist, pragmatist, positivist, existentialist, and structuralist interpretations, embracing most of the disciplines which have contributed significantly to the development of the *Geisteswissenschaften* in the nineteenth and twentieth centuries. It is both his strength and his weakness that this should be the case. His work is richly suggestive rather than systematic, a chaotic mixture of insight and archaism which leaves to the reader the task of finding some sort of coherence. To the historian, however, this plethora of contradictory interpretations amounts to the statement of a problem rather than a solution. The historian has, perhaps naively, taken Ranke's dictum to heart: he has determined to tell the story of events *wie es eigentlich gewesen ist;* and until he can produce a Vichian interpretation of Vico, he can consider his studies only as reports of work in progress.

The study of Vico, then, is fraught with methodological difficulties. On the one hand, we are faced with a series of interpretations that are strictly incompatible, a set of ideas that are said to have been derived from Vico but which have come to fruition very much later, and a group of disciplines of which he is said to have been the father but whose development has (in some cases) been a specifically twentieth-century phenomenon. In short, the received set of interpretations of Vico is, in the literal sense, anachronistic, and this anachronism has become part of the conventional wisdom of the history of ideas in the form of an assumption about originality on Vico's part. Vico's importance is seen as a source for ideas that would be systematically developed only after his death. Moreover, such development was normally effected not by serious study of Vico's work but by a belated recognition of intellectual affinity. Vico's ideas are not studied on their own terms, but for intimations of the future that they might be seen to contain. Vico's "providence" becomes Hegel's "cunning of reason"; his account of the conflict between groups that leads to a change of political arrangements is read as an anticipation of Marx's notion of class conflict; and, indeed, whenever difficulty arises, Vico is interpreted by a species of retrospective analogy. There is no attempt to try to discover what Vico was trying to convey by his specific form of words, and in many cases he is taken to be arguing for a position which he could not possibly have entertained.

On the other hand, even where there is a conscious awareness of the dangers of anachronism in dealing with a thinker such as Vico, it has proved seemingly impossible to avoid retrospective interpretation. Berlin, for instance, identifies the anachronistic snares that have posed insuperable problems for Vico's commentators but feels obliged, if he is to do justice to Vico, to engage in the same sort of procedure. He writes:

> It may be that in finding in Vico so much that became fully articulate only in the nineteenth or twentieth century, I, too, am guilty of the same fault. Yet I cannot persuade myself that this is so. Premature anticipations of the ideas of one age in another happen seldom, but they happen. An original thinker misunderstood or ignored by his contemporaries is not a mere romantic myth.[1]

In drawing attention to Berlin's remark, I do not want to claim that Vico is a romantic myth, only to point to some of the meth-

---

[1] Isaiah Berlin, "The Philosophical Ideas of Giambattista Vico," in *Art and Ideas in Eighteenth-Century Italy* (Rome: Edizioni di storia e letteratura, 1960), pp. 227-228.

odological difficulties involved in trying to characterize such a thinker accurately. And while Berlin's essay is sensitive to the historical context of Vico's thought, his interpretation is cast in a style that would, rightly or wrongly, make Vico and Berlin kindred philosophical spirits.[2]

These methodological considerations can be seen to have reduced Vichian studies to something of an impasse. To expect a uniformity of interpretation would be neither possible nor desirable. But despite the wealth of critical literature that has been produced in Italy since the appearance of Croce's monograph on Vico in 1911, the state of the field still gives the impression of being something of a scholarly free-for-all.[3] If disagreement centered upon points of exegetical detail, this would hardly be surprising in a writer such as Vico. His style is notoriously ambiguous and convoluted; and if commentators experienced difficulty trying to unravel the main thread of his argument, this would not be anything to remark upon in a thinker who seems to lose himself almost willfully in his digressions. We are accustomed to this sort of confusion. We meet it in Hobbes, Locke, Rousseau, Hegel, Marx, indeed all the leading figures of our intellectual tradition; and far from considering this state of affairs deplorable, we are inclined to see in it an indication of the vitality of our criticism. We can trace certain traditions of interpretation, but, for the most part, we do not find the dead hand of scholastic orthodoxy. The confusion that seems to be endemic in Vichian studies is of a different sort. Interpretation, in this case, is a function of assimilation to a previously existent philosophical school; and exegetical disputes tend to turn on the neatness with which Vico's thought can be assimilated to a particular orthodoxy. If we are to progress in our understanding of Vico's philosophy, it is imperative that we face these methodological dilemmas.

[2] For a comparison of Berlin's position with his interpretation of Vico, see his essay, "The Concept of Scientific History," in William H. Dray, ed., *Philosophical Analysis and History* (New York: Harper & Row, 1966), pp. 5–53.

[3] Benedetto Croce, *La filosofia di Giambattista Vico* (Bari: Laterza, 1911).

Texts and Contexts

It is only comparatively recently that students of the history of philosophy have come to face the possibility that there might be specific problems attached to writing the history of philosophy, as distinct from the normal problems encountered in the activity of thinking philosophically. From Plato to the eighteenth century, the Western philosophical tradition could be said to have been dominated by an abstract conception of reason, essentially time-less, such that a consideration of philosophical ideas could be con-ducted without regard to the time and place in which they were formulated. The philosopher's only interest was with the adequacy of this set of ideas as answers to the perennial questions which it was his concern to investigate. Hence, at the end of the seven-teenth century, it was possible to debate the relative merits of the "ancients" and "moderns," as if they offered answers to the same set of philosophical problems. Following what is glibly called "the nineteenth-century historical revolution," the debate seems rather queer; and to a man of historical disposition it is either of "historical" interest alone or simple nonsense.[4] But that the de-bate should have attracted the attention of learned men from the Renaissance to the beginning of the eighteenth century is testi-mony to the extratemporal terms of reference within which phi-losophy was conducted. Even Vico, before the formulation of his mature philosophy, made a small but not insignificant contri-bution to the debate.[5]

It is on the meaning of this notion of a perennial philosophical problem that attention has been focused in the debate about the appropriate manner of conducting the history of philosophy. Col-lingwood, in his *Autobiography*, explicitly concentrates his criti-cism on the assumption, dear to the Oxford "realists," that there exists a set of eternal questions in philosophy and that the great

---

[4] R. G. Collingwood, *An Autobiography* (Oxford: The Clarendon Press, 1939), p. 6.
[5] *De nostri temporis studiorum ratione* (1709), translated by Elio Gianturco as *On the Study Methods of Our Time* (Indianapolis: Bobbs-Merrill, 1965).

historic texts of philosophy constitute more or less inadequate answers to this set of questions. The corollary of this belief, in Collingwood's view, is that the various answers to these common questions can be examined in the form of propositions and compared with one another. Thus, in the view of the "realists," it would make perfect sense to compare Plato's *Republic* with Hobbes's *Leviathan* in order to ascertain which contained the most adequate presentation of the nature of the state.[6] All this Collingwood was concerned to deny. A proposition, for Collingwood, made no sense unless it was understood as an answer to a specific question; and until that question had been identified, there was nothing that the philosopher could say about it. Accordingly, a philosophical text had to be read not as a set of independently valid propositions but as a group of related answers to questions which it was the historian's task to identify. In this manner, to argue that, where Plato and Hobbes contradict one another, one of them must be wrong is to misunderstand the respective activities in which Plato and Hobbes were engaged. The history of thought, in this view, "is not the history of different answers given to one and the same question, but the history of a problem more or less constantly changing, whose solution was changing with it."[7] This original insight in the field of political theory Collingwood extended to the entire domain of critical thinking. To know what any man means by a specific utterance, it is necessary to reconstruct the problem to which his utterance is an answer. And a philosopher, examining an unfamiliar set of ideas, can be said to understand those ideas only when he is able to set them in the context of the questions to which they are an attempted solution.

These suggestions were largely ignored, and for many years the history of philosophy was conducted in precisely the manner that Collingwood had deplored. In the last decade, however, the revival of interest in his work has been accompanied by an acute

[6] Collingwood, *An Autobiography*, p. 61.
[7] *Ibid.*, p. 62.

methodological self-consciousness among historians of ideas. In particular, the union of philosophy and history that he advocated has been accompanied by detailed investigations of the implications of this recommendation for practicing historians.[8] It is no longer felt, at least in certain quarters, that it is legitimate to interpret texts by concentrating only upon the text itself and squeezing a plausible meaning out of the form of words that the author adopted. This procedure is seen as an open invitation to anachronism. A difficult passage may be capable of more than one interpretation, and if the text is to be the sole guide to our understanding of the author, we may well find ourselves imposing interpretations that have a certain contemporary relevance. If we want to know what Vico understands by "science," we search in vain if his text is our only source. And because we are accustomed to handling various conceptions of "science" in modern philosophy, we run the risk of imposing a conception of "science" on Vico which he could not possibly have held. We are urged,

---

[8] The leaders of this so-called "revisionist" movement in the history of ideas have been John Dunn, J. G. A. Pocock, and Quentin Skinner. See Dunn, "The Identity of the History of Ideas," in Peter Laslett, W. G. Runciman and Quentin Skinner, eds., *Philosophy, Politics and Society*, Fourth Series (Oxford: Blackwell, 1972), pp. 158–173; Pocock, "The History of Political Thought: A Methodological Enquiry," in Peter Laslett and W. G. Runciman, eds., *Philosophy, Politics and Society*, Second Series (Oxford: Blackwell, 1962), pp. 183–202, and *Politics, Language and Time* (London: Methuen, 1972); and Skinner, "Meaning and Understanding in the History of Ideas," *History and Theory* 8 (1969): 3–53, "On Two Traditions of English Political Thought," *The Historical Journal* 9 (1966): 136–139, and "Some Problems in the Analysis of Political Thought and Action," *Political Theory* 2 (1974): 277–303.

The work of this school has not been without criticism. See Bhikhu Parekh and R. N. Berki, "The History of Political Ideas," *Journal of the History of Ideas* 34 (1973): 163–184; Charles D. Tarlton, "Historicity, Meaning, and Revisionism in the Study of Political Thought," *History and Theory* 12 (1973): 307–328; Jonathon M. Wiener, "Quentin Skinner's Hobbes," *Political Theory* 2 (1974): 251–260; and Gordon J. Schochet, "Quentin Skinner's Method," *Political Theory* 2 (1974): 261–276.

In drawing attention to Collingwood's influence on the "revisionists," I do not want to suggest that he was the sole or necessarily the most important influence. In this respect it would be important to mention Oakeshott, Austin, and Wittgenstein. There are some seminal pages on matters herein discussed in Isaiah Berlin's "Does Political Theory Still Exist?" in Peter Laslett and W. G. Runciman, eds., *Philosophy, Politics and Society*, Second Series. pp. 1–33. See also my paper, "The History of Ideas and the Study of Politics," *Political Theory* 2 (1974): 420–431.

instead, to examine the context in which a writer formulated his thought, to specify the range of meanings which a term could have had for him. In short, we are told to ascertain an author's intention in using the words he did rather than to impose any interpretation that the words could be seen to imply in abstraction from their historical context. And while it is legitimate to say that an idea sketched in an earlier thinker was later developed by others into a coherent philosophy, it would be the grossest anachronism to use the later development as a key to the interpretation of the original work. In the case of Vico, for example, while it might be appropriate to look at his work within a tradition that later included existentialism, it would be historically meaningless to interpret the *New Science* as an existentialist work. In this view, the only legitimate interpretation would be cast in a form which the writer in question could possibly have intended, for the business of historical interpretation is seen as an attempt to reconstruct the intentions that would make a text intelligible.

It is not suggested that the recovery of an author's intentions is a simple or self-evident activity; rather, that if the procedure is not adopted, a text can be said to mean anything that its words can be constrained to mean. In the work of Quentin Skinner, this conception of the priority of intentions in the understanding of texts is supported by a sophisticated use of the techniques developed in recent years in the philosophy of language.[9] A text, whatever else it might be, is seen as an attempt to communicate something to somebody. It can, accordingly, only be seen in the context of a set of problems that the author in question can plausibly be supposed to have been concerned with. The only alternative to such a view would be to consider the text as a sort of private language-game. In this case, the historian would have no points of reference with which to begin his interpretation; and, following Wittgenstein, there are good reasons to suppose that

9 See Skinner's works cited in footnote 8. Skinner has particularly indicated his indebtedness to J. L. Austin.

the author of such a text must have been engaged in some sort of public language-game, no matter how esoteric, or simply writing nonsense.[10]   Skinner's positive recommendation to the historian is that the only way to reconstruct an author's intentions is to immerse oneself in detailed historical research.   The methodological recommendation is not itself new; it is simply an injunction to the historian of ideas to engage himself in the sort of grass-roots research which his colleagues investigating other types of human activity in the past have always regarded as a prerequisite for the achievement of historical explanations.

An author's intention, then, is an inference for which the text and its historical context serve as evidence.   An historian will seek to establish the problems with which his author is concerned and the level of generality at which he is addressing himself to those problems.[11]   This in itself is no mean undertaking.   In the history of political thought, the galaxy of "great" texts includes those by pamphleteers such as Burke, preoccupied with current political issues, and philosophers such as Hobbes, operating at the highest level of abstraction.   A single writer can, of course, operate at different levels of abstraction within a single work.   But this only serves to emphasize the difficulty of the historian's task in unraveling the complex interrelationship of intentions that are his guiding thread in the interpretation of texts.   What this school of thought is trying to establish is that, difficult though it may be, the historian has necessarily to engage in this sort of activity or he will find himself interpreting his author by the anachronistic imposition of his own assumptions.[12]   And this is precisely what has occurred in the study of Vico.   Whether this sort of anachronism is avoidable in Vico's case is something that I will be concerned to investigate.

[10] See Ludwig Wittgenstein, *Philosophical Investigations*, translated by G. E. M. Anscombe (Oxford: Blackwell, 1968), pp. 94–96.
[11] See J. G. A. Pocock, "The History of Political Thought: A Methodological Enquiry."
[12] See Quentin Skinner, "Meaning and Understanding in the History of Ideas," p. 7.

Paradigms and Presuppositions

If historians are intent on understanding past ideas without assimilating them to their own contemporary presuppositions, they are nevertheless obliged to reconstruct a set of presuppositions within which an author's intentions can be located. They cannot assume what it would be appropriate for a given historical agent to intend without sketching a reconstruction of an entire form of life. In Wittgenstein's words, "Our knowledge forms an enormous system. And only within this system has a particular bit the value we give it." [13] An historian, bent on reconstructing this "enormous system" in which to locate a set of ideas, might well have our sympathy if he felt that the attempt to locate an individual's thought within its appropriate "system" would involve him in an infinite regress. But again, his trepidation would be misplaced, for he would have misunderstood the sort of certainty that is necessary if his historical account is to make sense. To quote Wittgenstein again, "the questions that we raise and our doubts depend on the fact that some propositions are exempt from doubt, are as it were like hinges on which those turn." [14]

These methodological qualms have to some extent been allayed by the work of a recent historian of science, Thomas S. Kuhn.[15] Kuhn has sought to present the history of science in terms of the paradigms that characterize the manner in which the community of scientists are disposed to see the world. These paradigms constitute a frame of reference in periods of what Kuhn calls "normal science." They are a prior framework within which the puzzle-solving activity of "normal science" makes sense; indeed, the puzzles which a scientist is disposed to investigate are

[13] Ludwig Wittgenstein, *On Certainty*, edited by G. E. M. Anscombe and G. H. Von Wright, translated by Denis Paul and G. E. M. Anscombe (Oxford Blackwell, 1974), p. 52.

[14] *Ibid.*, p. 44.

[15] Thomas S. Kuhn, *The Structure of Scientific Revolutions* (Chicago: University of Chicago Press, 1970). Pocock, in particular, has been impressed by Kuhn's notion of a "paradigm," and has sought to use it as a general methodological canon for the history of ideas. See J. G. A. Pocock, *Politics, Language and Time*.

dictated by the requirements of a paradigm, and scientific activity in normal circumstances, constitutes a refinement of the logical structure of the paradigm. A scientist, in this view, cannot simply investigate a particular phenomenon, for his very conception of the phenomenon as a problem to be solved will be a function of his having accepted the authority of the paradigm. If the activity of "normal science" should produce a host of anomalous data, unintelligible within the framework of the paradigm, a scientific revolution occurs. This, for Kuhn, is simply the replacement of the old paradigm by a new one. Henceforth, scientists will be disposed to see their world in a different light. The new paradigm will engender new problems, and the puzzles associated with the old paradigm will no longer be recognized. To the practicing scientist they will be literally unintelligible and of "historical" interest alone. Kuhn's point, however, is that the scientist, lacking historical awareness, accepts as scientific whatever the current paradigm dignifies with that appellation. To the historian, the adjective "scientific" applies relative to a paradigm accepted by the community of scientists. In this sense, the old paradigm would be just as scientific as the new one. The methodological point is simple. The history of science need not be written as a sort of success story of the current paradigm but as the successive transformations of paradigms. And in the broader field of the history of ideas, it is held that something like Kuhn's notion of a paradigm will enable us to locate intentions within an historically viable framework.

Kuhn has drawn our attention to two distinct points, both of which must be borne in mind if we are to write the history of an intentional activity. If we are to understand intentions, it is essential that we be able to locate them within a specific context. And if we are to write a history of intentions, we must be able to characterize the manner in which the interrelationship between context and intention changes. The first point, stated rather differently, constitutes the crux of Wittgenstein's argument about what it makes sense to say in any situation. Before we can understand a statement, it is necessary to locate it within a language-game; and confusion about the meaning of a statement is the necessary consequence of a confusion about its appropriate language-game. The "priority of paradigms" that Kuhn stresses in his account of scientific activity is simply a prerequisite for that activity to make sense at all:

> All testing, all confirmation and disconfirmation of a hypothesis takes place already within a system. And this system is not a more or less arbitrary and doubtful point of departure for all our arguments: no, it belongs to the essence of what we call an argument. The system is not so much the point of departure, as the element in which arguments have their life.[16]

Our very understanding of a "fact," which for Kuhn is relative to a paradigm, is for Wittgenstein dependent on its place in a particular language-game; any change in our conception of matters of fact is necessarily associated with a change in a language-game:

> If we imagine the facts otherwise than as they are, certain language-games lose some of their importance, while others become important. And in this way there is an alteration—a gradual one—in the use of the vocabulary of a language.[17]

The historian's task, then, will be to locate his author's text within its appropriate language-game; and the language-game will be taken as a fixed "hinge" on which his interpretation will turn. The language-game, however, can be taken as a fixed point only for relative purposes. Something said within a language-game, as Wittgenstein implies, can produce changes in the structure of the language-game itself. And if the language-game is taken as the canon of interpretation, the historian may be faced with a situation in which his text has altered the framework in which it made sense. It is in such circumstances that interpretation in the history of ideas becomes problematical.

   This dilemma is central in Collingwood's work. He has shown us the importance of locating a text in a context of appropriate

---

[16] Wittgenstein, *On Certainty*, p. 16.
[17] *Ibid.*, p. 10.

questions, and has also identified the context of presuppositions upon which the questioning activity is dependent. To ask a question presupposes a state of affairs that makes the question meaningful. To use Collingwood's example, to ask a man whether he has stopped beating his wife presupposes that he had been in the habit of beating her.[18]   And this presupposition will itself be dependent on other presuppositions about the conventions surrounding the relations between men and women in a particular society. These presuppositions Collingwood calls "relative," in the sense that they can be shown to be related to other presuppositions in a chain of question and answer. We cannot, however, ask questions about the presuppositions of presuppositions without end; ultimately, we will be faced with a presupposition which it makes no sense to question, what Collingwood calls an "absolute presupposition." "Absolute presuppositions" constitute, for Collingwood, the "hinges" without which the rest of our questioning activity would be meaningless. But if we cannot ask questions about "absolute presuppositions," that does not mean that we can say nothing at all about them; for "absolute presuppositions" have a history, and a history of "absolute presuppositions" would constitute a critical frame of reference with which to examine the subordinate constellations of ideas that derive their intelligibility from the coherence of the whole.

Historical ideas, then, can be examined without recourse to anachronistic procedures; for what an idea means will depend on its location within the context of a set of "absolute presuppositions." But once again, we come up against a problem. While in broad terms it might be possible to look at a text in relation to the "absolute presuppositions" that characterize the period in which it was written, on points of detail we are faced with critical criteria that are themselves subject to change. We may, that is, have to deal with a text that is instrumental in changing the constellation of "absolute presuppositions" that made its initial formu-

---

[18] R. G. Collingwood, *An Essay on Metaphysics* (Oxford: The Clarendon Press, 1940), pp. 25–26. See especially pp. 3–77 for much of what follows in this paragraph.

lation intelligible. And though we might want to say that an author could not possibly have intended to change those "absolute presuppositions," we are clearly confronted with an interpretative problem if a text's frame of reference is as transient as the text itself is ambiguous.

The Problem of the Innovator

What we have seen in these last few pages is a convergence of views, formulated from very different perspectives, emphasizing the primacy of context in the understanding of any statement. And yet in each formulation we seem to encounter the same methodological difficulty. If we are to understand intentions, we need to locate them within their appropriate contexts; while contexts are themselves changeable and problematical. Whether we use the language of "paradigms," "language-games," or "absolute presuppositions," the structure that gives meaning to a specific utterance is as illusive as the meaning of the utterance itself. In everyday life we are able to take certain things for granted, to treat certain assumptions as if they were free from doubt. But it is precisely these assumptions that the historian has to reconstruct. And, the way I have presented his problem, his task might appear Promethean. His account will seem like a dubious inference from premises that derive their certainty only from the conclusion itself.

To an historian, however, the problem itself might appear somewhat unreal. Change is the currency of his profession. All he seeks to do is to make change intelligible. And if he can locate past human activities within a traditional mode of conduct, he is satisfied that he has fulfilled his professional duty. What he seeks are not "hinges" but continuities. If he can identify a tradition, it is, for him, a warrant for his explanation. Change will no longer appear inscrutable. And if his account lacks certainty, he will be content to say that "certainty" is not a noun that comes within the historian's province. His professional conduct belies his confidence. He is dissatisfied with previous accounts of change, and is perpetually engaged in an attempt to reach a goal in his explanations which he would not be foolish enough to specify. And his reliance on the concept of tradition has a familiar circularity about it. In normal circumstances it serves him well enough. If ideas are his province, he will be happy to have identified the nexus of traditional assumptions that make a text intelligible. But once again, it is the innovator who poses the problem. A writer, addressing himself to familiar difficulties, might come up with answers that are instrumental in changing the nature of a tradition. We seem to be back where we started.

The problem of the innovator is that he could not have intended to change the framework from which his work issued, but that framework has nevertheless been called into question. It is not simply that he is offering novel answers to an old set of questions; rather, he has, perhaps inadvertently, asked himself the old questions in a manner that is incompatible with conventional assumptions. Both Vico and Descartes were concerned with the problem of science, and in the first instance their terms of reference were remarkably similar; yet when Vico extended the discussion of science to the human studies, he was operating in a different world of discourse. The problems associated with Cartesian science are scarcely recognizable in the *New Science*, but these problems were fundamental to Vico in the first phase of his theory of knowledge. In Vico's case, we can trace the genesis of his mature philosophy from his early preoccupation with basically Cartesian problems; and we have the benefit of an autobiography that helps us to identify the particular problems that Vico was concerned with at various stages of his intellectual development. But if we were left to infer from the text of the *New Science* the questions to which that work is an answer, our task would be impossible. While the work is normally read as the development of the implications of Vico's dissatisfaction with Descartes' theory of knowledge, Descartes himself is referred to only once.[19]   The *New Science* is itself the product of successive revisions of a book that was written in positive form only as a result of what Vico calls "a stroke of bad luck." [20]   It had previously been written as a two-volume work criticizing the theories of society found in seventeenth-century writers such as Grotius, Selden, Pufendorf, Hobbes, Spinoza, Bayle, and Locke.   This manuscript is no longer extant, and we are deprived of a document that might have proved invaluable in our attempt to identify Vico's specific meaning in many difficult passages.   And the authoritative text of the *New Science* that we are left to interpret is the amalgam of various additions and revisions.   Vico had no doubt about the originality of his work, but he was always dissatisfied with its form.   He was, it seems, striving (unsuccessfully) to locate his own work within an appropriate frame of reference.   Vico felt himself to be engaged in the formulation of a new paradigm, yet his own relationship with that paradigm was, in Kuhn's sense, preparadigmatic.   He was unable to make his meaning clear because the rules and conventions that separate sense from nonsense in the new paradigm had not been articulated.

The historian's difficulty in this matter is but an extension of Vico's.   In the interpretation of a text, he needs to take certain things for granted.   And if his explanation is historically accurate, the things he takes for granted will be the unspoken assumptions that were the "hinges" of his author's conception of the world.   But if his author has, as it were, taken his own world off its "hinges," introduced a set of ideas that are irreconcilable with the established paradigm, he is obliged to attempt to construct a paradigm within which those ideas could have a place.   The dangers in this procedure are obvious.   If his author is genuinely original, he is unlikely to have succeeded in articulating a new

---

[19] *The New Science of Giambattista Vico* (hereinafter *NS*), translated by Thomas G. Bergin and Max H. Fisch (Ithaca: Cornell University Press, 1968), par. 706.

[20] *The Autobiography of Giambattista Vico*, translated by Max H. Fisch and Thomas G. Bergin (Ithaca: Cornell University Press, 1944), p. 166.

paradigm; and if such a paradigm is not readily identifiable, the historian runs the risk of imposing a paradigm of his own creation. Whatever else Vico's commentators might disagree about, on the question of his originality there is no dispute. An early English critic, John Kenrick, writing for a journal edited by Coleridge's disciples Hare and Thirlwall, has a remarkable passage identifying the difficulties implicit in the ascription of originality which is worth quoting in full:

> Without encroaching on the just claims of other men, to exalt the fame of Vico, we may safely pronounce him to have been one of the most original thinkers whom his country has produced. At the time at which he lived, it was perhaps impossible to do more than detect the falsehood of long-established opinions, to discover and demonstrate the truth which should be substituted for them, was necessarily the work of a succeeding age. But he who first shakes the foundation of an edifice of ancient error, should not be deprived of our gratitude, though he only leaves the ground encumbered with ruins, without being able to build up any thing in the room of what he has overthrown. Were he even as well qualified to construct as to destroy, he finds neither tools nor materials prepared for this second labour.[21]

In this view, if Vico had made himself understood, it would have required the preexistence of the paradigm for which his work provided a foundation. Any confusion in his thought would be explained by the fact that he was working in a critical void between paradigms. It is historically implausible that Vico should attain the coherence that was a function of the mature articulation of the paradigm; and the specific achievements associated with the later development of the paradigm could not be ascribed to him. An historian whose subject was the group of ideas associated with the mature paradigm might want to stress the importance of Vico's "influence" on the development of those ideas. But he must be careful not to attribute to Vico ideas that came to fruition after the paradigm had been established. If his task is the specific interpretation of Vico's thought, his dilemma is unenviable. While avoiding anachronism, he has to explain a set

---

21 "Vico," *The Philological Museum* 2 (1833): 644.

of ideas that exist in no readily identifiable intellectual framework, that are, in the literal sense, transitional.

With regard to specific interpretations of Vico, historians have succumbed to the temptation of anachronism. Lacking an unambiguous historical paradigm, a set of logically related concepts which can be shown to have served as Vico's frame of reference, they have interpreted him with the dubious wisdom of hindsight. Given the nature of Vico's work, it should not surprise us that this should have been the case. To understand the meaning of his words, it is necessary to locate them within some sort of structure; and the labor of fifteen years that Vico devoted to revisions of his *magnum opus* is evidence that he himself was by no means clear what that structure should be. Instead of attempting to characterize Vico's "transitional paradigm" (and the difficulties of such a task are implicit in the ambiguity of the concept), historians have been content to subsume his work under the categories of a paradigm which they consider to be "significant" for the future development of ideas. In adopting this procedure they have, paradoxically, contravened one of the axioms that served as a keystone for Vico's work:

> It is another property of the human mind that whenever men can form no idea of distant and unknown things, they judge them by what is familiar and at hand. This axiom points to the inexhaustible source of all the errors about the principles of humanity that have been adopted by entire nations and by all the scholars. For when the former began to take notice of them and the latter to investigate them, it was on the basis of their own enlightened, cultivated, and magnificent times that they judged the origins of humanity, which must nevertheless by the nature of things have been small, crude, and quite obscure.[22]

This lacuna in Vichian studies is the more unfortunate in that Vico's *New Science* is, among other things, a treatise on the methodology of the history of ideas. Having identified the "conceit of nations" and the "conceit of scholars" as probable sources of erroneous historical accounts, he proceeded to elaborate a set of principles which served as a regulative canon in the recon-

[22] *NS*, pars. 122–123.

struction of past modes of thought.[23]   Understanding human utterances in the past had been vitiated by the assumption of "the
three princes of the natural law of the gentes . . . that natural
equity in its perfect form had been understood by the gentile
nations from their first beginings." [24] The portrayal of primitive
societies was thus rendered anachronistic by the adoption of the
criteria of rationality of civilized nations as a standard to evaluate
the modes of thought of all times and all places. The realization
that reason has a history, however, engenders difficulties of its
own. If the principles of civil society are "to be found within
the modifications of our own human mind," how are we "to
descend from these human and refined natures of ours to those
quite wild and savage natures, which we cannot at all imagine and
can comprehend only with great effort"?[25] In other words, if the
verification of our historical accounts is to depend upon a species
of empathetic reenactment, how are we to avoid the anachronistic
imposition of our own "magnificent" opinions?

Vico's solution to the dilemma (if the anachronism may be ex-
cused) was to employ historical paradigms as a framework within
which the relations of ideas could be understood without recourse to eighteenth-century assumptions. His characterization
of the ages of gods, heroes, and men gave him a criterion to distinguish the limits of meanings which could be construed from
a specific form of words used in a specific period. Law, language,
ethics, poetry, each assumed a distinct character in the life of a
period, and the relation of these utterances to one another was
made intelligible by reference to the appropriate historical paradigm. Comparison of ideas was made possible within the compass of paradigms. In short, Vico had established the *sine qua non*
of a history of ideas, a criterion of judgment that avoided anachronism. It is a curious, but characteristic, tribute to Vico that this
aspect of his work should be identified at a time when historians
of ideas have become self-conscious about their procedures.

23 *NS*, pars. 125–128.
24 *NS*, par. 329.
25 *NS*, pars. 331, 338.

The Priority of Common Sense and Imagination: Vico's Philosophical Relevance Today

BY ERNESTO GRASSI

> I believe that a piece of work can only be understood . . . if it is realized at what points a structure of its kind transcends what it has set out to represent.
>
> —Theodore Adorno, *Lecture on the Introduction to Sociology*

Vico's *New Science* confronts traditional metaphysics and Cartesian rationalism with the outline of a new method of scientific thought which, simultaneously, takes the form of a novel restatement of the humanistic tradition. Before discussing this new method and its relevance today, I must first examine Vico's rejection of traditional metaphysics and of the Cartesian grounds for philosophy, insofar as they do not constitute a basis for the "formation" of man and for an understanding of history; and I must look briefly at two important contemporary critiques of humanistic ideas, represented by logistics and structuralism.

The Traditional System of Scientific Thought

According to traditional thought, empirical observations prove inadequate in forming a starting point for scientific statements because they can never go beyond a limited range of experiences; similarly, hypothetical statements are inadequate because they result in a consideration of mere possibilities. Statements can be of a scientific nature only if they are derived from universally valid and necessary premises. Through recourse to such premises, the statements are demonstrated and thereby "explained."

At the end of the Middle Ages, Dante, in his *De Monarchia,* provided the following definition for this system of scientific thought, which has its roots in the classical conception of metaphysics: "As every truth that is not primary can manifest itself only through the truth of a nondeducible principle, ever investigation must start from a principle to which analytical reference is made in order to deduce from it the certainty of all statements following from it." In other words, statements are scientifically valid only if they can be strictly deduced from an unquestionable, ultimate axiom in a necessary and universally valid manner. This is the traditional process of scientific thinking as Dante still construed it.

With Descartes, despite his starting point in the *cogito,* the structure of scientific thought does not depart from that pattern. He, too, wants to derive from a first truth, following the example of mathematics and geometry, all the conclusions that are deducible. As Vico points out: "[Cartesian] critical philosophy supplies a first truth of which you can be certain even when you doubt." [1] Because all sciences are to be derived from this first truth, the rational process of deduction assumes primary importance. "The aim of all investigations, the only object of aspiration, honor and universal praise today, is truth." [2]

Vico concludes that this process of thought above all depreciates and stifles common sense *(sensus communis),* which is essential to action; furthermore, it eliminates *prudentia,* or foresight, because

---

[1] *De nostri temporis studiorum ratione,* in *Opere di G. B. Vico* (hereinafter cited as *Opere*), edited by Fausto Nicolini, 8 vols. in 11 (Bari: Laterza, 1911–41), 1: 79.
[2] *Ibid.,* p. 78; cf. also p. 80.

a particular case cannot be derived from universal premises; and lastly, it depreciates fantasy, or imagination, because of its non-rational character.

Vico asks himself plaintively how such premises can lead to a fruitful education of the young: "Trained by this method of study, our young people will be unable in the future to act with requisite prudence in civic life, nor will they be able to enliven a speech with charm or warm it with the fire of emotion." [3]

Rational thought is further censured by Vico when he maintains that purely deductive knowledge, gleaned from first premises, bars the way to an understanding of history, because it excludes anything changeable and arbitrary. Vico realizes that the first rules of Descartes' method virtually imply a dismissal of history.

The clarity and certainty of cognition that Descartes strives to achieve, Vico reminds us, can belong only to the Creator with regard to his creations, while for human beings clarity is limited to what they themselves produce. As man has not created nature, he cannot know it. He can know only history, which is his own creation (*verum ipsum factum*). Yet "all philosophers have tried to arrive at knowledge through the realm of nature . . . and have neglected to reflect on the world of nations, or the historical world, which was created by man." [4] But with what kind of faculty have men created this world of theirs?

---

[3] *Ibid.*, p. 91.

[4] *Scienza nuova seconda*, in *Opere* 4: par. 331. (Translations of passages from the *Scienza nuova*, hereafter given as *NS*, are made from the Laterza edition of Nicolini, but with frequent reference to the admirable German text of Erich Auerbach, *Die neue Wissenschaft über die gemeinschaftliche Natur der Völker* [Rowohlts Klassiker, 1966]). See too *NS*, par. 2: "Hitherto philosophers have shown only part of providence by considering it merely in connection with natural order . . .; they have not yet considered it from the aspect that is peculiar to man: whose nature has the primary quality of being sociable." This brings out the distinction made by Vico between what he calls philology and philosophy: "Philology . . . [is] the theory of all those things that depend on the human will" (*NS*, par. 7): "Philosophy is concerned with reason, and this gives rise to the science of truth; philology observes what man's discretion has established as law, and this gives rise to the awareness of what is certain" (*NS*, par. 138). Here is the difference between philosophical theorems and those of philology: "these theorems [of philosophy] are the

The Approach of "Logistics"

Today logistics has, on the basis of other considerations, also rejected metaphysics as a process of scientific thought, but it dismisses "humanistic" ideas as well. Traditional logic differentiates between two methods by which to substantiate knowledge. The deductive method starts from premises and derives the inferences already inherent in them. Here it is indispensable for the premises to prove universally valid and necessary, otherwise the conclusions would be merely of a formal nature. The premises, however, are necessarily presupposed in the deduction, for the process is none other than derivation. The "finding," the *invenire,* of the premises is not part of the function.

Traditional logic, therefore, had to turn its attention to the inductive method to examine whether it was its function to "find" the original premises. If, in accordance with tradition, however, induction is understood as a process leading from the multiplicity of individual cases to a universal conclusion (induction as "reversed" deduction), all necessary and universally valid premises will remain unattainable, for the multiplicity used as a starting point will always be limited. Modern logistics also emphasizes this idea: " 'Inductive thinking' is to be understood as all types of inferences in which the conclusion goes beyond the content of the premises and hence cannot be asserted with absolute certainty." [5]

Induction leads to probability only. As scientific thought is thereby reduced to the stringency of a process of inference, the conclusion drawn by contemporary logistics is as follows: "In order to make a decision about the existence of such relationships, one need only know the meanings of the propositions, *not, how-*

---

nearer truth the more they rise to universal matters; while those others are the more certain the more they adhere to particular matters" (*NS,* par. 219).

5 Rudolf Carnap and Wolfgang Stegmüller, *Induktive Logik und Wahrscheinlichkeit* (Vienna: Springer, 1959), p. 1.

ever, their truth value." [6]   Logistics supplies a purely "formal" concept of knowledge, which claims to be the only possible concept.

If, in order to arrive at "truth value," one would have recourse to the self-evidence of original premises, *intuition* would become the ultimately valid criterion.   This would mean, as is pointed out by logistics, that scientific thought would be deprived of all its rigor and that its terminology, under the influence of the imagination, would be studied with metaphor and analogy.   It would be the end of strictly scientific reasoning.

This conclusion leads logistics to the need for a purely formal language, a "calculus," as an expression of a purely axiomatic system.   The development of modern logic of science correspondingly limits itself to being a theorem logic, for it does not concern itself with the "intellectual content" of theorems.   Conclusions reflected in calculus never attain a truth concept.   Logistics renounces the idea of leading to truth.

Accordingly, science does not claim to be metaphysical, nor is logistics capable of supplying an answer to the questions arising from life.   "The supposed propositions of metaphysics, of value philosophy, of ethics . . . are nothing but expressions of feelings that evoke corresponding feelings and attitudes of will in the hearer." [7]   Thus "Philosophy is to be replaced by the logic of science, i.e. by the logical analysis of the concepts and propositions of science." [8]   In this manner, human problems, those concerning concrete life, are never acknowledged as scientific questions.

The "Antihumanism" of Structuralism

In contemporary discussions on scientific methodology, a further antimetaphysical and antihumanistic theory of science is to be considered, that of structuralism.

[6] *Ibid.,* p. 30.
[7] Rudolf Carnap, *Logische Syntax der Sprache* (Vienna: Springer, 1934), p. 203.
[8] *Ibid.,* p. iii.

Structuralism sets out from the idea that a "human science" is feasible only if we examine, as a starting point, man in the various "contexts" or "structures" through which he realizes himself. What is meant is *not* man as the object of an abstract anthropology (Vico's definition of man is anthropological). Structuralism claims to establish a methodology for the *sciences humaines.*

The first "structure" taken into consideration is that of biology, because in it man appears as a being developing in a context of functions and stimuli (of a physiological and cultural nature).

Sociology represents the second "system," one through which man is grasped in his concrete entity. Production and consumption of goods (as essential aspects of work) form, in their complexity, the "structures" through which various human actions and conceptions become understandable. In the framework of the needs that man tries to satisfy, he enters into contact or conflict with his fellow men. It is through this struggle or harmony that he asserts himself.

Language is a third "structure" through which man in his concrete existence can be the object of scientific investigation. It represents a system of signs within which individual formulations can be understood and examined purely as deviations or variations within an existing, closely knit complex.

In all three fields, the *renunciation of the individual* is effected as the starting point of the investigation. "The true concern of human sciences is, therefore, *not a single subject,* the human being, but a *purely formal aspect.*" [9]

The antihumanist approach of Marxist structuralism is equally unequivocal. The mere knowledge of social structures in which man chances to live, and which are the results of the variable combinations of invariable elements—manpower, tools, and appropriation of products—are leads for disclosing his nature. Through the various combinations of these factors, the significance and function of the individual are simultaneously altered.

[9] Michel Foucault, *Les mots et les choses: une archéologie des sciences humaines* (Paris: Gallimard, 1966), p. 365.

In accordance with this thesis, Marxist structuralism has programmatically proclaimed the need for a theoretical "antihumanism," inasmuch as the previous idealistic, or bourgeois, philosophy begins, in all its branches (epistemology, interpretation of history, political economy), with an isolated and hence abstract set of problems regarding human nature. Althusser, who claims to provide the methodological key to the understanding of Marxism, states this radical thesis thus: "We can only know something about man under the absolute condition that the philosophical (theoretical) *myth about man is reduced to ashes.*" [10] According to Althusser, all the desires, dreams, images, and fancies of the individual, when divorced from the texture of social elements, are in fact mere "irrealities," or simply "ideology." What is "concrete" or "real" is *not* related to man as an individual, with his subjective passions, hopes, and questions.

Common Sense, Ingenuity, and Imagination

Having reviewed the basic system of traditional scientific thought and of Descartes' "critical philosophy," as well as logistics and structuralism, I come now to those questions on the basis of which the significance of Vico's *New Science* is properly discussed.

According to Vico's approach, the historical world arises from interdependencies of human requirements, from the elements needed by man. From these derive the necessity of intervening in nature, by humanizing it, as well as the necessity of establishing human institutions, social community, political organizations, and ways of life. What lies at the basis of this structure is neither philosophical considerations, nor theoretical or metaphysical conclusions, but common sense *(sensus communis)*. I shall quote only a crucial passage from Vico:

> The human will, highly unstable as it is by nature, is rendered firm and definite by the *sense common* to all men with respect to

[10] Louis Althusser and others, *Lire "Le capital"*, 2 vols. (Paris: Maspero, 1965), 2: 179.

what is needed by and useful to them: these are the two sources of the natural law of nations. The sense that is common to all is a judgment without reflection, universally felt by an entire group, an entire people, a whole nation or the whole of the human race.[11]

In order to understand Vico's idea, it is above all important to clarify the deeper structure of common sense. In the rationalistic tradition, common sense is considered "popular" or "common" thinking (in the negative sense of the term). This is already true of Descartes' interpretation of *bon sens,* and later we read in a passage from Kant:

> Common reasoning, which, as a merely sane (but not yet culti-vated) form of reasoning is considered as most inferior, . . . has the offensive honour of being burdened with the name of common sense (*sensus communis*); and that in such a manner that the word common . . . is understood to mean *vulgar,* that which is met with everywhere, which to possess is by no means a merit or a priv-ilege.[12]

Accordingly, the common sense inherent in all men possesses (fol-lowing Kant's formulations) a logical structure which "judges merely by obscurely conceived principles." Common sense plays only the part of a natural, uncultivated, preparative capacity, which is to lead on to the real, expanded activity of reason. The basic rationalistic scheme remains untouched.

Whether Vico's idea of common sense is to be interpreted in the same manner, and thus does not go beyond the rationalistic tradi-tion, can only be determined by first answering the question as to which faculty forms the basis of the structure of the human world, and consequently, which faculty leads to the *sensus communis.* Vico points to the *ingenium,* to which he attributes an "inventive" but by no means a "deductive" or rational function; on the same

11 *NS,* pars. 141–142. "Common sense is the criterion divine providence has taught man in order that he may determine what is certain in the natural law of nations" (*NS,* par. 145). Common sense is, therefore, the fundamental function inspiring the same ideas in entire nations that do not know each other.

12 *Kritik der Urteilskraft,* par. 40, in *Gesammelte Schriften,* 24 vols. (Berlin: Reimer, 1902–66), 5: 293.

grounds, he characterizes his own philosophy and system of scientific thought as "ingenious," "inventive," and "topical." [13]

In the *Vindiciae,* Vico maintains, with reference to geometry, that a look at isolated Euclidean theorems produces the impression that they are fragmentary and disconnected; but if they are put into relationship with each other, they lead to an insight into geometrical truths. Vico calls this function of establishing relationships the act of the *ingenium.*[14]

The following are some of Vico's fundamental statements in this context: "Ingenuity penetrates and binds together *in a common relationship* . . . things that appear to the workaday man uncommonly fragmentary and disparate." Through such a bond, "the things are shown to be connected and related." [15] In *De antiquissima Italorum sapientia* he says: "The faculty of knowing is the *ingenium,* through which man *observes and creates similarities.*" [16] And elsewhere: "*Ingenium* is the capacity to integrate disunited and dissimilar things." [17]

Ingenuity is the ability to reveal similitude as a common element in things which, as such, attains to universality. This concept of the *ingenium* has an entire tradition behind it, of which I can give here only two examples. Baltasar Gracián (1601–1658) defines ingenuity as the faculty "which expresses relationships among things." [18] The *concepto,* from which the term *conceptua-*

---

[13] "Topics is the discipline that makes the mind creative, criticism the one that makes it precise" (*NS,* par. 498).

[14] *Vindiciae,* in *Opere* 3: 303.

[15] *Ibid.,* p. 304.

[16] *Opere* 1: 183.

[17] *Ibid.,* p. 179. "For this is the order of human ideas: to observe similar things, first in order to express oneself, and later in order to demonstrate—first through the example, for which a single likeness is enough; . . . for undeveloped minds one similarity suffices" (*NS,* par. 424). "So in the days of returned barbarity one spoke of a 'fantastic man,' meaning a man of ingenuity. . . . Ingenuity is what shapes [things] and puts them into harmony and order" (*NS,* par. 819). "Metaphysics draws the mind away from the senses, poetic ability must submerge the mind fully in the senses" (*NS,* par. 821).

[18] Baltasar Gracián, *Agudeza y arte de ingenio,* in *Obras completas,* 3rd ed. Madrid: Aguilar, 1967), p. 242.

lismus in mannerism stems, is the "grasping" on the basis of this original vision.[19]   Ludovico Muratori (1672–1750) defines *ingegno* as "that faculty and active force through which the intellect collects and unites, and discovers the similarity, relation and foundation of things." [20]

The ingenious faculty assumes the important function of supplying arguments which the rational process itself is not capable of "finding":

> Descartes' geometrical method corresponds to the sorite or chain syllogism of the Stoics.   In geometry it is useful, because geometry admits it when there is a question of defining terms and postulating possibilities . . . [However] this method is not as useful for finding new things as it is for ordering things that have already been found.[21]

But it is exclusively on the basis of revealing common elements that a transfer can be made, and that is why Vico defines the ingenious faculty as a requisite for metaphorical thought.   "In sharp-witted [ingenious] statements, the metaphor prevails." [22] This has a rich tradition behind it.   Already Aristotle had called the metaphor "the perception of similarities": "a true transfer [*eu metapherein*] is the faculty to see similarities [*to homoion theorein*]." [23]

Based on the ingenious faculty, which establishes relationships or common factors, imagination, according to Vico, confers meanings on sense perceptions.   Through its transfers, imagination is the original faculty of "letting see" *(phainestai)*, so that Vico calls it "the eye of the ingenium." [24]

This faculty does not fall into the realm of playfulness.   Vico

---

19 *Ibid.*

20 Ludovico Muratori, *La perfetta poesia*, vol. 2, chap. 1.

21 *De antiquissima Italorum sapientia*, in *Opere* 1: 184.

22 *De studiorum ratione*, in *Opere* 1: 86.

23 *Poetics* 1459a4. Cf. *NS*, par 209: "The earliest men, as children of the human race, . . . felt the need to compose for themselves poetic characters, that is, imaginative genera or universals, in order to reduce, as it were, specific types to certain prototypes or idea portraits, each one to the species resembling it."

24 *De antiquissima Italorum sapientia*, in *Opere* 1: 185.

maintains that human beings live primarily in a world of imagination. Ingenuity and imagination belong from the very beginning
to the cognition and formation of the human world.

The part played by imagination in creating the human world
and its history is substantiated by Vico, among other things, by
his well-known statement that the very first language was a language of imagination or, in other words, that the first people were
poets:

> The fundamental principle of the origin of languages, as well as of
> letters, is shown in the fact that the first gentile peoples . . . were
> poets who spoke in poetic characters . . . . Poetic characters of this
> type appear in the form of imaginative genera and universals (or
> images, mainly of animate beings . . . formed by their imagination),
> to which they reduced all species or particular dispositions.[25]

While rational man tries to achieve cognition of reality through
definition (i.e., through the description of species and specific
types), the human being whose reason is as yet undeveloped does
it by relating particular species to images, to imaginative universals. "Imagination collects from the senses the sensory effects
of natural phenomena and combines and magnifies them to the
point of exaggeration, turning them into luminous images to suddenly dazzle the mind with their lightning and stir up human
passions in the thunder and roar of their wonder." [26]

It could be argued that Vico attributes to imaginative, metaphorical speech no more significance than that of "nonproper"
speech, which becomes "proper" only through logic, in that he
restricts this kind of language, and its corresponding formation
of the world, to an "earlier" period of history. We can answer this
objection only by going to the facts, that is, by clarifying the relationship between ingenious, imaginative activity and common

---

[25] *NS*, par. 34; cf. par. 699: "Since reason in those days had not been excessively
refined through the art of writing, nor spiritualized through the habit of arithmetic,
nor was its abstractive capacity developed through numerous abstract expressions,
it was not criticism or judgment that was practiced, but topics or inventiveness."

[26] *Orazione in morte di donn'Angela Cimmino marchesa della Petrella,* in *Opere*
7: 170.

sense, or by examining more deeply the concrete domain in which
ingenuity and imagination are capable of building up the human
world.

The Domain of Common Sense: Work

Common sense has as its aim, according to Vico's definition, to
provide man with what is useful to him, with what he needs.
Moreover, we have seen that ingenuity and imagination lie at
the basis of the emergence of the human world. We must therefore inquire whether and how ingenuity and imagination contribute to common sense, what the relationship is between them,
for merely referring to these three functions to clarify the internal
dialectics of the *New Science* does not reveal the real structure of
Vico's approach to historicity.

Vico clearly defines the function through which human needs
are fulfilled as *work*. The myth of Hercules lies at the base of
the making of history, because that mythical figure has always
been, according to Vico, the first to carry out the humanization of
nature. "Hercules figures were the founders of the first pagan
peoples because they wrought the first fields from the earth, sub-
duing it to farming." [27] The first human act consisted of adjusting
nature. I need not quote further well known passages from the
New Science in which man's original work is said to consist of
clearing the virgin forest and thereby creating the first space
unmistakably belonging to the human being, the *ara* as the origin
of the town, as the site of the community and its institutions.

The labor of Hercules presupposes an interpretation of nature
prior to its humanization, that is, as a reality serviceable to mankind, as well as an anticipated vision of success for the act in question. Work, therefore, is to be understood as a function both
of conferring a meaning and making use of a meaning, never as
a purely mechanical activity or a purely technical alteration of

[27] *NS*, par. 14.

nature detached from the general context of human functions. Otherwise it would consist merely of an inexplicable act of violence to devastate nature.

If it is the aim of common sense to supply man with what he needs, ingenuity and imagination must carry out their functions primarily in the domain of work, and this can be understood only in the following manner. By establishing relationships (similitudes) between what man needs (e.g., to quench a thirst) and what his senses report to him in each specific concrete situation in nature (e.g., the availability of water), man works out the transfer of meanings leading him to the appropriate action (e.g., looking for water and making it available to himself). This is the meaning of work. The establishment of relationships and the transfer of meanings to what the senses report (*metapherein*) are activities of an ingenious and imaginative nature, respectively. It is consequently within the "ingenious" structure of work, and not within the sphere of rational thought, that common sense originally functions. The *sensus communis* does not, therefore, consist, as the rationalistic interpretation would have it, of a "popular" or "common" way of thinking. It lies outside the rational process, within the sphere of ingenuity, so that it assumes an inventive character.

Work alone is capable of proving the objectivity of ingenious and imaginative activities; it makes it evident whether the relationships established have proved subjective, by their failure, or objective, by their success in leading to a result. It is through work, too, that the objectivity of nature itself is revealed, because nothing other than work provides us with the experience that we can by no means handle nature arbitrarily: only a certain material and a certain way of treating it, or adjusting it, leads us to the aim of our action.

Thus Vico maintains that it was for the satisfaction of their needs that nations were led to live in justice and to join in communities,[28] whereby he emphasizes the fact that this situation

[28] *NS*, par. 2.

emerged before the appearance of philosophers: "So the first nations, as children of the human race, first founded the world of *technai*, and then the philosophers, who came much later and were the old men of the nations, founded the world of science." [29]

If common sense has its roots in ingenious and imaginative activity, it radiates human spirituality and can be interpreted only as an expression of a fundamental experience, that of the absence of analogies or patterns between human needs and nature and of the need to look for them. Spirituality is to be interpreted here as a "lack," in the sense of a slackening of the originally firm union between imagination and impulse or need. Given a failure of the ingenious faculty, which must always assert itself in the face of new situations, man would be reduced to a standstill with rational conclusions resulting from already established relationships, revealing nothing new. This purely rational world would go to ruin for lack of spirituality: "those who command are forced by the eternal necessity of that natural order to turn again to the spirit . . . and if they discover that they cannot see the basic facts or cannot find them again, they will most certainly have to serve nations and states that have a better spirit." [30]

I will summarize what I have just said in a schematic way. The unity of action as a closed system within itself consists of the need which makes it possible to transfer meanings to neutral environmental factors and to set the action in motion. The realization of the meaning stills the need. Imagination is the "eye of ingenuity" because of its function to create original metaphors through the transfer of meanings. It is in this very structure of work that the *sensus communis* manifests itself.

---

[29] *NS*, par. 498.

[30] *NS*, par. 1114. The critique of the prevalence of rationale thought is also expressed in the following sentence: "In the course of long barbaric centuries, ru consumes the *grotesque subtleties of evil intellectual faculties* which, through th barbarity of reflection, had turned them into more inhuman beasts than they ha been in the first barbarity of sensual existence" (*NS*, par. 1106; my italics).

The Logic of Imagination

With these arguments in mind, we must now ask ourselves what Vico meant when he said that men originally thought in *generi fantastici* and *universali fantastici* rather than in rational concepts. A further essential problem ought to be discussed in this connection: is it possible—and if so, in what sense and within what limits—to develop Vico's tenets into a "logic of imagination" which would provide the *sensus communis* with a deeper dimension and which would be distinct from rational logic?

The terms *generi* and *universali* belong to the tools of traditional logic, which aims, by a process of abstraction (revealing common properties), to classify and subdivide individual objects into species and genera in order to grasp the essence or common factor existing within different elements and forming the prerequisite for their definition.

Vico builds up his theory of imaginative genera and universals not by means of abstraction but by creating, in his terms, "ideal portraits," "exemplary characters," in fact by means of symbols such as fables or mythical figures (e.g., those of Achilles or Hercules).

These poetic, fantastic figures belong to a special form of thinking, and at the same time create a reversal of traditional logic, since they by no means represent a poetic disguise of rational concepts. The fantastic, imaginative concept (the "conceiving" or "comprehending" that leads to a definition) grasps and circumscribes within itself (corresponding to the Greek term *oros*) a multiplicity through an image, so that it expresses the essence in terms of universals—for example, lion as the essence of strength, head as the essence of height. Just as rational thought determines differences between individuals in order to form species and genera by means of abstraction, so in the "imaginative concept" a being is crystallized through the ingenious act as a direct vision of a pictorial whole. This represents simultaneously the exemplary and the allegorical figure. The images of poetic logic are the expression of the imaginative act through which the relationship between "things that are remote from one another" (according to Vico's formulation) is predicated—the realization of the logic of the imagination. Vico says:

> Poetic wisdom, which was the first truth of the gentile world, had to begin with a kind of metaphysics, not of an abstract, rational type like that of the scholars, but one felt with the senses and presented by the imagination as would befit those first men who possessed no reflection but very strong senses and a *powerful imagination*.[31]

The logic corresponding to such poetic wisdom and metaphysics uses a "fantastic way of speaking," because it primarily uses metaphor "conveyed by analogy of physical properties to designate *abstract mental operations*." [32] Metaphor, therefore, is the original form of raising the particular to the universal by means of pictorial representation, to achieve an immediate revelation of the whole. An example: "So 'tignum' and 'culmen' really meant 'beam" and 'stalk' in the days of straw huts: later, when the towns became more beautiful, they came to designate the entire material and appurtenance of a building." [33]

In the logic of imagination, the "example" acts as the first form of the coordination of ideas, and this "example," which, as Vico puts it, "contents itself with a *single similar thing*" [34] and belongs to the domain of the logic of imagination, assumes the same function as induction does in rational logic. Vico explicitly distinguishes rational induction, "which *needs several similar things*," from the "example," which requires only *one* similarity in order to convince. To clarify this thesis, he mentions, among other things, the fable of Menenius Agrippa.

The need to speak of a logic of imagination thus arises from the following fact: if man does not form rational concepts of genera,

---

31 *NS*, par. 375; my italics.
32 *NS*, par. 404.
33 *NS*, par. 407.
34 *NS*, par. 424.

he still feels the need to create for himself "poetic characters"—
that is, concepts of genera or universals created by imagination in
order to reduce special types, as it were, to certain prototypes or
ideal portraits, to reduce each to the genus to which it belongs.[35]

Just as children follow up the idea and names of men, women,
and things they have first come to know by later conceiving and
naming accordingly all men, women, and things that are *similar*
to the first ones, so poetic truth is a metaphysical truth, "as opposed
to which the physical truth that does not correspond to it must
be considered as false . . . thus the true general, for example, is
Godfrey, as described by Torquato Tasso; and all those generals
who do not completely and in every way correspond to Godfrey
are not true generals." [36]

From a purely factual point of view, we can point out that the
justification of speaking of a *logic* of imagination, as against a
rational logic, lies in the following awareness: the noun "logic"
comes from the verb *legein,* that is, "to select" and "to collect."
The rational process of establishing relationships consists of combining or connecting related things and separating nonrelated
things. Explanation and proof are here the results of a process
of derivation of relations on the basis of given premises.

In rational logic, accordingly, the *universal*—which is to represent the "commonness" of a class—is attained by a process of abstraction whereby we proceed from the perception of individual
objects to the essentials formed by species and genera. In such
logic, moreover, the "connecting" is a result of a process of derivation. And similarly, the mental activity consists in the process of
derivation.

In the logic of imagination, on the other hand, the act of putting into relationship *(legein)* "things that are remote from one
another" is the result of an immediate, original connection, a connection which, because of its immediacy, can appear only in the
form of a momentary vision or, in other words, an image.

[35] *NS,* par. 209.
[36] *NS,* par. 205.

Correspondingly, the imaginative universals are also the results of an invention and, in contrast to rational universals, acquire an emotive effect by virtue of their pictorial character.

Finally, the mental activity in the logic of imagination does not consist of a rational process, but expresses itself in a primary, two-fold experience, that of the absence of, and the need to look for, necessary connections on the basis of which men can and must build up the world that is their due.

Here I must emphasize a very important point: it would be wrong, and it would amount to a fundamental misconception, to interpret Vico as though the logic of imagination were limited to a pure logic of symbolic forms, for instance in the sense of Ernst Cassirer. The essence of Vico's fantastic, imaginative logic does not consist in the design of any images, symbols, or analogies conceived in the abstract but in the constant need of establishing, by means of the ingenious and imaginative activity (forming the fundamental structure and root of the *sensus communis* and manifesting itself in work), and with the use of imaginative concepts, the relationships between what man needs for his realization and what his senses supply in constantly new situations. In other words: the logic of imagination must be put into the closest possible connection with work as the humanization of nature, otherwise imagination and its products would have to be defined as "unreal" activities diverting from historical reality.

The significance I attribute to the logic of imagination, therefore, should not be understood in the sense of a purely theoretical interest in a critique of the prevalence of rationalism. I must point out instead that this emphasis on the logic of imagination and my interpretation of it arises from an awareness that it represents the prerequisite for a common language as an expression of common sense, so that it prevails over rational language. With this I also provide evidence that the humanistic tradition, which reaches its peak in Vico, supplies an essential answer to questions arising today, for instance through Marxism, in the field of language. What I mean is the following: through its critique of idealism, its attack upon a dialectic of ideas evolving independently in a purely rational sphere and providing the premises for a subsequent *a priori* derivation of the dialectics of history, Marxism has pressed toward a recognition of the primacy and priority of a nonrational language—that is, a common language (cf. the theses of Antonio Gramsci) resulting from a concrete, historical process of work. This thesis acquires its theoretical legitimacy only through the logic of imagination.

Finally, Vico's thesis on the imaginative capacity of the first human beings should not be understood in a chronological sense, for ingenuity and imagination, metaphorical and analogical thought, belong to the original nature of man and consequently to work as the realization of the *sensus communis*. They provide the condition for the "finding" of the premises out of which rational activity will proceed to draw its conclusions in order to systematize what has been shown through insight.

Vico's reference to the return of barbarity confirms this interpretation. In his opinion, barbarity always reappears when the original ingenious and imaginative contact with reality is lost. It is then that human beings escape into purely rational considerations:

> So in the course of long barbaric centuries, rust consumes the grotesque subtleties of evil intellectual faculties which, *through the barbarity of reflection,* have turned them into more inhuman beasts than they had been during the first barbarity of sensual existence . . . . Therefore, enslaved by such *calculated malevolence,* people . . . finally lose their feeling for amenities, refinement, amusement, and luxury and only have feelings for the necessities of life: and with the small number of survivors and the abundance of the necessities of life, they become decent again in a natural way.[37]

The "Induction of Similarities"

The definition of work as the original concrete realm of common sense leads to significant conclusions regarding the various

---

[37] *NS,* par. 1106; my italics.

patterns of scientific thought discussed at the outset of this paper.

The traditional concept of induction consists of the reduction (*inductio, peri-agogè*) of a multiplicity to a common factor, or to what constantly remains "equal" within the multiplicity. It is only on the basis of the constant that multiple phenomena can be grasped in their essence through a deductive process. But if induction is regarded in the traditional way, it proves, for reasons already mentioned, inadequate as a way to knowledge.

Vico opposes this conception with his "induction of similarities," which he defines as insight into the "similitude" between man's needs and natural reality from which common sense in work takes its departure. Work is always characterized by this inductive structure:

> The person who uses syllogism does not so much combine a variety of things as release the type contained in a genus from the very womb of that genus . . . . The ancient philosphers of Italy approved neither of syllogism nor of sorites, but used *induction of similarities* in their arguments . . . . Ancient dialectics consisted of induction, of the *composition of similarities.*[38]

As in traditional metaphysics, Vico also derives the definition of reality from a primary principle: this axiom demonstrates the necessity, in view of the constantly new and varied needs (spiritual as well as material), of continually resuming the induction of similarities. So the specific responses to this essential demand can never claim to be formulated and thereby established in an abstract theorem valid for all times and all places. This is the significant historical value of Vico's thesis.

Against logistics the following should be kept in mind. The "induction of similarities" also opposes any formalism of a logistic nature: the inductive, ingenious act is invariably concerned with those questions which lead to the satisfaction of needs. It is attached, indeed, to a "truth value," to a "spiritual content."

Vico describes the original, imaginative, metaphorical language

---

[38] *De antiquissima Italorum sapientia,* in *Opere* 1: 183–184; my italics.

as "sharp" *(arguta)*, because it alone corresponds to the *argumen*, to the "sharp-wittedness" *(argutezza)* of ingenuity. Ingenious language can never be reduced to a calculus. It is formed in its very essence by analogy and metaphor, in obvious contrast to the tenets of logistics. Metaphor represents, in its vision of common characteristics, the fundamental structure of language; it never becomes a fantastic disguise for ideas, but is the source itself of constant new arguments for inference.

Logistics intends to overcome metaphorical speech by eradicating images from scientific language. The formalized language of calculus is to replace metaphorical language, which is rejected by logistics on the grounds of its being "improper," with mathematical symbols, which it praises as "proper" expressions, because they are not transferable. But precisely through this rational abstraction and through the fact of its being nontransferable, the purely logistic, deductive process grows rigid and cannot claim to be inventive.

As against structuralism in general and its Marxist proponents in particular, the following should be kept in mind. With Vico, the duality of subject and object is the result of man's fundamental experience of being constantly faced with possibilities. Man as a subject works on the basis of relationships of similitude that are not familiar to him from birth. He finds himself alien and alone in the face of nature, which he perceives through his senses. The singular man, man as subject, confronts nature as a reality to be defined and adjusted, so that as a subject he is not part of the original unity of nature. The argument of structuralism that the self-assertion of the subject is an abstract point of departure proves untenable.

Contrary to the reproach that structuralism levels against humanism, work, in Vico's opinion, is by no means the result of a generalized, abstract "creative" act. The adjustment of nature—that is, the product of work—is, in Vico's opinion, the result of constantly varied, concrete relationships (depending on the here and now), established between human needs and the

realities provided by nature. The determining and revealing factor each time is the specific "situation," as a section out of the
entirety of meaningful living and acting. Outside of this concrete
context, the function of ingenuity and imagination would remain
trivial. The continual invention and discovery of relationships
constantly leads to different kinds of production, distribution, and
consumption, and determines the respective form of the function
of work within society.

To conclude: rational thought, in the traditional sense, consists
of connecting *(legein)* and abstracting in order to define sensory
manifestations with a view to attaining universal and necessary
principles and in order to substantiate or explain the corresponding definitions. Vico confronts this process with metaphorical
thinking. This is also a process of combining, connecting *(legein)*
and abstracting, but not of a rational nature. The ingenious
vision of relationships between sensory manifestations, a vision
inherent in metaphor, represents the primary aspect of combining,
the aspect characteristic of sharp-wittedness. Again, the establishment of relationships is carried out with a view to satisfying
needs so that man can fulfill himself. In this respect, ingenious
discernment abstracts by eliminating all other possible meanings
of sensory phenomena and creating a meaningful human world
through the medium of work.

The connecting, abstracting function contained in the act of
the *ingenium* forms the essence of "real" or original thought and
speech.

The main themes of humanism—that is to say, the new interpretation and affirmation of the *sensus communis* (which we find
also in Lorenzo Valla and Nizolius), the defense of man as a subject faced with the task of defining and adjusting reality on the
basis of patterns to be discovered (as maintained by Pico della
Mirandola and Guarino Veronese), the rejection of the priority
of rational thought processes and their corresponding idiom
(Leonardo Bruni and Agnolo Poliziano)—all these attain their
highest philosophical expression and significance with Vico. His

is a defense of a tradition that had been given no philosophical attention since Descartes.

Translated by Azizeh Azodi

Comment on Professor Grassi's Paper

Professor Grassi undertakes to show that in the *New Science* the preeminence of "common sense" must be understood in reference to Vico's conception of the "logic of the imagination." He thereby extends the treatment of common sense given in Professor Pompa's recent book to include Vico's imaginative universals.[1] Moreover, Grassi argues that this imaginative logic is directly involved with human practice or work. I agree wth Grassi's attempt to show that Vico's view of common sense is dependent upon his theory of imaginative logic. To an extent, too, I agree with his wish to show that this logic is involved in man's concrete practical life. But Grassi's argument raises some questions for me, especially concerning what he considers the nature of man's work and "needs" to be and how these relate to imaginative universals in particular.

Vico's *New Science* is devoted to the problem of the common nature of "nations" or, as we might say today, "cultures." His aim is to show that there is a unity in the multiplicity of human societies, a unity that is more fundamental than the notion of a future international political unity. This unity Vico conceives as an "ideal eternal history," and he elaborates its specific phases and characteristics in the *New Science*. Central to this unity as Vico understands it is his theory of the multiple independent origin of cultures. "Uniform ideas originating among entire peoples unknown to each other must have a common ground of truth," he says.[2] This ground of truth he calls "common sense." Common sense is responsible for determining the highly unstable human will and giving it direction. This occurs on the basis

---

[1] Leon Pompa, *Vico: A Study of the New Science* (New York: Cambridge University Press, 1975).

[2] *The New Science of Giambattista Vico* (hereinafter *NS*), translated by Thomas G. Bergin and Max H. Fisch (Ithaca: Cornell University Press, 1968), par. 144.

of the three principles of common sense: belief in a provident deity, belief that the passions must be controlled, and belief that the soul is immortal. Together these beliefs control the first wild men.

Vico does not conceive the first men to hold these beliefs in order to fulfill any need or to soothe the irritation of intellectual doubt. Grassi also wants to avoid the view that common sense is based on intellectual concerns. Vico holds that the previously mentioned beliefs are spontaneous. "Common sense is judgment without reflection," says Vico.[3] Nonetheless, as Grassi indicates, Vico understood these commonsense beliefs as products of ingenious human activity and not as givens or simply as the original way in which things confront man. In later stages of the ideal eternal history, men reflect upon these commonsense beliefs; but the first men experience them as reality. Vico named those immediate forms of experience in which these commonsense principles originate "imaginative universals." Vico says that imaginative universals constitute the first type of "universality" by reducing all particular instances in a genus to an image and doing so univocally, *not* analogically.[4] This idea he calls the "master key" to his *New Science*.[5] Repeatedly Vico insists that it demands great effort to come to understand the poetic nature of the first men, that is, the "common sense" of peoples by which they come to religion, marriage, and the burial of the dead. This is because all these institutions depend upon the immediate imaginatively universal nature of experience for these men. Jove and other divinities confronted them, and human action was in accord with this fact.

The immediacy of poetic logic is not a point of contention here. There is nothing abstract about imaginative universals. On the contrary, they are images that pose as the ideal, and so they are the opposite of logical forms as these are normally understood. My difficulty with Grassi's view of imaginative universals concerns their relationship to work. The activity of imaginative or inventive thought, as Vico describes it in his *De antiquissma Italorum sapientia*, represents the chief means of solving problems. It is the logic of invention which interests Vico in that work, the logic of hypothesis. He contrasts this with mere induction by enumeration, which is not inventive. I think Grassi rightly argues that this logic is responsible for the establishment of the relationship between what man needs and what his senses sup-

---

[3] *NS*, par. 142.
[4] *NS*, par. 34.
[5] *NS*, par. 34.

ply him.   By means of invention, man comes to satisfy his needs.   This inventive logic leads men to different forms of production, distribution, and consumption, as Grassi says.   But this also serves to create diversity among peoples rather than to unify them, and so it represents a different function of the imagination than is present in "common sense."

The problem here is the relationship between "imagination" and *ingenium*.   Common sense depends upon the former for the imaginative universals upon which the institutions of social life are based.   The ingenious activity demanded by work also depends upon the imagination to unify what is diverse into "similarities."   But these similarities do not seem the same as those univocally understood imaginative universals of common sense.   The question is how do *these* stand in the "closest possible relationship to work"?   What does "work" mean in this context?   How does Jove and original poetic morality establish a relationship between a need and what the senses supply?

Regardless of the needs which the logic of imaginative universals may fulfill, it would seem that this logic serves also to *create* a distinctly human need.   Our thought is far removed from that of the first men.   Original poetic morality has been dissipated.   The unified world of the first men is now fragmented.   As a result, contemporary men feel the need for values that can unify their lives.   But the source of this need lies in man's original nature as a human being and not in his momentary situation.   Therefore, it cannot be fulfilled in the way we quench a thirst or solve other problems.   This problem shows how rightly Grassi criticizes the contemporary "objective" conception of man.   It also shows that even contemporary man stands in a relationship to the logic of the first men although the nature of this relationship is not immediately clear.   Contemporary men are not able to think like the first men without great effort, and yet they perceive a need because of this fact.   I hope that Grassi can clarify how he conceives this need to arise and in particular how the fundamental importance of work takes this kind of need into account.

JOHN MICHAEL KROIS

Response by the Author

The problem to which Dr. Krois refers is of fundamental importance. It can be reduced to the question of how "material" and "spiritual" work are to be distinguished.

Vico's basic problem consists in determining the principle and structure of human historicity. He identifies this with the *sensus communis*
and with the *ingenium* and *fantasia* (imagination) that it is based upon.
As I already mentioned, the essence of the *ingenium* consists in the
capacity to expose the relationship between sensory appearances and
needs whereby *fantasia* transfers the appropriate meanings to sensory
appearances. The satisfaction of needs is therefore produced through
ingenious and imaginative work and is its product.

In this regard the following should be noticed. The transformation
of nature accomplished through work at all levels of life, be it vegetative, sensitive, or human, displays a common basic structure. At the
biological level, the goal of self-preservation for the particular creature
as well as the continuation of the species is brought about by the satisfaction of desires and drives through the senses. At the human level,
life's work is carried out through the construction of plans that lead
to the humanization of nature.

Three things can be discerned here. At all these levels "work"—
as we have defined it—is applied as the determining force for the realization of life. Marx, for example, spoke in just this sense in a famous
passage in *Kapital* about the work of animals (he refers to spiders and
bees). Furthermore, at every level of life an ingenious and imaginative activity is visible because everywhere there is a construction of
relations between given circumstances and the transferal of meanings
to save life and preserve the species. Finally, surprisingly, we must
even attribute an allegorical and metaphorical character to vegetative
and sensitive reality. It has an allegorical character (*allegorein,* that
is, to say something and mean something else) because, for example,
when a phenomenon is said to be "good" or "useful," the meaning of
this particular phenomenon is thereby expressed with regard to the
realization of life and affirmed or regarded in this way. Here there
is also a "metaphorical" character insofar as life itself "transfers" in
each case a meaning to reality. With this the terms allegory and
metaphor obtain a more fundamental and wider meaning than in the
field of literature.

What, now, is the essential difference between material and spiritual
work? From a purely formal perspective this division is obviously
justified only when a fundamentally different kind of structure can
be shown in human work than in organic biological work.

The first essential difference consists in the fact that animals complete
the work of satisfying organic needs, through the application of innate

schemata. Man, on the other hand, is forced to seek out schemata and determine their appropriateness. With men, the fulfilment of needs leads to the development of new kinds of needs, which themselves lead to new forms of work and hence to new forms of society. For this reason human society never "is"; it is always "becoming," and it is this essential aspect that makes it a "historical" world.

I want to point out that Marx, for example, thought he recognized and identified completely the specific nature of *human* work by just this characteristic. But in this case spiritual work (which is always specifically human work) originates, surprisingly, from a "lack" of innate schemata that leads to the necessity to *search* for schemata. This would mean that "spirituality"—surprisingly, I repeat—would be identical with a "deficiency."

On closer inspection of the situation which confronts man, however, completely different *other* needs can be shown. First, there is the need to know *why* man lacks innate schemata, that is, why he does not find himself bound within nature. This brings us to the all-important recognition of man's freedom. This question brings with it the second question of *how* man is torn from the unity of nature and is thereby opposed to it in a subject-object relationship. Animals live *in* nature, but we human beings live over and against it, because whoever knows he is not "bound" by nature does not recognize it as his home and thus sees it as something foreign and strange to him. The two problems are the basis of anthropology as science.

The third and further question is *if, how,* and *where* man may recognize ties that somehow bind. The Latins formulated this question as the question of *religio* (from *religare*).

All these questions demand an area of purely spiritual work that can never be derived from the process of meeting organic needs. Once more: we saw that the various given circumstances of vegetative and sensitive life represent allegories and metaphors of organic life, but the question is: of *what* is this new "free" spiritual world an allegory and metaphor?

One hint: an original form of spiritual work manifests itself in *art*. The previously mentioned "unboundedness" or "freedom" over and against nature leads man to "imaginative" works in which he is able to construct "possible" worlds. These also harbor the danger, however, of being directed to what is not an essential reality of being for man and thus becoming just a "game," restricted to pointless preoccupations. It then becomes purely aesthetic enjoyment apart from the obligations of life.

A further form of spiritual work consists in the clarification of man's behavior regarding the passions, which leads to *moral work*. The various meanings of the passions in different situations cannot be derived from the satisfaction of drives but only from the "boundedness" that is valid for human beings. With this, ethical work shows itself to stem always from the original and ever-present essence of *religio*.

From insight into the essential relationship between art, ethics, and religion, and from the recognition of the underivability of spiritual work from material work, Vico founded historical development on three essential works of culture. These are the ever-present recurring work of *religio*, the institutionalization of marriage and thus the family (as the control of drives), and finally the cult of the dead as a sign of humanity which Vico derives from *humare*, to bury.

ERNESTO GRASSI

The Primacy of Language in Vico

BY MICHAEL MOONEY

> With the most agreeable tie of speech reason bound together men who had hitherto been solitary.
>
> —Cicero, *De re publica* 3.2.3

Whom are we to believe? Arnauld, who rejects the *ars topica*, or Cicero, who asserts that his own eloquence is due chiefly to the practice of this art?" [1] Vico's rhetorical query, put some short way into his celebrated discourse on the Ancients and the Moderns, showed no particular boldness or courage. He was speaking after all in Naples, not Paris, and of his twenty-eight colleagues there assembled for the commencement of academic year 1708–09 fully twelve—and they the best paid and most prestigious—were from the faculty of law; certainly they were disposed to hear a rousing defense of the "copious" method of traditional rhetoric, a virtual adjunct to their own discipline, against the sterile practices of the Cartesians, then so fashionable to the north.[2] And surely the younger of Vico's listeners, disproportionately law and prelaw students, were receptive to an apology for the kind of prudential flexibility and sharp-witted ingenuity

---

[1] *De nostri temporis studiorum ratione*, in *Opere di G. B. Vico* [hereinafter *Opere*], edited by Fausto Nicolini, 8 vols. in 11 (Bari: Laterza, 1911–41), 1: 83.

[2] Of the twenty-nine chairs at the University, twenty-two were in "professional" studies—five each in theology and medicine, in addition to the twelve in law. There was a single tenured post *(perpetua)* in mathematics and one untenured *(quadriennale)* in physical philosophy. See Nino Cortese, "L'età spagnuola," in Francesco Torraca, ed., *Storia della università di Napoli* (Naples: Ricciardi, 1924), p. 304.

basic to the sundry careers in civil life for which most of them were training. Descartes could have his hearing in the various academies and literary salons of the city, but here at the Royal University, and in the society which it served, Cicero reigned supreme.

Whatever be the truth of Vico's alleged "politicality," now so much in debate,[3] it seems plain that he advanced to his startling theories on the birth of humanity by holding fast to the classical (and humanist) ideal of the public servant as "sage," as man of learned eloquence, and by embracing and extending the "philological" studies which, having already swelled by the time of Quintilian "to the dimensions of a brimming river" (*Institutio oratoria* 2.1.4), were the stock in trade of Renaissance humanists. Vico's "new science," in brief, emerged as a combination of principles adapted from classical rhetoric with philological discoveries and conjectures—some brilliant, others fanciful, all "fantastic"— in ancient poetry, myth, language, and law.[4]

[3] I am referring to recent studies by Nicola Badaloni, Biagio De Giovanni, Salvo Mastellone, Pietro Piovani, and others, and especially to the controversy surrounding the essay of Giuseppe Giarrizzo, "La politica di Vico," *Quaderni contemporanei*, no. 2: *Giambattista Vico nel terzo centenario della nascita*, edited by Fulvio Tessitore (Salerno: Istituto universitario di magistero, 1968), pp. 63–133. An assessment of the controversy is offered by Piovani, "Apoliticality and Politicality in Vico," in Giorgio Tagliacozzo and Donald P. Verene, eds., *Giambattista Vico's Science of Humanity* (Baltimore: The Johns Hopkins University Press, 1976), pp. 395–408.

[4] The centrality in Vico's development of the methods and paradigms of "philology," including humanist studies in jurisprudence, is impressively argued by Donald R. Kelley, "Vico's Road: From Philology to Jurisprudence and Back," in Tagliacozzo and Verene, *Giambattista Vico's Science of Humanity*, pp. 15–29. See also the paper by Kelley which follows in this journal. Kelley's thesis has now the firm, if nuanced, support of Sir Isaiah Berlin, *Vico and Herder: Two Studies in the History of Ideas* (New York: Viking Press, 1976), pp. 123–142.

My conclusion as to Vico's adaptation of classical rhetoric restates in large measure the thesis of Andrea Sorrentino presented in his much neglected work, *La retorica e poetica di Vico, ossia la prima concezione estetica del linguaggio* (Turin: Bocca, 1927): "Nelle *Institutiones oratoriae* [Vico's course manual of 1711] non solo si può avere un ragguaglio della cultura dell'autore e una sintesi dell'opera scolastica di un Maestro che è Vico, ma—e in ciò è l'importante—la germinazione prima dell'opera del genio; germinazione avvenuta nel lago morto della millenaria retorica tradizionale: di tra le forme consunte nasce la cellula nuova" (p. 115). Whatever the volume's shortcomings—it is often sketchy, for instance, where probing is

As Vico unfolded his theory of origins, moreover, he left behind in his writings—especially but not only in those of the "school"—if not a fully developed political theory, at least a pronounced and arguably consistent philosophy of culture that I will come, at the end of this paper, to call "Roman," one that continued in the conservative political and classical sociological traditions of the nineteenth century and awaits further development in our day. Basic to this contribution, however, as to that of his science of origins, is Vico's insistence on the primacy of language, that characteristic bias of traditional poetic and rhetoric. In his use and reformulation of this ancient conviction lies much of the excitement of his discovery and some considerable portion of his legacy.

---

needed, and pedantic where a word would suffice—its central thesis, I find, is sound: key tenets of Vico's eventual "new science" are already developed in significant degree as principles of rhetoric in his early course manual. Sorrentino, however, is concerned to follow the transformation of the principles into a mature (and revolutionary) aesthetic and linguistic theory, whereas I am more struck by the "logical" and "civil" (or sociological) character of Vico's rhetoric and thus its eventual use in a general theory of culture.

Attention to Vico as humanist rhetorician has also been given by more recent historians of linguistics: Antonino Pagliaro, "La dottrina linguistica di G. B. Vico," *Atti dell'Accademia nazionale dei Lincei, Memorie della Classe di scienze morali, storiche, critiche e filologiche*, ser. 8, 8 (1959): 379–486, reprinted as "Lingua e poesia secondo G. B. Vico" and "Omero e la poesia popolare in G. B. Vico," *Altri saggi di critica semantica* (Messina and Florence: D'Anna, 1961), pp. 299–474; Karl O. Apel, *Die Idee der Sprache in der Tradition des Humanismus: von Dante bis Vico* (Bonn: Bouvier, 1963); and Tullio De Mauro, "G. B. Vico dalla retorica allo storicismo linguistico," *La Cultura* 6 (1968); 167–183, reprinted in translation in Giorgio Tagliacozzo and Hayden V. White, eds., *Giambattista Vico: An International Symposium* (Baltimore: Johns Hopkins University Press, 1969), pp. 279–295. Yet none of these more recent commentators has considered directly the course manual of 1711, *Institutiones oratoriae,* available in full only in the seventh volume of the edition of Francesco Sav. Pomodoro (*Opere di Giambattista Vico*, 8 vols. [Naples: Morano, 1858–69]), or the variants, indicated by Nicolini (*Opere* 8: 197–203), in the text of 1738. A brief analysis of the 1711 version has recently been made by Alessandro Giuliani, "Vico's Rhetorical Philosophy and the New Rhetoric," in Tagliacozzo and Verene, *Giambattista Vico's Science of Humanity*, pp. 31–46, the first such study, to my knowledge, since the work of Sorrentino and the paper of Benvenuto Donati, "Le lezioni di 'Rettorica' del Vico," *Nuovi studi sulla filosofia civile di G. B. Vico* (Florence: Le Monnier, 1936), pp. 134–161.

Wisdom and Eloquence

While men still roamed the woods [wrote Horace], Orpheus, the holy prophet of the gods, made them shrink from bloodshed and brutal living; hence the fable that he tamed tigers and ravening lions; hence too the fable that Amphion, builder of Thebes' citadel, moved stones by the sound of his lyre, and led them whither he would by his supplicating spell. In days of yore, this was wisdom, to draw a line between public and private rights, between things sacred and things common, to check vagrant union, to give rules for wedded life, to build towns, and grave laws on tables of wood; and so honor and fame fell to bards and their songs, as divine.

In some marginal comments on this passage from the *Ars poetica* (vv. 391–401), Vico noted that while Horace's chronology was wrong, his claim was correct: for "first, or vulgar, wisdom was poetic in nature," wrote Vico, and "from poetic history are to be sought the origins of republics, laws, and all the arts and sciences that make civilization [*humanitatem*] complete." Thus my *"New Science* [of 1730], and especially its second book," is essentially "an extended commentary on this passage." [5]

And so it is. But the passage itself is but one in a long tradition of Greek and Roman authors, dating at least from Aristophanes and Isocrates, who held that speech, not reason, is the basis of culture, that poetic heroes, not philosopher kings, create human society. [6] The idea is stated most impressively by Cicero in *De inventione* (1.2.2–3), itself a summary of Hellenistic rhetoric. After speaking of "men scattered in the fields and hidden in sylvan retreats," he writes:

It does not seem possible that a mute and voiceless wisdom could have turned men suddenly from their [savage] habits and introduced them to different patterns of life. . . . [And] after cities had been established, how could it have been brought to pass that men should learn to keep faith and observe justice . . . unless men had

---

5 *Opere* 7: 76. The passage from Horace and the other classical references that follow are from the Loeb edition.

6 Aristophanes, *Frogs*, vv. 1031–1036; Isocrates, *Nicocles*, 5–9. On this tradition see Friedrich Solmsen, "Drei Rekonstruktionen zur antiken Rhetorik und Poetik," *Hermes* 67 (1932): 133–154.

been able by eloquence to persuade their fellows of the truth of what they had discovered by reason?

Or, as he says most simply in *De oratore* (1.8.33):

What other power [than eloquence] could have been strong enough either to gather scattered humanity into one place, or to lead it out of its brutish existence in the wilderness up to our present condition as men and as citizens, or, after the establishment of social communities, to give shape to laws, tribunals, and civic rights?

Fine humanist that he was, Vico himself, in his seminal Sixth Oration, set aside the rather trivial subquarrel among the poets and rhetors over ascendancy in the realm of language (and thus in the founding of culture), combined elements from both the Horatian and Ciceronean versions, and offered his own "reconstruction" of the ancient topos:

So too we learn from the fables of the wisest poet that Orpheus tamed beasts with the music of his lyre and Amphion moved stones with his singing, charming them into place of their own accord, and so built the walls of Thebes; and for these merits it was thought that the lyre of the former and the dolphin of the latter were borne aloft and painted in the stars. These stones, these beams, these beasts are human fools, and Orpheus and Amphion the sages who conjoined their theoretical knowledge of divine things and their practical knowledge of human things with eloquent speech, and by its compelling force led men from solitude into social bonds, i.e. from love of self to respect for humanity, from inertia to industry, from unbridled freedom to the obedience of law, thus uniting fierce and weak men under the stability of reason.[7]

---

[7] *Opere* 1: 60–61. As to the "dolphin of Amphion," did Vico confuse Amphion with the sea-goddess Amphitrite, persuaded by the Dolphin to marry his master, Poseidon, who thereupon rewarded his sea-servant with a constellation in his image? While the lyre of Orpheus became Lyra, Amphion was not, to my knowledge, rewarded in the heavens.

For Vico's final handling of the topos see the *Scienza nuova seconda*, in *Opere* 4: pars. 81, 523, 615, 661, and especially 734, where Horace's chronology is corrected. (Further references to the final edition of the *Scienza nuova* will be given as *NS* and by paragraph number alone; translations are drawn from the inestimable version of Thomas G. Bergin and Max H. Fisch, *The New Science of Giambattista Vico* [Ithaca: Cornell University Press, 1968]).

I cite these passages at length, not merely because, as will be plain to all, they form the distant background of the "new science," but because they embody, for me at least, the soul of Vico— and it is with the soul of Vico, for better or worse, that I must ultimately rest my case. Vico spent his whole life, both as pedagogue and as scholar, both in the classroom and in his writings, trying to combine wisdom and eloquence in such a way as to best serve the public good. Endlessly he inveighed against both a "voiceless wisdom" and an empty rhetoric. Societies fell apart when wisdom and eloquence became disjoined, when philosophers like the Cartesians forgot how to communicate and when rhetoricians like the Mannerists played games with language and sought merely to be clever, not true. The sign of utter social decadence, Vico noted—in a magnificent image also adapted from Cicero (*De re pub.* 1.17.28)—is when men, despite the great throng and press of their bodies, live in a deep solitude of spirit.[8] Despite his own penchant for solitude, there was nothing Vico so abhorred as a society of isolated individuals. Whether original brutishness or ultrasophistication caused it made no difference: solitude of spirit was a cultural disease. He went so far at one point, in fact, as to suggest a kind of state curriculum and civil religion not unlike that of Rousseau.[9] If Descartes' passion was indubitability, and Hobbes's was security, that of Vico was *civitas*, the well-functioning republic in which men acted as citizens.[10]

---

8 *NS*, par. 1106. See too his early formulation of this image, as a portrayal of fallen humanity, in the Sixth Oration: "Collectivities of men may appear to be societies, but the truth is that with all the massing of bodies there is a thoroughgoing isolation of souls" (*Opere* 1: 59).

9 *De studiorum ratione*, in *Opere* 1: 119.

10 This he shared, of course, with a distinct but significant tradition in Renaissance humanism, centered in fifteenth-century Florence. See Hans Baron, "Cicero and the Roman Civic Spirit in the Middle Ages and the Early Renaissance," *Bulletin of the John Rylands Library* 22 (1938): 3–28, and his full-length study, *The Crisis of the Early Italian Renaissance: Civic Humanism and Republic Liberty in the Age of Classicism and Tyranny*, 2 vols. (Princeton: Princeton University Press, 1955; 2d ed., 1 vol., 1966); Eugenio Garin, *L'umanesimo italiano: filosofia e vita civile nel Rinascimento* (Bari: Laterza, 1952); and Eugene F. Rice, Jr., *The Renaissance Idea of Wisdom* (Cambridge: Harvard University Press, 1958).

For this reason he castigated repeatedly the "individualistic ethic" of the Epicureans, off in their Garden, "blissful in the belief in their own happines," as Cicero had quipped (*De orat.* 3.17.64). The same implications he saw in the new method of Descartes, made pedagogically serviceable by Arnauld—that through it students would be rendered incapable of civic life. Intellectual giants they might become, but they would be mute, unimaginative fools in the forum, the courtroom, and the pulpit.[11] Bacon's method, on the other hand, he could tolerate, even affirm, for it was a science of ingenuity, based in the imagination, in the art of experimentation, of trying literally to recreate the processes of nature, and thus could only support the analogous arts of politics and rhetoric necessary for civil life.[12]

From Rhetoric to a Science of Origins

Convinced that the union of wisdom and eloquence was the nature of a true polity, Vico set out both as teacher and as scholar to argue their interpenetration. What is intriguing in this initiative is that the dual endeavors, initially separate, eventually merged with the happiest of issue, but presented in turn a tormenting dilemma.

[11] See section VII of the *De studiorum ratione*, in *Opere* 1: 90–96, beyond question the core of his discourse, as indeed of his entire early works. It bears remembering that Vico's objection to Descartes was not scientific, and only derivatively epistemological; in the first instance it was "moral" or "civil": applied beyond the fairly narrow realm in which it was serviceable, Cartesian analysis would wreck public life.

[12] Though Vico does speak of Bacon's "inductive method" (e.g. *NS*, par. 499), it seems clear that he understands (and treasures) it as an "inventive" or experimental procedure. See the *De antiquissima Italorum sapientia*, in *Opere* 1: 180–185, where it is presented, following Book V of the *De dignitate et augmentis scientiarum*, as "topics" or the art of discovery; and the conclusion of the work, *Opere* 1: 191, where it is set forth as the model of the *verum/factum* principle: "id pro vero in natura habeamus, cuius quid simile per experimenta faciamus"; and the *Vindiciae*, in *Opere* 3: 303, where it is related to the *ingenium*, "the divinum omnium inventionum parentem"; and the *De mente heroica*, in *Opere* 7: 18, where the reading of Bacon is recommended to the heroic mind as an impulse to advance the sciences and add to the inventions of our "still young" world.

In his teaching and pedagogical orations, Vico's principal concern was to maintain the vision of classical rhetoric. Classical
rhetoric had always held that its art had a share in the task of reasoning, that it was indeed the logic of social discourse, the kind of
reasoning that went on among nonspecialists (*inter rudes* was Vico's
telling phrase [13]) in matters that were merely or mainly probable,
and that to be successful the rhetorician had to discover the most
appropriate things to say (the *topoi* or *res*), arrange them in the
right order, and find the most suitable language (*verba*)—the
tropes and figures of speech—with which to make his case.[14] Now
it was the dubious accomplishment of Peter Ramus, as we know,
to have simplified the liberal arts curriculum by transferring
rhetoric's "logical" tasks of discovery (*inventio*) and arrangement
(*dispositio*) to the field of logic; the result was to destroy rhetoric
as the logic of discourse, and in time it became largely an art of
ornamentation, grandeur, or witticism. "The attitude toward
speech has changed," writes Ong of the sequels of Ramism:

> Speech is no longer a medium in which the human mind and
> sensibility lives. It is resented, rather, as an accretion to thought,
> hereupon imagined as ranging noiseless concepts or "ideas" in a
> silent field of mental space. Here the perfect rhetoric would be to
> have no rhetoric at all. Thought becomes a private, or even an
> antisocial enterprise.[15]

Vico rejected this artificial separation of *res* and *verba*, of
thought and language, for he saw in it the ruin of civil life. Public
life required its peculiar form of discourse; it was too complex and

---

13 Sixth Oration, *Opere* 1: 62. "Eloquentia multitudini et vulgo facta est," he
wrote, more conventionally, in his *Institutiones oratoriae* [cf. n. 4], p. 2.

14 Of the copious literature on classical rhetoric, see the historical survey of
Wilhelm Kroll, "Rhetorik," in Pauly-Wissowa, *Realencyclopädie der classischen
Altertums*, Supplementband 7 (Stuttgart: Metzler, 1940), cols. 1039–1138, and the
systematic presentation of Heinrich Lausberg, *Handbuch der literarischen Rhetorik*,
2 vols. (Munich: Hueber, 1960).

15 Walter J. Ong, *Ramus, Method, and the Decay of Dialogue: From the Art of
Discourse to the Art of Reason* (Cambridge: Harvard University Press, 1958), p. 291.
See also Wilbur S. Howell, *Logic and Rhetoric in England, 1500–1700* (Princeton:
Princeton University Press, 1956) and *Eighteenth-Century British Logic and
Rhetoric* (Princton: Princeton University Press, 1971).

uncertain to be managed by scientific logic, and too important to be left to bombast. It required an imaginative mind to show a jury, a judge, or an assembly connections between seemingly unrelated things and to devise tropes for situations in life that had no names, for, as he liked to quote from Aristotle (*De Soph. El.* 165a11–12), there are more things in the world than there are words, and therefore, as Cicero maintained (*De orat.* 3.38.155), metaphor is not mere ornamentation but a necessity of communication arising from the poverty of language.[16]

In his annual course on the principles of oratory, Vico held firmly to a notion of rhetoric as the art of persuasion, paradigmatically practiced in a court of law, bent on serving the true and the equitable in matters of deliberate human action, the reality of which must be established through appropriate language. Though he adhered to the traditional practice of treating successively the two "offices" of rhetoric concerned with *res* (the discovery and arrangement of "places"), followed by that concerned with *verba* ("elocution" or "style"), he was plainly uncomfortable with any separation of content and form. Thus, in discussing "legal issues" *(status qualitatis legalis)* in his section on the *topica*, Vico stressed the intrinsic ambiguity of normative legal texts and the consequent necessity of living speech to make them applicable: the legal reality of a past deed (and thus the fate of the accused) depends on the ability of competing attorneys to sharpen the issue through speech.[17] Similarly, in the section on style, Vico favored "figures of thought" over "figures of speech," since the former "occupy the mind, not the ears"; [18] he reduced the tropes to an economic four, not by the way in which they adorn, but by the

[16] *Institutiones oratoriae*, p. 101.

[17] *Ibid.*, pp. 34–38. In the prologue to his *Diritto universale* (1720–22), Vico would write that "the whole of jurisprudence consists of three parts: philosophy, history, and that peculiar art of adjusting law to the facts." This latter art Vico went on to identify as rhetoric. Cf. *Opere* 2: 26–28. This extends a theme of the *De studiorum ratione*, in *Opere* 1: 101.

[18] *Ibid.*, p. 115.

way in which they transfer meaning; [19] and most significantly, in the fullest discussion in his unusually spare treatise, he related the "conceits" of seventeenth-century rhetoric with the "maxims" or *gnomai* of Aristotle (*Rhet.* 1394a19–1395b19) and the *sententiae* of the Roman orators (Quintilian 8.5.1–8). Properly understood, *concetti* are not those pithy, witty one-liners (*dicta arguta*) of the Mannerists by which an agile tongue dazzles and regales an audience, snaps back heads with laughter, and demonstrates his own cleverness; such conceits discover no truths, advance no civil ends. Rather, *concetti* are brief, sharp-witted statements (*dicta acuta*) having enthymematic force, with incisiveness equal to their conciseness, born of imaginative, ingenious minds intent on discovering the true; through them listeners see novel visions and discover new relationships, sinners are reduced to tears, implausible cases are won in court, legislation is gotten through intractable assemblies.[20]

Meanwhile, as philologist, equally convinced of the unity of wisdom and eloquence, of *res* and *verba*, Vico set out to discover ancient Italic wisdom by tracing the origin and meaning of Latin

---

19 *Ibid.*, pp. 101–109.

20 *Ibid.*, pp. 90–101. When a reviewer of the first *New Science* remarked that its author was "more clever than true" ("ingenio magis indulget quam veritati"), Vico took the occasion to rescue *ingenium* from its increasingly poor reputation among logicians (as mere "wit," not discernment: Hobbes, Locke) and Baroque rhetoricians (as "wittiness" or "cleverness"). Returning to its classical meaning (via Bacon, Matteo Peregrini, and Baltasar Gracián), Vico declared the *ingenium* the source of all freshness, novelty, and invention, making it indeed a distinct faculty of ingenuity. Its products, in the realm of language, are the *dicta acuta*, identified above. *Dicta arguta* ("witty remarks"), on the other hand, arise from a "feeble and narrow imagination" and out of a spirit of playfulness and trickery: led to expect one thing, the hearer is told another, and thus convulses with laughter. Laughter, however, Vico continues (following Aristotle and Cicero), rests in the *subturpe*, the "moderately base," and not for naught have the poets pictured *risores* as satyrs, halfway between men and animals. Cf. the *Vindiciae*, in *Opere* 3: 302–306. Thus the melancholy portraits of Vico that have come down to us, both the canvas and the *Autobiography*, receive confirmation: one does not imagine Vico enjoying a good knee-slapping joke.

On the sources of Vico's rhetoric see Sorrentino, *La retorica e poetica di Vico*, pp. 46–73, and for the context of the debate over *acutezza*, *ibid.*, pp. 85–105.

words.[21] And he failed abysmally. The problem, his anonymous reviewer suggested, was his approach: the etymological method, the critic argued, will only give rise to endless wrangling; why not dig up the ruins of ancient Etruria, since it was the Etruscans who gave the Romans their first laws and sacred rites? But that approach, replied Vico, would be even less certain, for ancient myths were purposely enshrouded in mystery, and as for laws, the number of those derived from the Etruscans are relatively few compared with those imported from Greece! [22]

It is not the least irony in intellectual history that Vico progressed to his new science by disproving the substance of his own objections: not only would ancient fables be deprived of their esoteric character, but the Law of the Twelve Tables would be given indigenous origins. Vico did not join in any archeological dig, nor did he abandon his fascination with etymologies, but he widened his philological concerns to include, among other things, the epics of Homer and ancient Roman law, and precisely through the kinds of curious conjectures and transmutations noticed by Max Fisch and Donald Kelley, he came to see them, not as esoteric philosophic products, but as gradually evolving, imaginative efforts by peoples, at first separated, to form themselves into nations.[23]

---

[21] *De antiquissima Italorum sapientia ex linguae latinae originibus eruenda* (1710), in *Opere* 1: 123–194.

[22] *Opere* 1: 236–238, 242–248.

[23] Max H. Fisch, "Vico and Roman Law," in Milton R. Konvitz and Arthur E. Murphy, eds., *Essays in Political Theory: Presented to George H. Sabine* (Ithaca: Cornell University Press, 1948), pp. 62–88; Donald R. Kelley, "Vico's Road." See also Dino Pasini, *Diritto, società e stato in Vico* (Naples, 1970). Vico's philological "conversion" is signaled in the *Diritto universale*, bk. 2: *De constantia jurisprudentis*, in *Opere* 2: 308, 341, and is consolidated in the *Scienza nuova prima*, in *Opere* 3: pars. 10–11 and 249–252. The first hint Vico had of the "barbaric" nature of the Law of the Twelve Tables was apparently its "horrid and coarse" language, duly noted in his *Institutiones oratoriae*, p. 76. His research on the Twelve Tables is reported on progressively throughout the three books of the *Diritto universale* and in the *Scienza nuova prima*, and is summarized in the *Ragionamento primo*, in *Opere* 4: pars. 1412–1454, once slated for inclusion in the *New Science*. The *Ragionamento* is thus the counterpart to the third book of the final *New Science*, which summarizes Vico's Homeric research; indeed the latter takes note, in its

Suddenly, his work as pedagogue merged with his work as philologist and legal scholar: he recalled the logic of discourse he had been maintaining in his lectures and orations; he recalled Cicero's view that tropes are necessary, since things are more numerous than words; [24] he remembered the line from Aristotle's *Rhetoric* (1395b1–4) that simple minds like to hear stated as universal truth the opinions they hold about particular cases,[25] and the lines from the *Poetics* (1451b5–7) that poetic statements, unlike those of history, have the nature of universals.[26] All this he combined, in typically transmuted form, with his philological research and—in one of the most singular instances of *ingenium* on record—drew his famous conclusion: poetry is the native tongue of the race, the clarion call of humanity's birth.[27] Poetry is not a product of mind, but the logic of the mind's development.[28] Not philosophy or human wisdom, but *poetic* wisdom was the wisdom of the ancients.[29] Here, in a single phrase adapted from the Stoics, he had the perfect synthesis of wisdom and eloquence, of *res* and *verba*, he had striven for his whole life.

In its primary sense, of course, "poetic wisdom" means simply "wisdom that is made": Vico is quite explicit in saying that the first men were "poets" in the Greek sense of "creators." [30] Never one to use central concepts univocally, however, Vico also considers the first men poets because "they spoke in poetic characters"—the discovery of this fact being the "master key" of the *New Science*.[31] The etymological meaning of "poetic wisdom"

---

final paragraph (par. 904), of the parallel character of the poems of Homer and the Law of the Twelve Tables as representative of Early Greece and Rome, respectively.

24 *NS*, pars. 34, 456, 830.

25 *NS*, pars. 209, 816.

26 *NS*, pars. 205–206.

27 *NS*, pars. 34, 199. *Cf. Diritto universale*, bk. 2: *De constantia jurisprudentis*, in *Opere* 2: 363–385, and *Scienza nuova prima*, in *Opere* 3: pars. 253–262, where the discovery, "following twenty-five years of continuous hard thought," is announced.

28 *NS*, pars. 400–411.

29 *NS*, pars. 360–363, 375, 779–780.

30 *NS*, par. 376.

31 *NS*, par. 34.

is thus conjoined with the traditional notion of the poet as creator of culture: the "self-making" which is poetic wisdom is in the first instance—as vulgar "metaphysics" and its corresponding "logic"—a matter of language. Language, however, has now a fuller, more profound meaning than it had in the ancient topos. The earliest language, Vico argues, was fully nonverbal—the "mute" language of myth and fable and the (to him) "natural" signs of hieroglyphs and ideograms. The first human act was literally mute, wholly sensory and corporeal, scarcely imaginable: hearing thunder sound in the heavens, the *giganti* raised up their eyes, became aware of the sky, and "saw" it as a great animated body, Jove.[32] In this action, no longer mere reaction but act of "poetic" imagination, of the transfer of meaning *(metapherein)* through the "ingenious" discovery of relationships heretofore unnoticed, the *grossi bestioni* quit their spiritual isolation, established communication and community, and became men. Through their "collective sense" *(sensus communis)* of Jove, life in society began. The rhetorical act, the art of speaking effectively *inter rudes*—of discerning new relationships, fashioning appropriate language, appealing never to abstract truths but always to the *sensus communis,* to "what is held generally or by most" (Aristotle, *An. Pr.* 24b11, 70a3; *Top.* 100a30; *Rhet.* 1357a35), and so persuading men to civil action—this act of the rhetor is here generalized, made the common, universal, and necessary act of the ancestors of the race.[33] And so too the act remained, Vico argues—not a studied device, but a "necessity of nature" owing to the youth of mind and the poverty of language [34]—through the second or "heroic" stage of humanity, when emblems, blazonings,

[32] *NS,* par. 377.

[33] *NS,* pars. 495–498. Cf. *Diritto universale,* bk. 2: *De constantia jurisprudentis,* in *Opere* 2: 279: "Poesis necessitate naturae orta, quam hactenus omnes ex hominum consilio et arte natam putarunt." Thus did Vico decide, to his satisfaction, the ancient debate as to whether poetry is a matter of "nature" or "art" (i.e., human design). On this controversy, see Lausberg, *Handbuch der literarischen Rhetorik,* pars. 37–41.

[34] *NS,* pars. 830, 832.

symbols, metaphors, images, similes developed—in short, the entire world of folklore and poetry in the narrower, contemporary sense.[35]

How seriously Vico took this priority of poetry in the formation of culture has been shown recently in a particularly acute article by Hayden White: in yet another curious transmutation of rhetorical doctrine, Vico used the four principal tropes—metaphor, metonomy, synecdoche, and irony (an enumeration deriving, ironically, from Peter Ramus [36])—to demonstrate not

---

[35] This entire "metaphysical" and "logical" output of the poetic and heroic ages Vico calls "imaginative universals" (*universali fantistici: NS*, pars. 933–934) or, variously, "poetic maxims" (*sentenze poetiche: NS*, par. 825), defined as "*concetti di passioni vere*" and distinguished from the "*sentenze di filosofi*" (*ibid.*). Plainly, this too is an adaptation of rhetorical theory, specifically the doctrine of "rhetorical maxims" (*sententiae particulares*), discussed above, which Vico related to both the *gnomai* of Aristotle and the *concetti* of the moderns, and to which he gave such prominent treatment in his course manual. Of the traditional understanding of the *sententia* Lausberg writes: "Die *sententia* ist ein 'infiniter' (d.h. nicht auf einen Individualfall begrenzter), in einem Satz formulierter Gedanke, der in einer *quaestio finita* als Beweis oder als *ornatus* verwandt wird. Als Beweis gibt die *sententia* eine *auctoritas* ab und steht dem *iudicatum* nahe. Als *ornatus* gibt die *sententia* dem finiten Hauptgedankengang eine infinite und damit philosophische Erhellung. . . . Der infinite Charakter und die Beweisfunktion der *sententia* kommen daher, dass die *sententia* im sozialen Milieu ihres Geltungs- und Anwendungsbereiches als einem Richterspruch oder einem Gesetzestext ähnliche autoritätshaltige und auf viele konkrete ('finite') Fälle anwendbare Weisheit gilt" (*Handbuch der literarischen Rhetorik*, par 872; cross references omitted). Vico's adaptation of the doctrine may be followed through the *Diritto universale*, bk. 2: *De constantia jurisprudentis*, in *Opere* 2: 370–374, and the *Scienza nuova prima*, in *Opere* 3: pars. 253–266, 309–316. *Sententia*, Vico notes, is related to *sentire*, and the first men, scarcely more than mere bodies, thought and judged through their senses. Significantly, by 1738, and probably much earlier, Vico had excised the part on the *sententiae* from his course manual, having treated the matter more thoroughly in his published works. See Nicolini's note, *Opere* 8: 203.

There are of course other sources for Vico's "imaginative universals." Mario Fubini, for instance, "Ancora dell' 'universale fantastico' vichiano," *Stile e umanità de G. B. Vico*, 2nd ed. (Milan and Naples: Ricciardi, 1965), pp. 201–204, has emphasized the passage from Aristotle's *Poetics* (1451b5–7) that I indicated above, stressing the lively discussion of the idea in the late Renaissance. (See also Pagliaro, *Altri saggi di critica semantica*, pp. 394–411.) I believe, nonetheless, that the "logic" of the idea derives rather from classical, especially Aristotelian, dialectic and rhetoric.

[36] See Andrea Battistini, "Tradizione e innovazione nella tassonomia tropologica vichiana," *Bollettino del Centro di studi vichiani* 3 (1973): 67–81.

merely the development of language but the entire *corso* of the
nations in all their intellectual and social forms as they proceed
from the divine to the heroic to the human age. In the *New
Science*, White argues, the development of consciousness from
metaphorical identification to metonymic reduction to synec-
dochic construction to ironic statement is strictly analogous to
transformations in social structure from the rule of the gods to
the rule of the aristocrats to the rule of the people to a state of
lawlessness. Thus Vico's dialectic is not that of the syllogism
(thesis, antithesis, synthesis) but of "the exchange between language on the one side and the reality it seeks to contain on the
other." [37]

The Roman Theory of Culture

But here is where the dilemma emerges, for men do eventually
develop prose, and the poetic tropes, once necessary modes of expression and being, become mere figures of speech.[38] The mind
unfolded, man moves from his natural ambience of simile and
metaphor, of poetic universals, to the land of genera and species,
capable of formulating abstract principles for areas of inquiry and
industry for which previously he had only a tradition of imaginative trials and errors, expressed in tropological form. He moves
on, for instance, from a civil equity based on authority to a

---

[37] Hayden V. White, "The Tropics of History: The Deep Structure of the *New
Science*," in Tagliacozzo and Verene, *Giambattista Vico's Science of Humanity*,
pp. 65–85, at 78. See also Sorrentino, *La retorica e poesia di Vico*, pp. 123–130;
Pagliaro, *Altri saggi di critica semantica*, pp. 365–371; and in the same symposium
in which White's paper appears, the paper of Nancy S. Struever, "Vico, Valla, and
the Logic of Humanist Inquiry," pp. 173–185, esp. 179–180. The adaptation of the
theory of the tropes begins in the *Diritto universale*, bk. 2: *De constantia jurisprudentis*, in *Opere* 2: 365–368, continues in the third book of the *Scienza nuova
prima*, in *Opere* 3: pars. 303 ff, 307 ff, 366 ff, and is concluded in the final *New
Science*, where the doctrine becomes "poetic logic" (pars. 400–411). By 1738, the
section on the tropes and figures was also omitted from Vico's course manual.

[38] *NS*, par. 409.

natural equity based in reason,[39] from customs that are pious and punctilious to ones that are truly dutiful, taught to each man by his own sense of right.[40]   In sum:

> man is properly only mind, body, and speech, and speech stands as it were midway between mind and body.   Hence with regard to what is just, *the certain* began in mute times with the body. Then when the so-called articulate languages were invented, it advanced to ideas made certain by spoken formulae.   And finally, when our human reason was fully developed, it *reached its end in the true* in the ideas themselves with regard to what is just, as determined by reason from the detailed circumstances of the facts.[41]

What becomes now of the primacy of language?   Having been validated as a logic of social discourse by being shown to be the logic of mankind's earliest formation, is rhetoric now to be abandoned in an enlightened age?   Has it lost its function of mediating experience and discovering the true?   Is Vico in the end another Hobbes, discarding metaphor as a hindrance to science?

Vico did argue of course that in even the best of circumstances, in a Christian Europe blessed with revelation, a hearty eloquence must accompany abstract truth, inflaming the people to do the things they know by reason to be true.[42]   But is this not the very separation of wisdom and eloquence that Vico sought steadfastly to resist?   Has eloquence lost its logical, truth-seeking function and become merely hortatory, following fast on the heels of science?   Having so brilliantly rewritten the first half of Cicero's topos—that eloquence alone can establish society—is Vico now content to repeat its second half slavishly—that once society matures, eloquence is needed to persuade men of the truth of what they have discovered by reason?

It is also true, on Vico's view, that in even the worst of circumstances, in nations beyond the pale of Christianity, men can and do indulge that specifically "human" trope, irony, made possible

---

39 *NS*, pars. 947–953.
40 *NS*, pars. 912–921.
41 *NS*, par. 1045; my emphasis.
42 *NS*, pars. 1101, 1110.

by the same awareness of the difference between truth and falsity on which science itself rests; [43] but this, Vico thought, is false eloquence, falsity parading as truth, the very separation between tongue and brain that Cicero warned against (*De orat.* 3.16.61). Irony isolates men from one another and brings on the dissolution of social bonds. It is the very antithesis of the union of wisdom and eloquence.[44]

It would be all too handy at this point to follow Croce and other neo-Idealist interpreters in arguing that Vico, in an unfortunate confusion, made historical-chronological eras of universal forms of the spirit: imagination could thus be spared, and with it the sundry linguistic forms through which it operates, and the entire apparatus assured a permanent role in the functioning of culture.[45] But Vico was far too attuned to the rhythm of history, far too conscious of the dialectic of social and linguistic development, far too engaged with the actual rise and demise of cultures to permit such a rendering of his thought. More plausibly, one might appeal to the unfinished character of the *New Science,* far more concerned with the birth of humanity than ever it was with its maturity; and one might recall the obvious fact, often remarked, that for all their "haughty, avaricious, and cruel"

---

[43] *NS,* par. 408.

[44] While irony is treated by the ancients quite casually as simply another rhetorical possibility (e.g., Quintilian 8.6.54–56), it assumes in Vico the ominous character of "calculated falsity" or deceit, a distinctly "human" posture unavailable to the childlike, spontaneous, "naturally truthful" poets and heroes (*NS,* par. 817). In this it is similar in structure to the *dicta arguta* so roundly condemned by Vico in his course manual and especially in the *Vindiciae.* (See Croce's note, "La dottrina del riso e dell'ironia in Giambattista Vico," *Saggio sullo Hegel e altri scritti di storia della filosofia,* 3rd rev. ed. [Bari: Laterza, 1927], pp. 277–283.) And indeed, it was not until the second edition of the *New Science* (1730), published a year after the *Vindiciae,* that irony became part of Vico's tropological dialectic of history.

[45] Benedetto Croce, *La filosofia di Giambattista Vico* (Bari: Laterza, 1911), esp. chaps. 3–4. Vico does remark in passing that "poetic speech . . . continued for long time into the historical period" (*NS,* par. 412) and that the "three languages [mute, symbolic, articulate] began at the same time" (*NS,* par. 446)—passages which Pagliaro sees as an inchoate "phenomenology of language," in contrast to the chronology of language which Vico developed at length (*Altri saggi di critica semantica,* p. 421–424, 474). Croce, however, treats them as mere signs of Vico's confusion.

ways,[46] it was "heroic" spirits that Vico admired and praised effusively in his final academic address (1732); and one might further insist that in the portrait of a culture served equally by reason and eloquence there is something too trite—while in the image of a nation of ironists, each man knowing "the truth," there is something more novel and genuine—for us ever to believe that Vico considered a fully mature culture anything more than an illusion. But this is all to appeal to the soul of Vico, not to his actual words.

Yet words we have too; for if the dynamic of the human age occupied Vico so little in the *New Science,* it was of pressing concern to him as teacher and citizen: he was living, after all—in his own terms—in the "returned age of man," and he cared dearly about the health of his own society.[47] So I depart the firm ground of his final *New Science* and wade back into those dark, fertile waters of his earlier "school" writings. Before departing, though, I pause to read another gloss on Horace written in 1738: "When it first arose, poetry had utility for an end, the utility by which the nations were founded. Utility gradually declined in importance until it was replaced by pleasure. No poetry is useful to a republic, however, unless, with pleasure as its means, it take utility as its principal end."[48] Is Vico not, I wonder, struggling to retain metaphor as part of the civil process itself, and not simply as the necessary modality of its earliest phases? I return to his famous letter to Francesco Estevan, written in 1729 while preparing his second *New Science,* and there I find him pressing

---

[46] *NS,* par. 272; cf. pars. 708, 787.

[47] Did he not prepare (if only to suppress) a "Practic of the New Science, hoping to offer therein some aid to human prudence "toward delaying if no preventing the ruin of nations in decay" (*NS,* par. 1405)? A translation of th "Practic" by Thomas G. Bergin and Max H. Fisch appears in Tagliacozzo an Verene, *Giambattista Vico's Science of Humanity,* pp. 451–454. See too in the sam symposium the articles by Angela Maria Jacobelli (pp. 409–421), Max H. Fisc (pp. 423–430), and Alain Pons (pp. 431–448), each of whom treats, though fro different perspectives, the issue I am now addressing.

[48] *Opere* 7: 74. The gloss is on Horace's famous lines: "Aut prodesse volunt au delectare poetae/ aut simul et iucunda et idonea dicere vitae" (*Ars poetica,* vv. 33; 334).

anew the case of the *De studiorum ratione* made twenty years before: we neglect at our peril the study of language and letters and the practice of topics and oratory, for these alone prepare us for life in the public forum, while Cartesian analysis dulls the common sense and suspends the truth that unites us.[49] I return to the very first statement of cultural *corso* and *ricorso*, in the Second *Risposta* of 1712, and there I find him urging that philosophy in general, and particularly that in his day, be content with the realm of the probable lest, in striving for mathematical perfection, it touch off that skepticism which causes nations to decline.[50] And I return finally to the *De studiorum ratione* of 1708, to its section on jurisprudence, where Vico first attempts to set forth the development of Roman law and compare it with the practice of law in his day; and there I find him ridiculing the attempts of the moderns to produce an absolute "art of equity," that is, to reduce the prudence of law to convenient preceptive manuals *(artes redactae)*. Nothing is more futile, he argues, for "such manuals foster a habit of abiding by general maxims whereas in real life nothing is more useless." "Our law groans under the bulk of its books and forensic oratory has fallen mute." Better to follow the heroic Romans, who kept laws to a minimum and forced equity to emerge from the skill of an eloquent barrister.[51] Did Vico find, I wonder, in the logic of jurisprudence, in the dialectic between prose and poetry, between codified law and the eloquence of the lawyer, the model for a vital *human* society (or for a perpetually *heroic* society forever striving to become human), even as the specter of a "voiceless wisdom" once impelled him to discover the primacy of poetry in the origins of mankind?

With about as much accuracy as we speak of the *mos Gallicus*

---

[49] *Opere* 5: 212–218.

[50] *Opere* 1: 273–275.

[51] *Opere* 1: 99–113, at 99 and 106. Here Vico follows late humanist and seventeenth-century authors, notably Francis Bacon, in reacting against the earlier humanist effort to "reduce to arts" the various disciplines of the curriculum. On his see Neal W. Gilbert, *Renaissance Concepts of Method* (New York: Columbia University Press, 1960), pp. 92–98, 112–115.

(as fully Italian as ever was the *mos Italicus*), I choose to call this the "Roman" theory of culture, in contrast to the "Greek." On the Greek view, the apogee of human culture is science and abstract thought; on the Roman, it is eloquence and the prudence of law. This was the position of the ancient sophists—of the more thoughtful ones, if not of those who so rightly exercised Socrates. It was the position of the "prudential" Aristotle, the Aristotle of the *Ethics* and *Politics,* of the *Topics,* the *Rhetoric,* and the *Poetics.* It was consummately the position of the "reformed" school of Roman orators, headed by Cicero, and of the "civic humanists" of the early Italian Renaissance, who in their writings and practice gave new meaning and dignity to the *vita activa.* And it was the position of Giambattista Vico, who delighted in mocking, most notably in the closing paragraph of every version of the *New Science,* the quip of Polybius that "if all men were wise there would be no need for religions and laws" (*Hist.* 6.56.10). "There is no other occupation," wrote Cicero, "in which human virtue approaches more closely the august function of the gods than that of founding new states or preserving those already in existence" (*De re pub.* 1.7.12). In his soul, if not in his every word, Vico was a faithful son of Rome.

In Vico Veritas: The True Philosophy and the New Science

BY DONALD R. KELLEY

Living in Vico's world of thought is an inspiring and sometimes intoxicating experience. So many things seem to fall into place, so many fields to open up, so much of the cultural future as well as past to become comprehensible. Vico's *New Science* is a cornucopia—or is it a Pandora's box?—of structured learning; and whether we regard its contents as a prophetic vision, a cosmic myth, a crazy quilt of curious erudition, or a paradigm of cultural science, we should not deny ourselves the experience of sharing in this magnificent, if sometimes intemperate effort to recreate the life cycle of civilization in a dynamic encyclopedia of interdisciplinary lore and superdisciplinary logic—a latter-day *speculum mundi*.

The effort alone would seem to justify extrapolations from Vico's system to modern systems of sociology, anthropology, psychology, and linguistics, even if specific connections must often remain in the eye of the beholder. If as a historian I am obliged to question such massive "precursoritis," as a historian of ideas I must acknowledge the life of disciplines and concepts apart from their practitioners and even terminologies. But as a historian of any sort I must shun the ways of the *speculator*, medieval or modern. Professionaly, I have condemned myself to the fate of the

false diviners in Dante's inferno, who are forced to proceed by looking backward. From this uncomfortable position I tend to see
Vico not so much as a progenitor as an inheritor, not so much a
herald of modern science as a minstrel of ancient learning; and
his system I take not so much as a *corso* as a *ricorso* of Western
thought.[1] Yet such an angle of vision, as Vico himself suggests,
may lead to insights denied to a more speculative examination of
his ideas.

From this Vichian standpoint the "new science" appears as a
summing-up of a long intellectual enterprise, or set of enterprises,
whose purpose was to erect a comprehensive and definitive social
cosmology. Placing his effort historically, tracing the provenance
of his conceptualizations, is no easy task; and it is made more difficult by his rampant eclecticism and intention of proceeding, so
he declared in his autobiography, "as if there were no books in
the world." Yet this was clearly a rationalization made in the
spirit not of historical or even autobiographical accuracy but
rather of his latter-day systematizing and in accordance with his
view of education, which was that the stage of pure reason succeeds that of memory and book learning. By then he had already
accumulated his store of "topics" and "examples" and established
his philological method. What he really admired, even in his
famous "four authors," was rather the form than the content of
their thinking, and what he wanted to be admired most in his own
thought was its "geometric" character. But age brings forgetfulness and distortion as well as wisdom. The primal truth is that, in
a longer psychological and pedagogical perspective, Vico's most
fundamental authorities were drawn from other sources than that
of formal philosophy. This becomes apparent when we abandon
the habit of looking at Vico's system statically and synchronically
and try to view it diachronically and genetically, in keeping with

---

[1] For the details and documentation of this interpretation see my "Vico's Road
From Philology to Jurisprudence and Back," in Giorgio Tagliacozzo and Donald P.
Verene, eds., *Giambattista Vico's Science of Humanity* (Baltimore: The Johns
Hopkins University Press, 1976), pp. 15–29.

Vico's own maxim that "doctrines must take their beginnings from that of the matters of which they treat." [2]

Jurisprudence, the True Philosophy

In broad outline, the trajectory of Vico's thought seems, like so many of his own conceptualizations, to fall into three phases. First comes what may be called the trivial stage, the time for studying language and literature. In the traditional scheme of Western education this corresponds to the period of childhood (specifically to that "third childhood" of Renaissance pedagogues) devoted to the liberal arts, especially grammar and rhetoric, the so-called *studia humanitatis,* which Vico referred to as "language and the study of topics." The root of the "new science," in other words, was the classical tradition, in particular the scholarly aspect of Renaissance humanism called philology, and of course as professor of rhetoric at the University of Naples Vico had a professional commitment to this tradition. The second stage was marked by a shift from the arts to science, and the particular science that attracted Vico was jurisprudence, although—in one of the traumatic experiences of his career—he failed to win appointment to the university's chair of law. Nonetheless, this discipline absorbed him for years and gave him access to another seminal intellectual tradition paralleling and enriching that of philology. Lastly, and in a very meaningful sense a synthesis of the first two phases, came Vico's several efforts to build a philosophical system, that "new science" which he variously presented as a "philosophy of authority," a "civil theology," a "rational chronology," a "philosophical grammar," and—most pertinently here—a "universal system of law."

The cycle just described is also congruent, and not accidentally,

---

[2] *La Scienza nuova seconda giusta l'edizione del 1744,* edited by Fausto Nicolini, th ed., rev. and enlarged (Bari: Laterza, 1953), par. 314.

with the general *corso* of human culture, from heroic or poetic wisdom, through human, finally to civil "wisdom." Psychologically this *iter* began in the realm of memory, passed into that of reason, and ended—like Dante's, as so often noted—in a transcendent vision.   Now although this vision has itself been the subject of endless exegesis and speculation, much less attention has been paid to the earlier phases, represented successively by the humanistic orations and especially by the *Universal Law*, except as background to the *New Science*.   Yet according to Vichian—and arguably Vico's—psychology, the essence, the *ingegno* of his philosophy ought to be drawn precisely from the more primitive stages.   From the first, the "trivial" stage, Vico derived his literary method and materials; from the second, the scientific stage, he derived much of the structure of his thought and ideas about history; and it was the synthesis and transmutation of these disciplines that underlay his final, never-quite-realized vision.   The first two stages were most fundamental in that each produced a crucial intellectual epiphany that was translated into an axiom of the new science.   The first was the assumption that the new science *(nova scientia)* was the direct result of philology. "Philology is the study of speech. . .," Vico explained, "but since words represent the ideas of things, philology must first treat the history of things . . ., hence human governments, customs, laws, institutions, intellectual disciplines, and the mechanical arts." [3]   The second epiphany, and the one at issue here, is that jurisprudence itself represented the "true philosophy," and the consequences of this assertion were even more momentous.   It was out of the union of these two insights, and out of the marriage of the associated antique traditions, that Vico's philosophical creation emerged. From *philologia* (to put it simply) came Vico's method and anti-Cartesian epistemology; from *jurisprudentia* came the original form

---

[3] *Il diritto universale*, edited by Fausto Nicolini, 3 vols. (Bari: Laterza, 1936) vol. 2: *De constantia jurisprudentis*, p. 308.

and much of the historical and linguistic substance of the "new science." [4]

What did Vico mean when he called jurisprudence the "true philosophy"? As usual, many things; as usual, not a static definition but an open continuum of meaning. In the first place, the statement represented one of those "topics" collected in the days of study and discipleship, specifically a formula taken from the very first title of the Digest, that anthology of classical jurisprudence which any beginning law student, and indeed most liberal arts students, would be familiar with. It is a passage from Ulpian in which jurisconsults are praised as veritable "priests of the law" and their discipline "true not counterfeit philosophy" (vera philosophia non simulata), a passage that was repeated and glossed and inflated by dozens of jurists from the sixth through the eighteenth century.[5] It was associated with the scarcely less famous formula defining law as "the knowledge of things divine and human," that is, wisdom (sapientia), a formula likewise cited by Vico in this context and justified in terms of Platonic and Aristotelian philosophy. By the late Middle Ages the justification of the equation jurisprudentia est vera philosophia was well established, and two arguments in particular were recognized. The first was that law represented the most perfect science because it was universal, construed the world in terms of cause and effect, and had its own independent method. The second was that, unlike natural philosophy, jurisprudence was concerned with action, not speculation, with public welfare, not private knowledge. As a lifelong student of civil law and its commentators, humanistic and scholastic, Vico was indelibly impressed by this central theme of Roman jurisprudence.

[4] On the modern tradition of "philology," see A. Bernardini and G. Righi, Il concetto di filologia e di cultura classica (Bari: Laterza, 1953). For jurisprudence there is no comparable study in terms of the history of ideas.

[5] On this theme see my "Vera Philosophia: The Philosophical Significance of Renaissance Jurisprudence," Journal of the History of Philosophy 14 (1976): 267–279.

Vico and the Legal Tradition

The general implications of this theme, and of the tradition i
celebrated, are more far-reaching than historians of ideas hav
realized, although students of Vico should be able to appreciate
them. The reason for the neglect of this tradition, it seems to me
is the overwhelming impact (though in some ways anachronistic
attraction) of natural science, as represented especially by the in
timidating figures of Descartes, Galileo, Bacon, Newton, Leibniz
and other devotees of mechanical or mathematical philosophy. A
a result, the history of philosophy has been dominated by the sys
tem-builders of natural law; the history of science has become ₐ
thriving scholarly industry (with nothing at all comparable for
social or cultural sciences); and there has been an epidemic o
precursoritis in the search for contributors to, or anticipators of
pre-Galilean mechanics, pre-Keplerian astronomy, and the like
Here I speak more out of envy than criticism. It is altogether ad
mirable to have the work of, say, the Merton school of the four
teenth century not only studied but incorporated into the history
of philosophy. But it is a pity, or at the least a curious imbalance
to neglect not merely figures of comparable significance in the
history of the legal tradition but entire genres of pre-Vichian and
pre-Montesquieuist social and cultural thought. At least one by
product of this massive neglect has been a distorted view of Vico
and his place in intellectual history.

This is certainly not the place to begin filling in this great
blank, but it should at least be noted that jurists, or authors work
ing primarily out of a juridical tradition, made significant contri
butions to social and cultural sciences before the establishment of
the particular disciplines.[6] They investigated and thought about
the process of historical change, for example; they discussed the
intricate relationship between man and society; they considered
problems of international and intercultural relations; and they

---

[6] I go further into this question in a paper on "The Prehistory of Sociology," forth
coming.

did these and other things with a richer empirical base and some-times greater conceptual sophistication than political philosophers (who again, a select few, figure so prominently in intellectual his-tories). They contributed also to many aspects of formal philos-ophy, including the problem of knowledge, the nature of man and the universe, the processes of cause and effect, the search for a proper scientific method, and the theory of hermeneutics. Per-haps most important, the legal tradition offered a viable alterna-tive to the structure and conventions of metaphysics. The ar-rangement of Justinian's Digest, Institutes, and Code, in other words, suggested a model all the more attractive in that its values and categories were human and not abstract, normative and not value-free, consisting in particular of persons, things, actions, and relationships, of public and private spheres of life, and especially of the human cosmos of the *respublica,* which could itself serve as a principle of organization and evaluation of the whole range of human behavior and knowledge. In short, jurisprudence consti-tuted its own world, its own encyclopedia, method, language, and even religion; and more than one author, especially from Bodin to Montesquieu, tried to build a philosophic system in its image. Of these perhaps the most successful was Vico, especially because he self-consciously set out to offer an alternative to the fashionable Cartesianism of his own day. Let me suggest just a few of the ways in which Vico carried on and extended the juridical ideal of *vera philosophia.*

To begin with, Vico, with characteristic eccentric traditional-ism, took as his principal model of historical experience *Romani-tas,* following in particular the pattern of Roman constitutional transformation summarized in the second title of the Digest based on Pomponius's work "On the Origin of Law." Many of the sem-inal themes of Vico's philosophy of history are derived from Roman law as conceived, arranged, and interpreted by Justinian; and many others from the later glossators and commentators, in-cluding the belief that civil law was itself virtually "written rea-son" *(ratio scripta).* So Vico emphasized the poetic character of early Roman law with reference to Justinian's prefatory remark about the "fables" to be found in earlier texts, and the law of the Twelve Tables in particular he characterized as essentially a "serious poem," reflecting that "poetic wisdom" of the first stage of civilization. He urged the thesis of the divine origin of law with reference to the passage praising the jurists as "priests of the law." He illustrated the primacy of words over thoughts in terms of the extreme reverence of the early Romans for the letter over the spirit of the law. "When the words fail," he liked to quote, "the cause is lost." He described legal development as a movement from the anarchy of private law, equivalent to the state of nature, to the principle of equity *(aequum bonum)* associated with the public sphere, and he regarded this as a primal reflection of his famous *verum-certum* concept. "In general," as he put it, "ancient jurisprudence neglected the true for the certain," that is, neglected equity for literal construction of sacred laws. More generally, jurisprudence—whose parts were philosophy, history, and judgment—exhibited the same triadic character as Vico's conceptions of psychology and politics, each reflecting facets of *humanitas.* In these and other ways (some detailed in a groundbreaking article of Max H. Fisch [7]), Vico attempted to transmute Roman legal tradition into a system of universal law.

What is important to understand in this context is that the legal tradition itself had for centuries accommodated efforts to rationalize and to systematize civil law and to raise it out of its Romanist environment. This effort was carried on largely under the rubric of the "law of nations" *(jus gentium).* Like Bodin two centuries before, Vico identified this field with that of universal history, which covered the life stories of all the *gentes,* their customs and institutions. In a typically historicizing fashion he distinguished between the law of the greater nations *(jus majorum gentium)* and that of the lesser *(jus minorum gentium),* which is to say between

7 Max H. Fisch, "Vico on Roman Law," in Milton R. Konvitz and Arthur E. Murphy, eds., *Essays in Political Theory: Presented to George H. Sabine* (Ithaca: Cornell University Press, 1948), pp. 62–88.

"heroic jurisprudence," the wisdom of the founding fathers, and the civil institutions of the first governments. Characteristically, he assumed that the life cycle of all *gentes* was similar; and so when he took up the old question of the origin of feudal law, he inverted the common opinion of jurists: "Roman law emerged from feudal law," he concluded, "not feudal from Roman." Feudalism, in other words, represented an adolescent stage in the life of every society. Vico's goal obviously was a universal law— a *jus naturale gentium* or (in the *New Science*) *diritto naturale delle genti*. In this effort Vico again was continuing the work of his juridical predecessors, often within their terminology and conceptual framework. "To understand laws," according to the formula of Celsus cited by Vico, "one must know not only their letter but also their spirit and intention." In legal jargon this "spirit of laws" *(mens* or *ratio legum)* referred basically to the intention of the lawgiver as contrasted with the *verba* of the law itself. In the Vichian reincarnation the *mens legis* had to do with authority, hence the realm of the *certum*, the *ratio legis* with its rationality, hence the *verum*. Consequently, for Vico as for Montesquieu, the "spirit of the laws" required both historical and legal—both philological and philosophical—analysis. These were the faces of the "true philosophy" according to Vico, and the bases of his new science.

In Vico's *Diritto universale*, representing the first version of this new science, the materials of the legal tradition were already twisted almost out of recognizable shape; in the *Scienza nuova* they are transmuted entirely. Yet the connecting links are by no means lost. They may be traced in two related ways: first through a reversion from primarily legal to primarily philological or poetic materials, which is to say the Homeric epics; and second through reversion from primarily Latin to primarily Greek historical experience. But the target remained the same: wisdom *(sapientia)*, and Vico explained the connection in this way: "To jurisprudence," he wrote in the introduction to his *Universal Law*, referring to the topos found in the first title of the Digest, "the Romans gave the same name as the Greeks gave to wisdom, 'the knowledge of things divine and human.'" What Vico did in a sense was to replace the terms of Roman jurisprudence, and especially that primal poem of the law, the Twelve Tables, with those derived from or suggested by Homer. Nevertheless, he explicitly preserved the goal of formulating "true philosophy" and a system of "universal law" in the sense intended by jurists. The difference was that Vico shifted from the normative emphasis of the applied science of law to the analytical emphasis of the theoretical science of society, and so he was led beyond the categories and structures of the law to seek the spirit, the *ingenium* of humanity in general.

In Vico's own terms this was a movement from the *certum* of legalities to the *verum* of civil wisdom, but looking beyond the eighteenth century his achievement has a significant bearing, it seems to me, on our view of the human sciences. From the present perspective Vico's new science illustrates something resembling a major paradigm shift (in Thomas Kuhn's sense of this term), that is, a shift from classical jurisprudence to modern social and anthropological thought. For what Kuhn has argued with respect to the enterprise of natural science applies also, though less neatly, to the sciences of man. Here too there is a "role for history," not only to correct myopic views of the history of sociology and anthropology but also to help construct "a new and dynamic image" of these human sciences.[8] In the continuum of social thought that extends from Aristotle to Durkheim, and likewise from Ulpian to Max Weber, Vico's system represents an illuminating and pivotal contribution. It was that other pioneering social thinker, Comte, who remarked that metaphysics

---

[8] Thomas S. Kuhn, *The Structure of Scientific Revolutions* (Chicago: University of Chicago Press, 1962). I am aware of the looseness of this analogy and of Kuhn's own reluctance to make such extrapolations, but I think the application has at least marginal utility.

was the ghost of dead theologies. On the basis of this reading of Vico I may conclude by suggesting—in all sobriety, if with some historical abandon—that in many ways the social and cultural sciences seem to be the ghosts of dead jurisprudences.

Vico's Political Thought in His Time and Ours

BY GUSTAVO COSTA

T HE interpreters of Vico have been rather reluctant to see his thought in political terms, and, when doing so, have usually been inclined to cast it in more or less incongruous molds that have nothing to do with the culture of the philosopher's time. This is the case of Nicola Badaloni's Marxian approach, founded on the idea that Vico is to be considered a kind of source of inspiration to the adversaries of capitalist society.[1] According to Badaloni, Vico shared with modern Marxists the aspiration to overcome the contradictions of modern civilization, in order to restore the dimension of nature, the true foundation of the universality of man. It is not my intention to follow this course of interpretation, which seems rather dangerous to me because it tries to adjust Vico's philosophy to a completely different system of thought, with the result that both are blurred. I will attempt, instead, to demonstrate the relevance and actuality of Vichian political principles without ignoring the historical reality of the eighteenth century.

In order to have a full understanding of Vico's political thought, we must keep in mind the following considerations:

1. Vichian philosophy is a systematic attempt to explain the

---

[1] See his introduction to G. B. Vico, *Opere filosofiche*, edited by Paolo Cristofolini (Florence: Sansoni, 1971), pp. lvi–lviii. An important exception to the widespread habit of superimposing preempted interpretations on Vichian political philosophy is Giuseppe Giarrizzo's stimulating article, "La politica di Vico," *Quaderni contemporanei*, no. 2: *Giambattista Vico nel terzo centenario della nascita*, edited by Fulvio Tessitore (Salerno: Istituto universitario di magistero, 1968), pp. 63–133.

ever-changing activity of man by means of rigorous interconnections among all aspects of that activity. In other words, the development of political institutions is always seen by Vico in a necessary relation to the development of the conception of the world (from "poetic theology" or mythology to rational philosophy) and of the other activities of man, including science and technology. It is therefore imperative to view Vico's political thought within the framework of his dynamic pattern of growth and decline, without losing touch with other forms of human creativity, such as poetry and science.

2. In spite of his efforts to maintain scientific impartiality in treating his subject matter, Vico shows a marked preference for the early phases of each cycle, for what he calls the childhood and youth of the "nations," or their barbaric ages. In fact, the beginning of each cycle appears to be endowed with a more intense creativity in every field of human activity, which progressively diminishes and almost disappears in the later stages of each cycle.

3. The process leading from primitive man to highly civilized man, although uniform in its pattern, involves various "nations" developing at various paces. In other words, "nations" still characterized by an archaic structure coexist with "nations" that have already attained their maturity or even the final stage of over-ripeness and dissolution. Hence Vico postulates the coexistence of civilized people and barbarians not only in the ancient world but also in our contemporary international reality.

4. According to the *New Science,* there is an unchangeable pattern of political development, according to which all civilizations "have their roots in . . . the divine governments, and . . . must proceed through this sequence of human things: first becoming commonwealths of optimates, later free popular commonwealths, and finally monarchies." [2] This political phenomenology, borrowed from classical thought, admits various combinations or

---

[2] *The New Science of Giambattista Vico* (hereinafter *NS*), translated from the third edition (1744) by Thomas G. Bergin and Max H. Fisch (Ithaca: Cornell University Press, 1948), par. 1004.

"mixtures . . . of a succeeding form with a preceding government." [3] Such a phenomenon is explained with a reference to axiom LXXI of the *New Science* which reads as follows: "Native customs, and above all that of natural liberty, do not change all at once but by degrees and over a long period of time." [4] It must also be noted that Vico applies to modern parliamentary states the labels of "commonwealths of optimates" or "heroic aristocracies," more or less tempered with "free popular commonwealths."

5. The Italian philosopher flourished in an age when absolutism triumphed in Catholic countries. This state of affairs was potentially challenged by Protestant England. In fact, the "Glorious Revolution," dethroning the Stuart dynasty, had preserved a parliamentary regime which became the focus of attention of European intellectuals who advocated more or less radical changes in the political and social structures of their own countries. But Rome still harbored the hope of restoring the Stuarts to the throne of England in the name of the divine right of kings. Only in 1745, with the epic failure of Bonnie Prince Charles, did it become clear that the Stuarts had no chance of recovering their lost kingdom, but at that time Vico was no longer among living men.

Northern Gothicism

Let us consider Vico's attitude toward contemporary Europe, keeping in mind the above stated considerations. Despite the Catholic orthodoxy professed by the Italian philosopher, the tension existing between Catholic and Protestant powers does not find any expression in the *New Science*. Vico plays down the religious split of contemporary Europe, referring to the latter in very broad religious terms as the center of Christianity: "in Europe, where the Christian religion is everywhere professed, in-

3 *NS,* par. 1004.
4 *NS,* par. 249.

culcating an infinitely pure and perfect idea of God and com-
manding charity to all mankind, there are great monarchies most
humane in their customs." [5] This view revives the medieval concept of Europe as the Christian stronghold, opposed to the rest
of the world, dominated by infidels.[6] Christianity makes Europe
"everywhere radiant with such humanity that it abounds in all
the good things that make for the happiness of human life, min-
istering to the comforts of the body as well as to the pleasures of
mind and spirit." [7]

But, beyond the supposedly uniform surface of Christian religion, Vico does not fail to see a political differentiation peculiar
to Europe: "In this part of the world alone, because it cultivates
the sciences, there are furthermore a great number of popular
commonwealths, which are not found at all in the other three
parts." [8] The causal link established by Vico between the development of science and that of free popular commonwealths requires
an explanation. As usual, we must refer to the whole body of
Vichian philosophy. Science and technology are considered by
the Italian thinker as two typical creations of primitive man, living in a more or less barbaric society. In fact, Vico was well aware
of the strict connection existing between the natural philosophy
of primitive man—that is, magic—and experimental science,
both founded on "*autopsia* or the evidence of the senses" and the
"unitive" or inductive method.[9] But primitive or barbaric man
also enjoys a liberty unknown to representatives of highly refined
civilizations. Thus Vico establishes an implicit link between liberty and scientific and technological creativity, without elaborating
on it, out of fear of ecclesiastical censorship. Moreover, since the
so-called "new science of nations" was created by Vico after the
pattern of experimental science, it was supposed to be a living

---

[5] *NS*, par. 1092.

[6] Carlo Curcio, *Europa: storia di un'idea*, 2 vols. (Florence: Vallecchi, 1958), 1: 389.

[7] *NS*, par. 1094.

[8] *NS*, par. 1092.

[9] *NS*, par. 499. See my article "G. B. Vico e la *Natura simpatetica*," *Giornale critico della filosofia italiana* 47 (1968): 401–418.

proof of the fact that the Italian philosopher's mind had not been spoiled by the rationalistic culture of the eighteenth century. In fact, Vico held that some exceptional personalities can validly resist the prevailing influence of their times, secluding themselves from contemporary society, or simply refusing to adhere to the main trends of contemporary culture, as can be gathered from the celebrated letter addressed by the author of the *New Science* to Gherardo degli Angioli in 1725.[10]

The "great number of popular commonwealths" attributed by Vico to the European scene has puzzled the interpreters of the *New Science*, including Fausto Nicolini.[11] Indeed, we cannot understand how the Italian philosopher can assert such a thing unless we keep in mind that the Vichian idea of "popular commonwealth" is a very broad one, and implies a tension with a pre-existing aristocracy, having in some cases the outward appearance of a monarchy. Thus Poland and England, "although they are monarchic in constitution, yet seem to be governed aristocratically," while "the Swiss cantons and the united provinces or states of Holland have organized a number of free popular cities into two aristocracies," and "the body of the German empire is a system of many free cities and sovereign princes . . . and in matters concerning the state of the empire it is governed aristocratically." [12] These relatively archaic and barbaric countries were the seats of parliamentary freedom and experimental science. In fact, they had produced Newton and Leibniz, "the two foremost minds of our age," [13] as Vico states, alluding to the controversy about calculus.

The Italian philosopher shows a marked preference for contemporary England, in spite of the fact that he had praised the Jaco-

10 G. B. Vico, *L'autobiografia, il carteggio e le poesie varie*, 2nd ed., edited by Benedetto Croce and Fausto Nicolini (Bari: Laterza, 1929), pp. 195–200.

11 Fausto Nicolini, *Commento storico alla seconda Scienza nuova*, 2 vols. (Rome: Edizioni di storia e letteratura, 1949–50), 2: 143–144.

12 *NS*, par. 1092.

13 *NS*, par. 347.

bite cause in an impeccable Latin inscription.[14] England appears
to Vico as a kind of heroic aristocracy whose members, "not yet
enervated by the effeminacy of our age, can enjoy only atrocious
tragedies,"[15] and are therefore very similar to the contemporaries
of Homer and Dante, barbarian poets flourishing in a barbaric
society. But England is above all the promised land of experimental science, firmly established by Francis Bacon, a master of
Vico himself: "Hence with great reason Bacon, great alike as
philosopher and statesman, proposes, commends, and illustrates
the inductive method in his *Organum,* and is still followed by the
English with great profit in experimental philosophy."[16] The
necessary link existing between the empirical approach and the
barbaric structure of English society, ruled by an aristocratic regime more flexible and loose than absolute monarchy, is stressed
again in this eulogy of Bacon. In fact, Vico attributes to this
philosopher the merit of having fostered the habit of *autopsia* or
the evidence of the senses, contributing in this way to the preserva-
tion of an archaic but happy phase of social and political development. The same praise could have been bestowed on John
Locke, whose psychology represents the backbone of the *New Science,* a pioneering work from the viewpoint of the psychological
school of sociology, were it not for the fact that the English philosopher had been explicitly condemned by Pope Clement XII in
1734.[17]

The prominent place held by northern Europe in Vico's political thought has its roots in the republican tradition of Italian culture as well as in the patriotic writings of northern authors who
glorified their ancestors, the ancient barbarians fighting against
the Romans, after the example set by Tacitus in his writings and
particularly in the *Germania.* I cannot dwell here on these

---

[14] G. B. Vico, *Scritti vari e pagine sparse,* edited by Fausto Nicolini (Bari:
Laterza, 1940), p. 214.
[15] Vico, *L'autobiografia, il carteggio e le poesie varie,* p. 199.
[16] *NS,* par. 499.
[17] See my article "Vico e Locke," *Giornale critico della filosofia italiana* 49 (1970):
344–361.

two components of Vico's political thought, which I have amply
illustrated in a book.[18] I will therefore limit myself to mentioning
writers such as Machiavelli, Ludovico Guicciardini, Boccalini,
Gregorio Leti, Vendramino Bianchi, and Maffei, representing the
highlights of Italian republicanism from the Renaissance to
Vico's time. As to the northern followers of Tacitus, it will be
sufficient to remind you of the fortune enjoyed by the *Germania*
in countries such as Germany, Holland, Scandinavia, and England.
In various cases, the study of German antiquities, founded mainly
on Tacitus, produced the important political result of amalga-
mating the racial pride of being the descendants of the Goths,
conquerors of Rome, and the drive to evolve a parliamentary form
of government, supposedly corresponding to the inbred love of
freedom traditionally attributed to the barbaric forefathers. The
strenuous struggle of the Goths against Rome became the symbol
of the eternal conflict of freedom-loving people against their op-
pressors, and of the contrast existing between Nordic and Latin
man: the former, pure and intolerant of any kind of political and
religious tyranny; the latter, corrupt and prone to accept the
despotic orders of a political or religious ruler. This Germanic
myth, developed mainly in the British world, appears also in the
writings of men who had a great influence in shaping America.
William Penn, the great Quaker, went back to Tacitus to find
evidence of a German predilection for liberty in order to justify
religious sects.[19] The same myth was alive in Thomas Jefferson,
firmly convinced that his conception of liberty had its origin in
the ancient barbarians of northern Europe.[20] This attitude was
also adopted by the nineteenth-century scholar and philologist
George Perkins Marsh (1801–1882), who held that the Goths came

---

[18] Gustavo Costa, *Le antichità germaniche nella tradizione culturale italiana da
Machiavelli a Vico* (Naples: Guida, 1977).

[19] Samuel Kliger, *The Goths in England: A Study in Seventeenth and Eighteenth
Century Thought* (Cambridge: Harvard University Press, 1952), pp. 80–82.

[20] *Ibid.*, pp. 110–111.

to America aboard the *Mayflower* and fought for American independence against the "Roman" tyranny of England.[21]

Vico had eagerly read the publications of northern scholars praising German or Gothic liberty, manliness, and virtue. He had a direct knowledge of the works published in Latin by important representatives of the antiquarian school that brought about a revival of the German past, such as Ole Worm, Olof Rudbeck, Johan Loccenius, and Daniel Georg Morhof, as it appears from the *New Science*, including a passage not accepted in the final edition of 1744.[22] Since Vico quotes Ole Worm's *De prisca Danorum poesi dissertatio,* published as an appendix to the work entitled *Runir seu Danica literatura antiquissima, vulgo Gothica dicta* (Copenhagen, 1636; 2nd ed. 1651), he also knew two very important specimens of Norse poetry, partially translated in the same book: the *Sonatorrek* by Egill Skallagrímsson and the *Krákumál.*[23] Last but not least, Vico had probably heard about Sir William Temple's essays *Of Heroic Virtue* and *Of Poetry,* two landmarks in the history of English gothicism, from his personal friend Paolo Mattia Doria, who referred to them in a work published in 1716.[24]

Unfortunately I cannot deal at length with this fascinating aspect of Vico's culture, hitherto ignored by his interpreters, although it appears to be extremely relevant not only to his aesthetics but also to his political and social thought. What I want to stress here is the fact that Vico did not consider republican

[21] *Ibid.,* pp. 106–110.

[22] *NS,* pars. 430, 471. Cf. also G. B. Vico, *La Scienza nuova, giusta l'edizione del 1744, con le varianti dell'edizione del 1730 e di due redazioni intermedie inedite,* edited by Fausto Nicolini, 4th ed., 2 vols. (Bari: Laterza, 1953), 2: par. 1237.

[23] On the relevance of the Norse poems quoted above see Stefán Einarsson, *A History of Icelandic Literature* (New York: Johns Hopkins Press for the American-Scandanavian Foundation, 1957), pp. 59, 68, 182; Mario Gabrieli, *Le letterature della Scandinavia* (Florence: Sansoni; Milan: Accademia, 1969), pp. 43, 62–70.

[24] *Ragionamenti di Paolo Mattia D'Oria, indirizzati alla Signora D. Aurelia d'Este, Duchessa di Limatola, ne' quali si dimostra la donna, in quasi che tutte le virtù più grandi, non essere all'uomo inferiore* (Frankfort, 1716), pp. 437–438. This matter is amply debated in my book, *Le antichità germaniche.*

liberty the exclusive prerogative of a race, although it was alive mainly in northern Europe. In fact, the Italian philosopher adopted the views of the northern gothicists only to transform them into a completely different political vision, conferring upon all "nations" the same historical destiny. The eulogy of the northern peoples, made by Tacitus and repeated by his numerous followers, becomes in Vico an hermeneutic instrument allowing a better understanding of primitive society. The study of German antiquities leads the Italian philosopher to a new interpretation of archaic Roman history, because he attributes to the forefathers of the Romans the same barbaric characteristics traditionally attributed to the ancient Germans. Germanism and Romanity, these conflicting terms of humanistic culture, are reconciled in a new synthesis of universal validity. The *Scienza nuova* does not fit into the history of the anthroporacial school of sociology.[25]

Cyclical Renewal

So far, this paper has illustrated Vico's attitude toward contemporary Europe, revealing his secret predilection for Protestant England. This makes the Italian thinker a much more complex and interesting figure to specialists in political thought of the eighteenth century. However, the relevance of Vichian philosophy cannot be confined within the limits of past and contemporary history, because it involves also a prediction of future events. Indeed, the core of the *New Science* is the ever-present myth of the Golden Age, having not only a retrospective significance but also a futuristic one.[26] From this point of view, Vico appears to be the heir of a prophetic tradition, fostered in Italy by writers such as Joachim of Floris, Dante, and Campanella. In fact, Book

25 P. A. Sorokin, *Contemporary Sociological Theories through the First Quarter of the Twentieth Century* (New York: Harper & Row, 1964), pp. 219 ff.

26 See the section on Vico in my book *La leggenda dei secoli d'oro nella letteratura italiana* (Bari: Laterza, 1972), pp. 177–188.

V of the *New Science,* dedicated to the "recurrence of human things in the resurgence of the nations," although sketchy in comparison with the others, is not only an original study of the Middle Ages but also an eloquent profession of faith in the capacity of mankind for a periodical rebirth, containing a new secular interpretation of the traditional religious idea of *renovatio.*

The cyclical pattern of history adopted by Vico after the classical tradition was certainly a major obstacle to the fortune of his philosophy in the eighteenth century, when the idea of linear progress became generally accepted. Yet the *New Science* proves that the crisis of modern man was already taking shape under the smooth surface of the Enlightenment, although it was noticed only in recent times, when it had reached its climax. As Sorokin remarked about twenty-five years ago, the twentieth century is an age of crisis, since the progressively linear theories of social evolution, dominating the so-called sensate period of Western culture, have been replaced by different kinds of philosophies of history, cyclical, eschatological, and apocalyptic.[27] In fact, the nostalgia for the lost paradise and the expectation of a new Golden Age are the main features of our contemporary society. As usual, they are accompanied by the feeling that we are living in an age of catastrophic transition and that our civilization has entered the final stage of dissolution.

Allow me to illustrate this apocalyptic attitude, referring to an Italian book recently translated into English: Roberto Vacca's *The Coming Dark Age.*[28] It opens with a quotation from the *Revelation of St. John the Divine,* prophesying the end of the world. However, the author makes it immediately clear that he does not intend to join the so-called doom-writers of our times who foresee a total catastrophe brought about by nuclear holocaust, overpopulation, pollution, and ecological disaster. Although

---

[27] P. A. Sorokin, *Modern Historical and Social Philosophies* [formerly titled *Social Philosophies of an Age of Crisis*] (New York: Dover, 1963), pp. 7–9.
[28] Roberto Vacca, *The Coming Dark Age,* translated by J. S. Whale (Garden City, N.Y.: Doubleday, 1973).

these factors appear to be extremely dangerous, Vacca calls our attention to another factor capable of bringing havoc upon us: "the fact that vast concentrations of human beings are involved in systems that are now so complicated that they are becoming uncontrollable." A catastrophic process leading to the end of our civilization is looming ahead, because "our great technological systems of human association . . . are continuously outgrowing ordered control." [29] This fascinating hypothesis of an apocalypse that is impersonal, casual, and unpremeditated has been judged favorably by Umberto Eco, a very acute observer of contemporary society.[30]

It is important to note that Vacca's pessimistic view rests on the optimistic assumption that the collapse of our technological civilization will be followed by rebirth, because of "the periodic alternation of all things human, which history seems to support." [31] There is no doubt whatsoever that this perspective of doom followed by palingenesis belongs to the same prophetic tradition that has in the *New Science* one of its more original manifestations. What makes it closer to Vichian thought is the fact that the catastrophe is attributed not to violent causes but to an overgrowth of rationality resulting in an overgrowth of technological systems. Indeed, Vico warns his readers of the dangers connected with the excessive development of human reason. In the *De nostri temporis studiorum ratione* (1709), this distrust of over-refined rationality is directed against the analytical geometry created by Descartes and Fermat. In fact, Vico states that the greatest inventions of modern times, such as the gun, the ship propelled by sails alone, the clock, and the dome, were made before, or independently from, the creation of analytical geometry. On the other hand, those who have tried to make new machines by relying

29 *Ibid.*, pp. 3, 4.
30 Umberto Eco, "Il Medioevo è già cominciato," *Documenti su "Il nuovo Medioevo"* (Milan: Bompiani, 1973), pp. 7–28.
31 Vacca, *The Coming Dark Age*, p. 6.

on analytical geometry have been doomed to failure, as happened in the case of a Father Perot who had "built a ship the proportions of which had been carefully calculated beforehand according to the rules of analytical geometry, expecting it to be the swiftest vessel in existence," but was cruelly disappointed because "it sank to the bottom of the sea and remained there as motionless as a rock." [32] Vico never abandoned this view of the deleterious effects brought about by reason, because he recognized the same essence in technology and poetry. In the *New Science*, commenting on axiom LII, he asserts that "the world in its infancy was composed of poetic nations" and that "poetry is nothing but imitation." [33] This remark is immediately followed by an important consideration attributing useful inventions to barbaric ages only and recognizing in technology a typical product of poetic activity: "This axiom will explain the fact that all the arts of things necessary, useful, convenient, and even in large part those of human pleasure, were invented in the poetic centuries before the philosophers came; for the arts are nothing but imitations of nature, poems in a certain way made of things." [34]

Vico was the first Western thinker to denounce the involution implicit in the so-called age of technological progress. But he saw also in England a kind of sanctuary where the good barbaric way of life was still alive. This political reality, a kind of dreamland to the Italian philosopher, who was more a poet than a thinker, was the perfect antithesis of France. In fact, the latter signified to Vico Cartesian rationalism and all evils connected with the overgrowth of human reason, while England signified barbaric poetry, heroic sociopolitical structures, and *autopsia* or experimental science. Indeed, the *New Science* is a landmark in the history of the so-called struggle against French rationalism,

---

[32] G. B. Vico, *On the Study Methods of Our Time*, translated by Elio Gianturco (Indianapolis: Bobbs-Merrill, 1965), p. 29.

[33] *NS*, par. 216.

[34] *NS*, par. 217.

fought in eighteenth-century Europe not only for aesthetic but also for political reasons.[35] It should also be noted that Vico did not embrace a completely pessimistic view of the future of Europe because of the political and cultural reality—sanguine, poetic, and barbaric—still existing in the northern countries and particularly in England. However, the pattern of ideal eternal history could not be escaped: even Poland and England, "if the natural course of human civil things is not impeded in their case by extraordinary causes . . . will arrive at perfect monarchies."[36] Did Vico envision the restoration of the Stuarts to the throne of England? It is highly probable, since nobody could foresee the final defeat inflicted on the Jacobite cause in 1745. In any case, the author of the *New Science* was convinced that the decline would start immediately after the triumph of absolute monarchy in England. After the pattern of Roman history, Caesar and Tiberius would be followed by "the dissolute and shameless madmen, like Caligula, Nero, and Domitian,"[37] who would destroy the state.

35 Carlo Antoni, *La lotta contro la ragione* (Florence: Sansoni, 1942), pp. 1–3.
36 *NS*, par. 1092.
37 *NS*, par. 243.

Vico and the Idea of Progress

BY ROBERT NISBET

D<small>R.</small> Johnson once told Boswell that he could repeat an entire chapter of a scholarly book from memory. The book, said Johnson, was *The Natural History of Iceland,* from the Danish of Horrebow. The chapter, No. LXXII, was titled "Concerning Snakes." It read, Johnson said, in its entirety: "There are no snakes to be met with throughout the whole island."

If this audience were fortunate, it could depart in a few seconds with the entire content of my remarks this evening memorized easily. It would consist simply of the words: "There is no idea of progress to be met with throughout the whole of Vico." I cannot, alas, be so generous with you, for while there is indeed much truth in that statement, it is not, as lawyers love to say, the whole truth, nothing but the truth.

To be sure, if what we mean by the idea of progress is what J. B. Bury declared it to be in his well-known book—the idea that mankind as a whole has progressed, slowly, gradually, and continuously, is now progressing, and will continue to progress in the distant future—then Vico is, as Bury himself states, devoid of the idea, immaculately so. This is the idea that lights up the pages of a distinguished succession of minds in the modern West: Turgot, Condorcet, the leaders of the French Revolution, Kant, Saint-Simon, Comte, Hegel, Spencer, Tylor, and many others. So stated, this formulation of the idea of progress must be counted among the central intellectual elements of modernity, down at least until the present century.

Vico most certainly doesn't belong to that succession. We find nothing in his writings answering to the description I have just given. All the same, Vico was profoundly interested in the *problem* of progress—that is, the conditions under which distinct intellectual advancement occurs in human history, assessed, however, against conditions under which decline and degeneration take place. Not, I think, until George Cornewall Lewis's *Treatise on Methods of Observation* appears in 1851 (a work, by the way, that specifically cites and clearly draws from Vico) do we have anything comparable to Vico's distinctive utilization of historical materials. And only in the present century in the writings of such figures as Flinders Petrie, Max Weber, Halford McKinder, Spengler, Toynbee, A. L. Kroeber, F. J. Teggart, and a few others do we come upon treatments of cultural change in historical contexts which might be said to go beyond Vico, though not, I believe, at any higher level of philosophical insight.

There is one interesting exception to what I have just said: Turgot. His famous discourses of 1750 and 1751 place him securely enough among the prophets of progress, and I do not question the fact that his largest historical significance lies in his formulation of the idea of necessary, universal progress that would be utilized so widely in the nineteenth century, made indeed the very basis of the science of society as conceived by Comte, Spencer, Tylor, and so many others for whom progress and evolution were synonomous words. But there is in Turgot's collected works a little-known, ambitious piece written several years before the Sorbonne discourses of 1750–51 were composed. It is Vichian in character—style as well as content—though I can find no evidence to support my belief that in some fashion the youthful Turgot had come upon the *New Science*.[1]

The title of Turgot's 1748 sketch is "Researches into the Causes

[1] Alain Pons has shown us how difficult it is to discern Vichian influence anywhere in the French eighteenth century. See his "Vico and French Thought," in Giorgio Tagliacozzo and Hayden V. White, eds., *Giambattista Vico: An International Symposium* (Baltimore: The Johns Hopkins Press, 1969), pp. 165–185. But see Giorgio Tagliacozzo, "Economic Vichianism: Vico, Galiani, Croce—Economics, Economic Liberalism," *ibid.*, pp. 349–368, especially pp. 353–354 and n. 29. [See too the "footnote" by Gustavo Costa which follows this paper.—Eds.]

of the Progress and Decline of the Sciences and Arts. . . ." It is more a set of notes, fragments, in outline form than an essay. What gives it interest is the fact that here we find no declaration, as we do in the later discourses, of universal, necessary, and immanent progress for mankind. Instead we are presented the problems of progress and decline in intellectual history. What are the circumstances of advancement of nations in history? Of decline? Through what social and cultural factors is the uneven distribution of human genius in different fields, different areas, different times, to be explained? He is struck by the tendency of scholars to read their own tastes and moods into the past, by, in sum, what Vico calls "scholarly conceit." So too is this young Turgot aware of what Vico had called "national conceit." It is of nations and peoples Turgot is writing when he says: "Men who gaze into deep waters cannot find the bottom; they see only their own image." There is an interesting likeness between Turgot's treatment of myth, metaphor, and poetry in the lives of nations and that of Vico. This Turgot is as interested as Vico in historical events, in problems of origin, development, diffusion, and also decline. There is much about Egyptians, Jews, Greeks, and Romans and what can be learned from their histories. Above all, there is the same sense of the multiplicity or pluralism of history that Vico gives us. It is, to repeat, a very different Turgot in this fragmentary work of 1748 from the Turgot of the later progress-intoxicated Sorbonne discourses. But as to whether in fact the young Turgot had been put in contact, directly or indirectly, with Vico's thought is a matter for conjecture.

Comparative Methods

There is, as everyone here knows only too well, nothing that comes easily out of Vico. Frank E. Manuel has astutely noted that Vico is one of those Janus-types which not infrequently confront us in the history of thought, at once looking back to ancient times for illumination and forward for inspiration.[2] Manuel is probably right also in characterizing Vico as a belated Renaissance mind rather than a harbinger of the nineteenth century, which is of course the age when he became suddenly famous. Vico, clearly, is one of William James's "tough-minded" rather than "tender-minded." Arnaldo Momigliano, in his review of Leon Pompa's recent book, observes how "events, anecdotes, images, simple words stimulated him and provoked questions."[3] Pompa himself stresses Vico's fascination with *events*.

This fascination is an aspect of Vico worth all the emphasis Pompa and Momigliano give it. For the idea of progress that stretches in the main line from Fontenelle's late seventeenth-century declaration "[M]en will never degenerate, and there will be no end to the growth and development of human wisdom" all the way to Herbert Spencer's celebrated late nineteenth-century "Progress, therefore, is not an accident, but a necessity" was based, as its most devout adherents readily conceded, not upon the record supplied us by the actual events in history but, instead, upon uses of reason, as advocated by Descartes, in search of laws or principles relating to the assumed nature of mankind and underlying all events and actualities. During the Quarrel of the Ancients and Moderns in the seventeenth century, the quarrel that precipitated Fontenelle's and Perrault's triumphant announcements of the permanence and invariability of the law of progress, it was acknowledged that the historical record, as evidenced by actual courses of events among individual peoples and nations, did *not* vindicate the principle of progress.

This emphasis, we find, never left the philosophy of unilinear progress. Auguste Comte, in so many words, declared the ideal to be an "eventless history," a history completely devoid of references to names, personages, events, dates, and places. Spencer

[2] Frank E. Manuel, *The Eighteenth Century Confronts the Gods* (Cambridge: Harvard University Press, 1959), pp. 149–167.

[3] Arnaldo Momigliano, "The One True History," *Times Literary Supplement*, September 5, 1975, p. 982, reviewing Pompa's *Vico: A Study of the New Science* (Cambridge: Cambridge University Press, 1975).

not only conceded but strongly emphasized the fact that the great principle of progress was not, could not be, substantiated by the actual histories of individual peoples. Throughout the eighteenth century there had been, side by side with the kind of history a Gibbon or Robertson wrote, that other kind of "history" well described in the French by the phrase *histoire raisonnée*: "conjectural," "hypothetical," "natural" history, the purpose of which was not to record and analyze actual events in time but, rather, to seek, through reason, the natural laws of the development, the progress, of mankind as a whole. Such history, so-called, was, obviously, a perfect vehicle for the idea of progress. Dugald Stewart, friend of Adam Smith and student of his writings, defended this approach by stating that it is more important to demonstrate through reason how something *may have been* produced than to show, through document or other record, exactly how it was produced. Stewart also stresses the Cartesian cast of such investigation, emphasizing the relation it has to mathematical modes of inquiry. Through such rationalist speculation, laws for the whole of mankind, not just concrete peoples, could be constructed.

Not that the peoples of the world were altogether dismissed. From Turgot's Sorbonne discourses throughout the nineteenth century we see in use what Comte called *The* Comparative Method. It is, however, comparative in name only. In actuality, it is a device by which in theory all extant peoples are arranged axonomically, from simplest to most advanced, using Western criteria, of course. The premise of ineluctable, unilinear progress in time is basic. Thus the spatial series of peoples yielded by observation miraculously becomes the *time series* through which mankind has moved over the ages. The sense of progress of kind that was revealed in the spatial series, the classificatory series of peoples on earth at this time, could so easily become the sense of an unbroken, continuous, necessary progress through time if one availed himself of the premise of progress as a master principle, of the view that all change tends to be, like individual organic growth, fulfilling, perfecting, and theoretically necessary.

Now the scantest reading of the *New Science* makes clear to us how impatient Vico would have been, indeed was, of such use of the geographical and historical record. Look at Book I and its Chronological Table where, in seven different columns, Vico sets down for us what he regards as the momentous events, places, and dates of the Hebrews, Chaldeans, Egyptians, Greeks, Romans, and others. Here is no compressing—through invocation of a master entity, mankind or human race—of diversity into a single, linear series such as we find in the works of the philosophers of progress. In that philosophy the unity of mankind was and is stressed, along with the unity of *origin* of man's culture. Differences are not really accepted as such in the works of Condorcet, Comte, Spencer, and others: they are converted into successive steps of one unified entity, mankind. It is *similarities* which came to occupy the attention of those anthropologists such as Tylor who constructed their developmental theories on the basis of the idea of progress. How very different with Vico. Differences fascinated him, led him at times almost to a state of ecstasy, at very least absence of ordered presentation. Just as he could not, as it were, get enough facts, real events, authoritative dates, to content him, neither could he get enough differences of history and culture to sate his appetite.

What Vico sought so presciently were conclusions resting not upon Cartesian principles achieved through a geometrical type of reasoning that in effect expunges the empirical world but rather, upon examination of actual histories of peoples—comparative examination. Such comparison is in another universe from the rationalist device I just described, the one called by Comte, Spencer, Tylor, and others *The* Comparative Method. If Vico repudiated ideas of necessity and of truth drawn only from Cartesian processes of deduction, he was equally antagonistic to ideas of mere chance or random coincidence, that is, the assumption of the principle of accident as sovereign. Fascinated though he was by the concreteness and uniqueness of events, he did not be long to the state of mind that in the nineteenth century Ranke would come to represent: the state that in effect declared events so unique, so peculiar to time and place, that one could describe them only in their uniqueness. What I draw from Vico is desire for a science that will, without rejecting events in time, without repudiating the multiplicity and plurality which the real record attests to, seek nevertheless, from comparative study of this record and those events, scientific generalizations.

Here is where Vico's acquired (slowly acquired, but in time relentless) distaste for Descartes and Cartesianism is so pertinent. Sir Isaiah Berlin, in his essay on Vico's "Concept of Knowledge," has brought out for us vividly and in detail the importance of Vico's distinction between *verum* and *certum* as types of knowledge. The first, *verum*, as Sir Isaiah stresses, is the a priori knowledge that mathematics best exemplifies. It is, of course, absolute in character and is the result of the pure use of reason. But, Sir Isaiah notes, "Such a priori knowledge can extend only to what the knower himself has created." [4]

Now, as I have already suggested, the conceptual foundations of the modern idea of progress, the idea that came out of the Quarrel of the Ancients and Moderns, that was given support in the eighteenth century by "conjectural history" and in the nineteenth by social evolution, are formed exactly by principles reached through the mathematical processes of *verum*. As I noted above, Dugald Stewart himself, in his contemporaneous analysis of the method, pointed to the necessity of using mathematical modes of reasoning if the "real" or "scientific" understanding of mankind's development in time was to be acquired—in contrast to what is available to us from use of our senses, from exploration of actual events, places, times, and people which can at best supply us with *certum*. Fontenelle and Perrault, in their pristine statements of the idea of continuous, necessary, and universal progress of knowledge in the arts and sciences, were adamant in insisting

[4] Isaiah Berlin, "A Note on Vico's Concept of Knowledge," in Tagliacozzo and White, *Giambattista Vico: An International Symposium*, pp. 371–377, at 371.

that the master principle of progress cannot be drawn from the actual records, which reveal all too often not progress but inertia or decline. This principle, as they and their successors realized full well, could be reached and understood only through Cartesian processes of thinking: processes which, in their disregard of the merely transitory and ephemeral, went, as was imagined, straight to the nature of man and society, directly to what came to be thought of as the *natural* history of mankind. In the Quarrel, the Moderns "won" their battle by clever use of Cartesian *verum* as the preferred form of knowledge. Never mind the actual record manifest in a comparison of the poetry and rhetoric of ancient Greece with that of seventeenth-century France. The superiority of an Aeschylus or Sophocles to a Racine or Corneille is apparent only. From the nature of mankind there may be deduced, following the rigorous procedures advocated by Descartes, definite proof of modern French superiority to ancient Greek. There is charming circularity of reasoning to be found in both Fontenelle and Perrault: we know that we, the Moderns, are superior to the Ancients because of the principle of progress that operates, leading to long-run advancement of quality. And we know the principle of progress operates because, plainly, Corneille and Racine are the superiors of Aeschylus and Sophocles in their insights into human nature.

Descartes, it might be pointed out here, didn't much like any poetry or rhetoric, and, as Sir Isaiah observes, expressed his full contempt for the kinds of investigations which scholars in the humanities carried on. How ridiculous, Descartes thought, to spend half a lifetime just to find out about Rome what Cicero' housemaid knew. Needless to say, Vico had, or in time came to have, very different ideas on the matter. He was the first to sense, and then to proclaim, the inappropriateness of Cartesian "science," *verum*, to the study of human beings and their history—or rather their histories. If he sometimes seems almost neurotically intense about the matter, we need only reflect on the fact that his warnings were almost totally disregarded; th lure of Cartesianism was altogether too great for those, from the time of Hobbes down to Comte, Spencer, and Tylor, who conceived their mission to be that of putting the study of man upon the same secure, absolute foundations which could be observed, it was thought, in the mathematical-physical sciences. When Bentham once observed that without leaving the recesses of his study he could legislate scientifically for all of India, the shade of Descartes must have been elated. One can imagine, however, the opposite reaction of Vico's shade. Only in the twentieth century have we begun to reach, in more and more areas, the philosophical level of problem-formation we can see, albeit darkly at times, in Vico's *New Science*.

Vico's History

There confronts us, of course, the difficult problem of what Vico called his "ideal eternal history." It has been the subject, and will continue to be, of a great deal of interpretative writing. It teases us with the implication of the very necessity Vico so thoroughly denounced. It has a proto-Hegelian ring. I am frank in confessing my wish that he had never used the phrase. But he did, and we must try to be as clear as possible about what he did and did not mean by it. In the first place, its referent is the individual people or nation, not some entity called Mankind or Civilization, as in the Turgots and Condorcets and Comtes. Vico believed that through careful study of many national histories there could be discerned a common line of historical change that went from genesis through development and progress to decline and eventual barbarism. His "ideal eternal history" is, in short, not monogenetic, monocentric, and unilinear, but rather the reverse of these. Plurality of peoples is the foundation on which Vico's law rests.

Second, I should like to advance the idea that in his use of the word "ideal" he suggests very strongly Max Weber, whose own "ideal type" was, by Weber's own prescription, a construct derived from the histories of concrete, actual peoples. In modern scientific language, it is, I think we are justified in saying, a theoretical model, resting upon a union of law and fact, principle and data, that Vico is offering us.

Third, as Pompa has stressed, following in this respect Pietro Piovani's excellent essay "Vico without Hegel," [5] we had better, before we think of Vico as an early Hegel, bear in mind the significant difference that in Vico, unlike Hegel, there is clear recognition of *deterioration* as a fixed phase of the process of change, one, moreover, brought about by the selfsame elements of reason which in the beginning had generated advancement. In this respect Vico is one with his beloved Greeks and Romans and their theories of the cycle. Furthermore, Vico's double-edged use of reason, or rationalism, is highly suggestive of the later use Weber would make in his own treatment of rationalization, its first positive function, its later destructive manifestations.

Finally, however troubling at times Vico's ideal eternal history may be for some of us, we cannot doubt that it rests upon, by design certainly, the comparative study of many peoples; it is the course that each and every people will travel in time as the result, Vico tells us, of common human nature reacting to recurrent challenges or circumstances: "The nature of things is based upon the fact that they come into being at certain times, in certain ways. Wherever the same circumstances are present, the same phenomena arise." I am reminded by Vico's statement, indeed by his whole approach, of the late Alexander Goldenweiser's "principle of limited possibilities." Given the nature of human beings, given the recurrent challenges of topography, climate, war, migration, need for food and security, etc., we are bound to find recurren responses to these challenges. A principle of limits is bound to prevail, thus making possible comparative history and, in Vico' sense, a science of history. And if one rests his eye, not upon th vast abstraction Mankind, but upon the concrete histories of actual peoples, decline and degeneration are as often to be seen as progress and advancement.

What Vico gives us, in striking contrast to the perspective contained in the mainline philosophy of progress that arose on Cartesian foundations in the late seventeenth and early eighteenth centuries, is the conception of human experience in time as a kind of storehouse or laboratory of data which become of value to us only insofar as we approach them with concrete questions in mind, and which are *not* amenable to arrangement, as Turgot, Comte, Hegel, Marx, Spencer, and so many others endeavored to arrange them, to reveal a *necessary* line of advancement of the whole of mankind, one reaching from the beginning of human culture all the way to some imagined condition in the distant future; the frank recognition of phenomena of decline and deterioration as well as of those of advancement and progress and the further recognition that decline is, on the evidence of history, just as probable in the future, if not actually certain, as advancement, and this holds true of knowledge as well as of social institutions; the immense importance Vico gives the role of ideas and of idea-systems underlying social structures and distinct historical ages, thus introducing a kind of continuing, wholly social *praxis* in human affairs; and, finally, Vico's recognition of the several configurations the process of change in time can assume, ranging from outright explosive advance or innovation, through sheer fixity or inertia, all the way to manifest decline and failure.

Overall is the unmistakable pluralism of Vico's contemplation of the world, society, and man. He disavowed monogenesis, as I have noted, and at the same time disavowed the unilinear in time, except insofar as his "ideal eternal history" fits this in its application to each and every nation or people. But, as Sir Isaiah Berlin emphasized in his 1960 essay on the philosophic ideas of Vico, this ideal eternal history "cannot, although it is metaphysically necessitated, be known a priori, but can be learnt only em-

pirically." [6]   That is, I believe, the central fact, the one that separates Vico utterly from the substance, the essence, of the idea of
progress as this idea is made manifest to us by the long line of
philosophers in the West stretching from Perrault and Fontenelle to the present day.

It may of course be said that Vico made providence serve where
others made progress the mainspring of history.   But I agree with
Pompa that the notion of transcendent providence can be eliminated from Vico's work without in any way damaging its principal
elements.   That cannot be said of the elimination of progress
from the works of the Condorcets, Comtes, and Spencers in the
mainline.   It is Vico, I think, more than anyone else prior to our
own century, who makes us so aware as we study the *New Science*
with its frank, nay joyful, acceptance of the pluralism and particularity of historical experience, how very much more than a
mere judgment of value the idea of progress actually is, or has
been, in the modern West.   It is its role as method, as perspective
as means of classifying and categorizing all human experience into
one, linear, and necessary unity that gives the idea of progress it
monumental importance in the rise and development of the social sciences.   For it was from the eighteenth century's vaunted
idea of progress that the nineteenth century's social evolution
social development, philosophy of history, and other crucial perspectives sprang.   It is not necessary to stress here the fact that
in no sense or degree did the nineteenth century's cherished theory
of social evolution emerge from the work of the biologists, Darwin
included.   The roots of the theory of social evolution are deep
in the whole Cartesian envisagement of reason, natural law, and
the force of "clear and simple ideas" that Vico was the first to attack, albeit impotently at the time.   In short, to repeat, the root
are deep in the idea of progress.

[6] Isaiah Berlin, "The Philosophical Ideas of G. B. Vico," in *Art and Ideas i
Eighteenth-Century Italy* (Rome: Edizioni di storia e letteratura, 1960), now ap
pearing in revised and longer form in Sir Isaiah's *Vico and Herder: Two Studie
in the History of Ideas* (New York: Viking Press, 1976).

I cannot close on a better note than a few lines from Croce's
History:

> It is a fact ... that there is in Vico's thought the most conspicuous
> and conscious opposition to Illuminism, which he studied, within
> the limits of his opportunities and functions, in its original aspects
> of natural law and Cartesianism and of polemical history based
> upon the ideals of modern European society and upon "clear and
> distinct ideas." In Vico we find all those aspects which intellectual
> rationalism abhorred as irrational; he promoted them first to the
> rank of special rational forms. . . .[7]

Vico's Influence on Eighteenth-Century European Culture: A Footnote to Professor Nisbet's Paper

I wish to call attention to some basic facts concerning the fortune of
Vico in Europe which, in my opinion, are likely to strengthen Pro-
fessor Nisbet's suggestion that Turgot may have been influenced by the
New Science.

The pivot of European culture in Vico's time was beyond any doubt
Paris. Was the *New Science* available to Parisian intellectuals? A
recent study has pointed out that a copy of the second edition of Vico's
masterpiece (printed in 1730) was in the library of a prominent physician and bibliophile of Paris, Camille Falconet, as can be gathered
from the *Catalogue de la bibliothèque de feu M. Falconet, Médecin
Consultant du Roi et Doyen des médecins de la Faculté de Paris* (Paris,
1763, II, p. 475, no. 19705). Falconet's library contained also the serial
in which Vico's *Autobiography* appeared (the *Raccolta d'opuscoli
scientifici e filologici*, edited by Father Angelo Calogerà). If one keeps
in mind that Falconet's house was the center of an intellectual gathering of freethinkers and antiquarians, and that Falconet's library was
a circulating one, since its owner was a generous lender of books to

---

[7] Benedetto Croce, *History As the Story of Liberty*, translated by Sylvia Sprigge
New York: Norton, 1941), p. 71.

needy intellectuals, one must admit that the *New Science* could not be an unknown work in Paris. From approximately 1732, when the book was acquired by Falconet, to 1762, when the bibliophile passed away, the *New Science* was within the reach of the Parisian *gens de lettres*. In fact, explicit references to Vico were made by Pierre-Nicolas Bonamy in a dissertation *Sur l'origine des loix des XII Tables*, read in 1735 at the Académie des Inscriptions, and by Antoine Terrasson in the *Histoire de la jurisprudence romaine*, published in 1750. In view of this, I believe that Professor Nisbet's suggestion of a Vichian influence on Turgot's sketch entitled *Researches into the Causes of the Progress and Decline of the Sciences and Arts* (1748) is perfectly legitimate.[1]

If attention is shifted from Paris to another important capital of eighteenth-century intellectual life, London, one must admit that Vico's name was not completely unknown there as well. In 1710, the *Memoirs of Literature* published a short review of the *De nostri temporis studiorum ratione*, borrowed from the *Journal des Savants*. A copy of the final edition of the *New Science* (1744) was in the library of a prominent London physician, Richard Mead, who received his doctorate from the University of Padua. In 1755, after Mead's death, this copy was sold for 6 shillings and 6 pence. The most important product of Vichian influence on eighteenth-century British culture was Thomas Blackwell's *Enquiry into the Life and Writings of Homer* (1735), which stimulated the intellectual activity of writers such as Warburton, Joseph and Thomas Warton, James Beattie, Monboddo, Gibbon, Hurd, Bodmer, Winckelmann, and Herder.[2]

Since I have just mentioned three writers belonging to the German-speaking world, I would like to conclude this *excursus* on Vico's fortunes in eighteenth-century Europe with a few words on the reception of Vichian ideas in Leipzig. In 1710, a periodical published by Gleditsch, the *Neuer Bücher-Saal der gelehrten Welt*, informed its readers that the *De antiquissima Italorum sapientia* was to appear in Naples. In 1751, a basic reference work, the *Allgemeines Gelehrten-Lexicon*, edited by Christian Gottlieb Jöcher, dedicated to Vico a detailed entry, founded on the *Autobiography*, in which the so-called "ideal eternal history" was explicitly mentioned. It may be interesting to note that the space allotted to Vico's biographical sketch is longer than the one

---

[1] See further my article "Vico, Camille Falconet e gli enciclopedisti," *Bollettino del centro di studi vichiani* 3 (1973): 147–162.

[2] See my article "Thomas Blackwell fra Gravina e Vico," *Bollettino del centro di studi vichiani* 5 (1975): 40–55.

allotted to entries dedicated to prominent European philosophers such as Spinoza, Locke, and Malebranche.[3]

In conclusion, factual evidence no longer allows us to be skeptical about Vico's influence on eighteenth-century European culture.

GUSTAVO COSTA

[3] See also my article "Vico, Johann Burckhard Mencke e Christian Gottlieb Jöcher," *Bollettino del centro di studi vichiani* 4 (1974): 143–148.

Vico and the Ideal of the Enlightenment

BY SIR ISAIAH BERLIN

My topic—the relationship of Vico's views to the notion of a perfect society—is not an issue central to Vico himself. He does not directly treat it, so far as I know, in any of his published works. But I hope to show that his central thesis is relevant to this ideal— one of the most persistent in the history of human thought—and indeed incompatible with it. It is one of the marks of writers of genius that what they say may, at times, touch a central nerve in the minds or feelings of men who belong to other times, cultures, or outlooks, and set up trains of thought and entail consequences which did not, or could not, occur to such writers, still less occupy their minds. This seems to me to be the case with regard to Vico's celebration of the power and beauty of primitive poetry, and the implications of this for the idea of progress in the arts, or culture, or the concept of an ideal society against which the imperfections of real societies can be assessed.

The concept of the perfect society is one of the oldest and most deeply pervasive elements in Western thought, wherever, indeed, the classical or Judaeo-Christian traditions are dominant. It has taken many forms—a Golden Age, a Garden of Eden in which men were innocent, happy, virtuous, peaceful, free, where everything was harmonious, and neither vice nor error nor violence nor misery were so much as thought of; where nature was bounteous and nothing was lacking, there was no conflict, and not even the passage of time affected the full, permanent, and complete satisfaction of all the needs, physical, mental, and spiritual, of the blessed dwellers in these regions. Then a catastrophe occurred which put an end to this condition; there are many variants of this—the Flood, man's first disobedience, original sin, the crime of Prometheus, the discovery of agriculture and metallurgy, primitive accumulation, and the like. Alternatively, the golden age was placed not in the beginning but in the end: in the millennial rule of the saints which will precede the Second Coming; or in life beyond the grave, in the Isles of the Blest, in Valhalla; or in the Paradise of the three monotheistic religions; Homer finds a semblance of earthly paradise on the isle of the Phaeacians, or among the blameless Ethiopians whom Zeus loved to visit. When the hold of myth and institutional religion weakened, secular, no longer wholly flawless, more human utopias began to succeed these—from the ideal communities of Plato, Crates, Zeno, Euhemerus, to Iambulus's Islands of the Sun, Plutarch's idealized Sparta, Atlantis, and the like. Whatever the origins of such visions, the conception itself rests on the conviction that there exist true, immutable, universal, timeless, objective values, valid for all men, everywhere, at all times; that these values are at least in principle realizable, whether or not human beings are, or have been, or ever will be, capable of realizing them on earth; that these values form a coherent system, a harmony which, conceived in social terms, constitutes the perfect state of society; that indeed, unless such perfection is at least conceivable, it is difficult or impossible to give sense to descriptions of existing states of affairs as imperfect; for the miseries, vices, and all the other shortcomings of existing human arrangements—cruelty, injustice, disease, scarcities, mental and physical torments, everything, indeed, that afflicts men—must be seen as so many fallings-short of the ideal or optimal state of affairs. How this optimum is to be attained is another question. But whether the answer is to be found in sacred texts, the visions of inspired prophets, institutionalized religion, metaphysical insights, or in more historically rooted social ideals, or the constellations of the simple human values of beings uncorrupted by destructive civilization, there is a common assumption which underlies all these conflicting doctrines: namely, that a perfect society is conceivable, whether it is an object of prayer and hope, a mere vision of unrealized and unrealizable human potentialities, a nostalgic sighing after a real or imaginary past, the final goal toward which history is inexorably marching, or a practical program which enough ability, energy, and moral clarity could in principle realize.

The neoclassicism of the Renaissance gave birth to a great revival of such visions of perfection. More and Patrizzi, Doni and Campanella, Christian utopians of the early seventeenth century, Francis Bacon, Harrington, Winstanley, Foigny, Fénelon, Swift, Defoe, mark only the beginning of such visions of society, which continued until comparatively recent times, when, for reasons that will be familiar to everyone, they suffered a considerable slump. The late seventeenth and early eighteenth centuries were singularly rich in such romances fed by fanciful accounts of the peace and harmony of primitive societies in America or elsewhere. All this is familiar enough. The principal point I wish to make is that not the least original attribute of the remarkable writer who is the subject of this conference is that in this instance, too, he took and independent line of his own and sailed his boat against the stream.

It might be said that since he felt himself to be a pious Christian, the temptation to construct a secular utopia was, in his case, not too strong: man cannot attain to perfection on this earth, the Kingdom of God is not of this world, man is weak and sinful, the attempt even to imagine a perfect kingdom on earth implies a denial of the irremediable finiteness of man and his works, even of the works of his mind and imagination. Yet Campanella was a monk and a Christian, whatever the Inquisition may have thought; so, indubitably, were Sir Thomas More, who died for his faith, and Samuel Gott, and Archbishop Fénelon, and the authors of *Antagil* and *Christianopolis,* and many others—but this did not seem to deter them from designing earthly utopias. Nor is there any emphasis in Vico's work on human impotence and wickedness; if anything, he stresses the opposite—man's magnificent creative capacities, which make him the instrument of Providence in trans-forming his social and cultural life. Nor is this all: there is the curious paradox of a faithful son of the Catholic Church who nevertheless advocates a cyclical theory of history, which seems to leave no room for the radical transformation of history, once and for all, by the incarnation and the resurrection of Christ, nor for the movement of history toward the single far-off divine event by which it is completed and transcended. To reconcile Vico's be-lief in *corsi* and *ricorsi* with Christian revelation has been (or should have been) a standing crux to his interpreters—greater, if anything, than the difficulty of fitting Plato's cyclical theory of suc-cessive social orders with his apparent belief in, at any rate, the theoretical possibility of an ideal state. Whatever the explanation in Plato's case, for Vico there can surely be no avenue to total fulfillment on earth: if no social structure can last, if collapse into the "barbarism of reflection" is inevitable before the new begin-ning, in the endless repetitive spiral of cultural development, the notion of a perfect society, which implies an unchanging, static order, seems automatically excluded. That, indeed, is perhaps why, for example, Polybius, who believes in cycles, offers no utopia. Nor does Machiavelli, who holds a similar view and predicts that even his neo-Roman state, which he regards as feasi-ble and not utopian, will not last. It is this doctrine, rather than the mounting empiricism of Vico's age, that seems to me to be a decisive antiutopian influence. For even if, like Bodin or Montesquieu, one pays due attention to the variety of human lives caused by differences in natural environment, climate, and so on, one can still suppose that every type of society is free to strive for, and certainly to conceive of, its own individual path to perfection. Moreover, Bodin and Montesquieu, while they main-tain that the means open to dissimilar societies may differ, seem to have no doubt about the universality, objectivity, immutability of ultimate values—peace, justice, happiness, rational organiza-tion, and, in Montesquieu's case, individual freedom to do what is right and avoid what is wrong. With Vico, matters are somewhat different. Let me try to explain why I believe this to be the case.

Vico is not essentially a relativist, though he has sometimes been called that. The world of primitive savages is utterly different from our own glorious age, but by means of an agonizing effort it is possible to enter the minds of those *grossi bestioni,* see or attempt to see the world with their eyes, and understand their *Weltanschauung,* their values, their motives, aims, categories, concepts. For Vico, to understand them and their world is to see their point, to grasp the way in which they necessarily belong to, and indeed express, a particular stage of social development, a stage which is the origin of our own condition, a phase of the creative process, to understand which is the only way to understand ourselves. Each epoch in Vico's *storia ideale eterna* is related by a species of social causation to both its predecessor and its successor in the great chain the links of which are connected in an unalterable, cyclical order. But whereas for those metaphysical thinkers who believe in progress nothing that is of permanent value need be lost irretrievably, for in some form it is preserved in the next higher stage; and whereas for those who contemplate the perfect society all ultimate values can be combined, like the pieces of a jigsaw puzzle, in the single, final solution, for Vico this cannot be so. For change—unavoidable change—rules all man's history, not determined by mechanical causes, as he thinks it is for the Stoics or Spinoza, nor due to chance, as it is for Epicurus and his modern followers. For it follows a divinely determined pattern of its own. But in the course of this process gains in one respect necessarily entail losses in another, losses which cannot be made good if the new values, which are part of the unalterable historical process, are, as indeed they must be, realized, each in its due season. If this is so, then some valuable forms of experience are doomed to disappearance, not always to be replaced by something necessarily more valuable than themselves. And this means that it must always be the case that some values are not compatible, historically compatible, with others, so that the notion of an order in which all true values are simultaneously present and harmonious with each other is ruled out, not on the ground of unrealizability due to human weakness or ignorance or other shortcomings (the overcoming of which could be at least imagined) but owing to the nature of reality itself.   This means that the idea of perfection is ruled out not so much for empirical reasons but because it is conceputally incoherent, not compatible with what we see history necessarily to be.

The Discovery of the True Homer

Let me give you the most vivid example of this in Vico's *New Science*. In the Third Book of the *New Science,* called "The Discovery of the True Homer," Vico declares that "the first men of the gentile nations, children of nascent mankind, created things according to their own ideas . . . by virtue of a wholly corporeal imagination. And because it was quite corporeal, they did it with marvelous sublimity; a sublimity such and so great that it excessively perturbed the very persons who by imagination did the creating, for which they were called 'poets,' which is Greek for 'creators.' " [1] And again: "The most sublime labor of poetry is to give sense and passion to insensate things," as children talk in play to inanimate things as if they were living persons.[2] For "in the world's childhood men were by nature sublime poets." [3] And again: "Imagination is more robust in proportion as reasoning power is weak." [4] Because men's senses were stronger when men were more brutish, since Providence gave these to them for physical self protection, and grew less so in the age of reflection

[1] He goes on to say that one of the labors "of great poetry is to invent sublime fables suited to the popular understanding." He then quotes Tacitus's *fingunt simul creduntque*—"no sooner imagine than they believe" (*The New Science of Giambattista Vico* [hereinafter *NS*], translated by Thomas G. Bergin and Max H. Fisch [Ithaca: Cornell University Press, 1968], par. 376).

[2] *NS*, par. 186.

[3] *NS*, par. 187.

[4] *NS*, par. 185.

—reflection which took the place of instinct—"the heroic descriptions, as we have them in Homer, are so luminously and splendidly clear, that all later poets have been unable to imitate them, to say nothing of equaling them." Yet the heroes of the age (toward the end of which Homer lived) are described by Vico as being "boorish, crude, harsh, wild, proud, difficult and obstinate." [5]

Vico has no illusions about either the Age of the Gods or that of the Heroes. He speaks of the practice of human sacrifice—by Phoenicians, Carthaginians, Gauls, Germans, American Indians, Scythians, in the golden age of Latium (Plautus's *Saturni hostiae*) —and remarks: "Such a mild, benign, sober, decent and well-behaved time was it!" [6] Such is man in "the innocence of the golden age!" [7] He does not doubt that it was this religious-Cyclopean authority,[8] based on terror, that was needed to create the first disciplined savage human societies.[9]

Then came the Heroes. The central figure of the heroic age is Achilles, the Achilles "who referred every right to the tip of his spear." [10] "This is the hero Homer sings of to the Greek peoples as an example of heroic virtue, and to whom he gives the fixed epithet 'blameless'!" [11] Vico compares this to the barbarian times of the *ricorso* (the age of medieval Christian chivalry) and the "vindictive satisfactions of the knights-errant of whom the romancers sing." [12] Such heroes are Brutus, who killed his sons; Scaevola, who burnt his hand; Manlius, who killed his children; Curtius, the Decii, Fabricius and the rest—"what did any of them do for the poor, unhappy Roman plebs?" [13] What they did, Vico tells us, was to ruin, rob, imprison, whip them. Anyone who tried to help the plebs—Manlius Capitolinus, or King

---

5 *NS*, pars. 707–708.
6 *NS*, par. 517.
7 *NS*, par. 518.
8 *NS*, par. 523.
9 *NS*, par. 518.
10 *NS*, par. 923.
11 *NS*, par. 667.
12 *NS*, par. 667.
13 *NS*, par. 668.

Agis in Sparta—was declared a traitor and killed. In these societies, according to Vico, there is no virtue, justice, mercy, but avarice, arrogance, inequality, cruelty. This is the heroic age, the age to which Homer belonged and which he celebrated. Heroic ages are times of "cruel laws," "supreme arrogance," "intolerable pride, profound avarice, pitiless cruelty": [14] "the haughty, avaricious and cruel practice of the nobles toward the plebeians which we see clearly portrayed in Roman history." [15]

Vico notes that "Scaliger is indignant at finding almost all Homer's comparisons to be drawn from beasts and other savage things," but this is part of his poetic genius. "To attain such success in them—for his comparisons are incomparable—is certainly not characteristic of a mind chastened and civilized by any kind of philosophy. Nor could the savage and truculent style in which he describes so many, such varied and such bloody battles, so many and such extravagantly cruel kinds of butchery as make up all the sublimity of the *Iliad* in particular, have originated in a mind touched and humanized by any philosophy." [16] Yet this barbarian poet made it difficult, according to Horace, to invent any new characters after him.[17] This is so because, Vico declares, "Homer, who preceded philosophy and the poetic and critical arts, was yet the most sublime of all the sublime poets," so that after the invention of philosophies and of the arts of poetry and criticism, there was no poet who could come within a long distance of competing with him. The sentiments and "the modes of speech" and actions of such sublime natures can be "wild, crude and terrible," and this can be produced only in a heroic age—at the end of one of which the Homeric poems were created; later this is no longer possible.[18]

According to Vico, this is so because this kind of sublimity is inseparable from being "sprung from the people." Homer's poetic

14 *NS*, par. 38.
15 *NS*, par. 272.
16 *NS*, par. 785.
17 *NS*, par. 806.
18 *NS*, pars. 807–808.

characters are "imaginative universals" to which all the attributes of a genus are attributed. They are generic types (not altogether dissimilar from Weber's ideal types), so that to these men Achilles *is* heroic valor, quick temper, pride, honor, and liability to anger and violence, right as might; Ulysses *is* heroic wisdom—wariness, patience, dissimulation, deception, duplicity.[19] Once true concepts—abstract universals—are created by the civilized reason and not the imagination of an entire society, this kind of sublimity comes to an end. This is so because, before writing is invented, men possess "vivid sensation," "strong imagination," "sharp wit," "robust memory," which they later lose.[20]

Homer is "the father and prince of all sublime poets." [21] He is "celestially sublime," possesses a "burning imagination." [22] "The frightfulness of Homeric battles and deaths gives to the Iliad all its marvelousness." [23] This could not have sprung from "a calm, cultivated, and gentle philosopher." [24] This is what makes Homer the greatest of poets for Vico. It is this that makes him a master of "wild and savage comparisons," [25] or "cruel and fearful descriptions of battles and deaths" [26] and "sentences filled with sublime passions," [27] with "expressiveness and splendor of style" impossible in the ages of philosophy, criticism, poetry as a civilized art, which came later.[28]

Vico's central point is that poetic feeling, which "plunges deep into particulars," cannot exist when men think in concepts: inspired singers, of whom Homer is the greatest, cannot coexist with philosophers. Whatever these later, milder, more rational times— the age of men—may create, namely, the arts and sciences of

19 *NS*, par. 809.
20 *NS*, par. 819.
21 *NS*, par. 823.
22 *NS*, par. 825.
23 *NS*, par. 827.
24 *NS*, par. 828.
25 *NS*, par. 893.
26 *NS*, par. 894.
27 *NS*, par. 895.
28 *NS*, pars. 896–897.

elaborate civilizations, they cannot give us within the same "cycle" "burning imagination" or "celestial sublimity." This has vanished. We can realize the splendor of this primitive poetry only by understanding the "wild, crude, and terrible" world from which it springs, we can do this only if we abandon the idea of the artistic superiority of "our own magnificent times."

All this was composed at a time when one of the dominant aesthetic theories was still that of timeless and objective criteria of excellence in the arts, in morality, in every other normative sphere. Some critics believed in steady progress in the arts, based on growth in rationality and the gradual elimination of the savage world of myth and fable and primitive unbridled imagination, the dark and brutal age which we have left behind us. There were also those who believed that classical poetry, and especially Roman, was superior to that of the moderns. In both cases, it was assumed without much question that there existed a single, timeless standard of judgment whereby some thought that they could demonstrate the superiority of, say, Racine or Addison to Milton or Shakespeare or Homer, while others believed that they could demonstrate that Sophocles or Virgil were greater poets than any poet of a later age. A corollary of this was that the quality, the degree of excellence, of an art was part and parcel of the general quality of an age and its culture. For Voltaire or Fontenelle, the art or poetry of classical Athens or Rome, or Renaissance Florence, or France under Louis XIV, were magnificent, inasmuch as they were produced by and for enlightened men like themselves, in contrast with the ages of ignorance, fanaticism, barbarism, persecution, the art of which was as degraded as the societies in which a few savage captains quarreled with a handful of fanatical bishops for control over a collection of idiotic serfs (to use Voltaire's summary of early medieval Europe).

Vico's position was radically different from this and a harbinger of things to come. He does not deny the cruelty, avarice, arrogance, inhumanity of the master class of the "heroic" ages. But a certain kind of sublime art can spring only from such soil.

Clearly, an age in which there is a recognized standard of justice for all men, in which human sacrifice is not practiced and rational methods of uncovering the facts of the past have superseded myth and legend, is in certain obvious respects superior to a culture in which Agamemnon causes his daughter to be slaughtered as an offering to the goddess, or men see the sky as a huge, animate body whose anger is expressed in thunder and lightning. But the increase in humanity and knowledge (which means the peak of a, cycle) is inevitably accompanied by a loss of primitive vigor, directness, imaginative force, beyond any made possible by the development of the critical intellect. Each succeeding age develops its own unique mode of expression, which is repeated, with perhaps some variation, at the corresponding stage of each successive cycle of the "ideal eternal history." There is no need to compare and grade on some single scale of merit each cultural phase and its creations and forms of life and action; indeed, it is not possible to do so, for they are evidently incommensurable. Nevertheless, the children of one culture can attain to an understanding of the life and activity—the thought, behavior, art, religion, the entire vision of life—of another culture, of what our ancestors could create while we cannot, because they were what they were, and we are what we are, occupying, as we do, different segments of the same cycle. This is not relativism, for we are able not merely to record but to understand the outlooks of other societies, however imperfectly, without assimilating them to our own; nor is it the old absolutism whereby we can pronounce their works to be superior or inferior to each other, or to our own, by the use of some unaltering criterion valid for all men, everywhere, at all times. But if this is so, then the very notion of a harmonious synthesis in one perfect whole of all that is best is not so much attainable or unattainable (even in principle) as unintelligible. The unparalleled power of the imagination in the early ages cannot, conceptually cannot, be combined with a developed critical capacity, philosophical or scientific knowledge, depth of intellectual analysis. It is absurd to ask whether Aeschylus's *Agamemnon* is a better or worse play than *King Lear*. When (I think) Shaw spoke of the

Ninth Symphony of Beethoven as being profounder than anything in the Bible, he uttered (if Vico is right) a proposition which was neither true nor false but one that, on examination, turns out to be senseless. To a disciple of Vico, the ideal of some of the thinkers of the Enlightenment, the notion of even the abstract possibility of a perfect society, is necessarily an attempt to weld together incompatible attributes—characteristics, ideals, gifts, properties, values that belong to different patterns of thought, action, life, and therefore cannot be detached and sewn together into one garment. For a Vichian this notion must be literally absurd: absurd because there is a conceptual clash between, let us say, what gives splendor to Achilles and what causes Socrates or Michelangelo or Spinoza or Mozart or the Buddha to be admired; and since this applies to the respective cultures, in the context of which alone men's achievements can be understood and judged, this fact alone makes this particular dream of the Enlightenment incoherent. The skepticism or pessimism of a good many thinkers of the Enlightenment—Voltaire, Hume, Gibbon, Grimm, Rousseau—about the possibility of realizing this condition is beside the point. The point is that even they were animated by a conception of ideal possibilities, however unattainable in practice. In this, at least, they seem to be at one with the more optimistic Turgot and Condorcet. After Vico, the conflict of monism and pluralism, timeless values and historicism, was bound sooner or later to become a central issue. If Vico had done no more than raise it, indirectly yet at its profoundest level, in his seminal chapter on "The Discovery of the True Homer," this alone should have been sufficient to reveal the power and originality of this thought.

The Workings of Providence

I should like to add a brief note on another notion in Vico, at once central to his thought and relevant to the ideal of a perfect society—his idea of Providence. It has been compared both to Hegel's "cunning of reason" (or of history) and to Adam Smith's "hidden hand," but it differs from both. It is true that in Vico Providence preserves and improves human societies by means of the unintended consequences of the operation of human passions and desires, and especially of human vices, which it turns to good account into social virtues in a fashion not unlike that described in Mandeville's *Fable of the Bees*. Like Hegel, he conceives human passions and desires and needs (Vico stressed particularly class conflict) as the dynamic force which generates social change—this is the stuff which is "used" in Hegel by the Idea, in Vico by Providence, to compass its ends. But in Hegel the cunning of reason leads, at least in theory, to an ulti-mate goal, when the Idea has become fully conscious of itself (how-ever this is interpreted, whether as an attainable culmination of the cosmic process or as an asymptotic approach to a consumma-tion destined never to be reached), while Smith's "hidden hand" guarantees the harmony and felicific results generated by the ac-tivities of individuals motivated solely by rational self-interest. In Vico's vision of history, men seek, not necessarily by rational meth-ods or from rational motives, to satisfy wants created by basic "drives"—by fear, ambition, shame, awe, desire for security, for survival, the need to understand, express, communicate, dominate, obey, worship, love, hate; and the creative activities originated thereby serve to create social tensions which transform their lives, ideas, and themselves and so create new forms of social life—a view later richly developed by Saint-Simon, Marx, and their followers. But for Vico this process is a succession of phases in the life of each separate culture, sometimes developing upward to peaks of strength and splendor, at other times declining to the loss of hu-man solidarity, the alienation of individuals and groups, disinte-gration of the social texture, weakness, decadence, collapse. An identical order of stages is determined by Providence for each "gentile" society, but no final goal; there is no vision of the march of mankind toward final perfection, whether inspired by a conscious realization of it (as the more optimistic *philosophes* hoped was the case) or driven by hidden but beneficent forces. Such a conception of progress, whether "linear" or "dialectical," would, for Vico, in the first place, be incompatible with his view of the eternal cycles of history; and, in the second place, would constitute the usurpation of the role of Providence as he conceives it. If the attempt to prove the existence of God is, for him, absurd and blasphemous because all proof is creation, and to prove the existence of God is to create the very God whose existence one is purporting to demonstrate, then it must follow that to attempt to *demonstrate* by logical or metaphysical argument the nature of the far-off divine event, the new heaven and the new earth, the end of human history, is to claim to be able to construct by human means what God alone can create. For Vico, as a Christian, this can only be a matter of faith, not (even finite) reason: the beneficent ways of Providence may be observed, described, believed in, but not demonstrated, without making man, not (man-made) Providence, the sole creative force in the universe. Human history, or at least its most general characteristics, may for Vico be philosophically demonstrable, because creative human activity is the providentially ordained agency which causes societies to rise or fall; but its ultimate purpose must lie beyond human control, or, indeed, reason; else the purposes of God would be man-made. It seems to me that this marks a decisive difference between Vico's position and that of Hegel and his followers of all schools, from Absolute Idealists to Marxists and materialists whose theodicy or philosophy of history denies transcendence, that is, any impassable gulf between matter and spirit, between God and the world. And while, admittedly, Vico's conception of Providence is not among the clearest of his basic notions, whether in the *New Science* or his other writings, it is incompatible with any attempt to dissolve it into an intelligible teleology—the unalterable march toward the final, universal goal, the solution of all the problems of which "it is and knows itself to be the solution," whether as this was conceived by the *philosophes* of the eighteenth century, or by the Idealist metaphysicians or utopian socialists of the nineteenth, or by the neo-Hegelians of our own "glorious times."

Notes on Contributors

Sir Isaiah Berlin
is Fellow of all Souls College, Oxford, and President of the British Academy. His most recent book is *Vico and Herder: Two Studies in the History of Ideas* (1976).

Gustavo Costa
is Professor and Chairman of the Department of Italian at the University of California, Berkeley. His most recent book is *La leggenda dei secoli d'oro nella letteratura italiana* (1972).

Max H. Fisch
is Adjunct Professor of Philosophy at Indiana University-Purdue University in Indianapolis, where he is directing the Peirce Edition Project. With Thomas G. Bergin, he is the translator of Vico's *New Science* and *Autobiography*.

Ernesto Grassi
is Professor and Director of the Centro italiano di studi umanistici e filosofici at the University of Munich. His most recent book is *Humanismus und Marxismus* (1973).

B. A. Haddock
is Lecturer in Political Theory and Government at University College in Swansea, Wales.

Robert Welsh Jordan
is Assistant Professor of Philosophy at Colorado State University, Fort Collins.

Donald R. Kelley
is Professor of History at the University of Rochester. His most recent book is *François Hotman: A Revolutionary's Ordeal* (1973).

John Michael Krois
is Assistant Professor of Philosophy at the Technical University of Braunschweig, West Germany.

Ernan McMullin
is Professor of Philosophy at Notre Dame University. He edited *The Concept of Matter in Modern Philosophy* (1976)

Michael Mooney
is Special Assistant to the Executive Vice President for Academic Affairs at Columbia University and Associate Director of the Institute for Vico Studies, New York.

Robert Nisbet
is Albert Schweitzer Professor in the Humanities at Columbia University. His most recent book is *Sociology as an Art Form* (1976).

Leon Pompa
is Lecturer in Philosophy at the University of Edinburgh. He is the author of *Vico: A Study of the New Science* (1975)

Lionel Rubinoff
is Professor of Philosophy and Chairman of the Academic Board of Julian Blackborn College, Trent University, Peterborough, Ontario. He is the author of *Collingwood and the Reform of Metaphysics* (1970).

Giorgio Tagliacozzo
is Director of the Institute for Vico Studies, New York. With Donald Phillip Verene he edited *Giambattista Vico's Science of Humanity* (1976).

Howard Tuttle
is Associate Professor and Chairman of the Department of Philosophy at the University of New Mexico, Albuquerque. He wrote *Wilhelm Dilthey's Philosophy of Historical Understanding* (1969).

Donald Phillip Verene
is Associate Professor of Philosophy at Pennsylvania State University. With Giorgio Tagliacozzo he edited *Giambattista Vico's Science of Humanity* (1976).

VICO AND CONTEMPORARY THOUGHT—2

Table of Contents

Developmental Psychology and Vico's Concept of Universal History

BY SHELDON H. WHITE

DEVELOPMENTAL psychologists have repeatedly linked the growth of the child's mind with growth processes in history. Jean Piaget argues for a resemblance between the cognitive development of the child and the movement of the history of science. Heinz Werner has argued that there are many cross-correspondences between the thinking of younger versus older children as compared with the thought of primitive versus advanced societies and thus, by implication, that the advancing thought of the young child recapitulates an advancement sequence in the history of culture. At the turn of this century, G. Stanley Hall exuberantly pursued the notion of recapitulationisms governing child development, cultural development, and evolution. It is interesting that the point has failed to carry. Developmental psychologists today remain generally uninterested in the argument. For that matter, many developmental psychologists today remain unconvinced by only a portion of that argument, one much closer to home, the claim that there is a universal history governing children's cognitive development.

Individual Development and Cultural Evolution

Yet one remains curious about this peculiar pattern of theoretical investment. Before the twentieth century we do not find counterparts of our modern developmental psychologists. But we find, still, writings that propose such far-reaching and all-embracing universal processes of development that one must regard them as ancestral to the twentieth-century arguments. Herbert Spencer proposes a Development Hypothesis under which he assumes that a common kind of movement through time governs change in geology, phylogeny, the history of nations, the history of mind, and almost everything else. Behind Spencer there is Hegel, with his universal history governing the growth of human sociality toward Reason, God, the state, and freedom—the four taken as, somehow, the same thing. And then, behind Hegel, there is Giambattista Vico, in whose writings, once again explicitly, the argument is made that there is a linkage between the growth of the thought of the child and the development process governing the universal history of human societies.

One cannot conscientiously evade this pattern of distinguished sponsorship of an idea. The most modern and most limited form of the idea is Piaget's claim that the social construction of reality in science resembles the construction of reality in the mind of the child. I find that if one pursues this idea, and if one looks for such resemblances, they seem to be there. But Piaget is essentially arguing that an individual process of knowledge-gathering ought to show some resemblances to a communal process of knowledge-gathering, and perhaps this is not a very startling kind of resemblance. What of the larger claim?

There is one predominant reason why the more modern protagonists of the idea have been discounted. Their analyses of culture and history have been forced. Hall, Werner, and Spencer assumed that one could easily arrive at an ordering of human cultures from the most primitive to the most advanced. They did so using an outlook that we would today characterize as elitist and notions about diverse cultures that we would today regard as beneath the consideration of serious ethnographers. Indeed Hegel, after he writes the systematic preface to his *Philosophy of History*, launches into a characterization of the societies of the world that one can only fairly describe as an essay in ethnocentric bigotry. So one is tempted to dismiss the idea as one of those forced contrivances of the oversystematic mind, chance resemblances forced together to create an overarching metaphor, a kind of ratiocinative poetry transmitted from one systematist to another in the last several centuries. One could easily dismiss this persistent line of argument as a peculiar infusion into modern thought of what Vico would call the "conceit of nations."

But what gives one pause is the extraordinary degree of contemporary validity of these writers and their ideas. Generally, the trend of modern thought is toward a reaffirmation of much that they had to say. After Heinz Werner wrote his treatment of comparative developmental psychology, he proceeded, with Bernard Kaplan, to write a curiously prophetic treatment of symbol formation. The book did not have much apparent impact a decade ago, but now we find that the drift of current analyses of cognitive development is toward a more and more serious consideration of symbol formation as the primary nexus of cognitive growth. G. Stanley Hall's exuberant recapitulationism and evolutionism have long been discounted. But today there are significant writings in ethology and sociobiology that are quite in line with his ideas. His ideas reemerge in contemporary writings, clothed in evidence, and there is again the attempt to link the development of the child with evolutionary processes. Recapitulationism, neotony, and pedomorphism are live issues. I believe that Herbert Spencer's writings, translated into modern lingo and salted and peppered with up-to-date footnotes, might serve as a (much needed) modern psychological textbook in which the current analyses of information-processing and genetic epistemology are brought into theoretical alignment.

And, finally, there is Hegel. There is no need for me to argue that we are today revisiting Hegel, because the revival of Hegel is now proclaimed on all sides. The modern psychologist who revisits Hegel is surprised and intrigued. In his writings he finds embryonic fragments of Freud, Piaget, Marx, modern doctrines of the unconscious and of consciousness-raising, phenomenological writings, Harry Stack Sullivan's theory of anxiety, evolutionism, progressivism all jumbled and juxtaposed in the most interesting ways. So one considers again the claim of these varied sources that the development of the child is tied in with universal history.

Vico and the Developmentalists

Vico's treatment of the claim is older. It rests on different grounds and comes out of a somewhat different scholarly tradition. The, most important difference between his treatment and those succeeding is that he divorces the argument from other arguments having to do with the validity of rationalism as a basic analysis of human epistemology. All of the modern lineage of developmentalists, Piaget not excluded, appear to be rationalists. They mix the claim that the world is known through constructive acts of the mind, this claim ines capably true, with another claim that the highest and mos sophisticated knowledge humans have of the world come through reason, this claim somewhat more problematic. Vic argues that human knowledge of the world arises in the imag inative, the poetic, and the intuitive faculties, and that highe forms of thought seem to reconstitute these properties. Vic too, speaks of the highest forms of human thought as consti tuted in reason, the *certum*, but in the context of his othe arguments one must see his reason as not of the same stuff as, say, formal operations.

I am not a Vico scholar and so I propose in the rest of this paper to develop some arguments that might lead one to relate the development of the child to some aspects of human history. Some of these arguments are common to Vico and other developmentalists, but one seems to be unique to Vico and an important insight for the modern treatment of developmental psychology. It is easiest for me to convey these arguments in my own terms without going through the apparatus of scholarship necessary to link them directly with passages in his writings. Let me say only that these were arguments that arose in my mind as I read his writings and those of explanatory commentators; I give them as they appear in my reason.

1. *Things which remain the same but change have some significant common properties.*

Not only Vico, but all developmentalists, may be regarded as having recognized some issues in what we today call systems analysis. When Spencer and Werner apply a uniform notion of development across a rather astonishing range of phenomena, they are in fact recognizing an issue that a contemporary engineer might put as one of "control systems analysis." Bernard Kaplan, in his "Meditations on Genesis," argues that the developmental processes one finds in childhood transcend the processes of age change and have some more general applicability. But, in fact, the notion of development does not particularly originate in the phenomena of childhood. It arises wherever and whenever we find an organization that retains its integrity as an organization—that is called by the same name and seems to persist in the same functions—even as it undergoes modification. In this sense, "development" may be a property of an enlarging business corporation, a nervous or circulatory system that undergoes modification in evolution, or the mental processes of a child.

There are peculiar constraints on the changes an organization can undergo if we insist that all functions be retained during change. Consider an infant. We think of an infant as helpless, but an infant does a surprising number of complicated things to keep itself alive. It breathes. It regulates oxygen. It ingests and excretes. It regulates its own pH level and a surprising number of other parameters of metabolism. It even has a simple repertoire of behaviors, perhaps behavior systems designed to elicit caretaking behavior, perhaps behavior systems designed to bring about learning and intellectual development. The infant is a viable organism. One of its problems is to grow and change without dying in the process. It must change conservatively.

Consider, as an analogy, a rather trivial example. We have a car with a windshield wiper and we wish to install a new and better windshield wiper, but we are bound by the rule that we must always at every instant in time have a functioning windshield wiper. We cannot take out the windshield wiper and put in a new one because this would, in our analogy, lead to "death." So we would contrive to put a new windshield wiper function on the car in some rather complicated ways. We might install a secondary windshield wiper, operating to extend the action of the first, to cover functions the first does not cover. But this secondary wiper operates independently of the first. Or we might install a whole new windshield wiper, better than the first, but leave it inoperative until it is fully installed. Then, appropriate wiring might contain an "inhibit" of the older so that, at the exact instant the new system begins to function, the older one ceases. Either of these higher-order inventions would have an interesting conservative property. If there was something defective about our new installation, or if it ever failed, the system would "regress" to first-order, more primitive function and the essential property of windshield wiping would be preserved.

One finds hierarchical arrangements exactly like those of our fanciful example in the evolutionary design of the brain

And one imagines that one finds them in the progressive elaboration of the child's thought. I believe that the well-known maxim of Spencer and Werner that development proceeds by differentiation and hierarchical integration represents a superficial and somewhat misleading account of the necessities induced by function-preserving change. But all of the avid developmentalists have, I believe, recognized the force of the issue.

2. *Social systems reconstitute individual principles or motives, but in so doing they engage different human motives.*

A second kind of systems analytic argument is rather different, and it has to do with the differences that occur when individuals versus groups of individuals attempt to execute the same function. This argument arises quite clearly in Vico when he discusses the functions of law, but it seems implicit in the writings of other authors and it seems to be by no means restricted to law.

Certain properties of human action are socially desirable and necessary. Take the human ability to be just or to be curious. Societies need those abilities. A simple society works well only if there is a king who is just, who can settle disputes evenhandedly, who can enforce the laws fairly. And that simple society is better off if it contains individuals who are curious, who explore and invent, and who create new knowledge and new technology so that the society can better adapt to its circumstances.

Truly just or curious individuals are in relatively short supply, so sooner or later societies tend to bureaucratize those functions. They constitute social subgroupings to recreate justice and curiosity. The first, justice, is recreated by the system of courts and the legal profession. The second, curiosity, is recreated by institutions for research and development, both within and without the university. These social recreations are not ideal, in part because they emerge developmentally. Old systems are permuted or extended, always retaining function, until gradually newer systems controlling these functions are installed. It is characteristic of our courts and our universities that they retain archaisms and that they are not fully expressive of what a rational man might design if he had the option of designing them *de novo*. But we are here not interested in the conservative features of their design as much as their relatively radical features.

Courts are designed to serve justice but, as people are endlessly fond of pointing out, it is hard to find just men in them. The court's activity is grounded on the adversary system, one lawyer engaged in verbal combat with another. The judge adjudicates their argument, but his function is not left at the mercy of his sense of justice. He is bound by the strictures of procedure and precedent, and by an appeals court system which in a very real sense is designed to "keep him honest." It is an irony of the modern legal system that men with a strong sense of justice—or, rather, men with *only* a strong sense of justice—probably do not do well in it. One needs to be combative. One needs strong legal scholarship, or else the managerial ability to deploy strong legal scholarship. So the individual must be gifted and motivated in quite different ways if he is to participate in a bureaucratic system for creating justice.

Exactly the same kind of argument might be elaborated with respect to our modern bureaucratic system for research and development. If we examine the life of one of the most relentlessly curious and eccentric individuals of modern times, Sir Francis Galton, it is hard to imagine him surviving and flourishing in an environment of publish-or-perish, research grants and contracts, committees, and the sea of distractions and side issues that exist for research workers in modern universities. One does find relentlessly intellectual and bureaucratically inept individuals within the modern university surviving and even cherished by their colleagues. Things are not always quite as fierce within the bureaucracy as Vico makes out. But his point is well taken. Social systems establish a principle or motive of the whole that is often quite differen in kind from the principles that are necessary to the individuals who constitute those systems.

3. *Social systems reconstitute human knowledge-gathering. In so doing they extend the human* umwelt.

The third argument to be offered here is not particularly Vico's. It is a strong feature of the other developmental arguments I am considering here and will assist, ultimately, in our consideration of the child.

Spencer made a strong case for the rise of intelligence during the course of evolution. His intelligence was not the intelligence we are familiar with in modern days, the intelligence that the intelligence test tests, but a more abstract entity akin to Piaget's intelligence or Von Uexkull's *umwelt*. In this sense, the term refers to the scope of human understanding rather than its power. The intelligence of Spencer is sentience, breadth of awareness of the world, not computational or analytic ability.

Spencer arranged the evolutionary order of creatures in the homocentric way that the nineteenth century was fond of contemplating, all creatures of the earth arranged on a linear great chain of being that culminates in man. When one does this, the grand sequence of evolution is posed as a quest for intelligence. Nature has striven for more and more of it and Man is her finest flower. But a less grandiose version of the argument is possible. One finds it in Harry Jerison's recent book, *Evolution of the Brain and Intelligence*, or summarized in his recent *Scientific American* article, "Paleoneurology and the Evolution of Mind." Suppose we explore the consequences of an evolutionary expansion of brain mass, considering it as a specialization or a line of development in evolution and disregarding the question of a Grand Plan. We can fairly conclude that such an expansion leads to an expansion of *umwelt*, awareness, sentience, intelligence.

With Jerison's perspective, one can then take Herbert Spencer's all-important next step without falling into the pitfalls of Social Darwinism. One can now argue that cultures reconstitute intelligence by bureaucratic devices. Perception of the world is enlarged by technologies—the microscope, the space capsule, radio-carbon dating. Pooled perceptions are created by merging the observations of individuals through the reconciliatory mechanisms of discourse, media, scholarship, and science. A social *umwelt* arises and in this *umwelt* one looks back and forth across a billion years of time, one knows the shape of a molecule, one senses radiation, one studies the pattern of the raindrop. We reachieve the Spencerian synthesis. Culture extends a specialization in evolution, sentience, by a transposition from brain and sensory knowingness to a bureaucratized knowingness.

4. *The cultural* umwelt *is a collective act of imagination, regulated by reason but not composed of reason.*

Please notice that I have conducted my talk thus far with the aid of some imaginary playmates called Vico, Hegel, Spencer, Hall, Werner, and Piaget. I have never seen any of them, although for all practical purposes I treat them as flesh and blood, as real as anyone I have seen but transposed across lines of time and space that are, themselves, creatures of imagination. We live in a scientific world which is abundant with legends, myths, fantasies, and the unseen. For that matter, our nonscientific culture abounds in the legendary, including (for me) Akron, Ohio, the dollar crunch, mugging, etc. We readily mix perceived, conceived, and received terms in the play of our minds, as convinced of the reality of the remote and contrived as we are of the near and simple. We are emotional about the unreal, feel delight or anger or fear about fantasy events as readily as we do about the seen and the directly experienced.

How does this unreal world come to be so real? Jerome Singer and his associates have studied the development of make-believe play in children, arguing that at about 6 or 7 such play tends to cease, goes underground so to speak to become reexpressed in adult daydreaming and fantasy. Perhaps the imagination of the young child reemerges in some more central facets of human thought. Perhaps it emerges in socially given knowledge of the unseen, in what Vygotsky would call "scientific concepts," concepts not given to the child out of his own experience but transmitted by others. The child receives knowledge about people, places, dimensions, and schematizations. He grasps that knowledge by regulated acts of imagination.

The poetry and the fantasy of childhood live on in adulthood, reconstituted in the individual's participation in the social construction of reality. Society creates regulated acts of imagination, demanding not that the unseen be dismissed from human experience but that the unseen is permissible only within acceptable frameworks of justification, verification, and inference. This regulatory apparatus we generally characterize as "reason," but reason, logic, formal operations are not the stuff of thought. They are to thought what the adversary system is to law, not the stuff of justice but the mechanism by which justice is recreated in the midst of a social framework. So reason extends and directs the child's thought, allows it to tease out the objective (the intersubjective) aspects of its experience, allows the conceived to be extrapolated from the perceived and ultimately to stand beside it. Not all those extensions that reason permits to the mind are social in origin or intent, but most of them are. For the most part the cognitive development of the older child is an aspect of social development, the private *umwelt* merging into the social.

5. *Generally, the child begins life with private knowledge, thought, systems of inquiry, and motives. To develop, the child must advance in an orderly fashion into the social reconstitutions of its society. In this sequence from private to public knowingness, grossly, the sequences of childhood and human history are alike.*

Why have so many argued for likeness between the development of the mind of the child and the presumed developmental forces of human history?

(a) They have seen that the development of the child must

take place through a process of function-preserving change, and they have seen that, over the course of historical time, important social institutions tend to undergo function-preserving change. From a systems-analytic view, certain diagrammatic features of these change processes may be identical.

(b) They have seen that in history social control principles vested in the function of individuals tend to evolve toward bureaucratic recreations in which the same basic social control principles are now vested in groups of individuals. Committees do things that, once, individuals used to do. With regard to such groups, the motive or control principle of the whole is not a full specification of the motives necessary for individuals who are members. Lawyers need qualities other than a sense of justice; researchers need qualities other than curiosity.

(c) They have seen that one line of evolutionary specialization, the line that goes toward humans, involves an enlargement of *umwelt* or intelligence. And they have seen that human culture bureaucratizes and extends the growth of this specialty, cultural adaptation extending an evolutionary adaptation. It seems worth noting, again, that this is not an argument about the intelligence that the intelligence test tests but a systems-analytic argument about the growth of knowingness over time. And it also seems worth noting that this argument does not imply a universal history of cognitive development. Different cultures may well extend the evolutionary *umwelt* in different ways, toward different realms of possible experience, and all these bureaucratic extensions may validly be considered to be extensions of intelligence. The principle can hold without in any way implying a monolithic great chain of being for species, for societies, or for human cognitive development.

(d) Some, like Vico, have seen that the social reconstitution of intelligence involves not the suppression of human imagination and poetry but its regulation. The child mixes the perceived and the conceived in make-believe play and then later, in daydreaming. But the serious and scientific though of the adult is no less metaphoric. The child's thought at older ages becomes regulated by reason, as we say. We make a mistake if we take this to mean that the child cannot conceptualize, induce, deduce, or infer in the early years of life. What we really are implying is that the child begins to learn those devices by which he separates out of his own experience those parts that are "objective," knowable by all. The child learns symbol systems and procedures by which he enters into the cultural dialectic that perpetuates and extends the social *umwelt*. In this special, social sense the child's thought becomes reasonable.

(e) And, finally, all have seen that the child begins life with private experience and private knowledge and in the course of its cognitive development in some general way retraverses the paths once taken by its culture in historical time from private to public systems of control, not only in intellectual matters but also in other aspects of human sociality as well. There is no reason to argue for exact recapitulation in human development, but there seem to be many and sound reasons arguing for a gross analogy between childhood and history, a gross recapitulation.

Vico, Developmental Psychology, and Human Nature*

BY AUGUSTO BLASI

THIS New Science or metaphysic, studying the common nature of nations in the light of divine providence, discovers the origins of divine and human institutions."[1] These words, by which Vico summarizes the intent of his own work, also suggest certain fundamental similarities and differences between Vico and developmental psychology. Like Vico, developmental psychology is also concerned with origins and progress and attempts to bring into relief that which is common and universal. Vico is interested in institutions and societies, while developmental psychology focuses primarily on individuals; this difference, however, is not basic, as Vico does not separate human development, viewed historically, from the development of societies. The crucial difference is indicated by the words "in the light of divine providence." When Vico's concept of providence is stripped of its religious connotations, it reveals certain basic assumptions about human nature and development that are quite different and even incompatible with the assumptions, often implicit, of contemporary developmental psychology and of social sciences in general.

It is my intention, in this essay, to center the comparison between Vico and developmental psychology on their respective understandings of human nature by analyzing their constitutive elements and by uncovering their implications. One

[1] *The New Science of Giambattista Vico* (hereinafter *NS*), translated by Thomas G. Bergin and Max H. Fisch (Ithaca: Cornell University Press, 1968), par. 31.

point I intend to make in this context is that some important work being done within developmental psychology cannot really be integrated into the broader conceptual framework that is common to the social sciences. The discussion around human nature will be the second part of the present essay; in the first part, I will draw a parallel between Vico's *New Science* and Lawrence Kohlberg's empirical and theoretical work on the development of moral thinking. In a way, this comparison between Kohlberg and Vico will serve a preliminary function: it will help me to make more concrete the objectives, the hypotheses, and the findings of one area in developmental psychology; it will facilitate extracting what I believe to be the central characteristics of the general field; finally, by showing how close the similarities are between Vico's historico-philosophical ideas and some of the concepts and empirical descriptions of developmental psychology, it will establish Vico's relevance and his right to enter into a dialogue with contemporary psychology.

Throughout this essay, I will try to maintain the perspective of a developmental psychologist in dialogue with other psychologists, emphasizing what appears to be inconsistent or inadequate in our own work. Vico's theory will be looked at with the purpose of finding there new insights and new ideas which may help us to reexamine our assumptions about and our approach to human development.

Vico and Kohlberg

Parallels between various aspects of contemporary developmental psychology and Vico's thinking have previously been pointed out—for example, in the areas of cognition, language, and aesthetic development.[2] The domain of moral

[2] Silvano Arieti, "Giambattista Vico and Modern Psychiatry," unpublished and undated manuscript; Fernando Dogana, "Il pensiero di G. B. Vico alla luce delle moderne dottrine psicologiche," *Archivio di psicologia, neurologia e psichiatria* 31 (1970): 514–530; Howard Gardner, "Vico's Theories of Knowledge in the Light of Contem-

development and of the development of legal and civic concepts, the core of Vico's work, may offer the most striking parallelism yet between Vico and contemporary developmental thinking, particularly as represented in Lawrence Kohlberg's theory.

Kohlberg believes that there are six different modes of thinking about moral matters; each mode, being internally consistent and general in its application, constitutes a real, though perhaps unarticulated, moral philosophy. These structures of moral judgment, he thinks, follow a well-defined order of appearance in the individual development, an order which is invariant and universal. The evidence for these propositions has been gathered through interviews and is based on what individuals of different ages and cultures say when faced with a specific set of moral dilemmas, the ways in which they reason, and the criteria they use to arrive at solutions. The descriptions of these stages of moral judgment, first reported by Kohlberg himself in the late 1950s, have been repeatedly confirmed since then, not only in Kohlberg's own laboratory but also by other independent researchers.[3]

Kohlberg usually groups the six stages in three more general levels with two stages per level. Similarities can be found between these three levels of moral thinking and Vico's three natures of man.[4]

porary Social Science," in Giorgio Tagliacozzo and Donald P. Verene, eds., *Giambattista Vico's Science of Humanity* (Baltimore: Johns Hopkins University Press, 1976), pp. 351–364; George Mora, "Vico, Piaget, and Genetic Epistemology," *ibid.*, pp. 365–392. See also the articles by George Mora and Silvano Arieti in this issue of *Social Research*.

[3] For recent reports of this work, see Lawrence Kohlberg, "Stage and Sequence: The Cognitive-Developmental Approach to Socialization," in David A. Goslin, ed., *Handbook of Socialization Theory and Research* (Chicago: Rand McNally, 1969); "From Is to Ought," in Theodore Mischel, ed., *Cognitive Development and Epistemology* (New York: Academic Press, 1971); "Moral Stages and Moralization: The Cognitive-Developmental Approach," in T. Lickona, ed., *Moral Development and Behavior: Theory, Research, and Social Issues* (New York: Holt, Rinehart & Winston, 1976).

[4] Even greater similarities could probably be found between Vico's three natures and Loevinger's stages of ego development. See Jane Loevinger, "The Meaning and Measurement of Ego Development," *American Psychologist* 21 (1966): 195–206; also Jane Loevinger, *Ego Development: Conceptions and Theories* (San Francisco: Jossey-Bass, 1976).

Kohlberg's first and most primitive level is called Preconventional or, sometimes, Premoral. Individuals using this mode of thinking draw their criteria for right and wrong not from society's standards—society's moral force is not yet understood—but from their own personal needs, predominantly physical in nature. For the young child of six, at the stage of "heteronomous morality," "authority" means mainly physical power and the right to exercise it; fear of punishment is frequently mentioned as the ultimate reason why rules should be observed and authority should be obeyed. Later, the emphasis on the overwhelming power of authorities disappears and fear of punishment is no longer used as the fundamental criterion. At the stage of "individualism and instrumental purpose," the child, more confident and less impressed by physical power, becomes aware of his own special needs and desires and of the differences between his needs and those of others. At this point, "right" is anything that facilitates the satisfaction of one's wishes, "wrong" anything that brings frustration. Reciprocity and compromise, and therefore social arrangements, are understood and accepted on the same basis, as the best way for everybody to get what each wants. This is a pragmatic and basically individualistic morality by which only the results count and the ends justify the means.

The morality of Vico's "first men" has some similarity with Kohlberg's Preconventional Level. The poetic nature was, in fact, characterized by a blend of bodily and primitive impulses, only recently and still precariously subjugated, and a form of sacred terror for a superstitious divinity: ". . . it was a fanaticism of superstition which kept the first men of the gentiles, savage, proud, and most cruel as they were, in some sort of restraint by main terror of a divinity they had imagined."[5] Their newly conquered temperance was thus a result of fear of divine punishment; their prudence was expressed in attempts to avoid punishment through auspices.

[5] NS, par. 518.

Like Kohlberg's children, people of this age were "entirely immersed in the senses . . . buried in the body";[6] the body was the focal point for their self-perception.[7] Their virtues were "virtues of the senses,"[8] their laws were concrete,[9] and their punishments were exemplary and not governed by general laws.[10] Their justice consisted in not meddling in one another's affairs.[11]

Kohlberg's second level, labeled Conventional, begins to develop among Western middle-class children around the age of nine or ten and also constitutes the prevalent moral philosophy among adults. The basic criteria for right and wrong during the Conventional Level refer to norms and regulations of social groups, large and small, and to the authorities. What counts is not so much the contents of what is socially prescribed or proscribed, contents that may vary widely from group to group, but the acts of prescribing, forbidding, or simply expecting, all of which are essential to the functioning of societies and to the role of authorities. In contrast with the younger child, the conventional child or adult understands the moral force of authority, irrespective of its physical power; he also understands the intrinsic moral validity of rules and laws, regardless of their consequences, favorable or unfavorable, to himself. The ends no longer justify the means.

In the first stage of this level, the stage of "mutual interpersonal expectations and interpersonal conformity," moral criteria are derived from those interpersonal feelings that characterize the functioning of small groups (families, tribes): love, acceptance, feeling of belonging, and identity. Something is right because it brings approval, praise, and trust, or because it expresses one's loyalty to people and groups. At the next stage, the "social system and conscience stage," by con-

---

[6] NS, par. 378.
[7] NS, par. 1045.
[8] NS, par. 516.
[9] NS, par. 500.
[10] NS, par. 501.
[11] NS, par. 516.

trast, the individual understands the value of laws and rules, simply for their being rules and laws, that is, for their function in maintaining the social order in which one lives. Their moral validity does not derive from this or that specific authority, nor from one's love and loyalty, nor even from the desire to be accepted, even though civic reputation is a powerful motive; it derives, rather, from the fact that laws govern and express a network of abstract relations of roles, offices, rights, and duties. The maintenance of such social organization—the abstract role of authority may come to symbolize it—is now the basic moral motive.

It is more difficult to outline the parallels between this level of moral judgment and Vico's heroic nature, in which men, confident of their nobility and privileged origin from the gods, were "pious, wise, chaste, strong, and magnanimous,"[12] but, in their attempt to defend their class privileges, were also unconcerned for, and even cruel to, the weak and the poor. Perhaps the central elements of similarity between Kohlberg's conventionals and Vico's heroes lie in the emphasis on a rigid legalism and in the reliance on "common sense." Reason and truth come later, in the third age.

> In the meantime the nations were governed by the certainty of authority, that is, by the same criterion which is used by our metaphysical criticism, namely, the common sense of the human race . . . so that . . . our Science comes to be a philosophy of authority, which is the fount of the outer justice. . . .[13]

The third of Kohlberg's levels, the Postconventional or Principled, does not reject the legitimacy of authority and its function in society, though not infrequently its title is misinterpreted to mean just such a position. This level of thinking derives, instead, from the capacity of standing back and of questioning critically the bases for the moral validity of societies and authorities. As a result, social prescriptions, ex-

[12] *NS*, par. 1099.
[13] *NS*, par. 350.

pectations, and customs are looked at from within a framework which is both more encompassing and more radical. Thus, while the postconventional individual frees himself from the direct and immediate influence of social agencies, he also finds within himself, in his capacity for reflection, for logical reasoning, and for responsibility, the inner source of morality and justice. This justice is seen to transcend any tribalism and ethnocentrism and to reach the universal basis of humanity.

Within the Postconventional Level, the stage of "social contract and individual rights" finds the ultimate criteria for right and wrong, as the title suggests, in the individual's active participation in the process of devising and establishing laws and in the implicit or explicit commitment by which he freely binds himself to respect them and to curtail some of his independence. The last stage, the stage of "universal ethical principles," by contrast, looks for the ultimate justification of morality in the supreme value of the individual conscience and in the rights that derive from it.

Vico's "human nature," the latest to develop, seems to share many traits with Kohlberg's Postconventional Level. Cognitively, there is a well-developed capacity for abstract concepts and reasoning. There is also an emphasis on self-reflection and self-knowledge that leads to the understanding of common humanity and, hence, of the basic equality of men. As a result, virtues and values are approached for their intrinsic validity and not by custom: "Since virtuous actions were no longer prompted by religious sentiments as formerly, philosophy should make the virtues understood in their idea, and by dint of reflection thereon. . . ."[14] Laws start to be founded on reason, to be universal, and to be concerned with the welfare of everyone:

> With the coming of the human times . . . the intellect was brought into play . . . and universal legal concepts abstracted by

[14] *NS*, par. 1101.

the intellect were thenceforward said to have their being in the
understanding of the law. . . . This understanding is concerned
with the intention which the lawmaker has expressed in his law
. . ., an intention which was that of the citizens brought into
agreement upon an idea of common rational utility.[15]

In sum, Vico's fully developed man is "intelligent and hence
modest, benign, and reasonable, recognizing for laws conscience, reason, and duty";[16] he is characterized by "will without passion" and by "the interest itself in truth."[17] "In such
commonwealths the entire peoples, who have in common the
desire for justice, command laws that are just because they are
good for all."[18]

The parallel between Vico's three natures and Kohlberg's
levels of moral thinking is striking. Of course, it is not perfect.
There are some dissimilar elements; more important, it is not
certain whether, behind the descriptions, the structural elements that constitute Kohlberg's levels are the same as those
that underlie Vico's natures. The old philosopher and the
contemporary theorist rely on different data, which they approach with different questions in mind and different
methods. It is altogether surprising, under these conditions,
that such a high degree of match exists.

Whatever one will conclude on the similarities between
Vico's and Kohlberg's descriptions, it is undeniable that a
much closer, and by far more important, match exists between
the principles that each respectively uses in explaining development through stages and ages. These principles are simply listed here without elaboration or comment. Some of them
will reappear in the context of the discussion in the second
part of this essay.

According to Kohlberg:[19]

1. Morality is not given to us ready-made at birth, but is the

---

[15] NS, par. 1038.
[16] NS, par. 918.
[17] NS, par. 1101.
[18] NS, par. 1101.
[19] See particularly Kohlberg, "From Is to Ought."

result of a long process of development through a number of well-defined stages.

2. Each stage has at its center an internally consistent structure of thinking; as a consequence, it is impossible to grasp other stages from the point of view of one's own.

3. The stages form a sequence in which moral criteria become increasingly differentiated from nonmoral criteria, moral aspects become increasingly integrated with each other, and morality as a whole becomes increasingly adequate. The process, thus, is one of increasing moralization.

4. The stages are related to each other hierarchically, as elements of previous stages become integrant parts of later stages. No jumps or regressions are then considered to be possible.

5. Thus each stage is oriented to and acquires meaning from the final mature stage.

6. This sequence is universal, in the sense that development, wherever it takes place, follows the same order and tends toward the same moral maturity.

7. The universality of moral development is not based on common genetic make-up nor on cultural transmission of common values.

8. Each stage is acquired by the individual's effort to construct a system which makes sense of his own experience. The universality is based, therefore, on the fact that human beings share a few fundamental institutions and experiences, from which they actively construct a system of moral understanding.

9. Moral development is cognitive, not only in the sense that each stage constitutes an internally consistent structure, but, more important, in the sense that it is made possible by the development of logical capacities. Here Kohlberg relies on Piaget's theory and findings.

According to Vico:

1. Human nature is the result of a long process of historical development, proceeding through a number of ages.

2. Each age is composed of traits that are logically related to each other;[20] one cannot understand earlier ages by simply projecting onto them one's own understanding.[21]

3. The ages constitute the history of increasing humanization, toward the "complete humanity."[22]

4. The sequence is hierarchical, as each age becomes the matter for the form of the next age.[23] It is impossible for individuals of one age to function according to the characteristics of earlier ages.[24]

5. Thus each age, regardless of traits which in isolation may seem undesirable, is providential, because it performs a necessary role in the development of human nature.[25]

6. In spite of "innumerable variety of customs"[26] across peoples, the sequence of ages is universal; in fact, it constitutes an "ideal eternal history," necessarily present in every possible world.[27]

7. Such universality cannot be explained by common teachings or by societies having a common origin.[28]

8a. The universality of history should be explained by the universality of certain institutions, by common sense, and ultimately by Providence.[29]

8b. From the viewpoint of individual human beings, development is a result of their free activity, not of fate or chance.[30]

---

[20] Gardner, in "Vico's Theories of Knowledge in the Light of Contemporary Social Science," believes that the concept of structure cannot be applied to Vico's ages. In my opinion, Gardner assumes an unnecessarily narrow definition of structure.
[21] NS, pars. 329, 374.
[22] NS, pars. 927, 973, 1089.
[23] NS, par. 629.
[24] NS, par. 677.
[25] NS, par. 518.
[26] NS, par. 341.
[27] NS, pars. 348, 349, 915, 1096.
[28] NS, par. 146.
[29] NS, pars. 144–145, 308–328, 332–333.
[30] NS, pars. 130, 134–136, 179, 345.

9. Men's cognitive capacities, different at different ages, play a crucial role in determining the nature of each age.[31]

There are important differences between Kohlberg's theory of moralization and Vico's theory of humanization. One concerns the reciprocal influence that social institutions and individual development have in Vico's account.[32] Social institutions, by contrast, though recognized as an important factor, are not given by Kohlberg the kind of explicit attention that they deserve. This difference, however, seems to be a result of selective attention in a strategy of inquiry and of the temporary state of a theory's development and not an indication of real differences in assumptions and principles.

In spite of this and other differences, and in spite of areas where the doctrine is uncertain or its interpretation ambiguous, there is no doubt that Kohlberg's view of development is very close to Vico's. Neither Kohlberg, however, nor the cognitive-developmental approach which he represents, covers the whole field of developmental psychology; Vico's work, on the other hand, may contain valuable insights and implications for the study of human development in general, beyond any parochial restriction of domain or of theory. The rest of this essay will thus maintain as broad a perspective as possible.

Developmental Psychology and Human Nature

Developmental psychology is rather recent as a specific field of inquiry. This statement may be surprising but is defensible if the following minimal criteria are used to delimit the discipline: development is conceptually differentiated from other

---

[31] NS, pars. 284, 350, 375–378, 384, 405, 424, 768–769, 920, 923, 1101.

[32] Max Fisch, in his introduction to NS, writes: "When he [Vico] calls the world of nations the world of men, he means that what were beasts in the world of nature become men in the world of nations, and it is by the becoming of the world of nations that they become men, or, as he puts it otherwise, in a sense they make the world of nations, and in the same sense they make themselves by making it" (NS, p. xxvii).

psychological processes such as learning;[33] there is a real concern with the general laws of development, beyond the description of age differences; there is a specific methodological paradigm guiding the collection of observations and the critical formulation of inferences.[34] The area characterized by these criteria cannot be older than two or three decades; even now, it represents only a minor part of what goes on in child psychology.[35]

Within developmental psychology, one can find a number of rather different theories with contrasting, and perhaps incompatible, assumptions. It is possible, however, to abstract a limited number of traits which seem to be shared across the theoretical orientations and which may well characterize the field as it stands at present. These include: (a) The acceptance that the appropriate unity for developmental analysis is the structure and not an elementary bit of behavior. (b) The assumption that there is an order among age-related psychological structures and, thus, the attempt to study the properties of a sequence. Frequently, this sequential order is assumed to form some sort of progressive hierarchy.[36] (c) The search for universal features of development. Group and individual variations are not neglected but are frequently viewed

[33] The learning-theory approach assumes that development, as a psychological process, cannot be differentiated conceptually from more general processes such as learning, reinforcement, discrimination, and so on. This approach, therefore, while studying developmental "facts," does not construct from them a theory of development. See Donald Baer, "An Age-Irrelevant Concept of Development," *Merrill-Palmer Quarterly* 16 (1970): 238.

[34] An indication of how novel is developmental psychology can be gathered from the fact that Joachim Wohlwill's *The Study of Behavioral Development* (New York: Academic Press, 1973) is probably the first attempt to systematize and to discuss critically the empirical methods that are characteristic of the field.

[35] Prior to this time, there were psychologists, such as J. M. Baldwin, with developmental ideas but without an empirical paradigm; or there were isolated developmental psychologists, such as Piaget, but not yet a field. Child psychology, as Milton J. E. Senn recently testified in "Insights on the Child Development Movement in the United States" (*SRCD Monographs* 40 [1975], No. 161), has been essentially atheoretical, almost exclusively interested in describing age differences.

[36] For a discussion of this aspect in developmental theories, see D. C. Phillips and M. E. Kelly, "Hierarchical Theories of Development in Education and Psychology," *Harvard Educational Review* 45 (August 1975): 351.

against the background of universal traits. (d) The emphasis on cognitive processes, namely, on those processes by which the organism selects and transforms information from the environment. Activity, and even autonomy to a lesser extent, are now accepted characteristics of the developing organism. These features, then, perhaps with varying emphases, are present in contemporary developmental research and thinking, whether the specific domain of inquiry is perception or aesthetics, language or humor, early attachment or epistemological concepts, role-taking and social interaction or emotions, self-identity or the overall ego.

The field of developmental psychology, probably because of precisely those characteristics that at present seem to establish its identity, has been showing, in my opinion, signs of stress and discomfort. I am not referring to conceptual and methodological difficulties that any expanding field must encounter, but to recurrent difficulties in accepting and integrating certain hypotheses and findings. A number of ideas, more or less empirically supported, at times seem to be resisted, at other times to be systematically misinterpreted or minimized in their implications.

For example, while Piaget repeatedly insisted that his theory is not maturational and that the explanation for the universal sequence of cognitive development cannot reside in genetic blueprints,[37] many still consider him to be a maturationist at heart.[38] Of course, they do accept that genes cannot operate in isolation, and that stages are a result of interactions between the genes and the environment. But this unspecific and rather banal understanding of Piaget does not ultimately differentiate his theory from standard maturational theories. Thus, though Piaget's own statements are heard, they are also misinterpreted or reinterpreted or denied in order to fit them with

[37] See, e.g., Jean Piaget, *Six Psychological Studies* (New York: Random House, 1967) and *Structuralism* (New York: Basic Books, 1970).

[38] Harry Beilin, "The Development of Physical Concepts," in Mischel, *Cognitive Development and Epistemology*; on this issue see also Marx W. Wartofsky, "From Praxis to Logos," *ibid.*, and Charles Taylor, "What Is Involved in Genetic Psychology?" *ibid.*

more familiar assumptions. If there is such a universal order in development, it is reasoned, its explanation cannot but be maturational.

Another instance of stress within developmental psychology concerns the claim of universality for certain developmental sequences. Kohlberg's moral judgment is the primary example, though the same comments apply to Erikson's sequence of psychosocial development or Loevinger's sequence of ego development. Given the nature of these areas, a genetic-biological explanation may not appear sensible. Universality is then flatly denied because, it is explained, its empirical support is insufficient.[39] However, the response to the universality hypothesis, besides frequently distorting the theory and deriving from it unwarranted implications, is at times too strong and emotional to be simply based on the quantity of confirmatory research. After all, lack of sufficient empirical support is more normal than unusual in psychological theorizing.

A third example of uneasiness concerns specifically Kohlberg's theory of moral development. Not infrequently, his highest level of moral development, the Postconventional Level, is misinterpreted to mean a rejection of society's values and norms and a return to the egocentric individualism typical of the Preconventional Level. These misunderstandings occur even though Kohlberg described at length the differences between the pre- and the postconventional thinking and repeatedly emphasized the integrative nature of development by which the achievements of one level are not lost at the successive.

The reasons for such "resistance" and "distortion" are multiple: for instance, the a priori rejection of the idea that there is a universal goal in development may be motivated by its obvious social and political implications; the confusions around the Postconventional Level could be explained by the

[39] Elizabeth L. Simpson, "Moral Development Research: A Case Study of Scientific Cultural Bias," *Human Development* 71 (1974): 81–106.

intrinsic difficulties that the highest stages of any sequence frequently present to our grasp. While recognizing the validity of these and other explanations, I am offering here another diagnosis for what I identified as signs of stress within developmental psychology. I am suggesting that, at the basis of many confusions, paradoxes, antinomies, and cognitive stresses in general, there is a lack of appropriate conceptual categories. What is missing, specifically, is a concept of human nature, or at least a concept of human nature which is not limited to the biological side of man.

As a result of the general cultural climate prevalent at its birth and of other specific influences, scientific psychology, particularly in America, was born with a set of definite assumptions about human nature. During the nineteenth century, different and at times opposed philosophical movements conspired together to bring about a radical shift in the concept of mankind. Romanticism, the organicism of Comte and Hegel, the special brand of progressivism of J. S. Mill, Arnold, and Huxley, historicism in its varied forms, and finally Darwinism, administered a fatal blow to the belief, predominant in the preceding centuries, that there is a human nature, that is, a fixed, universal, and essential core of psychological and moral traits characterizing the human species. This belief was replaced by what Mandelbaum calls "the doctrine of man's malleability," with the central thesis that "there are no specific ways of thinking and acting which are so deeply entrenched in human nature that they cannot be supplanted by the effects of the circumstances in which men are placed or by means of man's own efforts."[40] This doctrine, which we also inherited, implied that "in a new age, man's individual and social life could undergo almost unlimited change: a radical new order of social relationships could be established, and in that new order there would be fundamental transformations in human nature."[41]

---

[40] Maurice Mandelbaum, *History, Man, and Reason* (Baltimore: Johns Hopkins Press, 1971), p. 141.

[41] *Ibid.*, p. 142.

Besides this pervasive assumption of nineteenth-century thinking, psychology in America had its own specific influences, a dominant one being evolutionary theory. Darwin and Spencer directly, and indirectly through William James and John Dewey, eventually led to functionalism, which has dominated American psychology to this day.[42] Functionalism translated the basic evolutionary concerns with survival and adaptation, in psychological terms, by shifting the emphasis from mental structures to the processes of change and by focusing on human responses as expressing the organism's adaptation to an ever-changing and varied environment.

The concept of human nature now prevalent in the social sciences can be characterized by the following elements: There are indeed a number of traits, relatively fixed and common to all human beings. These concern primarily the biological functioning but may also include a few elementary psychological traits. Though scientists vary in the number of psychological characteristics that they are willing to include in the standard human make-up, they all seem to agree that a trait, to the extent that it is universal, is also heavily dependent on the characteristic human genetic pool. All of the other psychological characteristics, the large majority and by far the most specific for human beings, are acquired through a variety of processes, whose common ultimate result is adaptation to the environment. Since environments are varied geographically and changeable historically, it follows that there is no psychological human nature. The only human nature that is recognized is biological in its character and in its source.

A recent controversy centered on the new field of sociobiology can be used to illustrate this set of assumptions. Without attempting to simplify the issues or to diminish the importance of the controversy, one could say that the differences between the two sides consist in the range of behaviors that each considers to be universal among humans and thus to be

[42] Ernest R. Hilgard, "Psychology after Darwin," in Sol Tax, ed., *Evolution after Darwin*, vol. 2 (Chicago: University of Chicago Press, 1960); Edwin G. Boring, *A History of Experimental Psychology*, 2nd ed. (New York: Appleton-Century-Crofts, 1950).

genetically determined. While one side believes that most human behaviors, including altruism, are so characterized,[43] the other thinks "that human biological universals are to be discovered more in the generalities of eating, excreting and sleeping. . . ."[44] However, neither side questions the basic parameters of the controversy, namely, that human nature is based on universal behaviors, behaviors that are actually present in all normal individuals, and that universal behaviors can be explained only genetically and biologically. Even the possibility of rather different premises is not considered: that universality may not require the actual presence of traits in all individuals but simply a universal tendency to develop them; that the explanation of such developmental potentials may not be either genetic or evolutionary (except in a very broad sense); and finally that human nature in its distinctive characteristics may not be biological but genuinely psychological.

From the assumptions about human nature that presently operate, the Piagetian idea of a nonmaturational development which is nevertheless universal and in some sense necessary makes absolutely no sense. And since moral values are usually considered nonbiological in nature, Kohlberg's proposition that the development of moral judgment is not determined by cultural variations also becomes incomprehensible. What is not biological *must* be culturally determined, and what is culturally determined *must* be relative. For the same reasons—that is, because of this prevalent concept of human nature—it also becomes difficult, if not impossible, to understand what Kohlberg means by postconventional thinking. When the conceptual field is divided between the biological and the cultural, it is easy to understand an egocentric and selfish individualism, motivated by biological or quasi-biological needs, and also to understand conformity to sociocultural norms. But

---

[43] See Edward O. Wilson, *Sociobiology: The New Synthesis* (Cambridge: Harvard University Press, 1975); see also Donald T. Campbell, "On the Conflicts between Biological and Social Evolution and between Psychology and Moral Tradition," *American Psychologist* 30 (December 1975): 1103.

[44] "Against 'Sociobiology'," *New York Review of Books* 22 (Nov. 13, 1975): 43.

the notion of a nonconforming thinking which is not selfish or asocial just does not have a category under which it could be classified.

I am not suggesting that the concept of human nature implicit in much of contemporary social sciences is necessarily incorrect or inadequate, nor that Piaget's theory and Kohlberg's hypotheses are necessarily correct. I am saying, however, that Piaget's and Kohlberg's theories, as well as other theories that share with them the hypothesis of a universal nonmaturational developmental sequence, are incompatible in some basic respect with certain fundamental assumptions of social science and cannot be integrated without distortion. To the extent that cognitive-developmentalism should appear empirically solid, a paradigmatic clash should be expected in developmental psychology and in psychology as a whole.

The Concept of Human Nature in Vico

Vico does have a clear and firm concept of human nature. One reason why some historians[45] concluded that he did not may be that Vico's concept is radically different both from the concept that was prevalent at his time and from that which is prevalent now. During the sixteenth and seventeenth centuries, nature was understood to be identical with fixed essence, namely, with that which is actually present in every individual of a species and establishes at the same time its identifying common core and its distinctiveness from other species. Essence denoted more the form, or the static aspect, of a species, and nature referred more to its characteristic operations and functions; but the two notions were considered

---

[45] One such historian is Bruce Mazlish, who writes in *The Riddle of History* (New York: Harper & Row, 1966), p. 55: "Vico's break with natural law allowed him to see that humanity evolved; and he traced this evolution in a naturalistic, empirical manner." His judgment is based on the assumptions that there can be only one concept of nature, which identifies nature with fixed essences, and that development and history are incompatible with human nature.

to be intimately related. It is interesting that this concept of nature, devoid of its metaphysical superstructures, is frequently the only concept available today, even implicit among those who reject the very idea of human nature. Nature is still what is *actually* found in every member of a species, but translated, in contemporary language, in terms of genetic pool or genetic make-up.

From such a viewpoint, it is impossible to understand what Vico was attempting to do, as he did away with the notion of nature-essence while retaining the concept of human nature. There is indeed a human nature, he argued, even though it cannot be determined by what is *actually* found in every member of the human race.

Human nature, in Vico's *New Science*, consists in a well-determined developmental pattern leading to a definite goal, pattern and goal being shared, as such, by all human beings. Not every individual needs to go through the end of such a pattern and to reach the common goal; in fact, since Vico's sequence of three ages is historical and not developmental, many—even the large majority of—humans did not and will not have the opportunity to arrive at the goal. Nevertheless, they are part of a common dynamic movement which leads to the same end. Human nature then consists in being a part of what Vico calls the "ideal eternal history":

> There will then be fully unfolded before us, not the particular history in time of the laws and deeds of the Romans or the Greeks, but (by virtue of the identity of the intelligible *substance* in the diversity of their *modes* of development) the ideal history of the eternal laws which are instanced by the deeds of all nations in their rise, progress, maturity, decadence, and dissolution, [and which would be so instanced] even if (as is certainly not the case) there were infinite worlds being born from time to time throughout eternity.[46]

Human nature is not simply process, becoming, or developing. Vico is no Heraclitus, nor a precursor of nineteenth-

---

[46] *NS*, par. 1096; see also pars. 245, 294, 349, 393.

century historicism. What makes the pattern he describes so important is that it is development toward full humanity. It is a process of "humanization." Though there are three different human natures, according to the three main historical ages, there is only one fully developed human nature; the other natures are human in virtue of being necessary precursors of the goal. "The third [natural law] is the human law dictated by fully developed human reason;"[47] . . . [the] benign law . . . the immutable law of the rational humanity, which is the true and proper nature of man."[48]

Vico, therefore, adopts for his *New Science* Aristotle's view that an object's nature can be identified only by its developmental end.[49] However, Vico, to a much greater extent than Aristotle, emphasizes the importance of the beginnings and of the intermediate natures as necessary steps to the goal, and thus the whole process of history and development. He points out examples of nations that, for different reasons, "failed to accomplish this course of human civil institutions."[50] "But the Romans . . .," he adds, "proceeded with even steps. . . . Today a complete humanity seems to be spread abroad through all nations. . . ."[51]

In what sense does this common development toward the same goal constitute a nature? Certainly because it is universal in the sense determined above. Universality alone, however, is not sufficient, if universality is established on a purely empirical-inductive basis. From an empirical-inductive viewpoint, two questions can be raised about the universality proposed by Vico. First, since few individuals across the centuries arrived at the stage of "full humanity," how does one know that their developmental pattern is the same? Second, what guarantee

[47] *NS*, par. 924.
[48] *NS*, par. 973; see also par. 326.
[49] "For by the nature of anything—whether of a man or a horse or a family household—we mean what it is in its full development. The end or essential aim of anything is its highest good . . ." (*Politics* 1, 2; translation by Philip Wheelwright).
[50] *NS*, par. 1088.
[51] *NS*, par. 1089.

do we have that the same pattern will occur in the future and that it is truly universal, on the basis exclusively of what we know from the past?

These are basically the arguments with which developmental psychologists, much more inclined than Vico's contemporaries to trust the ultimate validity of bare facts, dismiss Piaget's and Kohlberg's theories as metaphysical fantasies. How can one speak of universal development, they reason? It is enough to look around to immediately recognize that relatively few attain the stage of formal operations and even fewer the Postconventional Level of moral thinking. The usual reply, that everybody would arrive at the most mature stage if the proper circumstances were available, is most unsatisfactory to an empirically minded person. How would one know, since the circumstances are *in fact* what they are? The fact is that no empirically established universality can be adequate support for that kind of general universality on which a true concept of human nature should be based.

Vico's solution to this problem is, I believe, the only possible one. His particular historical sequence determines human nature because the sequence is necessary in principle, even though it may be *accidentally* interrupted. The sequence is in principle necessary because of the necessary connections tying certain events with their outcomes and these outcomes with other outcomes, and so on. The sequence is necessary because, once the first crucial steps have been posited, it has an internal logic of its own.

"Necessary" and "necessity" are perhaps the words most frequently used by Vico to describe the connections among events. Here are some examples chosen at random:

. . . the early gentile peoples, by a demonstrated necessity of nature, were poets . . .;[52] For all this [the fear and cruelty of the first nature] was necessary to tame the sons of the cyclopes and reduce them to the humanity of an Aristides . . .;[53] For all these

[52] *NS*, par. 34.
[53] *NS*, par. 191.

reasons the *famuli* must have revolted against the heroes. And this is that "necessity" which we conjectured to have been imposed by the *famuli* upon the heroic fathers . . .;[54] . . . by a common sense of utility the heroes were constrained to satisfy the multitude of their rebellious clients;[55] This language belongs to religions . . . and it was necessary in the earliest times when men did not yet possess articulate speech.[56]

The most expressive summarizing formula is:

> . . . since these institutions have been established by divine providence, the course of the institutions of the nations had to be, must now be, and will have to be such as our Science demonstrates, even if infinite worlds were born from time to time through eternity, which is certainly not the case. Our Science therefore comes to describe at the same time an ideal eternal history traversed in time by the history of every nation in its rise, development, maturity, decline, and fall.[57]

Vico insists several times[58] that the universality of his sequence is not a result of the nations having a common origin or of peoples communicating with each other. The fact that there were independent and separate origins indicates that the essential traits that humans go through in the course of their histories, as well as the essential characteristics of human and legal institutions,[59] are not results of arbitrary conventions but imply a deeper intrinsic "truth":

> Uniform ideas originating among entire peoples unknown to each other must have a common ground of truth. This axiom is a great principle which establishes the common sense of the human race as the criterion taught . . . by divine providence to define what is certain in the natural law of the gentes. . . . If that had been the case [that common laws came out of one first nation], it would have been a civil law communicated to other peoples by human provision, and not a law which divine pro-

[54] *NS*, par. 583.
[55] *NS*, par. 597.
[56] *NS*, par. 929.
[57] *NS*, pars. 348–349; see also par. 360.
[58] *NS*, pars. 144–146, 198, 332 ff.
[59] Vico's distinction between *jus gentium* and civil law corresponds to the distinction between what is natural, and thus universal regardless of communication, and what is conventional, and thus particular and changeable in principle.

vidence instituted naturally in all nations along with human customs themselves. . . .[60]

Thus Vico's historical pattern and the common goal it leads to constitute human nature, not simply because it is in fact present in everybody, which is not the case and which could be explained in any event by human convention, but because it indicates an intrinsic and necessary truth or principle about human beings.[61]

In trying to understand what might be this intrinsic truth on which human nature is established, it is impossible to avoid Vico's key concept of providence. Much has been written about it; no doubt, providence is no easy concept to understand and to integrate in our modern mentality. It seems to me, however, that it can be interpreted in a way which is both consistent with Vico's ideas and purpose and is hopefully relevant to contemporary developmental theory.[62]

First of all, Vico's providence, while compatible with a theological metaphysics, can be analyzed independently of one. Vico distinguishes very carefully the direct and extrinsic intervention of God in human affairs from the workings of

[60] *NS*, pars. 144–146.

[61] Vico touches here again on another issue of central concern to social scientists i.e., the distinction between what is genetic and what is acquired, which translate rather accurately into the distinction between nature and convention. As already mentioned, one basic assumption of present-day thinking is that much is a result of convention, particularly in the domains of psychology and sociology. John Passmore expresses this view when, discussing Aristotle's teleological approach to perfection, he writes: "Tasks are not set by Nature but by men, within particular forms of social organization: it would not be in the least surprising if man as such . . . had no task to perform, no end to pursue. This, indeed, is precisely what we should expect. . . . No doubt there are natural differences between human beings; men cannot give birth to babies nor can women fertilize a womb. But even the 'functions' of men and women beyond this elementary point, are fixed by men, not by Nature. It is not Nature who decides whether women shall work in industry, in agriculture, or in the house, or what they shall take as their objective in those pursuits. The so-called 'natural ends' indeed, should more accurately be described as 'conventional' ends" (John Passmore *The Perfectibility of Man* [New York: Charles Scribner's Sons, 1970], pp. 16–17).

[62] My interpretation seems to be consistent with Max Fisch's understanding (*NS*, pp. xxxv–xxxviii) and with the main lines of Leon Pompa's interpretation in *Vico: A Study of the New Science* (New York: Cambridge University Press, 1975), particularly chap. 5

providence through natural causes. For this reason he always separates the case of the Hebrews from the history of gentile nations.[63]

In a more positive sense, the fundamental properties of Vico's providence could be summarized as follows: (a) It is the main agency leading humankind through history to its complete and perfect state. (b) It does so, not in a random manner nor in an absolutely deterministic way, but in such an intermediate way that will lead to the goal while respecting man's freedom. (c) It operates, in fact, through the natural connections that things and events have with each other; since human beings may be unaware of such connections and particularly of their long-term implications, providence may be thought to produce its results besides and beyond the immediate human purposes. So described, the notion of providence is not very different from the notion of internal logic. There is a logic to actions and events; thus there is a logic to the sequence of events, to history and development. Man's behavior, even when freely performed, cannot be outside such a logic; this is precisely what it means to have a nature. The necessity discussed above is simply the expression of such internal logic. Under certain conditions, given man's characteristics at the time, religion must arise; the serfs must rebel against the nobles and the nobles are constrained to yield, and thus the commonwealth necessarily develops;[64] ownership must follow power and precarious ownership must follow limited power;[65] under other conditions, men come naturally to the feudal system,[66] and so on. This logic is not added to things, either by a decree of God or by men's conventions; it is what things and events really are. As Vico would say, they are things' "eternal properties." Providence-as-internal-logic, then, is the essence of history, history's "truth," or the "ideal eternal

---

[63] NS, par. 313.
[64] NS, pars. 583, 597.
[65] NS, par. 597.
[66] NS, par. 599.

history." "These [eleven] triadic special unities, with many others that derive from them . . . are all embraced by one general unity. This is the unity of the religion of a provident divinity, which is the unity of spirit that informs and gives life to this world of nations."[67]

Conclusion

In this essay I have tried to explicate the underlying meaning of what I think are the empirical and theoretical trends of developmental psychology, particularly the search for universal developmental patterns and for ideal developmental goals; I then suggested that the implications of these trends stand in opposition to the basic assumptions about human nature that have been dominant in the social sciences. Current developmental work is much more consonant with Vico's views of man, history, and natural laws than with the traditional psychological views on the same matters.

As I have already mentioned, demonstrating a set of logical, whether consistent or inconsistent, relations does not *ipso facto* indicate the truth-value of any one position. I did not intend to conclude that Piaget's or Kohlberg's theories are empirically correct, nor that Vico's *New Science* is empirically supported. I certainly did not imply that it is even possible, exclusively on the basis of empirical evidence, to determine that one concept of human nature is more correct than another.

"Human nature" is a complex concept, and the way to determine it is fraught with ambiguities. Besides the difficulties involved in determining which relations and developmental sequences are necessary,[68] there are problems in determining how central a universal sequence is to the understanding of human functioning, human growth, and human inter-

---

[67] *NS*, par. 915.
[68] See Phillips and Kelly, "Hierarchical Theories of Development in Education and Psychology."

course. I believe that Piaget built a reasonably solid case for his universal and necessary sequence in the development of logicomathematical operations: logicomathematical operations, in fact, do have a clear internal logic. Kohlberg, by similarly demonstrating the hierarchical logical relations between his stages of justice, has a solid argument for the propositions that higher stages are more adequate, in terms of justice, then the lower ones, and that one can get to the higher stages only through the lower stages. But the concept of human nature says more than this. It implies that, without it, a person is less of a human being, and, with it, nothing else is needed for a person's humanity. Even if Piaget and Kohlberg are correct in their hypotheses, it does not follow that an individual, who is better than others in resolving logical problems or even better than others in resolving problems of justice, is also a better human being or, to use Vico's expression, has a "full humanity."

The seriousness of these difficulties alone, on the other hand, does not justify maintaining the biological and functionalist view of man prevalent in psychology. That view, with its emphasis on adaptation to the immediate environment, renders the social sciences helpless every time issues of direction and goal arise that go beyond the pure technology of change. The world, moreover, has become so small that we may be forced, exclusively on functionalist grounds, to discover again our common humanity. It is here that the efforts of developmental psychology, limited and at times absurd as they may seem, can offer a valuable contribution. Vico's views, broad and sweeping as they are, can present then helpful insights.

* Work leading to this paper was partially supported by a grant from the Spencer Foundation.

Vico and Piaget: Parallels and Differences

BY GEORGE MORA

T HE silence which surrounded Vico's main work for the past two and a half centuries appears finally to have been replaced by a careful assessment of his role as a pioneer in historical and social sciences. As for the psychological sciences, his many pioneering insights into the human mind could not be properly considered during the various periods of different emphases in approach to the study of the mind: first philosophical; then, in the latter part of the nineteenth century, positivistic; later on, at the beginning of our century, mainly under Freud's influence, dynamic.

It is only quite recently that psychology, having reached the mature stage of a universally accepted field of knowledge, has begun to look at its past not in the old-fashioned sense of priorities according to the "Great Men" sequence, but in terms of beginnings, derivations, and relations of concepts and of practices. From this perspective, two important points have emerged: first, these concepts and practices cannot be viewed in isolation in space and time, but along a dimension of continuity marked by gaps and differences in emphasis from the early times to the present; second, psychology appears to have overcome the stage of narrow reliance on "hard" and "objective" data to enter, or rather reenter, a stage of broad acceptance in its domain of all kinds of phenomena of the mind. This is particularly evident for genetic psychology, wherein we are now leaning toward an integration of the study of the emotional and intellectual aspects of the development of the mind by Freud's and Piaget's schools, respectively.[1]

All this naturally leads us back to the main tenet of Vico's philosophy, that is, to his conviction that the only approach to the study of phenomena, whether related to the individual, the nation, or the species in its totality, is a developmental one. Yet the study of Vico's relevance for psychology has begun only very recently. One important point to keep in mind for anyone interested in such a study is that, over and above the *New Science*, attention should be given to all Vico's other writings, unfortunately not all available in English. Then it will be possible to ascertain how pervasive some of his concepts have been and how they have been repeated time and time again in refined and modified form in his various legal, educational, and historical works.

In this paper, I first present a comparison of Vico's and Piaget's genetic approaches to human psychology, then I discuss their respective views on education. After a brief mention of methodological aspects, I present a comprehensive view of Vico and Piaget and conclude with some remarks concerning Vico and genetic epistemology on the *Zeitgeist* of the eighteenth century which may be of help for the followers of Piaget.

Comparison between Vico's and Piaget's Genetic Approach to Human Psychology

In his many publications, Piaget has described three periods in the development of the mind: in the first period, the first

---

[1] The main trend of ego psychology in psychoanalysis is naturally conducive to the study of cognitive factors. This movement may slowly lead to the integration of the psychoanalytic and the psychogenetic methods, as Piaget himself has indicated (Jean Piaget, "Affective Unconscious and Cognitive Unconscious," in his *The Child and Reality: Problems of Genetic Psychology* [New York: Grossman, 1973], pp. 31–48). For an attempt to bridge the gap between the psychoanalytic and the psychogenetic methods, see Melvin L. Weiner, *The Cognitive Unconscious: A Piagetian Approach to Psychotherapy* Davis, Calif.: International Psychological Press, 1975).

eighteen months of life, sensory-motor schemes develop; in the second, from age two to eleven, concrete operations based on schemes of action internalized through semiotic relations, thought, and interpersonal connections take place; in the third, around the age of twelve, abstract reasoning evolves. In a famous axiom of the *New Science* Vico said: "Men at first feel without perceiving, then they perceive with a troubled and agitated spirit, finally they refelect with a clear mind."[2]

Similarities between Vico and Piaget can be found in regard to the main characteristics of the child's mind as described by the latter.

Egocentrism is a stage in which all social exchanges are perceived from the point of view of the subject, and centered upon the child and his own activity from the point of view of the observer. Vico says: "Because of the indefinite nature of the human mind, wherever it is lost in ignorance man makes himself the measure of all things."[3]

Animism is characterized by Piaget as a magic conception of reality based on the belief that all things, including inanimate ones, are endowed with the same movement, awareness, finality, and will of animate beings. Vico says: "When men are ignorant of the natural causes producing things, and cannot even explain them by analogy with similar things, they attribute their own nature to them."[4] At times the similarities are striking. In one of Piaget's books, in response to the question of the origin of the stars, a child answered: "People took little stones and made them into stars."[5] In his book on jurisprudence Vico says, "Children think that stars are nails fixed in the sky."[6]

---

[2] *The New Science of Giambattista Vico* (hereinafter *NS*), translated by Thomas G. Bergin and Max H. Fisch (Ithaca: Cornell University Press, 1968), par. 218.

[3] *NS*, pars. 120, 181.

[4] *NS*, par. 180.

[5] Jean Piaget, *The Child's Conception of the World* (Totowa, N.J.: Littlefield, Adams, 1969), p. 267.

[6] G. B. Vico, *Il diritto universale*, in *Opere giuridiche*, edited by Paolo Cristofolini (Florence: Sansoni, 1974), p. 462.

Artificialism is defined by Piaget as the belief that everything not only is made *for* man but is made *by* man. Vico says: "The nature of the human mind leads it to attribute its own nature to the effect. . . . [the giants, i.e., the early men, comparable to children] pictured the sky to themselves as a great animated body which in that aspect they called Jove, the first god";[7] "and to all of the universe that came within their scope, and to all its parts, they gave the being of animate substance."[8]

Other examples of similarities between Vico and Piaget are relevant to the concepts of imitation, imagination, and construction of reality, and, in regard to this latter, relate in particular to the well-known Piagetian studies on the development of the notions of number, sensorial functions, class, and movement. Two examples may suffice.

Piaget has shown that between the ages of four-and-a-half and five-and-a-half children are able to count (i.e., a number of bottles and an equal number of glasses), but the equality of number is determined solely by the equality of lengths, and counting is an extraneous and irrelevant act. Only around the age of six is the child able to establish the equivalence between two sets of objects by the method of one-to-one correspondence. In one of his early lectures Vico says:

> In the early times, when a decision had to be taken concerning a matter on which opinions were divided, all the people were convoked, the facts were exposed and they were told that Smith was of this opinion, Jones of that opinion and someone else of a third opinion. Then, each of those present left his place to move either to Jones's side or to Smith's side, or to someone else's side; finally the decision was given to the group which appeared most numerous. That happened because those primitive men were unable to say "Jones has one hundred votes, Smith fifty," etc.; in fact, it took at least two thousand years of civilization before a thing as abstract as numeration developed.[9]

Also, Piaget has found that children believe that one sees

[7] *NS*, par. 377.
[8] *NS*, par. 379.
[9] G. B. Vico, *Opere*, edited by Fausto Nicolini (Milan: Ricciardi, 1953), p. 964.

because the light is in the eye.[10] In discussing the activities of the senses in the heroic times, Vico says that "seeing distinctly was called *cernere oculis* (hence, perhaps, the Italian *scernere*) for the eyes are like a sieve and the pupils like two holes, and as from the sieve sticks of dust issue to touch the earth, so from the eyes, through the pupils, sticks of light issue to touch the objects which are distinctly seen."[11]

The role of language for the development of the child has been a key issue in Piaget's studies: while he first took the view that the child's intellectual development was strictly related to language and social factors, in recent years he has stressed action as source of thought.[12] Vico says: "It is noteworthy that in all languages the greater part of the expressions relating to inanimate things are formed by metaphor from the human body and its parts and from the human senses and passions."[13]

Even more recently Piaget has admitted the existence of "universals," characteristics of the cognitive structures of all human organisms,[14] as typified by the "scheme," defined by him as "what there is in common among several different and analogous actions" or as "practical, i.e., prelinguistic concepts."[15] Vico in his early treatise of 1709 on education de-

[10] Piaget, *The Child's Conception of the World*, p. 40.

[11] *NS*, par. 706.

[12] "This is, in fact, my hypothesis," he stated in a short interview on genetic epistemology, "that the roots of logical thought are not to be found in language alone, even though language coordinations are important. Rather, the roots of logic are to be found more generally in the coordination of actions, which are the basis of reflective abstraction" (Jean Piaget, "Genetic Epistemology," *The Columbia Forum* 12 [1969]; reprinted in Richard I. Evans, *Jean Piaget: The Man and His Ideas* [New York: Dutton, 1973], p. xlvii).

[13] *NS*, par. 405.

[14] In his dialogue with Evans, Piaget accepts the latter's statement in regard to developmental stages: "You are talking about universals, things that are characteristic of the cognitive structures of all human organisms, and you would probably say, in effect, that you could go to every single culture and you would find these same universals. . . . What you are really saying is that all societies have certain unique characteristics and all individuals in their cognitive development have universal characteristics" (Evans, *Jean Piaget*, pp. 71–72).

[15] *Ibid.*, p. 18.

fined topics as "the middle term . . . the 'medium' . . . what the Latins call *argumentum*,"[16] that is, topics are the commonplace, the hypothetical or verisimilar postulates subsumed in any form of reasoning. In the *New Science* and elsewhere he spoke at various times of the "universal words,"[17] of "imaginative class concepts or universals,"[18] especially as related to the way of communication between men of the heroic times,[19] and stemming from his well-known notion of common sense. In simple words, these topics or imaginative universals appear to be a half-way stage making possible the transition from concrete to abstract thinking.

The relevance of Piaget's genetic concepts for education centers on three areas: (1) the importance of definite stages of development; (2) the role attributed to the child's inner activity in construing his reality; (3) the recognition of an intrinsic structure of each intellectual operation as reflected in the child's action and thought.

Although criticized as too rigidly linked to developmental stages and too neglectful of the role played by emotional factors, Piaget's ideas on education are increasingly finding acceptance by many, also in this country. Central to these ideas is his emphasis on the role of action in the acquisition of knowledge, be this at the sensory-motor stage, at the stage of concrete operations, or at the stage of formal operations. As he recently put it: "To me the essential aspect of thought is its operative aspects: I think that human knowledge is essentially active."[20] In line with this, Piaget's followers have stressed the importance of allowing children to manipulate things and of

[16] Giambattista Vico, *On the Study Methods of Our Time*, translated by Elio Gianturco (Indianapolis: Bobbs-Merrill, 1965), p. 15.

[17] Vico, *Opere*, p. 264. In the *New Science* he said: "The first men, the children, as it were, of the human race, not being able to form intelligible class concepts of things, had a natural need to create poetic characters; that is, imaginative class concepts or universals, to which, as to certain models or ideal portraits, to reduce all the particular species which resembled them" (*NS*, par. 209).

[18] *NS*, par. 209.

[19] *NS*, par. 934.

[20] Evans, *Jean Piaget*, p. xliv.

providing them with potentially interesting experiences. As a matter of fact, in Piaget's study of children—as a critic has put it—"One experimenter (the psychologist) arranges for the opportunities for the other experimenter (the child) to carry on his or her own experiments."[21]

Vico, too, was aware of developmental stages in human life, and made reference to them as early as in his *Second Oration* of 1700.[22] As one of his students put it:

Vico believes in the existence of a *psychogenetic law*, by which the individual develops through a certain series of phases, the sequential order of which is immutable and fixed by nature. These stages parallel an equally immutable set of "culture stages" which the whole of mankind has traversed in its growth from infancy to adulthood, from primitivism to civilization.[23]

Interestingly enough, Piaget has found that there is a correspondence between the three stages of mathematical thought throughout history and throughout the development of the child: the first period of Euclidean geometry corresponds to preoperational thought in the child, the second period of analytic geometry (17th century) to concrete operational thought, the third period of sets with structures (late 19th century) to formal operational thought.[24]

As for the importance of the creative momentum for learning, Vico said:

Geometry should be taught not analytically, but synthetically, so as to arrive at the demonstration by combining; which means *to create the truth instead of finding it*. To find is a work of chance, to create, of industriousness; for this reason I have asked that geometry be taught *not with the help of numbers and genders, but of forms*; so that, in learning it, the fantasy, which is the core of talent, rather than talent itself, be strengthened.[25]

---

[21] *Ibid.*, p. 68.

[22] G. B. Vico, *Opere filosofiche*, edited by Paolo Cristofolini (Florence: Sansoni, 1971) p. 726; see also Vico, *Opere giuridiche*, p. 338.

[23] Elio Gianturco, "Introduction," in Vico, *On the Study Methods of Our Time*, p. xxvi

[24] Jean Piaget, Bärbel Inhelder, and Alina Szeminska, *The Child's Conception of Geometry* (New York: Basic Books, 1960), *passim*.

[25] Vico, *Opere*, p. 303; my italics.

Likewise, in regard to language, Vico says that "in forming a speech, children use a certain *geometrical synthesis*, with which they run through all the elements of language, gather those which they need and combine them into unity;"[26] and writing itself derives from geometry.[27] Indeed, these themes are at the heart of Vico's conviction that the true (*verum*) and the made (*factum*) are convertible—that is, that we can know for certain only that which we ourselves have made or created.

The analogies between Vico and Piaget extend also to the notions of truth and morality. For Piaget, children are always sincere in their approach to reality; the different interpretations that they offer of reality during their development is related to their different operational levels. Irony can occur only at adolescence, when "the subject becomes capable of reasoning correctly about propositions he does not believe, or at least not yet; that is, propositions that he considers pure hypothesis."[28] Vico says: "Since the first men of the gentile world had the simplicity of children, who are truthful by nature, the first fables could not feign anything false. . . . Irony certainly could not have begun until the period of reflection, because it is fashioned by falsehood by dint of a reflection which wears the mask of truth."[29]

Finally, as for the development of morality, Vico says that "men were for a long period incapable of truth and of reason, which is the fount of that *inner justice* by which the intellect is satisfied . . . the nations were governed by the certainty of authority . . . that is a philosophy of authority, which is the fount of the *outer justice*."[30] The "outer justice" is what Piaget has called "heteronomy," that is, the affective reactions and peculiarities of the morality of the child before the age of

---

[26] G. B. Vico, *La scienza nuova prima*, in *Tutte le opere di Giambattista Vico*, edited by Francesco Flora (Milan: Mondadori, 1957), 1: 784; my italics.

[27] Vico, *Opere giuridiche*, p. 480.

[28] Jean Piaget and Bärbel Inhelder, *The Psychology of the Child* (New York: Basic Books, 1969), p. 132.

[29] *NS*, par. 498.

[30] *NS*, par. 350; my italics.

seven or eight, which is strictly dependent upon the presence of the person who gives orders and which, later on, will develop into the "autonomy" of the "sense of justice,"[31] that is, into Vico's "inner justice."

Methodological Considerations

Piaget in his studies on children has employed, for infants, the observation of their behavior and, for older children, what he has called the "clinical method," consisting of eliciting verbal or nonverbal responses (through manipulation of objects, drawings, etc.) to questions and issues arising in the most neutral way, so as to avoid possible influence by the researcher. Considering the fact that he studied his own three children extensively, his method has been attacked by behavioral scientists on various grounds, partially accounting for the relative neglect of his work in this country until the last decade or so. On the positive side stand the advantage of longitudinal studies, the high level of consistency reached by the same researcher, and the comparable results obtained by independent investigators. Moreover, Freud's main tenets, which have achieved wide acceptance, were arrived at, too, from the study of only a few subjects.

Like Piaget, Vico was aware of the methodological difficulties related to his philosophical inquiry.

To discover the way in which this first human thinking arose in the gentile world, we encountered exasperating difficulties which have cost us the research of a good twenty years. We had to descend from these human and refined natures of ours to those quite wild and savage natures, which we cannot at all imagine and can comprehend only with great effort.[32]

How, then, did he gain the tremendous insight into the psychogenetic development of the mind? His *Autobiography* is

[31] Jean Piaget, *The Moral Judgment of the Child* (New York: Harcourt, Brace, 1932), *passim*.
[32] *NS*, par. 338.

not helpful on this matter, except for the casual observation
that he applied himself too early in life to the study of logic,
with the result that he got discouraged and stayed away from
it for a year and a half[33]—an early recognition of the importance of developmental stages. What is certain is that he lived
most of his life surrounded by children: he was, himself, the
sixth of eight children; at the age of eighteen he accepted a
position as tutor for the four children (then ranging in age from
nine to thirteen) of the Rocca family in Vatolla, south of
Naples, and remained there for nine years; later on, after his
marriage in 1699 at thirty-one, he had plenty of opportunity
to follow the development of his own children, eight in all,
born between 1700 and 1720, of whom five survived beyond
early childhood.[34]

Moreover, though somewhat influenced by the educational
ideas of the classical (Xenophon, Plato, Aristotle, Quintilian),
Christian (St. Augustine), Renaissance (Erasmus, Vives,
Rabelais, Montaigne) and seventeenth-century (Fénelon) tra-
ditions, it is unlikely that he was familiar with Locke's book
Some Thoughts Concerning Education, published in 1693.[35]

Vico and Piaget: A Comprehensive Assessment

Having thus far brought forward a number of similarities
between Piaget and Vico, it is now time to stress their most
striking difference: while in Piaget the psychogenetic tenets of
the child are presented as a well-construed comprehensive
theory of development of the personality, in Vico they represent occasional and scattered remarks in support of his views
on the development of humanity through various stages.

Of course, outstanding differences between Vico and Piaget
are easily found: their places of work and of residence—the

---

[33] *The Autobiography of Giambattista Vico*, translated by Max H. Fisch and Thomas G.
Bergin (Ithaca: Cornell University Press, 1944), p. 113.

[34] *Ibid., passim.*

[35] Remo Fornaca, *Il pensiero educativo di Giambattista Vico* (Turin: Giappichelli, 1957).

Catholic, exuberant, often tyranically run Naples versus the Calvinist, austere, democratic Geneva; their backgrounds— humanistic in Vico, as proven by his respect for eloquence and by his admiration for his four favorite authors (Plato, Tacitus, Grotius, and Bacon), scientific in Piaget, who first achieved renown for his studies on zoology and who has constantly shied away from philosophical speculations in favor of a biological orientation; their styles—colorful, impetuous, uneven in Vico, rational, dry, and consistent in Piaget; their personalities—irritable, rather distrustful in Vico, patient, conciliatory (typically in his attitude toward the disregard and unproven criticism of his concepts by psychoanalysts) in Piaget; finally, the tremendous differences in the reactions to their work—in Vico's case, puzzlement (even on the part of those well disposed toward him), opposition, and, worst of all, neglect, in Piaget's case, enthusiasm in some quarters in the twenties and thirties, followed by some degree of supercilious neglect in the forties, and, since then, overwhelming acceptance, as shown by the translations of his books, by all kinds of awards, and by the founding of the International Center for Genetic Epistemology in Geneva in 1956.

Yet, for all these differences, there are also many similarities between Vico and Piaget. Interestingly enough, each experienced an emotional crisis early in his life, essentially characterized by a period of isolation and by a disbelief in his own religious upbringing.[36] Although each resolved his crisis in different ways—Vico plunged into the humanities, Piaget into the sciences—these crises may have spurred their creativity,

---

[36] For Vico's crisis, see *The Autobiography of Giambattista Vico*; Fausto Nicolini, *La giovinezza di Giambattista Vico* (Bari: Laterza, 1932); Henry P. Adams, *The Life and Writings of Giambattista Vico* (London: Allen & Unwin, 1935); Antonio Corsano, *Umanesimo e religione di G. B. Vico* (Bari: Laterza, 1935) and *Giambattista Vico* (Bari: Laterza, 1956); Angela M. Jacobelli Isoldi, *G. B. Vico: la vita e le opere* (Bologna: Cappelli, 1960). For Piaget's crisis, see Jean Piaget, "Jean Piaget," in Edwin G. Boring and others, eds., *A History of Psychology in Autobiography*, vol. 4 (Worcester, Mass.: Clark University Press, 1952), p. 241 (reprinted in Evans, *Jean Piaget*, p. 109).

according to the recently developed notion of "creative illness."[37]

Both Vico and Piaget can be considered self-taught men
inclined by nature toward crossing and blending disciplines:
history, mythology, and language in Vico; biology, mathematics, and psychology in Piaget. The main difference between
them lies, of course, in the fact that Piaget developed his own
cross-disciplinary interest *after* the various above-mentioned
scientific fields had achieved a considerable development,
Vico *before* that.

Vico himself was aware of the need for new paths in the
sciences of men and wrote in *On The Study Methods of Our Time*
in 1707: "We neglect that discipline which deals with the
differential features of the virtues and vices, with good and
bad behavior patterns, with the typical characteristics of the
various ages of man, of the two sexes, of social and economic
class, race, and nation, and with the art of seemly conduct of
life, the most difficult of all arts."[38] Indeed, these were the
very disciplines of psychology and sociology which were to
develop in the nineteenth century.

For Vico the problem consisted in reaching scientific—or at
least sufficiently scientific—conclusions from the study of literature, history, and language. In fact, for lack of a psychological nomenclature, he was compelled to use figures of speech
to express his concepts; for instance, he called "diversiloquia"
the principle by which a concrete example signifies an abstract
concept, "as Achilles connotes an idea of valor common to all
strong men, or Ulysses an idea of prudence common to all
wise men."[39]

For Piaget the problem was to free himself from the strictures of scientific knowledge accumulated in the fields of

---

[37] H. Ellenberger, "The Concept of Creative Illness," *Psychoanalytic Review* 55
(1968): 442–456.
[38] Vico, *On the Study Methods of Our Time*, p. 33.
[39] *NS*, par. 403; see also pars. 210, 890.

biology, mathematics, and psychology in order to look at the child in a candid way and, eventually, to discover the common principles underlying these various fields.

Both Vico and Piaget, however, came to the awareness of a fundamental parallelism between the developmental stages of the child and the developmental stages of humanity. In his keynote address at a conference convened in his honor in Ellenville, New York, in June 1975, Piaget stated, on the basis of several examples, that "understanding what goes on in children can shed light on understanding the history of science, and vice versa."[40]

Finally, because of their tremendous originality and cross-disciplinary interests, both Vico and Piaget are difficult to categorize, and their places in the field of knowledge have remained uncertain. Perhaps the intrinsic reason for this difficulty is that both attempted in different ways to bridge the gap between the sciences and the humanities—an issue so crucial in our day.

Vico and Genetic Epistemology

At present, there is no history of genetic epistemology, defined by Piaget as "the attempt to identify the roots of the different varieties of knowledge from their most elementary forms and to follow their development through their successive stages up to their conceptualization in scientific terms."[41]

Like Freud, Piaget has been so involved in his pioneering studies that he has had no time or interest in tracing back antecedents and derivatives of his concepts. Now that genetic epistemology has reached the stage of universal acceptance, it is time to begin such an historical investigation; and Vico is naturally the point of reference for such an investigation.

[40] *The New York Times*, June 15, 1975.
[41] Jean Piaget, *L'épistémologie génétique* (Paris: Presses Universitaires de France, 1972), p. 6.

In terms of the interest in the child, the early students of child psychology in the second half of the nineteenth century were interested primarily in the developmental stages of the child rather than in epistemological research. Having lived more than a century earlier, Vico certainly could not be expected to be interested in this kind of research. But he anticipated it in his emphasis on the analogy between the mind of the child and that of the primitive, for which he found confirmation from three themes closely related to the idea of childhood as a distinct stage of the individual (a fundamental discovery of the eighteenth century),[42] that is, the themes of memory[43] (through his novel revival of the past), of autobiography[44] (through an account of his intellectual journey), and of adolescence[45] (through the impetuous style of life reflected in his writings).

Both solitary giants of knowledge in unexplored fields, Vico and Piaget could not be more apart for their different styles: emotional and perplexing in Vico, rational and scientifically convincing in Piaget. Their emphasis also has been opposite: on humanity in Vico, on the individual in Piaget.

Their paths cross, however. From the study of humanity, Vico derived insights into the psychogenetic law of the individual. From the study of the individual, Piaget is now moving toward the study of humanity. By construing his reality in the act of knowledge, "the child is a philosopher," Piaget has said.[46] This appears to echo Vico's statement, in his First Ora-

---

[42] Philippe Aries, *Centuries of Childhood* (New York: Vintage, 1965); George Boas, *The Cult of Childhood* (London: Warburg Institute of the University of London, 1966).

[43] Georges Poulet, *Studies in Human Time* (Baltimore: Johns Hopkins Press, 1956), pp. 23–24; J. Starobinski, "The Idea of Nostalgia," *Diogenes* 54 (1966): 81–103.

[44] G. Gusdorf, "Conditions et limites de l'autobiographie," in Günter Reichenkron and Erich Haase, eds., *Formen der Selbstdarstellung: Analekten zu einer Geschichte des literarischen Selbstportraits* (Berlin: Duncker & Humblot, 1956), p. 107; Roy Pascal, *Design and Truth in Autobiography* (Cambridge: Harvard University Press, 1960), chaps. 3 and 4.

[45] Hans H. Muchow, "Die Flegeljahre als Zivilisationsphänomen: Eine Theorie der Vorpubertät," *Studium Generale* 5 (1952): 280–286; Hans H. Muchow, *Flegeljahre: Beiträge zur Psychologie und Pädagogik der "Vorpubertät"* (Ravensburg: Maier, 1953).

[46] Jean Piaget, "Children's Philosophies," in Carl A. Murchinson, ed., *A Handbook of Child Psychology* (Worcester, Mass.: Clark University Press, 1931), pp. 377–391.

tion of 1699 directed to his students of rhetoric at the University of Naples: "Each of you, during childhood, is a great philosopher." And later, in the same oration: "Already at the age of two or three we memorize such an amount of ideas and words which exhaust the experience of everyday life, to combine and order which a philologist would have to write numerous big volumes."[47] What Vico, for lack of a better terminology, attributed to philology was later to be attributed to psychology; prophetically, two centuries later Jean Piaget would write the "big volumes." Regardless of the difference in style, a bold search for the truth unites Vico and Piaget. For as Vico himself put it: "The poet teaches by delighting what the philosopher teaches austerely."[48]

With this I terminate my study of the parallels and differences between Vico and Piaget. I trust that the points which I brought forward in my paper clearly show that Vico plays a central role in the historical approach to Piaget's epistemology and that those interested in this field may benefit from a study of Vico.

Comment on Dr. Mora's Paper

Dr. Mora's paper reveals striking similarities between Vico's and Piaget's developmental theories of mind. The real difference between these two thinkers, I would suggest, lies not so much in their views about the nature of the development of the mind as in their attitudes toward this development or certain aspects of it. Dr. Mora referred to this difference of attitude when he indicated that Vico "plunged" into the humanities while Piaget plunged into the sciences, and when he said that Vico's orientation was philosophical while Piaget's is ultimately biological.

[47] Vico, *Opere filosofiche*, p. 714.
[48] Vico, *On the Study Methods of Our Time*, p. 43.

The significance of Vico's and Piaget's attitudes toward the humanistic and scientific fields of knowledge may be seen in the importance which they conceive these fields to have for education. Although they agree about the creative nature of cognition, they emphasize the importance of different aspects of the learning process in their theories of education. In his oration *On the Study Methods of Our Time* Vico calls for education to concentrate at the outset on developing fantasy and memory and warns that the study of critical thinking, if it is begun too early, has a stifling effect. This is because the invention of arguments is prior to their critical evaluation, and this invention demands a developed imagination. More important for Vico, however, are the ethical effects of education. In the previously mentioned work he says:

> The greatest drawback of our educational methods is that we pay an excessive amount of attention to the natural sciences and not enough to ethics. Our chief fault is that we disregard that part of ethics which treats of human character, of its dispositions, its passions, and of the manner of adjusting these to public life.[1]

Later, in the *New Science*, he conceives this educational problem in terms of barbarism. There he states that it is possible to have barbarism arise from the intellect as well as from the senses. He says that the barbarism of reflection makes men more inhuman than the barbarism of the senses because it takes the form of premeditated malice.[2] Such men Vico describes as no longer sensible to anything outside life's necessities. They no longer possess a sense of community or humanity. Here Vico sees the educational value of the humanities. For Vico poetry and philosophy teach moral duties, albeit in very different ways, one by example and the other generically.[3] Like religion, they unite people's actions and teach a sense of community. Vico's view of education is an expression of his interest in community.

Piaget's approach to education reflects a different attitude. A summary of his suggestions for future education has been published with the Vichian-sounding title *To Understand Is to Invent*.[4] In this

[1] Giambattista Vico, *On the Study Methods of Our Time*, translated by Elio Gianturco (Indianapolis: Bobbs-Merrill, 1965), p. 33.

[2] *The New Science of Giambattista Vico*, translated by Max H. Fisch and Thomas G. Bergin (Ithaca: Cornell University Press, 1968), par. 1106.

[3] Vico, *On the Study Methods of Our Time*, p. 43.

[4] Jean Piaget, *To Understand Is to Invent* (New York: Viking, 1974).

book Piaget says that the integrity of the stages in which the child develops should be recognized and respected. Attempts to accelerate them, he says, could be harmful and future research will have to determine the optimal speed for the transition from one to the next.[5] He does not contradict Vico here. But upon closer inspection a basic difference in attitude emerges. In education Piaget is most interested in "cultivating the experimental mind." Of course this is not all that he is concerned with cultivating. Ethical education is the second main heading in his sketch for future education.[6] In his study on *The Moral Judgment of the Child* he showed the close relationship between cognitive and moral development.[7] Both logical and moral thought are normative, and the development of such normative thought depends upon cooperation.[8] This occurs by overcoming the absence of self-awareness that Piaget has called "egocentrism" and the merely submissive attitude to authority that accompanies it. Education should make us tolerant of other groups, he emphasizes.[9] But what does it do to positively build up a sense of belonging and humanity? Unlike Vico he does not give any importance to the humanities. In fact, he hardly treats them at all; they are peripheral to his real interest, which is the development of scientific cognition.

Piaget's relationship to philosophy is an interesting example of his relationship to the humanities. In his book *Insights and Illusions of Philosophy* he voices skepticism about philosophy's suggestive nature because the verification of philosophical theories seems impossible.[10] Because of its inability to become one of the sciences Piaget calls philosophy into question as a "centralizing discipline" and "headquarters for interdisciplinary research." He proposes that education should now center upon a "scientific structuralism."[11]

Piaget speaks as a representative of contemporary thought. Vico suggests a change or rather a broadening of our perspectives regarding education and what we should consider important generally. He represents the philosophical attitude that self-knowledge is most important. Any discussion of Vico and Piaget must take this fact into account.

JOHN MICHAEL KROIS

[5] *Ibid.*, pp. 22–23.
[6] *Ibid.*, pp. 109–126.
[7] Jean Piaget, *The Moral Judgment of the Child* (London: Routledge & Kegan Paul, 1932).
[8] *Ibid.*, p. 404.
[9] Piaget, *To Understand Is to Invent*, pp. 139–140.
[10] Jean Piaget, *Insights and Illusions of Philosophy* (New York; World, 1971), p. 11.
[11] Piaget, *To Understand Is to Invent*, pp. 32–33.

Vico's Insight and the Scientific Study of the Stream of Consciousness

BY JEROME L. SINGER

Psychological research on the nature of human thought has developed a new burst of vigor with the emergence of cognitive or information-processing models of human experience. The very thing that gave so much power to the psychodynamic points of view—the emphasis on drives, conflicts, and unconscious wishes—hindered psychology from developing a fuller sense of process in relation to human thought. Focusing upon the rise and fall of body-centered drives, psychologists representing psychoanalytic orientations or the drive-reduction learning schools tended toward a sensual reductionism. The most complex thought processes were explained predominantly as defensive maneuvers or, at best, as sublimated titrations of sexual or aggressive energies tied closely to biological functioning.

Since about 1960, the confluence of strains of research evidence and theorizing drawn from (1) studies of the nature of brain function,[1] (2) studies of information-processing,[2] (3) the examination of the importance of emotions rather than

[1] Donald O. Hebb, "Drives and the C.N.S. (Conceptual Nervous System)," *Psychological Review* 62 (1955): 243–253; Karl H. Pribram, "Reinforcement Revisited: A Structural View," in Marshall R. Jones, ed., *Human Motivation: A Symposium* (Lincoln: University of Nebraska Press, 1965).

[2] George A. Miller, Eugene Galanter, and Karl H. Pribram, *Plans and the Structure of Behavior* (New York: Holt, 1960); Ulrich Neisser, *Cognitive Psychology* (New York: Appleton-Century-Crofts, 1967).

drives as keys to motivational behavior,[3] as well as (4) research on imagination[4] have led to a different view of human behavior that brings psychology perhaps more into line with Vico's conceptions.

The cognitive perspective in psychology may be summarized perhaps in the following terms:

The human being is striving ceaselessly to organize complex information drawn from both the external environment and long-term memory systems. Torn between curiosity and the anxiety generated by excessive ambiguity or incongruity, humans must learn rules for anticipating sets of environment (physical or social) and also for limiting the range and complexity of information that is processed. The major human emotions—from terror, anger, or despair to the positive emotions of interest, surprise, and joy—can themselves be related to specific characteristics of the information-processing tasks which confront all of us.[5] Thus emotion and cognition are closely intertwined as the major human motivational systems.

Vico's View of the Human Imagination

Let us now review some of Vico's major propositions about human knowledge and imagination. First of all, there is the famous quotation (in Pompa's retranslation):

But in the night of thick darkness enveloping the earliest antiquity so remote from ourselves, there shines the eternal and

[3] Silvan S. Tomkins, *Affect, Imagery, Consciousness*, 2 vols. (New York: Springer, 1962–63); Carroll E. Izard, *The Face of Emotion* (New York: Appleton-Century-Crofts, 1971).

[4] Jerome L. Singer, *Daydreaming* (New York: Random House, 1966); Jerome L. Singer, *The Child's World of Make-Believe: Experimental Studies of Imaginative Play* (New York: Academic Press, 1973); Jerome L. Singer, *The Inner World of Daydreaming* (New York: Harper & Row, 1975); Jerome L. Singer, "Navigating the Stream of Consciousness: Research in Daydreaming and Related Inner Experiences," *American Psychologist* 30 (1975): 727–738.

[5] Tomkins, *Affect, Imagery, Consciousness*; Jerome L. Singer, *Imagery and Daydream Methods in Psychotherapy and Behavior Modification* (New York: Academic Press, 1974).

never failing light of a truth beyond all question: that this world of civil society has certainly been made by men and that its principles are therefore to be rediscovered within the modifications of our own human mind. Whoever reflects upon this cannot but marvel that the philosophers should have bent all their energies to the world of nature, which, since God made it, He alone knows; and that they should have neglected the study of the world of nations, which, since men made it, men could come to know.[6]

This profound view of human experience is elaborated further in the emphasis on the fact that humans, having grown up in social settings, inevitably reflect their experience in these settings and that this reflection in itself represents a reality of our environment much in the same way or perhaps more so than do abstract geometric or mathematical propositions. By examining their own thoughts, human beings, having already been actors in events, can go the next step and begin to generate propositions about causality. In effect Vico, at least as interpreted by Berlin and Pompa,[7] were aware that what we understand as causality inheres in the very manner in which humans interact with the environment. Indeed, it is a remarkable prefiguring of many current notions advanced by behaviorally oriented psychologists as well as phenomenologists and, most recently, attribution theorists. All have pointed to the necessity, in conceptualizing animal as well as human behavior, of taking into account what might be called the "causal texture of the environment" or the purposive behavior of animals and men.[8]

If we are to understand the development of social systems we can also examine them in relation to societies of different

[6] Leon Pompa, *Vico: A Study of the New Science* (New York: Cambridge University Press, 1975), pp. 154–155.

[7] Isaiah Berlin, "A Note on Vico's Concept of Knowledge," in Giorgio Tagliacozzo and Hayden V. White, eds., *Giambattista Vico: An International Symposium* (Baltimore: Johns Hopkins Press, 1969); Pompa, *Vico: A Study of the New Science*.

[8] Edward C. Tolman, *Purposive Behavior in Animals and Men* (New York: Appleton, 1932); R. Rescorla, "Conditioned Inhibition of Fear," in N. J. Mackintosh and W. K. Honig, eds., *Fundamental Issues in Associative Learning* (Halifax: Dalhousie University Press, 1969); Fritz Heider, *The Psychology of Interpersonal Relations* (New York: Wiley, 1958).

degrees of complexity because we can also, as adults, recall how we behaved as children or indeed observe the thinking of children as a clue to the potential of the mind at different stages. In this sense Vico was anticipating some other important developmental concepts. He wrote, for example, "In childhood memory is most vigorous and imagination is therefore excessively vivid, for imagination is nothing but extended or compounded memory. . . . This axiom is the principle of the expressiveness of the poetic images that the world formed in its first childhood."[9]

Vico seemed unusually sensitive to the special quality of childhood experience in his emphasis on its closeness to the immediate senses. Thus the child is characterized more by a concrete imagery related very much to the particular sensory modality through which information has been originally organized. By comparison, the adult retains this earlier potential but adds to it the capacity for reflection. This distinction between *coscienza* and *scienza*, or concrete sensory experience and reflective, abstract processes, certainly seems to foreshadow our current view of the imagery-parallel processing system and the verbal-analytic or sequential system. The directness of childhood experience has formed the basis for a brilliant analysis by Schachtel of the origin of so-called childhood amnesia or repression.[10] Schachtel has proposed that many early childhood experiences are not forgotten because of active conflict and internal repressive mechanism as Freud would have argued. Often the intellectual capacities of the child are lacking in that reflective capacity that allows for reorganizing, labeling, and classifying schema in ways available only to the adult.

In effect, Vico seems to be taking the position that the human being is a mythmaker or poet who organizes the unknown world into groups of metaphors that seem to give it

[9] Pompa, *Vico: A Study of the New Science*, p. 165.
[10] Ernest G. Schachtel, *Metamorphosis* (New York: Basic Books, 1959).

some structure in relation to what he has experienced in his interaction with others. In the case of the physical world and natural science, the tendency has been to believe that what is being studied is necessarily "out there," but Vico raises the profound question that humans have simply not examined the fact that their organization depends inevitably upon their own social experience. At least in the case of the social sciences, one can get perhaps an even better feeling of the reality of propositions about the human condition since some make more sense than others in the light of our actual day-to-day experiences and memories.

The notion of relation between the history of different civilizations and social groups and the structural characteristics of the human mind at different stages of development within a given individual's life has of course been one of the most popular implications of Vico's work. This view has been given a hauntingly complex representation in James Joyce's *Finnegan's Wake*, where the mind of a sleeping man in its concrete and unreflective associational juxtapositions relives again and again the history of the Irish culture. A developmental psychologist, Heinz Werner, has used similar notions in attempting to show that certain types of thinking characteristic of childhood in Western civilization are also observable in adults from presumably less complicated and verbal or literate cultures.[11] While this proposition has most recently been rather seriously questioned as we get to understand more of the complexity of the so-called "primitive cultures" that still dwell in the world, there seems little doubt that the absence of complex written material which can be accumulated and made available to children and adults may lead to very different patterns of thought and imagination. In a remarkable new work, Jaynes has raised the question whether we may be experiencing a particular evolutionary development in the greater differentiation of the "bicameral mind," that is, the

[11] Heinz Werner, *The Comparative Psychology of Mental Development* (Chicago: Follett, 1948).

distinction between the verbal-lexical-sequential properties of the left side of the brain and the imagery-concrete-parallel-process properties of the right side of the brain.[12] He has examined early literature, myth, and poetry and has questioned whether human beings in the period prior to the first millennium B.C. were indeed capable of distinguishing between dreams, early childhood memories, fantasies, and other images and their externally derived sensory impression. In effect he seems to be arguing that *coscienza* was indeed a characteristic of all human thought. Thus it was natural for a man of Odysseus's time to accept the fact that a dream which urged him to a particular course of action represented a genuine visitation from an external source rather than a product of his own memory and wishes.

Lewis's fascinating collection of dream literature from the ancient world demonstrates the sharp contrast between the literal belief in the dream as a visitation which can be found in Homer or earlier writings and the calm voice of reason that emerges from Aristotle writing in the fourth century B.C.[13] The latter points to the fact that in effect some dreams seem to come true because we have a great variety of intentions, some of which we manage to carry out but many of which are not possible of fulfillment. Here we see most clearly the distinction between the *scienza* of the classic Greek protoscientist and the *coscienza* of the earlier writers.

Current Research Approaches in Relation to
Vico's Orientation

The cognitive movement in psychology, as suggested, has grown out of extensive experimental research. It might be useful to point to some of the main trends at least with respect to imagination, as they might bear on Vico's orientation.

[12] Julian Jaynes, *The Evolution of Consciousness* (Oxford: Oxford University Press, 1976).
[13] N. Lewis, *The Interpretation of Dreams and Portents* (Toronto: Stevens, 1976).

The extensive nature of ongoing play behavior and the use of pretending and make-believe characteristic of childhood has been increasingly documented by a whole series of systematic observations of children at play in natural settings.[14] It seems pretty clear that children do follow something like Piaget's accommodation-assimilation cycle in which they attempt to imitate snatches of adult conversation or actions and fit these into the limited range of available schema. This accounts for the novelty and quaintness of some of their play behaviors or verbalizations, but it also puts them in touch with an additional novel environment which they can manipulate and from which they can elicit further knowledge of causal interrelationships.

A four-year-old child of my acquaintance was noticed by his mother to be lining up a whole group of toy soldiers on the kitchen floor. When asked about why this large battle array had been set up, he replied, "I heard you talking on the telephone and saying 'Daddy was all tied up at work.' I'm getting my soldiers ready to see if we can go and rescue him!" Here a child is attempting to cope with ambiguities in communication in the best way he can and establishing organizing principles on the basis of its limited range of cognitive schema. In this case the cliché phrase ("tied up") could be taken only in a concrete sense by the child.

Within childhood play we see the directness of experience and limitation of reflective capacities; at the same time we can discern origins of mythmaking and the development of new organizing principles. Space prevents an elaboration on the whole question of make-believe and pretending as human capacities. It could certainly be argued that the "as if" dimension, or what Kurt Goldstein called "the attitude toward the possible," is one of the highest of human capacities.

[14] Jean Piaget, *Play, Dreams, and Imitation in Childhood* (New York: Norton, 1962); J. L. Singer, *The Child's World of Make-Believe*: J. L. Singer and D. G. Singer, "Imaginative Play and Pretending in Early Childhood: Some Experimental Approaches," in Anthony Davids, ed., *Child Personality and Psychopathology* (New York: Wiley, 1976).

Vico regarded thought as an active, continuous process and an evolving one. We can see this position exemplified most clearly in the play of children, since they tend to verbalize and act out in sociodramatic form much of what presumably passes through their minds. Recent research has increasingly sampled the continuous play behavior of children as an important method for evaluating the development of imagination and emotion.[15]

It has often been thought that imagination or fantasy eventually disappears from adult mental life, surfacing only during night dreams or occasional fantasies. Indeed, Vico himself may have erred in overemphasizing the power of *scienza* once it has developed, much as Freud tended to overemphasize the power of the verbal and analytic human capacities once individuals were freed of neurotic conflict. It seems much more likely from recent research[16] that adult thought is often characterized by a complex mixture of concrete imagery and sensory-related experience with verbal-lexical and analytic coding systems. Indeed, it is likely that only a very small percentage of thought is truly carried out in the most purely "propositional" or abstract form and that most of our thinking involves remembrance of conversations, anticipated conversations, or visual images of particular human interaction.[17]

Even Piaget's conservation principle, which does not emerge until ages six or seven, can be shown to depend upon the experimenters' relying chiefly upon verbal reports. When children of five are asked whether two rows of candy containing an equal number of pieces are equivalent, they will tend to choose the longer row as having "more." Children by the age

[15] J. L. Singer and D. G. Singer, "Imaginative Play and Pretending in Early Childhood."

[16] J. L. Singer, *The Child's World of Make-Believe*; J. L. Singer and D. G. Singer, "Imaginative Play and Pretending in Early Childhood"; K. Pope and J. L. Singer, "Regulation of the Stream of Consciousness: Toward a Theory of Ongoing Thought," in Gary E. Schwartz and David Shapiro, eds., *Consciousness and Self-Regulation: Advances in Research*, vol. 2 (New York: Plenum, 1977).

[17] J. L. Singer, *The Inner World of Daydreaming*; J. L. Singer, "Navigating the Stream of Consciousness."

of seven can usually make a complete distinction at the verbal level between the two lengths of candy once they have ascertained by counting that the numbers are the same in both lines. Obviously, adults easily make the distinction between appearance and reality in the sense of sheer quantity. When however, children and adults are given the option of choosing only one of the two rows *to eat*, the adults tend to prefer the line of candies that "looks longer." In other words, all of us may continually be "hedging" our bets by the use of imagery processes.[18]

As suggested, however, it is quite possible that the representational or imagery form of thought need not be viewed as necessarily a childlike pattern. Imaginal thought has important adaptive properties. If we are trying to anticipate significant social encounters that are pending, we can often make effective use of our pictorial or verbal anticipatory capacities. And, of course, detective fiction such as the stories about Sherlock Holmes or Lord Peter Wimsey are replete with the effective use by the detectives of careful initial observation subsequently replayed mentally in relation to sets of events. By examining in one's mind's eye the entire layout of a room or the pattern of interaction of witnesses, one notices a setting or a gesture that had been too rapidly passed over before. In this sense we have probably as adults underestimated the great advantages of our capacities for vivid sensory experience. Indeed, this is one of the proposals made by Schachtel concerning the relation of creative experience and the sensory modalities.[19] Artists and poets, of course, are especially effective at recapturing this early sense of *coscienza*. A study by Kaplan and Singer indicated that individuals who as adults retained the capacity for fine discriminations in the so-called more primitive near-receptors of olfaction, touch, and gustation were also more likely to be more differentiated in their

[18] D. G. Singer and B. R. Cornfield, "Conserving and Consuming: A Developmental Study of Abstract and Action Choices," *Developmental Psychology* 8 (1973): 314.
[19] Schachtel, *Metamorphosis*.

belief-systems and less prone to clichés and gross prejudices in their social attitudes.[20]

A whole series of experiments has now begun to demonstrate the much greater complexity of adult thought when an attempt is made to tap in on its ongoing flow rather than simply examining the product in the form of a response to a question or problem.[21]

It seems clear that examination of the stream of thought from this vantage point supports, for one thing, the literary presentations of the flow of thought by writers such as Joyce. In addition, this research makes clear that ongoing thought in normal adults lacks the formal structure and precision that Freud, and to a somewhat lesser extent Vico, have attributed to it. What emerges from these experiments is evidence of a rapid shifting of attention to external stimuli, evaluation of the stimuli, resort to recall of early memories, anticipations of the immediate or long-term forthcoming events, and occasionally even elaborate fantasies of events of unlikely possibility in the individual's life.

Extensive questionnaire studies point up the great range of normal daydreaming activity and also call attention to three major structural patterns of normal daydreaming.[22] In effect it can be argued that the human being is not only forever exploring the external environment through the direct use of senses, but is constantly replaying associations mentally, some generated from external cues and others commonly representing chained sequences derived from one's own long-term memory system. In literature, the famous recovery of the memories of the town of Combray by the protagonist of *Swann's Way* following a taste of a cookie soaked in tea is a

---

[20] N. Kaplan and E. Singer, "Dogmatism and Sensory Alienation: An Empirical Investigation," *Journal of Consulting Psychology* 27 (1963): 486–491.

[21] J. L. Singer, *The Inner World of Daydreaming*; J. L. Singer, "Navigating the Stream of Consciousness"; Pope and J. L. Singer, "Regulation of the Stream of Consciousness."

[22] J. L. Singer, *The Inner World of Daydreaming*; J. L. Singer, "Navigating the Stream of Consciousness."

clear example. Humphrey has been able to analyze Molly Bloom's stream of consciousness in the last chapter of Joyce's *Ulysses*.[23] Having been awakened by the late return of her husband, the woman first experiences predominant associations to *actual* sounds she hears in the environment; gradually, as she drifts off into sleep, her associations are increasingly to privately generated memories, and these spin out longer and longer sequences of memory.

Analyses of such literary exemplifications of ongoing thought by *quantitative* means are also possible and revealing. Steinberg has effectively demonstrated that despite popular belief the predominant orientation and mood of Molly in her long interior monologue in *Ulysses* is one of negation, which only terminates finally with the famous "yes."[24] More structural and content analyses of ongoing thought obtained from normal individuals in the course of reporting their thought samples while carrying on tasks of varying degrees of complexity have further supported the notion of the extensive shift between imagery and fantasy processes and more logical or verbal-focused processes.[25]

What I am suggesting is that while Vico has opened the way for a remarkably full and flexible view of the human approach to experience, it is possible that he may have overplayed the sequential mode and a more reflective process as common to adults. Of course, if we take him to mean that reflection is a *possibility* that does not exist for children, without assuming that it is a predominant mode of the adult, then his position is not out of keeping with the current evidence. Thus it seems important that we recognize that his distinction between the poetic and the rational in the human imagination is not simply a set of alternatives that are inherently opposed.

---

[23] Robert Humphrey, *Stream of Consciousness in the Modern Novel* (Berkeley: University of California Press, 1954).

[24] Erwin R. Steinberg, *The Stream of Consciousness and Beyond in Ulysses* (Pittsburgh: University of Pittsburgh Press, 1973).

[25] Pope and J. L. Singer, "Regulation of the Stream of Consciousness."

Rather, it seems likely that both kinds of processes, just as both kinds of thinking from left and right hemispheres of our brain, seem to contribute together to the making for the fullest kind of human experience. Reports of scientists' own creative activity indicate how often they have hit upon important solutions to very technical problems through the accounts of striking visual or auditory images. Einstein's fantasy of the man shooting out into space and in effect looking back at himself when he travels faster than the speed of light; Kekulé's image of figures dancing in circles; Kettering's vision of a flower which suggested the possibilities of a particular engine-gasoline mixture—all are instances in which the poetic mode seems to emerge in imagery form prior to its translation into the more rational verbal-sequential abstractions of pure science.

With the discovery of more subatomic particles and (at the level of celestial physics) the discovery of "black holes" and "quasars," scientists are going to have to come up with new kinds of images and metaphors from which formal theories can be organized if we are to make sense of our universe in the next phase of this century. As Vico has suggested, in the social sciences we have a better sense of the metaphors that immediately do not work. We should take his advice and rely more fully on our own direct experiences of ourselves, our memories, fantasies, and dreams, as well as our sensitive understandings of the thoughts and actions of others in order to build better models of the human imagination and of social interaction.

Vico and Humanistic Psychology

BY AMEDEO GIORGI

Humanistic psychology is an amorphous movement within psychology that was initiated in America during the 1950s—and has since developed and spread into an international movement—by psychologists dissatisfied with both the status quo and the direction that traditional psychology was taking. The movement is amorphous because it began as a protest movement that evolved into a program.[1] Since different members protested against different aspects of traditional psychology, when the time came for a positive articulation of the movement, clashes and tensions prevailed rather than harmony. This in and of itself is not bad, especially since the humanistic psychology movement is exceedingly young. There are, however, certain other characteristics of the movement that I perceive to be weaknesses that are essentially correctable if sufficient notice of the right type were given to them. In this paper I propose to outline briefly the strengths and weaknesses of humanistic psychology and then to relate them to the thought of Vico. More specifically, I want to raise and attempt to answer the following question: How would humanistic psychology fare if it were cognizant of and grounded in the thought of Vico?

[1] Henryk Misiak and Virginia S. Sexton, *Phenomenological, Existential, and Humanistic Psychologies: A Historical Survey* (New York: Grune & Stratton, 1973).

Humanistic Psychology: Strengths and Weaknesses

In this section I will of necessity have to speak generally, and I am aware of the fact that exceptions to my statements exist. In addition, due to time considerations, I must present my points without supporting argumentation, but a more extensive discussion of these points is available.[2]

Before proceeding to the strengths and weaknesses of humanistic psychology, however, the traditional psychology it was protesting against must first be briefly described. When psychology broke from philosophy during the late nineteenth century, it allied itself with the most prestigious and fast developing scholarly context then existing—the natural sciences.[3] Thus every attempt was made, first, to meet the criteria that the natural sciences had developed for objective knowledge; only secondly did psychology turn to its subject matter in order to study it. This approach resulted in the adoption of numerous explicit and implicit alien presuppositions about psychological subject matter (e.g., man is continuous with nature, man can be studied only from an external viewpoint, etc.) because the presuppositions had already been determined by the history of the natural sciences, which is the history of man-nature, not man-man, relationships. Behaviorism and Freud's naturalistic approach to man were the end-products of this approach to psychology. Man's image was either mechanomorphic or biological in the pejorative sense. This was the state of affairs against which humanistic psychology rebelled in the mid-'50s, for it wanted to affirm "that the individual person as a patterned entity must serve as the center of gravity for psychology. The intention . . . is to rewrite the science of mental life entirely around this focus."[4]

    [2] Amedeo Giorgi, "Humanistic Psychology and Metapsychology," in J. Royce, ed., *Conceptual Issues in Humanistic Psychology* (in press).
    [3] Amedeo Giorgi, *Psychology as a Human Science* (New York: Harper & Row, 1970).
    [4] Gordon W. Allport, "The Person in Psychology," in F. T. Severin, ed., *Humanistic Viewpoints in Psychology* (New York: McGraw-Hill, 1965).

Secondly, it should be pointed out that, with one or two notable exceptions, humanistic psychology was founded and developed by psychologists who were mostly psychotherapists, clinicians, and personality theorists—in other words, primarily by psychologists who were practitioners and not academicians. This helps to account for the nature of the strengths and weaknesses that follow.

The strengths of humanistic psychology with respect to a psychology of man are the following:

(1) Its focal point is explicitly man as an experiencing person with an emphasis on distinctively human qualities.

(2) It is more willing to consider as sources of data human expressions as found in the arts and humanities and is open to a broader range of methodological procedures such as qualitative descriptions, interviews, and histories.

(3) Its emphasis is on healthy personality, it takes an interest in depth analyses of the healthy person.

(4) Its praxis is geared to real problems of individuals in everyday life and develops procedures to meet them in spontaneous ways.

Some of the weaknesses of the humanistic psychology movement, as I see them, are as follows:

(1) Humanistic psychology is more "humanistic" than scientific, in traditional senses, and by that very fact perpetuates the dichotomy between humanities and science rather than overcomes it.

(2) Like traditional psychology itself, humanistic psychology is not yet adequately founded and thus needs both rigorous theoretical and methodological articulation and direction.

(3) There is often great slippage between its ideals and its reality. Hence, while it claims social awareness and uses social rhetoric[5] and while some of its proponents are sensitive to the historical dimension of human reality,[6] most supporters do

---

[5] E.g., Abraham H. Maslow, "A Philosophy of Psychology: The Need for a Mature Science of Human Nature," *ibid*.

[6] E.g., H. A. Murray, "Explorations in Personality," *ibid*.

not consistently and systematically take full cognizance of the social and historical dimensions of humans, and thus actually fail to be genuinely humanistic.[7] This factor is, of course, related to the lack of adequate conceptualization and the lack of concern for foundations that also exists in traditional psychology.

(4) It overemphasizes feelings and emotions as properly human and intellectualizing as dehumanizing. While intellectualizing can be less than human, humanistic psychology's counteremphasis is less integrative than it might be.

In brief, humanistic psychology's emphases are too closely tied to traditional psychology's emphases in the sense that it has emphasized the gaps, the lacks, and the limits of traditional psychology, but has not related to traditional psychology in a dialectically healthy way in the sense that it could have transformed what traditional psychology was actually doing in a better way. However, to assume the latter project would have meant to create a systematic frame of reference comprehensive enough to incorporate the best of traditional psychology as well as the themes introduced by humanistic psychology to meet the deficiencies of traditional psychology. In a sense, this is what Vico's new science is all about and we shall now turn to it.

Vico's New Science

As Fisch states: "Vico's ambition was to create a science of human society, a science that should do for 'the world of nations' what men like Galileo and Newton had done for 'the world of nature'."[8] Briefly, Vico created this science by first

---

[7] C. F. Graumann, "Psychology: Humanistic or Human?", in Royce, *Conceptual Issues in Humanistic Psychology.*

[8] Max H. Fisch, "Introduction," in *The New Science of Giambattista Vico* (hereinafter *NS*), translated by Thomas G. Bergin and Max H. Fisch (Ithaca: Cornell University Press, 1968), p. xxxviii.

critiquing the interpretations of the development of the human nations held by his predecessors and then by trying to set forth the development of human customs by a chronology of seven early nations (Hebrew, Chaldean, Scythian, Phoenician, Egyptian, Greek and Roman). It was while attempting the latter effort that he discovered the critical method for differentiating between the true history of nations and their popular traditions. The critical method begins at "the beginnings of sacred history" and consists of (1) ideas, whereby historical principles of geography, chronology, philosophy, and metaphysics are discovered that help comprehend the morality, politics, and jurisprudence of the early nations as well as the developmental changes the forms of government undergo, and (2) languages, whereby the emergence of poetry (song and verse) is seen to be due to the same natural necessity in all the first nations, such that its development can be charted. By systematically relating the investigation of ideas with the investigation of languages, Vico claims to establish an ideal universal history based on providence and consisting of laws that all nations must follow in their rise, development, acme, decline, and fall. Power is given to this science because for every given stage of development Vico claims that certain determinate forms of language, customs, government, classes, alliances, etc., must exist.[9]

Relationship Between
Vico and Humanistic Psychology

We see that both humanistic psychology and Vico have the intention to develop a "new science" of man, and both realize that imitating the actual development of the natural sciences is not the way to do it. What differentiates them, however, is that Vico did reach a level of scientific articulation, whereas

[9] *The Autobiography of Giambattista Vico*, translated by Max H. Fisch and Thomas G. Bergin (Ithaca: Cornell University Press, 1944), pp. 165–172.

humanistic psychology is still groping. That is why humanistic psychology could benefit from knowledge of Vico; but I cannot find a single reference to him in the literature of humanistic psychology.

How can humanistic psychology benefit from a close reading of Vico? Obviously, in these circumstances I shall have to be selective, but I would like to point out some general areas of clarification that Vichian thought might provide. First of all, I do think that some basic principles of human behavior can be fruitfully obtained by carefully studying Vico's elements or axioms. Though many are questionable or dated (e.g., that imagination is nothing but extended or compounded memory),[10] others might be quite appropriate even in our times (e.g., that man in his ignorance makes himself the rule of the universe).[11] A research effort of this type might well yield an image of psychological man that could prove extremely fruitful for humanistic psychology and certainly would be better than the images of either behaviorism or strict Freudian psychology.

More important than content, however, is the way in which Vico went about establishing his new science. When one reads the above brief description, what seems to stand out most in Vico's effort, at least for me, is his theoretical rigor and his emphasis on sociality and historicity, and humanistic psychology would benefit if it paid as much attention to all three. Vico's theoretical rigor is seen in how he consistently attempts to interrelate stages of development with institutions, customs, language, etc. A tight network of relationships for human phenomena is simply missing in humanistic psychology. Perhaps the nearest thing to it would be Maslow's hierarchical theory of motivation,[12] although its systematic expression peters out quickly and there are numerous loose ends. The defin-

---

[10] NS, par. 211.
[11] NS, par. 405.
[12] Abraham H. Maslow, *Motivation and Personality* (New York: Harper & Row, 1970).

ition of human for Vico is intrinsically historical and social, whereas, as we noted above, despite a few exceptions, in humanistic psychology an extraordinary emphasis is placed on an individualistic perspective, such that one wonders if a truly human conception of man is assumed.[13]

If one looks at the strengths of humanistic psychology as listed above, none of them are incompatible with Vico and practically all were presupposed by him. The only possible exception is the last one—praxis—because Vico was a scholar rather than a doer, but his scholarly praxis certainly would be compatible with humanistic psychology research praxis. Similarly, if one took the leading concepts of humanistic psychology, such as self-actualization (Goldstein, Maslow), becoming (Allport), holistic emphasis on the total person (Murray, Rogers), or even self-disclosure (Jourard), one would find that in one way or another all of these concepts would be implied in Vico's understanding of human (thus the poet is a maker; nature is nascence; man is intrinsically historical and social and expresses himself in his institutions). In addition, however, the relationship among all of the concepts would be better known because they would all be part of a unified system.

This last point leads directly to the consideration of the weaknesses of humanistic psychology. It should be obvious by now that Vico could easily fill a current systematic void, both in terms of methodology and in terms of a clarified understanding of what it means to be human. Curiously enough, if one stands back and takes a Vichian perspective toward humanistic psychology, then there is a way in which one can make good sense of humanistic psychology as it actually exists now. I mentioned above that humanistic psychology was strongest in praxis and weakest in terms of founding itself. Vico's distinction between the certain and the true seems ap-

---

[13] Giorgi, "Humanistic Psychology and Metapsychology"; Graumann, "Psychology: Humanistic or Human?"

plicable here. Vico writes: "In good Latin *certum* means particularized, or, as the schools say, individuated;"[14] whereas
"the foundation of the true [knowledge] . . . has to do with
what is universal and eternal."[15] He also says: "Men who do
not know what is true of things take care to hold fast to what is
certain, so that, if they cannot satisfy their intellects by knowledge [*scienza*] their wills at least may rest on consciousness
[*coscienza*]."[16] What this says, in effect, is that when the truth,
in the strict sense of the term, is not known, then people will
fall back upon their experiences, and while there certainly is a
relationship between experience and truth, the two are not
identical. Since humanistic psychology consists so much of
experiential techniques, of clinical intuitions used by practitioners, of demonstrations and examples, we seem to have a
discipline that operates on the level of the certain in Vico's
sense of the term. There is a kind of operational empirical
generalization that is carried over from situation to situation
and modified according to need, rather than clearly articulated guiding principles that have emerged from these experiences.

It should be added, however, that it is generally known that
whatever the drawbacks of humanistic psychology, it seems to
be meeting a real cultural need. There are many individuals in
America who seek out and are helped by the services
humanistic psychology provides. What are some of these activities like? Humanistic psychological praxis is built in large
measure upon techniques and procedures for awakening feelings, intuitions, gestures, body language, and other nonverbal
methods of communication, and makes use of drama, literature, poetry, and music for helping people to get "together"
again. Vico, of course, understood the founders of humanity
to be not sages but "men" who relied more on "instinct, feeling, intuitions, manipulatory inventiveness (i.e., the apprehen-

---

[14] *NS*, par. 321.
[15] *NS*, par. 163.
[16] *NS*, par. 137.

sion not of the universal but of the particular)"; and he posited "as the primitive and basic modes of generalization not the universals of science and philosophy but those of poetry."[17] Could it be that our culture is beginning a new cycle and that humanistic psychology is itself a spontaneous response to the needs of the people and is correct in deliberately avoiding universals and knowledge and sticking to particulars and the certain?

Humanistic or Human Scientific Psychology?

Even if the last-mentioned conclusion is correct, it does not eliminate the need to understand why the specific praxis humanistic psychology is performing is meeting the needs of the times, and that leads us back to the question of a scientific endeavor. Pompa has summarized Vico's science as follows: "Knowledge of human activities must involve an account of man's nature which can be confirmed empirically. Man's nature is socially and historically conditioned so that the account in question can only be confirmed by the facts of history."[18] Thus Vico is calling for both a systematic understanding of man and empirical confirmation of that understanding, and as commentators on Vico have pointed out, he is calling for nothing less than an intrinsic relation between philosophy and science. Among the competing philosophies that could be used to ground humanistic psychology and provide it with a sound theoretical framework, my own bias is phenomenology, and while the relationship between phenomenology and Vico has been referred to before,[19] it may be worthwhile to note some of the convergences in this context.

[17] Max H. Fisch, "Introduction," in *The Autobiography of Giambattista Vico*, p. 43.

[18] Leon Pompa, "Vico's Science," *History and Theory* 10 (1971): 70.

[19] James Edie, "Vico and Existential Philosophy," in Giorgio Tagliacozzo and Hayden V. White, eds., *Giambattista Vico: An International Symposium* (Baltimore: Johns Hopkins Press, 1969), pp. 483–495; Robert Welsh Jordan, "Vico and Husserl: History and Historical Science," in Giorgio Tagliacozzo and Donald P. Verene, eds., *Giambattista Vico's Science of Humanity* (Baltimore: Johns Hopkins University Press, 1976), pp. 251–262; Robert Welsh Jordan, "Vico and the Phenomenology of the Moral Sphere," *Social Research* 43 (Autumn 1976): 520–531.

Some of the more important convergences between Vico and phenomenology that would help humanistic psychology become human scientific psychology are: (1) Phenomenology requires that one make effective contact with a phenomenon in order to describe it and come up with its intelligible structure; it holds that nothing can be described without relating it to the structure of the consciousness of the describer. This meets Vico's criteria for a genuine human science as articulated by Pompa.[20] (2) Vico argued against the "conceit of scholars," the presumption on the part of scholars that the ancients' understanding of their world was like theirs. In the same way, Merleau-Ponty argued against using the clear and distinct categories of rational thought for interpreting the functioning of the body. He spoke, rather, of doing an archeology of consciousness, and Vico did something like an archeology of institutions. (3) Vico's dictum that theories must begin where the matters they treat begin, of course, stresses genesis, and Merleau-Ponty and Husserl have spoken of a genetic phenomenology. (4) When Vico says that the new science must comprehend the vulgar or creative wisdom because it is the origin and presupposition of all science and philosophy, and that the new science must question its own foundations, he converges with phenomenology's stress on the *Lebenswelt* as the absolute foundation of knowledge and its intention to question its own foundations.

In essence, humanistic psychology is a praxis searching for its guiding principles. Vico has established principles for a human scientific approach that have practically been begging to be applied again. The two should complement each other well.

---

[20] Pompa, "Vico's Science."

Comment on Professor Giorgi's Paper

Our position in this country, as I see it, is an illustration of the historical cycle of which Vico writes. Nations rise, develop, experience their acme, and fall. We now are in the final phase of the cycle of society that began with the Renaissance. Vico would have understood this very well.

In a disintegrating society like our own, psychotherapy and psychoanalysis flourish. This occurs because individuals in the society have no reliable guides for their values or morals. Everybody has to look within himself in such a transitional age. Like boats tossed upon a turbulent ocean, we have no mooring places. Anxiety, alienation, insecurity are visible on all sides. As a time of vast and widespread preoccupation with psychology, our own age is parallel to the Hellenistic age in Greek times. Or the fourteenth and fifteenth centuries, the time of disintegration and transition of the Middle Ages.

In such times the central problem seems to me to be the disintegration of myths. Myths furnish the intellectual and spiritual framework of the society. There are nonmaterial forms of relationship between significant elements in the society. Vico would have understood this exceedingly well, as we know in reading his analysis of poetry and language. (I hope it is entirely clear that I am rejecting the common definition of myth in our day as "falsehood," and instead am defining myth as the moral pattern by which a society knows itself and thus finds its own identity.) One symptom of this disintegration is the tremendous growth of different religious sects in our country, as in meditation, yoga, etc. The yearning for these forms of "myth" is to some extent genuine, but the way it is approached is ungenuine. Each movement seems to be given the attribute of absolute truth and the devotee treats it as such, but then in a year or so he is off to give his devotion to another quasi-religious or quasi-psychological sect.

Another symptom of the time of transition is humanistic psychology. This brings us to Dr. Giorgi's paper. I must say to start with that there is nothing in Dr. Giorgi's paper that I radically disagree with; but I wish to make an addition in an area that is omitted from Giorgi's paper.

He is right that humanistic psychology began as a protest against Freudianism and behaviorism. But in this protest the individual actions and feelings—doing one's own thing, immediate emotions, and encounter—were all inevitably overemphasized. There was in this development a certain self-centeredness, a narcissism—such as an article last October in *Harper's* magazine indicated.[1] People flocked to the movement because it was a gathering point for anti-intellectuals.

The last few years, however, have brought out a new and different emphasis in humanistic psychology: a concern with theory. There have been a number of individuals and groups within the humanistic movement who have been searching for a theory that will inform our actions and will be genuinely humanist. First, this theory must be scientific in a sense which transcends the usual empirical emphasis, in which modern science has itself become a new myth. The science we seek must be not only inductive but deductive as well. It must posit, as Gregory Bateson has indicated, not only the existence of facts but also the existence of fundamental laws of science, the latter being the source of deductive thinking. This will make humanistic psychology a combination of hypotheses that will have a degree of *universality*. Second, this theory will deal with human beings as *symbolizing* creatures. Vico would have applauded this, for he knew that the awareness of our human capacity to think in symbols is the beginning of the discovery of new forms of mythology. Third, the new theory must be rooted in a positive approach to human nature rather than merely a negative. By that I mean we define human beings not in terms of neurosis but, rather, in terms of health; not in terms of boredom but of creativity, as creatures with imagination.

These developments are obviously only in the beginning stage. Many of us experience them as a yearning, which needs to be translated into actual theory building. Some of us who seek such a theory will be reading Vico with zest.

How would humanistic psychology fare if it incorporated Vico? Vico could well be the philosophical foundation for this new development.

ROLLO MAY

---

[1] Peter Marin, "The New Narcissism," *Harper's Magazine* 251 (October 1975): 45–56.

Vico and Modern Psychiatry

BY SILVANO ARIETI

This symposium reveals again the magnitude of Giambattista Vico's impact on contemporary thought. Since psychiatry, especially in its psychodynamic and psychoanalytic branches, plays such an important role in twentieth-century thinking, it is appropriate to inquire whether connections can be found between Vico and this discipline. In my opinion connections are not difficult to find, but generally they have been overlooked. To the best of my knowledge, I was the first psychiatrist to point out the connections between my field and Giambattista Vico. I did so in articles published in 1950 and 1952, and in the first edition of my book, *Interpretation of Schizophrenia*, published in 1955. Dr. Blasi and Dr. Mora have made my task easier with their discussions, respectively, of Vico and developmental psychology and Vico and Piaget. I shall first discuss Vico as precursor of Freud and Jung. Then I shall describe how Vico's conceptions helped me to interpret schizophrenia.

Vico and Freud

Both Vico and Freud engaged in a search for a deep psychological meaning in the apparently irrational myths, habits, and ways of thinking of ancient people. Vico was actually the first to describe some mental mechanisms, for instance, projection; but Freud was the one to present them in obvious psychologic terms, to include them in the framework of a Darwinian biology, and to make them available to people living in a cultural climate much more receptive to these ideas.

Was Freud influenced by Vico? I don't know whether we can answer this question. The great German psychologist Wilhelm Wundt knew Vico's work, to which he referred in his book *Völkerpsychologie*; and it could be that Freud was influenced by Vico through Wundt, but I am not in a position to prove this possibility.

What Vico studied concerning the mind of ancient people may be connected with what Freud called the primary process. In Chapter 7 of his main book, *The Interpretation of Dreams* (1901), Freud advanced the hypothesis that there are two fundamentally different kinds of mental processes, which he termed primary and secondary.[1] According to Jones, "Freud's revolutionary contribution to psychology was not so much his demonstrating the existence of an unconscious, and perhaps not even his exploration of its content, as his proposition" that there are these two kinds of mental processes.[2]

Freud gave the first description of the two processes and tried to differentiate the particular laws or principles that rule the primary process only. He called the primary process "primary" because, according to him, it occurs earlier in the ontogenetic development and not because it is more important than the secondary. Later Freud postulated that the primary process occurs earlier phylogenetically, too. The secondary process is the process of the normal adult who is awake; it is the process that follows the rules of thought of ordinary logic.

Now if we want to find correlates in the field of philosophy, we can say that Vico is the philosopher of the primary process and Descartes, with his "clear and distinct ideas," is the philosopher of the secondary process. It was much easier, of course, for Descartes to be understood by the intellectual masses, already educated in secondary process matter from the time of Plato and Aristotle. Vico, as a striking innovator, encountered more difficulty in making his ideas understood.

[1] Sigmund Freud, *The Interpretation of Dreams* (New York: Basic Books, 1960).
[2] Ernest Jones, *The Life and Work of Sigmund Freud*, vol. 1 (New York: Basic Books, 1953).

It is difficult to compare Freud's views on the primary process with Vico's views, for several reasons. Some of these reasons are connected with the different purposes of the two authors; others have to do with recent developments that have occurred in the psychoanalytic school. At first it seemed that in the study of the primary process classic psychoanalysis focused on the cognitive or symbolic processes that belong to the unconscious. When Freud later divided the psyche into three agencies (id, ego, superego), the unconscious did not correspond exactly to the id. The id was seen predominantly as a reservoir of psychic energy (or libido), and the primary process was conceived of, predominantly, not as a type of cognition but as a way of dealing with psychic energy. It is obvious, however, that any comparison between Vichian and Freudian conceptions must be made in the field of cognition.

At this point I will outline the major points of agreement between Freud's conceptions and Vico's:

(1) Both Vico and Freud give great importance to the nature and origin of mental processes. Both authors believe that things cannot be understood from the ways they are at the time they are considered but from the ways they came to be. Vico writes: "The nature of things is nothing but their coming into being at certain times and in certain special ways. These times and ways being as they are and not otherwise, things come to be as they are and not otherwise."[3] Vico applies this point of view not only psychologically but also, as Auerbach put it, as a form of justification of historical relativism as well as an affirmation that history is subject to law and order.[4] Freud applies this basic idea predominantly at a psychological level; what occurs in the adult psyche has its foundation in early childhood. As revolutionary as Vico's affirmation was for sociology and history, so was Freud's affirmation, at a time

[3] *The New Science of Giambattista Vico* (hereinafter *NS*), translated by Thomas G. Bergin and Max H. Fisch (Ithaca: Cornell University Press, 1968), par. 147.

[4] Erich Auerbach, *Literary Language and Its Public in Late Latin Antiquity and in the Middle Ages* (New York: Pantheon Books, 1965).

when psychological phenomena and psychiatric conditions were studied in cross section, that is, in their present aspect, not in a longitudinal section or unfolding in time. There is no doubt that to know the origin of things is a gigantic step toward the understanding of their nature.

(2) Both Vico and Freud compare primitive or ancient people to children of modern time. The underlying presupposition, which could not be formulated in this way by Vico, is that ontogeny recapitulates phylogeny. Vico speaks of the ancient or primitive world as *primo mondo fanciullo* (first childlike world).[5] The comparison between the primitive world and childhood is made all through the *Scienza nuova*.

(3) Both Vico and Freud see the development of the human mind as a progressive succession of stages, from the most primitive to the most complex. According to both Vico and Freud, society and history mirror the development of the individual, and the development of the modern individual recapitulates the development of society. The relationship between all these points of view is obvious. As I have already mentioned, Freud had the benefit of Darwin's contributions. Vico did not have such benefit and could not draw his conclusions from biological data, only from historical and literary sources.

A comparison between the mental stages described by Vico and those described by Freud is not easy because of their different terminologies and approaches. Vico speaks of the *bestioni* (big, beastlike humans) and of civilized men; he also refers to the ages of Gods, Heroes, and Men. Freud gives the following various classifications: (a) unconscious, preconscious, conscious; (b) id, ego, superego; (c) oral, anal, genital stages of libido. Again we could stress that Vico's levels are predominantly phylogenetic and Freud's predominantly ontogenetic. However, Freud's oral stage, characterized by a feeling of omnipotence, narcissistic traits, godlike attitudes,

[5] *NS*, par. 69.

and an impelling tendency to satisfy wishes, has many points in common with Vico's primitive stages.

(4) Both Vico and Freud reach the conclusion that man projects his own beliefs and feelings into the world and tries to interpret the world through this projection. According to Vico, man in his ignorance makes himself the ruler of the cosmos and makes an entire world out of himself:

> When men do not know the natural causes which produce things and cannot even give analogical explanation, they attribute to things their own nature. For instance, uneducated people say that the magnet loves the iron. . . . The human mind, because of its indefinite nature, wherever it wanders in ignorance, makes itself the rule of the universe concerning whatever it does not know.[6]

Vico could not use the word "projection," which was coined by Freud in 1896, and formulated the concept that man attributes his own nature to the world.

(5) Both Vico and Freud believe in a mental language common to all nations; that is, they both believe in the symbolic function of the human mind and in the existence of universal symbols.

Psychoanalysis studies symbols that are private and individualistic and those that are universal or recur among a large number of people everywhere. Whereas psychoanalysis studies symbols as they appear in dreams and in symptoms of psychopathologic conditions, Vico studies symbols as they appear in myths. The universal symbols in some respects correspond to Vico's "fantastic universals." In psychoanalytic theory, the symbol is conscious, the symbolized idea is unconscious.[7] Although Vico could not express himself in these words, it is obvious in reading the *Scienza nuova* that he felt that ancient people were not fully aware of the meaning implicit in their myths.

[6] *NS*, par. 180
[7] Otto Fenichel, *The Psychoanalytic Theory of Neurosis* (New York: Norton, 1945).

(6) Both Vico and Freud believe that incest is forbidden by man, not by nature, contrary to what Socrates thought.[8]

At this point, it may be important to underline some basic differences between Vico's and Freud's basic concepts:

(1) Both thinkers are very much concerned with primitive mentality, but their emphases are different. Freud wants to interpret and clarify the irrationality of the mental processes that follow the primary process. He stresses that these mental processes are irrational, primitive, and inferior to normal activities of the psyche. They are so inferior that the normal person is ashamed of them, feels guilty because of them, and therefore represses them. Psychoanalysis will uncover them ("Where id was, ego must be"), so that the person can discard them altogether. Vico, too, realizes that the mentality of what he calls *bestioni* was a lower form, but in this apparent irrationality he sees some rationality, some truth that appears in symbolic universals, expressed in disguised, poetical forms, especially in the medium of myth.

(2) Whereas Freud relies mostly on the study of dreams for an understanding of the archaic mind, Vico relies mostly on the study of myths and poetry. Myths and poetry are to Vico what dreams and symptoms are to Freud. They occupy approximately an equal role in the two systems. Fantasies and imagination in the waking state are as important in Vico's system as dreams are in Freud's.

(3) Both Vico and Freud deal with what in today's psychological terminology we call cognition and motivation. However, whereas Freud stresses motivation by far, Vico stresses cognition.

Vico and Jung

Jung's work also deserves special consideration in a study of the relation between Vico and modern psychiatry.

---

[8] *NS,* par. 336.

(1) The main point in common between Vico and Jung is the paramount role that archaic thinking plays in their systems. What in the Freudian system is included in the primary process becomes the collective unconscious in Jung's theoretical framework. Whereas Freud embraced Darwin's major concepts in evolution and applied them to his new psychoanalytic science, Jung followed Lamarck; that is, he believed in the inheritability of characteristics acquired from the environment. The collective unconscious would contain deposits of constantly repeated experiences of humanity.[9] For instance, one of the commonest experiences is the apparent daily movement of the sun. This experience reappears in numerous modifications in the myth of the sun-hero among various peoples.

Although modern biology has disproved the validity of the concept of the inheritance of acquired characteristics, Jung's scholarly search for similarities in the customs, beliefs, and ways of thinking of ancient people has led to important psychological conceptions. I have no evidence that Jung derived his major concepts from Vico, but certainly both authors' search for similarities in ancient people must be considered an important common characteristic. Vico, of course, did not attempt any biological interpretation of the recurrence of myths.

(2) For Jung, the archetype is the unity of psychological deposits, originated from the environment. The archetype is, by definition, an innate state of readiness to produce again and again similar or identical mythical or primitive ideas. These components of the collective unconscious are called by Jung not simply archetypes but various names: primordial images, mythological images, and behavior problems. To some extent they correspond to a mixture of Vico's fantastic universals and Vico's recurring common principles in human beings. Like Vico's fantastic universals, the archetypes tend to repeat

---

[9] Carl G. Jung, *Two Essays on Analytical Psychology* (New York: Pantheon Books, 1953).

archaic forms of cognition. The three common principles of Vico are divination, marriage, and burial, which give origin respectively to religion, morality, and belief in immortality. Although there is no exact parallel between Vico's fundamental principles and Jung's archetypes, the similarities are conspicuous.

The theory of recurrence, as formulated by Vico, may be more simply reformulated as the recurrence at various historical periods of various expressions of archaic mentality. Although the expressions of archaic mentality are part of the potential repertory of the human mind at any time, they may be elicited in clusters or in large numbers by particular historico-cultural and geographical factors.

(3) Unlike Freud, who saw predominantly pathology and irrationality in the recurrence of the forms of archaic mentality, Jung stressed that myths as well as the other archaic mental processes may be rational or irrational. They may be either symptoms of disease or constructive symbols. Jung is thus in this respect closer to Vico, who saw in the ancient myths the wisdom of past ages.

Vico's Influence on My Work

When I started my research on schizophrenia, approximately thirty-five years ago, I found myself in an advantageous position on account of two factors. One of them was the discovery made shortly after my arrival in America of a book by Heinz Werner, which opened to my understanding the vast vistas of a comparative developmental approach. But the other advantageous position was my knowledge of Giambattista Vico, which I had acquired during my premedical studies in Italy, at the Liceo Galileo in Pisa. As a matter of fact, I soon discovered the great parallel between Vico's and Werner's approaches.

In my early studies of schizophrenia I became particularly interested in the modalities of thinking of the schizophrenic patient. I soon realized that the schizophrenic patient, when he thinks in a typically schizophrenic way, adopts a type of cognition that corresponds not only to Freud's primary process thinking but also to Vico's archaic mentality. As a matter of fact, I called the special "logic" of the schizophrenic "paleologic," or archaic logic. I wrote that what seem schizophrenic forms of irrationality are instead reemerging archaic forms of rationality.

Paleologic is founded mainly on Von Domarus's principle, which, in a slightly modified form, is as follows: "Whereas the normal person accepts identity only upon the basis of identical subjects, the paleologician accepts identity based upon identical predicates."[10] For instance, a patient thought that she was the Virgin Mary. Her delusional thought process was the following: "The Virgin Mary was a virgin; I am a virgin; therefore, I am the Virgin Mary." The delusional conclusion was reached because the identity of the predicate of the two premises (the state of being virgin) made the patient accept the identity of the two subjects (the Virgin Mary and the patient). In order to remove her feeling of utter inadequacy, the patient needed to identify with the Virgin Mary, who was her ideal of feminine perfection. She also felt extreme closeness and spiritual kinship to the Virgin Mary. Nevertheless, she would not have been able to implement this identification had she not regressed to an archaic modality of thinking.

In primitive societies the same paleologic mode of thought prevails. For instance, Lévy-Bruhl reported a Congo native saying to a European that an evil man, a crocodile, and a wildcat were one and the same person because all of them had an evil spirit.[11] The common characteristic or predicate (hav-

[10] E. Von Domarus, "The Specific Laws of Logic in Schizophrenia," in J. S. Kasanin, ed., *Language and Thought in Schizophrenia* (Berkeley: University of California Press, 1944).

[11] Lucien Lévy-Bruhl, *Les fonctions mentales dans les sociétés inférieures* (Paris: Alcan, 1910).

ing an evil spirit) led to the identification. Books of anthropology are replete with similar examples. The paleologician does not respect Aristotle's three laws of thought. Vico advanced similar ideas about the origin of mythological figures such as satyrs and centaurs. He wrote that the ancients, being unable to abstract the same property from two different bodies, united the bodies in their minds. Vico explained mythological metamorphoses in a similar way; if a subject acquires a new property that is more characteristic of a second subject, the first is transformed into the second. For instance, if a woman who used to travel or to change in many ways finally stopped at a certain place, and no further change occurred in her life, in the myth she might appear as transformed into a plant. In logical language we could say that the paleologician has difficulty separating predicates from subjects and tends to identify with subjects that have one or more predicates in common.

Another characteristic that I described in the schizophrenic is the concretization of the concept. What in a normal person is conceived of in an abstract way assumes a concrete, perceptual, or quasi-perceptual representation in schizophrenic thinking. Vico described similar processes in ancient people. He gave numerous examples of how the idea is replaced by an image; how a concept becomes a fantastic universal. The immediate, the particular, and the concrete replace a concept that can be applied to a whole class. For instance, Jupiter becomes a vast animate and sensitive body that replaces the concept of supreme heroism and power; Hercules becomes the concrete embodiment of the abstract concept of strength. Thus concepts become personified, anthropomorphized. In some mentally ill patients, particularly the schizophrenic, the abstract idea is translated into a perception, in the form of a hallucination, fantasy, or delusion which is mediated by images.

Vico gave great importance to visual images. According to him, the fables of the ancients, before they were expressed in words, consisted chiefly of visual images. Language, or poetry, subsequently transcribed what was at first predominantly "imaged" in the visual field.

In the last fifty years images have lost the important position they held in the older books of psychology. The loss of interest in images in American psychology and psychiatry was possible because their most important functions had not been recognized and also because they did not lend themselves to objective or behavioristic investigations.

An image is a memory trace that assumes the form of a representation. It is an internal quasi-reproduction of a perception that, in order to be experienced, does not require the corresponding external stimulus. Although we cannot deny that at least rudimentary images occur in subhuman animals, there seems to be no doubt that they are predominantly a human characteristic. In fact, we can affirm that images are among the earliest and most important foundations of human symbolism. If we use the term "symbol" to mean something that stands for something else which is not present, the image must be considered one of the first symbols. For instance, I close my eyes and visualize my mother. She may not be present, but her image is with me; it stands for her. The image is obviously based on the memory traces of previous perceptions of my mother. My mother then acquires a psychic reality that is not tied to her physical presence.

Image formation is actually the basis for all high mental processes. It introduces us into the inner world that I have called fantasmic.[12] It enables the human being not only to reevoke what is not present but also to retain an affective disposition for the absent object. For instance, the image of my mother may evoke the love I feel for her. Primitive forms of cognition, which do not make use of language, are mediated predominantly by images.

In dreams, too, concepts are transformed into images predominantly visual in type. Psychoanalysis has given a great

[12] Silvano Arieti, *The Intrapsychic Self: Feeling, Cognition, and Creativity in Health and Mental Illness* (New York: Basic Books, 1967).

deal of attention to the images of dreams but not enough to the other types. Under the influence of Vico, I have called attention to the importance of the fantasmic stage of development. This is a stage in which images prevail over other cognitive constructs. This stage cannot be found in pure form either ontogenetically or phylogenetically, but there cannot be any doubt about its existence, as I have described elsewhere.[13]

The fantasmic stage represents an important intermediary form of organization that the evolving mind goes through while on its way toward an ultimate level, where universals, or concepts, or Descartes' clear and distinct ideas are possible. The fantasmic stage reappears in various stages of schizophrenia in the form of hallucinations, or in thoughts that rely more on images than on abstract concepts.

There is an additional point that I have derived from Vico, and which I think has influenced my psychotherapeutic approach toward all categories of patients. First of all, I must state that modern psychiatry has advanced different concepts and hypotheses about the goal of human mental health. At first, for many psychiatrists the goal seemed to be adjustment; that is, a state of psychological harmony with the environment, a concept that is a derivation of biological adaptational theories. Later, many psychologists and psychiatrists—for instance, Fromm, Horney, and Maslow—came to feel that adjustment cannot possibly be considered man's ultimate goal. Adjustment may actually stultify or limit the individuality of man, especially if it is adjustment to an unhealthy society. These authors believe that self-realization or self-actualization is man's goal. Although this point of view constitutes a certain progress over the concept of adjustment, in my opinion it also fails to explain the human condition. For instance, Horney refers to self-realization as the fulfillment of one's potentialities, just as an oak tree is the fulfilled potentiality of an acorn. This example of the acorn, first found in Aristotle's

---

[13] *Ibid.*; Silvano Arieti, *Interpretation of Schizophrenia*, 2nd ed. (New York: Basic Books, 1974).

writings, cannot be appropriately applied to man. The unfolding of man's psychological development is not necessarily inherent in a potentiality. Inasmuch as the human symbolic functions are susceptible of infinite combinations, man is forever an unending product, capable of unpredictable growth. We should not confuse potentiality with possibility.

According to Caponigri, the first principle of the modification of the human mind is to be found in the definition of man that Vico advances in the *Diritto universale,* namely, *posse, nosse, velle, finitum quod tendit ad infinitum,* a finite principle of possibility, of knowing, and of willing that tends to the infinite.[14] The *posse* of this definition, according to Caponigri, indicates Vico's insight into man's "indefinite nature." "This is the insight that the being of man cannot be enclosed within a determinate structure of possibilities, such, for example, as might be fixed by any law of cause and effect, but that it moves, rather, among *indeterminable alternatives,* and even further, by its own movement, generates these alternatives."[15]

The existentialist Italian philosopher Abbagnano has further elaborated the concept of possibility as differentiated from that of potentiality.[16] Also the French author Lapassade describes man as always *inachevé.*[17]

I have gradually come to see the goal of mental health not as self-realization or actualization of alleged potentialities but as self-expansion. The self of man evolves indefinitely along certain alternatives, which it generates. As I wrote elsewhere:

This is not to say that man is infinite; he is indeed finite, but in his own finitude he is always unfinished. Biological growth stops at a certain stage of development, but psychological growth may continue as long as life does. By psychological growth we mean the expansion of feelings, understandings, and possibilities of choices and actions with agreeable and often unforeseeable ef-

---

[14] Aloysius R. Caponigri, *Time and Idea: The Theory of History in Giambattista Vico* (Chicago:Regnery, 1953).

[15] *Ibid.;* my italics.

[16] Nicola Abbagnano, *Possibilità e libertà* (Turin: Taylor, 1956).

[17] Georges Lapassade, *L'entrée dans la vie* (Paris: Éditions de Minuit, 1963).

fects. Man thus cannot aim at self-realization but at an un-known, undetermined, and undeterminable self-expansion. The quality and extent of this expansion will depend on what he can make of his inner experiences, conceptual life, interpersonal relations, work, and actions.[18]

I believe that these words portray an indirect but very strong Vichian influence.

[18] Arieti, *The Intrapsychic Self*.

Vico and the Methods of Study of Our Time

BY HENRY J. PERKINSON

In 1706, Giambattista Vico, Professor of Rhetoric at the University of Naples, delivered his seventh annual oration. "Which," he asked, "are the better methods of study—ours or those of the Ancients?" In his six previous annual speeches, Vico had developed the traditional theme that the aim of education was nothing less than the pursuit of wisdom. In this seventh and most famous oration, Vico boldly declared that the methods of study of his time simply would not fulfill this aim.

He traced the inadequacy of those methods of study of his time to the then prevalent theory of education—a theory derived from, or inspired by, the philosophy of Descartes.

The Cartesians believed that one pursued wisdom through the accumulation of ideas that were absolutely certain. They counseled people to accept only those ideas that are clear and distinct—that is, absolutely certain. Vico's criticism was that this strict criterion ruled out what he called *verisimilia*, or "likely truths"—ideas that are not certain but are probably true. He argued that those educated in the Cartesian method to accept only ideas that are certain would find themselves out of touch with the rest of their fellows who accepted or rejected ideas by using common sense rather than the criterion of clearness and distinctness. These Cartesian intellectuals, Vico concluded, could never lead or guide the people; their education actually alienated them from the populace.

This argument, of course, harkens back to those of Isocrates against Plato in the fourth century B.C. Back then, Isocrates—also a professor of rhetoric—had insisted that the philosopher's quest for so-called certain knowledge was simply inappropriate for the education of leaders. More appropriate, he claimed, was an education in what he called "right opinion." Right opinion rested on probable or likely truths—what Vico later called *verisimilia*.

According to Isocrates, one got right opinion from the study of the humanities. The humanities—literature and history—preserved records of the wisest and most admirable sayings, presenting glowing accounts of the great and noble deeds of the past—all of which served as exemplars for the future leader. An education in the humanities, Isocrates concluded, initiated the young into their culture, or *paideia*, so that when they became leaders they would act in ways that accorded with their own culture—accepting those ideas that did conform to the common sense of those who shared that culture, rejecting those that did not.

So far it sounds as if Vico in his seventh oration was simply perpetuating a long-standing territorial feud among academicians—that perennial battle between philosophy and the humanities (reinstituted in our times as a battle between science and the humanities). Now Vico, to be sure, was deeply involved in the fight over what knowledge is of most worth. Indeed, one *could* construe his *New Science* as an attempted synthesis between philosophy and the humanities—recall his attempted synthesis between philosophy and philology (history), where he claimed to reduce philology to a science.

Yet I think Vico's theory of education was both broader and deeper than simply a theory of curriculum. Let me try to explain what I take to be his broader and deeper significance for educational thought and practice.

Man a Fallible Creator

At its deepest level, Vico's rejection of the Cartesian approach to education rested on his belief that Descartes had erred in thinking that human beings could ever attain certain knowledge. As Vico saw them, human beings are not gods; they are fallible. So, in spite of what Descartes believed, human beings have no criterion for certain truth, nor can they ever have such a criterion. And as for the Cartesians' prototype of certain knowledge, mathematics, Vico makes this astounding comment: "We can demonstrate geometrical things because we make them; if we were able to demonstrate physical things, we would make them."[1]

Here Vico is saying that the certain knowledge we have in mathematics is due to the fact that man has created mathematics, whereas he has not created the physical universe and, therefore, cannot have certainty or certain knowledge about it. This marks the first appearance of Vico's revolutionary epistemological theory that man makes his knowledge. Later, in his *Metaphysics* and in his *Universal Law*, he further developed this theory, adding to it the notion that man does create his ideas or theories about the physical universe and makes these theories certain through experiments. But these theories are always human knowledge, not to be confused with the divine knowledge God alone possesses, since He, only, created the physical universe. Hence man's knowledge of the physical universe is always fallible, never perfect.

Still later Vico expanded this conception of man as a fallible creator to include the institutions and arrangements of society. This became the basis for his *New Science*. Recall the first principle of that *New Science*: "But in the night of thick darkness enveloping the earliest antiquity, so remote from our selves, there shines the eternal and never-failing light of a

---

[1] G. B. Vico, *Il metodo degli studi del tempo nostro*, in *Opere*, edited by Fausto Nicolini (Milan: Ricciardi, 1953), p. 184.

truth beyond all question: that the world of civil society has certainly been made by men. . . ."[2]

Vico never directly applied to education this epistemological theory of man as a fallible creator of his knowledge.[3] Yet it does have profound significance for the practice of education. And today the modern methods of study are all based on this notion of man as the creator of knowledge. The modern methods of education reject the old spectator epistemology that resulted in "receptor" classrooms where students received knowledge (or—according to the pedagogical metaphor used—where students absorbed, accumulated, or swallowed knowledge). In place of receptor classrooms we now have modern activity classrooms where students construct and create knowledge. The names of John Dewey in the United States, Maria Montessori in Italy, Decroly in Belgium, Kerchensteiner in Germany, and Piaget in Switzerland all immediately spring to mind as the major modern educational theorists who have conceived and developed the active methods of study of our time. And all these theorists share the fundamental tenet that man makes knowledge, a tenet that each came up with independently.

None of these educational theorists ever evidenced any awareness of the work of Giambattista Vico—which, of course, given the history of Vichian scholarship, is quite understandable. Yet one wishes they had studied Vico, if only because his works contain suggested solutions to some of the contradictions inherent in the methods of study of our time.

Socialization versus Growth

The basic contradiction within the activity methods of our time comes from educators using activity as a means—a means

---

[2] *The New Science of Giambattista Vico* (hereinafter *NS*), translated by Thomas G. Bergin and Max H. Fisch (Ithaca: Cornell University Press, 1968), par. 331.

[3] Except in very general ways in parts of the *New Science*; see *NS*, pars. 238–240 and 1406–1408. See also my "Giambattista Vico: Philosopher of Education," *Pedagogica Historica* 14 (1974): 404–433.

to acquire the final or correct manner or mode of human behavior. John Dewey, for example, prescribed activity methods so that students could learn the scientific method. According to Dewey, the scientific method was *the* way mankind has, can, and will continue to solve all problems. By insisting that this is the final or correct mode of behavior which all must learn, Dewey ends up as an authoritarian educational theorist. For him the process of education becomes the socialization of the young, inculcating them with *the* correct method of human thought and behavior.

In the work of Montessori, Kerchensteiner, and Decroly we find a similar kind of authoritarianism in that all take the ongoing, existing society as the standard, or pattern, for the young. They all construe education as the process of initiating the young into that world. The activity method is prized as the most effective means of developing in the student the skills needed to function within the society. Moreover, through this method the schools secure student commitment to perpetuate the existing society.

Piaget uses the language of biology to indicate his agreement with this conception of education. "To educate," Piaget wrote, "is to adapt the child to an adult environment, in other words to change the individual's psychological constitution in terms of the totality of the collective realities to which the community consciously attributes a certain value."[4]

When construed in the way modern theorists do it, the activity method winds up no different from the traditional receptor method of the past. With both methods the young are socialized to the ongoing adult world. The only thing different about the activity methods of our time is that such methods enlist the children themselves in the process of socialization. Here is Piaget:

. . . The traditional school reduced all socialization, whether intellectual or moral, to a mechanism of constraint. The active

[4] Jean Piaget, *Science of Education and the Psychology of the Child* (New York: Viking Press, 1971), p. 137.

school, on the contrary, makes a careful distinction in almost all its achievements between two processes that have very different results and become complementary only with much care and tact: the constraint exercised by the adult and the cooperation of the children with each other. The constraint exercised by the adult achieves results that are all the more considerable in that they answer to very profound tendencies in the child's mentality.[5]

Now, since the older, receptive, methods of study, *and* the activity methods of our time, *both* construe education as socialization, what is wrong with that? Well, to state it baldly, socialization stymies growth, prevents advancement, cuts off improvement. Thus the critics of the notion of education as socialization—usually dubbed romantics—decry it because it sacrifices the growth of the individual to the status quo of society: socialization, they point out, is nothing more than the channeling, the molding, the processing, of young people into personnel to maintain and aggrandize the ongoing, established system.[6]

Instead of socialization, the romantic critics construe education as the process of individual growth and development. Here we reach the heart of the contradiction inherent in the methods of study of our time. For these romantic critics share the belief that man creates his knowledge, and so they endorse and use activity methods of instruction. For them, however, these activity methods are supposed to promote the fullest growth of the individual, *not* socialization to predetermined patterns of behavior. Since they advocate the growth of the individual in opposition (if need be) to the expectations of the society, the romantic educators are not without their critics. At best, the criticism goes, this individualistic education alienates the student from his society, and at worst it subverts the social order, generating chaos and anarchy.

[5] *Ibid.*, p. 178.
[6] See, for example, Paul Goodman, *People or Personnel* (New York: Random House, 1964); Neil Postman and Charles Weingartner, *Teaching as a Subversive Activity* (New York: Delacorte Press, 1969); Ivan Illich, *Deschooling Society* (New York: Harper & Row, 1970); A. S. Neill, *Summerhill* (New York: Hart, 1960).

Thus we find two contradictory expectations of the activity methods of our time: socialization versus individual growth. Critics of the former say it stymies advancement and improvement, critics of the latter say it can estrange students from the society.

In the writings of Giambattista Vico, who first proposed the notion that man creates knowledge, we can, I think, find some guidelines for overcoming the contradiction now inherent in the activity methods of study of our time.

But before turning to Vico, there is another, related criticism of our modern methods I wish to mention: the loss of curriculum content.

When Montessori, Dewey, and Piaget each developed the epistemological theory that man makes his knowledge into a theory of education, each concluded that the main function of the school is to help students to develop the skills and methods for making knowledge. In other words, they rejected the traditional receptor classroom. This makes sense: if man is a creator of knowledge, then, yes, schools and teachers should no longer function as the transmitters of knowledge. But this had far-reaching consequences. For with the arrival of the modern activity methods, the importance of the content of studies began to fade. The subject matter now had no intrinsic worth: it functioned solely to help develop the students' cognitive and manual powers and skills—those powers and skills used to create knowledge. Thus Dewey would have students learn problem-solving. Piaget has said that the aim of intellectual training is to form the intelligence rather than to stock the memory, to produce intelligent explorers rather than mere erudition.

By stressing the instrumental value of the subject matter, these theorists have brought about a reduced emphasis on the content of the curriculum, resulting in what I have called the loss of curriculum content. This raises for many the question of whether or not the activity methods of our time really do educate the young—the young today, besides being less skilled in reading, writing, and arithmetic, seem to know less history, geography, science, and literature.

Here, too, I think the work of Giambattista Vico can supply guidance.

Creation by Modification

For educators, the significance of Giambattista Vico's theory that man creates knowledge lies in the manner or mode of that creation. Vico says man does this through the modifications of the mind. In that famous paragraph of the *New Science* I quoted earlier he wrote: "But in the night of thick darkness enveloping the earliest antiquity, so remote from ourselves, there shines the eternal and never-failing light of a truth beyond all question: That the world of civil society has certainly been made by men, *and that its principles are therefore to be found within the modifications of our own human mind*."[7]

What does this mean? I take it to mean that man, unlike God, does not create *ex nihilo*, out of nothing. Whatever man creates—his theories, his behavior, as well as his institutions and his social arrangements—are all modifications of what he has previously created.

What Vico presents us is an historical theory of knowledge: man, in time, creates knowledge and utilities by modifying *existing* knowledge and *existing* utilities. The spring, or source, of each modification is the recognition of the inadequacy—moral, intellectual, or methodological—of what already exists. As Vico puts it in the *New Science*: "Men at first feel without paying attention, then they pay attention with a troubled and agitated spirit, finally they reflect with pure mind."[8]

In that sentence Vico lays out the stages of progress or advancement. Initially men pay little or no attention to what

[7] *NS*, par. 331; my italics.
[8] *NS*, par. 218.

they have created, then they become critical of it, and finally they reflect on it and improve it. Everything that man creates advances in this way—all knowledge, all behavior, all social institutions. Initially the child is inattentive to his own behavior, the scientist pays no heed to some of the theories he uses in his work, the citizen regards not his society's institutions. But when the child recognizes the inadequacy of his behavior, when the scientist sees the inadequacy of his theories, when the citizen perceives the inadequacy of the institutions of his society—then each becomes agitated. Then, in time, through reflection, each tries to modify, refine, change the concrete behavior, the current theories, the existing institutions.

For Vico, then, man is, like God, a creator. But unlike God, he is a fallible creator. Man cannot create out of nothing. Man creates only by modifying what he has previously created. In this way he can continually improve. In the *Universal Law* Vico defines man as: "a finite being, able to know and to will, who tends toward the infinite."[9] So, according to Vico, because he is finite, all that man creates (his knowledge, his behavior, his institutions) is never perfect, never complete, never totally true, never absolutely good. But, although man can never attain perfection, he does, or can, move closer to it. He can always advance his knowledge, can always improve his behavior—man does tend toward perfection. Yet—and this is most crucial for Vico's theory—man does not do this directly nor with facility. Man is not upright; he is corrupt. Therefore he seeks selfish ends, he does not seek the good; he seeks those theories and ideas that most comfort him, he does not seek truth.

And here we come to Vico's major theme in the *New Science*:

God has so ordained and disposed human affairs that men, having fallen from complete justice by original sin, and while

---

[9] G. B. Vico, *Dell'unico principio e fine del diritto universale* (Naples, 1839). See also *The Autobiography of Giambattista Vico*, translated by Max H. Fisch and Thomas G. Bergin (Ithaca: Cornell University Press, 1944), pp. 145–146.

intending almost always to do something quite different and often quite the contrary—so that for private utility they would live alone like wild beasts—have been led by this same utility and along the aforesaid different and contrary paths to live like men in justice and to keep themselves in society and thus to observe their social nature.[10]

According to Vico, man seeks his own utility—his own selfish ends—and he seeks theories that comfort him. But in so doing he actually advances toward the infinite, toward perfection, toward increased truth and goodness. The pedagogical significance of this notion is enormous. But before discussing this, let me briefly describe how Vico depicts this advancement.

First, man's knowledge. This advances or improves because man has a disposition toward unity or order. As Vico expresses it in the *New Science*: "The human mind is naturally impelled to take delight in uniformity."[11] Thus man seeks comforting theories, those that harmonize and cohere with those he already has. Contradictions are not comforting. Therefore men try to ignore, avoid, or eliminate contradictions. But since man is finite, the knowledge that he creates is never without some contradiction. It is this recognition of contradictions that leads men to modify their theories and ideas. Man improves his theories and ideas by eliminating the contradictions among them.

This is not to say that noncontradiction is a criterion for truth—man, being fallible, has no criterion for truth. But contradictions do signal that one or the other theory, or both, are false. So in eliminating contradictions, man reduces the falsity content of his knowledge and thus moves closer to truth. Vico's explanation of the logic of the advancement of knowledge has, in recent times, been carefully developed by

[10] *NS*, par. 2.
[11] *NS*, par. 204.

the work of Sir Karl Popper (although Popper nowhere makes any reference to Vico).[12]

Vico's theory of how man improves his knowledge has great significance for the role of the teacher in the educative process. Traditionally, in the older receptor classrooms, the teacher had the job of imposing knowledge on the young. In the modern activity classrooms, as we saw, the teacher no longer transmits knowledge; here the role of the teacher is to help students learn how to think. But one of the unwanted consequences of this modern approach is the loss of curriculum content.

If we apply Vico's theory to the teaching process, the content of the curriculum is not lost, nor is it imposed on the student either (as it was in the old receptor classrooms). The teacher merely presents the curriculum content as something to be criticized and improved. Through these continual critical encounters the student is initiated into the process by which knowledge, human knowledge, advances. The main task of the teacher is the Socratic one of helping students discover the contradictions within their own thought and between their thoughts and the thoughts of others. As a result of the teacher's critical probings, the students are encouraged to modify or refine their theories in order to overcome the contradictions. In this way students advance knowledge.

Private Utility, Social Good

Man does not only tend toward truth, he also tends toward the good. How? In the *New Science* Vico wrote:

But men, because of their corrupted nature, are under the tyranny of self-love, which compels them to make private utility

---

[12] Karl Popper, *The Logic of Scientific Discovery* (New York: Science Editions, 1961); *Conjectures and Refutations* (London: Routledge & Kegan Paul, 1963); *Objective Knowledge* (Oxford: Oxford University Press, 1972); *The Philosophy of Karl Popper*, edited by Paul A. Schilpp, 2 vols. (LaSalle, Ill.: Open Court, 1974).

their chief guide. Seeking everything useful for themselves and nothing for their companions, they cannot bring their passions under control to direct them toward justice. We thereby establish the fact that man in the bestial state desires only his own welfare; having taken wife and begotten children, he desires his own welfare along with that of his family; having entered upon civil life, he desires his own welfare along with that of his city; when its rule is extended over several peoples, he desires his own welfare along with that of the nation; when the nations are united by wars, treaties of peace, alliances and commerce, he desires his own welfare along with that of the entire human race. In all these conditions man desires principally his own utility.[13]

According to Vico, then, man is a member of the human race but he seeks solely his own utility—as he perceives it. And since he is always a member of a group larger than what he can actually perceive, this means his own behavior has consequences for others—consequences of which he is unaware and often unconcerned. But when those consequences adversely affect others, they complain—if they can—or threaten or even retaliate. What adversely affects people will vary in time and place in accordance with the common sense of the people, that is, those judgments of what is right, proper, good, etc., shared by a given people at a given time.[14]

As a result, since he seeks his own utility, man accommodates to others (out of fear for his own well-being), adjusting to ever-larger groups. And he does this by modifying his own behavior in light of the adverse repercussions it generates for him.

Thus, because he seeks his own utility, man becomes better, or improves his behavior, by modifying or restraining those acts that adversely affect others. In the *New Science* Vico identifies some of the beliefs, customs, laws, rules, and institutions men have created to restrain human passions and moderate behavior. Here Vico cites the belief in immortality (leading to

[13] *NS*, par. 341.
[14] Leon Pompa, *Vico: A Study of the New Science* (New York: Cambridge University Press, 1975), pp. 21 ff.

the custom of burial of the dead), belief in God (leading to the creation of the rules, customs, and institutions of religion), and the belief that human passions should be controlled (leading to the institution of marriage).

This theory of moral improvement has profound implications for education. The older, receptor, form of moral education had teachers trying to shape and control the behavior of the young by imposing on them the established beliefs, rules, customs, laws, and institutional restrictions that mankind had so far created to restrain people from acting in ways that adversely affect others. Education was socialization. The modern activity methods of Montessori, Dewey, and Piaget encouraged students to *discover* or *recreate*, through their own activity, these same restrictions on human behavior. Yet the modern theorists continued to construe education as socialization to existing arrangements and beliefs. The romantic educators, however, would use the activity methods to allow students freely to create their own beliefs, rules, regulations, and moral values. These are contradictory expectations of the activity method.

When we apply Vico's theory to the methods of moral education we must begin with the teacher. The teacher must understand (and, in time, help students to understand) that certain beliefs, customs, institutions, and the like are human creations intended to restrain people from behaving in ways that adversely affect others. Since these are human creations, they are not perfect but are improvable. Yet they are the best we've got; they have developed, over time, and have undergone modifications in the light of human experience. Thus the Vichian educator thinks it neither necessary nor wise to have the young begin to create *de novo* those restrictions and restraints on human behavior. Here the Vichian educator differs from the romantic educator. But the Vichian educator does not try to dogmatically socialize the young, either. And here he differs from the other educators—both old fashioned and modern—who do try to impose moral education on the young.

What the Vichian educator tries to do is to set up critical encounters (not confrontations) between the students' behavior, or their theories about behavior, and the traditional restrictions on human behavior. In these encounters the teacher tries to develop a critical dialogue about these existing restrictions in order to probe the students' behavior and their theories about behavior, which then, hopefully, will lead them to modify their own behavior in light of the criticisms.

In developing this critical dialogue, the teacher does not preach. Recognizing that, as Vico says, all people seek their personal utility, the teacher simply tries to see to it that students know when their behavior has adverse consequences for others. The classroom then becomes the place where adverse feedback is made manifest to students. Thus students discover that the pursuit of their own utilities necessitates restraining or modifying their own behavior in light of the criticisms or adverse response from others who are hurt by that behavior. With such a method, students, in time, realize that this is how finite or fallible human beings improve, individually and as groups: by eliminating or modifying those behaviors that adversely affect others. They come to see that individuals and groups are always improvable, and become themselves open to improvement—that is, open to modification of their own or their group's behavior.

This method of education initiates students to participation in the never-ending pursuit of the good. Man's pursuit of the good, like his pursuit of truth, is endless, precisely because it takes place through the continual modification of what man has already created—modifications made in light of criticisms that reveal the contradictions in his theories, the nonutility of his behavior. Through his efforts to escape contradictions and adversities man tends toward wisdom.

There are as many different ways to interpret the writings of Giambattista Vico as there are students of the thought of that gnomic genius. On the last page of his *Autobiography* Vico recorded some of the interpretations that had been made of his work by friends and foes. Among them he recounts the "grand praise" that "he was worthy to give good directions to teachers themselves." In this paper I have tried to suggest how appropriate this "grand praise" was.

General Education as Unity of Knowledge: A Theory Based on Vichian Principles*

BY GIORGIO TAGLIACOZZO

1 In a lecture broadcast over the Italian network some time ago I stated: "If I were asked who is the thinker, of any period, who can help us most in our attempt to solve the problem, so pressing in our time, of the unity of knowledge, my answer would unhesitatingly be that such a thinker is Giambattista Vico."[1] That opinion was not improvised. It was the outcome of: (a) several years devoted to the study and teaching of the ideas of leading thinkers on the problem of the unity of knowledge; (b) the realization that all those ideas were wanting; (c) my achievement of a solution which appeared to me (and has been judged by others) as being Vichian in nature.[2] In this paper I shall try to explain the above statement more fully than I was able to do in the broadcast. I shall: (a) briefly point out my reactions to the leading viewpoints concerning the problem of the unity of knowledge that I have investigated; (b) explain and appraise

---

[1] "Unità della cultura e cultura generale," in *Università internazionale Guglielmo Marconi* series of RAI-TV (Dec. 23, 1964).

[2] See, for example, Enzo Paci, "Vico, Structuralism, and the Phenomenological Encyclopedia of the Sciences," in Giorgio Tagliacozzo and Hayden V. White, eds., *Giambattista Vico: An International Symposium* (Baltimore: Johns Hopkins Press, 1969), p. 498. My Vichian viewpoint on the unity of knowledge has been commented upon by a number of reviewers of this volume, including Gustavo Costa (*Journal of the History of the Behavioral Sciences*, October 1972), Dario Faucci (*Giornale critico della filosofia italiana*, fasc. 3, 1973), Michael Littleford (*The Educational Forum*, March 1972), Leon Pompa (*Studi internazionali di filosofia*, 1973), and Donald P. Verene (*Man and World*, August 1971).

Vico's solution to that problem; (c) outline my solution, derived, directly and/or indirectly, from Vico's thought; (d) outline what appears to me as a genuine, rigorous solution to the problem of general education stemming, as a corollary, from the solution mentioned in (c).

The Problem of the Unity of Knowledge

2. In the course of my study and teaching, I found all the following ideas on the problem of the unity of knowledge unsatisfactory: (a) Bacon's ordering of the "sciences of nature" ("natural history," "physics," "metaphysics") in relation to one another in such a way as to reflect—as in a pyramid—the ascent from the multiplicity of individual things to their ultimate unity in the summary law of nature,[3] and his view of natural philosophy as being discontinuous with any other kind of inquiry;[4] (b) Descartes' idea of distinguishing sciences within a single comprehensive deductive system and comparing philosophy as a whole to a tree "whose roots are metaphysics, whose trunk is physics, and whose branches, issuing from the trunk, are all other sciences" (reduced to three principal ones: medicine, mechanics and morals);[5] (c) Leibnitz's idea that when the catalogue of human thought has been achieved, and each concept has been given its characteristic number and sign, we shall have secured a complete demonstrative encyclopedia of all knowledge;[6] (d) the Encyclopedists' view that the unity of human knowledge is not a unity in diversity, nor the unity of a whole in relation to its parts, but unity of continuity among parts wherever such continuity may be found;[7] (e) Kant's insistence on the need to *isolate* the

[3] See Robert McRae, *The Problem of the Unity of the Sciences: Bacon to Kant* (Toronto: University of Toronto Press, 1961), p. 34.
[4] *Ibid.*, p. 44
[5] *Ibid.*, p. 57.
[6] *Ibid.*, p. 81.
[7] *Ibid.*, p. 119.

various modes of knowledge according to kind and origin,[8] complemented by his equal insistence that all the sciences taken together have the unity of a single organized whole[9] and that the unity of science has its foundation in the nature of reason itself,[10] which demands that knowledge be brought into systematic unity;[11] (f) Comte's classification of the sciences, based on the idea of arranging them in such a way that each science is dependent on those preceding it and independent of those which follow;[12] (g) the logical-empiricist philosophers' view of the unification of science as the reduction of all sciences to physics—that is, the reduction of all phenomena to physical events—through the unification of the vocabulary of the sciences.[13]

One fundamental reason for my discarding all the above ideas was somehow related to, or of the same nature as, Vico's principle that "doctrines must take their beginning from that of the matters of which they treat"[14] and his remarks that "the philosophers failed by half in not giving certainty to their reasoning by appeal to the authority of the philologians,"[15] that "our Science" [the New Science] "took its start when the first men began to think humanly, and not when the philosophers began to reflect on human ideas,"[16] and that, "just the opposite of . . . Bacon in his Novus orbis scientiarum . . . where he considers how the sciences as they now stand may be

[8] Ibid., p. 125.
[9] Ibid., p. 128.
[10] Ibid., p. 130.
[11] Ibid., p. 133.
[12] See Auguste Comte, Cours de philosophie positive (Paris: Librairie Garnier Frères, 1949), vol. 1, Second Lesson, esp. VI, p. 138.
[13] For an authoritative presentation of the logical-empiricist approach to the unity of science, see Paul Oppenheim and Hilary Putnam, "Unity of Science as a Working Hypothesis," in Herbert Feigl and others, eds., Minnesota Studies in the Philosophy of Science, vol. 2 (Minneapolis: University of Minnesota Press, 1958). See also Paul Oppenheim, "A Natural Order of Scientific Disciplines," Revue internationale de philosophie, 1959, fasc. 3, and "Dimensions of Knowledge," ibid., 1957, fasc. 2.
[14] The New Science of Giambattista Vico (hereinafter NS), translated by Thomas G. Bergin and Max H. Fisch (Ithaca: Cornell University Press, 1968), par. 314.
[15] NS, par. 140.
[16] NS, par. 347.

carried to perfection," his science "discovers the ancient world of the sciences, how rough they had been at birth, and how gradually refined, until they reached the form in which we have received them."[17] This criticism will be discussed in Section 6.

3. On the other hand, some ideas of Ernst Cassirer and of a few other contemporary thinkers appealed to me considerably. Cassirer's philosophy of symbolic forms[18] (influenced at its origins, to a significant extent, by Vico's *New Science*[19]), which encompasses the study of myth, religion, language, art, history, and science,[20] was the springboard of my conceiving the idea, published in 1958 in a chart (the "Tree of Knowledge")[21] of human knowledge (in the sense of "culture")[22] as a tree whose trunk is "symbolism" and whose branches, issuing

[17] *Scienza nuova* of 1730, par. 37, quoted by Max H. Fisch in his introduction to *NS*, par. K6.

[18] Ernst Cassirer, *The Philosophy of Symbolic Forms*, 3 vols. (New Haven: Yale University Press, 1953–57).

[19] Since an earlier version of this paper was written in 1973 (see note on p. 796), Donald Phillip Verene has shown convincingly that Vico's influence on Cassirer goes back as far as Cassirer's graduate studies and can be traced through many of his works. See Donald P. Verene, "Vico's Science of Imaginative Universals and the Philosophy of Symbolic Forms," in Giorgio Tagliacozzo and Donald P. Verene, eds., *Giambattista Vico' Science of Humanity* (Baltimore: Johns Hopkins University Press, 1976), pp. 295–317 and ns. 37–39.

[20] See also Ernst Cassirer, *An Essay on Man* (New Haven: Yale University Press, 1944).

[21] The publication took place in connection with a course bearing the same title that I delivered at the New School for Social Research in 1959 and repeated a few times thereafter. The original "Tree of Knowledge," measuring 45 in. x 28 in., was designed by Hildegarde Bergheim according to my specifications. The first official presentation of my "Tree of Knowledge" chart was made in August 1960: see Giorgio Tagliacozzo, "Branches, Tree and Taxonomy of Knowledge," in International Congress for Logic, Methodology, and Philosophy of Science (Stanford University, August 24 to September 2, 1960), *Abstracts of Contributed Papers*, pp. 155–156. The tree was later reproduced in smaller format on the cover of *The American Behavioral Scientist* 4 (October 1960), which contained an article of mine bearing the same title. A brief description of it can be found in my "Epilogue" in Tagliacozzo and White, *Giambattista Vico: An International Symposium,* pp. 599–613.

[22] See my articles "General Education: The Mirror of Culture," *American Behavioral Scientist* 6 (October 1962): 22–25, "Culture and Education: The Origins," *ibid.*, 6 (April 1963): 8–13, and "Culture and Education: The Founding of the Classical Tradition," *ibid.*, 7 (January 1964): 20–25. See also Donald P. Verene, ed., *Man and Culture* (New York: Dell, 1970).

The "Tree of Knowledge" developed by Giorgio Tagliacozzo according to Vichian principles

from the trunk, are "symbolic forms" (analogous to Vico's "modifications of the human mind"[23]): magic, myth, religion, art, science. The Vichian nature of the tree—a feature which is absent in Cassirer (see Section 7)—will be explained in Sections 4, 5, and 6.

Concerning the influence of Cassirer's philosophy on the development of my ideas, I must also mention here that his relating the "forms of human culture" to the development of "different types of spatial and temporal experience,"[24] and more specifically his distinction of magical, mythical, and geometric space,[25] helped me indirectly to realize that different conceptions of space and time are the key factors that gave rise to, and then permeated, the various "views of the world" that have followed one another in historic time. The latter conviction was strengthened by Hans Reichenbach's[26] (and later by Bertrand Russell's[27]) suggestion that Greek geometry and mathematics were the conceptual model and springboard of the development of the Platonic theory of ideas, and hence of much of the thought clustered around it or derived therefrom. This suggestion contributed in turn to my distinguishing, in my tree of knowledge, three successive world views (Euclidean, Non-Euclidean, Organismic-Transactional) in the development of Western "science" from ancient Greece to the present time (see Section 9 f), and to my further search for, and formulation of, other less comprehensive historical-genetic-integrative concepts characterizing different branches and subbranches of knowledge, and groups and subgroups of disciplines, within each of those world views (see Section 9). That search was encouraged by Ludwig von Bertalanffy's general systems theory, which generalizes, and gives scientific

[23] NS, par. 349.

[24] Cassirer, An Essay on Man, p. 42.

[25] Ibid., p. 49.

[26] Hans Reichenbach, The Rise of Scientific Philosophy (Berkeley: University of California Press, 1951), p. 19 and passim.

[27] Bertrand Russell, Wisdom of the West (New York: Doubleday, 1959), p. 23 and passim.

status to, the well-known fact that similar viewpoints are present in all branches of science, irrespective of whether inanimate things, organisms, or mental or social phenomena are concerned, and which implies a systematic use of the formal correspondence, or isomorphy, of laws in different sciences, fields, or strata of reality for the purpose of the integration of knowledge.[28] Thomas S. Kuhn's theory of "paradigms,"[29] which vaguely resembles some aspects of my Vichian viewpoint (see below, Section 9*l*) appeared too late to influence its formulation.

Vico's Solution

4. If, as I said in Section 1, my proposed solution to the problem of the unity of knowledge is Vichian in nature, in what way and to what extent has it been directly influenced by the *New Science*, beyond the indirect Vichian influence it received—as a springboard—from Cassirer's philosophy? In more general terms: in what way and to what extent can Vico's thought contribute to a modern solution to that problem? In the attempt to answer these questions, I shall begin by outlining what appears to me to be Vico's solution to the problem of the unity of knowledge and by appraising the significance of that solution both in itself and as compared with other ones. I shall use the graphic image of a tree in order to make my explanations clearer. Such an image—which has a long and noble tradition[30]—was employed by Vico himself, as we shall

[28] Ludwig von Bertalanffy, "Philosophy of Science and Scientific Education," *Scientific Monthly* 77 (November 1953): 233–239; "General Systems Theory: A New Approach to Unity of Science," *Human Biology*, December 1951; "General Systems Theory," *Main Currents in Modern Thought*, March 1955; and *General Systems Theory* (New York: Braziller, 1968).

[29] Thomas S. Kuhn, *The Structure of Scientific Revolutions* (Chicago: University of Chicago Press, 1962).

[30] See Paolo Rossi, *Clavis universalis* (Milan: Ricciardi, 1960) and Frances Yates, *The Art of Memory* (Chicago: University of Chicago Press, 1966). Vico's *New Science*, in spite of its great novelty, seems to have some roots in common with the tradition of the "art

see in Section 5, and has been very helpful to me in developing my own viewpoint. As I mentioned in Section 3, Cassirer did not avail himself of it. However, his theory of symbolic forms can easily be visualized in this way for the purpose of comparison with Vico's viewpoint (see Section 7).

5. Vico compared his "poetic wisdom" to a "trunk" (i.e., "a crude metaphysics"), from one limb of which "there branch out . . . logic, morals, economics and politics, all poetic; from another, physics, the mother of cosmography and astronomy, the latter of which gives their certainty to two daughters, chronology and geography—all likewise poetic."[31] From this description of Vico's "poetic wisdom" it is not difficult to reconstruct his conception of an overall tree of knowledge. His distinction of "three kinds of natures," divine, heroic, and

---

of memory" (and hence of the *arbores scientiarum*), particularly in its seventeenth-century stage, when Bacon, Descartes, Leibnitz, and other thinkers turned it "from a method of memorizing the encyclopedia of knowledge, of reflecting the world in memory, to an aid for investigating the encyclopedia of the world with the object of discovering new knowledge" (Yates, *The Art of Memory*, pp. 368–369). This affinity is confirmed by the frontispiece used by Vico in the second *New Science* in the hope that "it may serve to give the reader some conception of this work before he reads it, and, with such aid as imagination may afford, to call it back to mind after he has read it" (see Rossi, *Clavis universalis*, p. 39). Further confirmation is given, in a sense, by Vico himself in his discussion of the "Corollaries Concerning the Principal Aspects of this Science" (*NS*, pars. 385–399). According to Enzo Paci (see "Vico and Cassirer" in Tagliacozzo and White, *Giambattista Vico: An International Symposium*, p. 467), "The New Science was meant to be—as in many respects it is—an encyclopedia of the sciences, of culture, and of history." Vico's use of the image of a tree to outline the "Division of Poetic Wisdom" (*NS*, par. 367) is a specific confirmation of his acquaintance with the tradition of the *arbores scientiarum* or, in any case, with the use of the tree image by Bacon in his *De dignitate et augmentis scientiarum* (see McRae, *The Problem of the Unity of the Sciences*, p. 26; Rossi, *Clavis universalis*, p. xii and *passim*) and by Descartes in his letter to Mersenne (see McRae, *The Problem of the Unity of the Sciences*, p. 57; Rossi, *Clavis universalis*, p. xii and *passim*). It is doubtful whether Vico was acquainted with the trees of the universe of knowledge proposed by Alsted and by Comenius as a basis for a reform of education. (On Alsted and Comenius, see Rossi, *Clavis universalis*, chap. 6, pp. 179–200, and Eugenio Garin, *L'educazione in Europa* [Bari: Laterza, 1957], esp. chap. 7.) The image of a tree of science has been frequently used in recent times by George Sarton; see, for instance, his essay "History of Science" (1956) in Dorothy Stimson, ed., *Sarton on the History of Science* (Cambridge: Harvard University Press, 1962), pp. 1–14.

[31] *NS*, par. 367.

human;[32] his giving the "poetic sciences" the same names as those of the corresponding "human" ones and considering them "poetic" precursors of the latter;[33] his discovery of a full correspondence between the former and the latter; his conviction that his science "discovers the ancient world of the sciences, how rough they had been at birth, and how gradually refined, until they reached the form in which we have received them"[34]: all this clearly reveals that, had he cared to describe his tree of knowledge in full, he would have presented it as a trunk (the "human mind," the maker of the "world of civil society"[35]) subdivided, according to the "modifications of the human mind,"[36] into three main branches—"religious wisdom," "poetic wisdom," "human wisdom"—all equally made up of identically named sciences, and that the name of each science would have appeared in the "tree" three times, once in each of those branches, with those three appearances, in a sense, outlining the historical-genetic transformation of that science.

If a confirmation of this interpretation were needed, it would be sufficient to recall the following statements by Vico: "As much as the poets had first sensed in the way of vulgar wisdom, the philosophers later understood in the way of esoteric wisdom;"[37] and: "Just as poetic metaphysics was above divided into all its subordinate sciences, each sharing the poetic nature of their mother, so this history of ideas [the *New Science*] will present the rough origins both of the practical sciences in use among the nations and of the speculative sci-

[32] *NS*, pars. 916–918.

[33] *NS*, par. 779: "it may be said that in the fables the nations have in a rough way and in the language of the human senses described the beginnings of this world of sciences, which the specialized studies of scholars have since clarified for us by reasoning and generalization."

[34] See n. 17.

[35] *NS*, par. 331.

[36] *NS*, par. 331.

[37] *NS*, par. 363.

ences which are now cultivated by the learned."[38] Needless to say, Vico's tree of knowledge, when fully described, would be nothing but a schematic picture of the *New Science*—a "history of human ideas, on which it seems the metaphysics of the human mind must proceed."[39]

What I have just said about Vico's "tree" does not, of course, mean that, had he actually undertaken to outline it in full, the three main branches issuing from the trunk—"religious wisdom," "poetic wisdom," and "human wisdom"—would have been identical in the sense that he would have found it necessary to treat them in equal detail. For instance, while remaining faithful to the scheme indicated and to the name and organization of the basic sciences, he would probably have enriched the "human wisdom" branch by further subdividing the sciences composing it and perhaps by adding others. Furthermore, had Vico lived in our time—and hence been aware of the "non-Euclidean" world view that began to emerge with Boole, Gauss, and Riemann around the midnineteenth century, and of the "organismic-transactional" world view dominating so many aspects of contemporary thought—he would probably have subdivided the "human wisdom" branch (as well as the others, if he had developed them—see Section 9*e*) into something analogous to my Euclidean World View, Non-Euclidean World View, and Organismic-Transactional World View subbranches of "science"[40] (for a brief explanation of this statement, see Section 9, especially *e* and *f*). Finally,

---

[38] *NS*, par. 391. Max Fisch points out that, according to Vico, "the sciences are themselves institutions, and the same vulgar wisdom that created families, commonwealths, and laws created also a poetic metaphysics, logic, morals, economics, politics, physics, etc. . . ." (*NS*, par. K7).

[39] *NS*, par. 347.

[40] Vico recognized that "every epoch is dominated by a 'spirit,' a genius of its own" (Giambattista Vico, *On the Study Methods of Our Time*, translated by Elio Gianturco [Indianapolis: Bobbs-Merrill, 1965], p. 73). This statement has some vague relationship with Thomas Kuhn's theory of "paradigms" (see the last sentence of Section 3 and n. 29, above).

it must be pointed out that "religious wisdom," "poetic wisdom," "human wisdom," and their elaborate subdivisions would probably have been represented by Vico, in his "tree," as coexisting: this because, although the types of thought represented respectively by those branches and subdivisions might have been born at different times, or might have had a comparatively different relevance at the time of their respective births, once born they survive indefinitely (see Section 10*b*). That this would be the case according to Vico is a corollary of his principle that "doctrines must take their beginning from that of the matters of which they treat,"[41] and is confirmed not only by the whole context of the *New Science* but also by such specific statements as "these three languages began at the same time,"[42] "poetic style arose before prose style,"[43] "poetic speech . . . continued for a long time into the historical period, much as great and rapid rivers continue far into the sea, keeping sweet the waters borne on by the force of their flow."[44]

6. If we compare Vico's "tree" with any of the many *arbores scientiae* that preceded it throughout the centuries,[45] or with any of the ideas mentioned in Section 2, we immediately discover the novelty and revolutionary nature of these key features: (a) three main branches (secondary trunks) issuing from the main trunk (instead of the latter directly ramifying into branches of knowledge and disciplines), because of Vico's discovery of two previously unknown modes of "wisdom": "religious wisdom" and "poetic wisdom"; (b) identical names, number, and organization of the key "sciences" in the three

[41] *NS*, par. 314.
[42] *NS*, par. 446.
[43] *NS*, par. 460.
[44] *NS*, par. 412; see also par. 629. Antonino Pagliaro has pointed out that, after giving a diachronic image of the three stages of language—divine, heroic, and human—Vico realized, and explicitly declared, that the different factors are present in each of them and operating synchronically (Antonio Pagliaro, *La dottrina linguistica di G. B. Vico* [Rome: Accademia Nazionale dei Lincei, Memorie, Classe di scienze morali, storiche e filologiche, 1959, ser. 8, vol. 8, fasc. 6], p. 486).
[45] See Rossi, *Clavis universalis*, and Yates, *The Art of Memory*.

coexisting branches—which indicates the "religious" and "poetic" origin of each "science" and, more generally, the idea that any "science" (as well as any of its "daughters," "granddaughters," etc.) goes through an unlimited series of stages, while old stages tend to survive indefinitely; (c) repeated, rather than unique, appearance of each "science" in the "tree".

It is easy to realize that the above features are corollaries of the "master key" of the *New Science*, the "discovery" that "the early peoples, by a demonstrated necessity of nature, were poets, who spoke in poetic characters."[46] In other words, as "within the picture of the *New Science* the theory of language occupies a central place, or rather is the nucleus around which . . . the edifice of Vico's thought . . . has . . . developed,"[47] so within the picture of Vico's "tree" of knowledge the historical-genetic-semantical factor is the most essential. In fact, the failure of all the attempts hitherto made to solve the problem of the unity of knowledge to produce convincing results may probably be attributed to the following reasons: (i) all those attempts, except, to some extent, the one made by Cassirer (but see below, Section 7), have overlooked modes of thought (e.g., myth, religion, art), "views of the world," philosophical trends, scientific theories, etc., which, however outdated they might be judged at a certain moment, are still with us, perhaps disguised in a modern version, as part of our culture; (ii) in most cases exclusive attention has been paid to a given viewpoint, considered as the ultimate one, in spite of the fact that theories born at different times often coexist, that science is continually developing new concepts, and that at times it combines several viewpoints or awakens dormant ones;[48] (iii) as a consequence of (i) and (ii) the name of each science has appeared only once in any scheme other than

[46] *NS*, par. 34.
[47] Pagliaro, *La dottrina linguistica di G. B. Vico*, p. 379.
[48] See Vico, *On the Study Methods of Our Time*, p. 73: "I remember eminent scholars who roundly condemned some branches of research; now they have changed their minds and are totally absorbed by the pursuit of those subjects."

Vico's; (iv) each science, in other words, has been considered *in abstracto*, like a monolith, that is, independent of its origin, history, stages, multiple strains, rather than in its historical-genetic-semantical reality, that is, as something similar to a mosaic of strains, born at different times and often having little in common except their name and their deepest roots (in the basic necessities of men and activities of the human mind); (v) like islands of an archipelago, whose submerged connections are invisible and hence tend to remain unknown, sciences *in abstracto* are either, at times, unifiable within a very limited range or entirely nonunifiable, due to the impossibility of discovering and disentangling their multiple roots, defining their common aspects and comparing them. Vico swept away all the above errors in one blow by substituting a dynamic-developmental "tree" for the static ones devised before and after him, and in so doing he laid the foundations of a modern solution to the problem of the unity of knowledge that even outstrips Cassirer's solution, as will be explained in Section 7.

It must be further pointed out that: (a) Vico's use of "mother" and "daughter" in outlining the subdivisions of "poetic wisdom" confirms the historical-genetic viewpoint on which his "tree" is based; (b) such a viewpoint lends itself to a modern taxonomic presentation—the first ever attempted in this field (see Section 9); (c) the taxonomic presentation of the tree is capable, perhaps uniquely so, of yielding a number of vital corollaries, upholding the above description of Vico's "tree" and shedding light on many aspects of my Vichian solution to the problem of the unity of knowledge (see Section 10); (d) one of the corollaries stemming from the repeated appearance of the same science in all the branches of the "tree" is that all sciences have an analogous "macroscopic" history, which runs in accordance with the general history of culture (see Section 10 *f*).

7. The foregoing should have given the reader some clear indication as to why Vico's, or a Vichian, viewpoint on the

problem of the unity of knowledge is more satisfactory than Cassirer's. In fact, although it might be true that Cassirer's discussion of "symbolic forms" (myth, language, art, history, and science) lends itself better than Vico's terminology to a modern treatment of that problem (this explains my use of terms borrowed from Cassirer in building my Vichian "tree"), Cassirer presents no general theory of the concept formation for mythical mind[49]—a theory indispensable as a foundation stone for the building of a genetic-historical tree of knowledge. This explains why in my broadcast I called Vico, rather than Cassirer, the thinker who can help us most today in our attempt to solve the problem of the unity of knowledge.

The Vichian Tree Updated

8. In the above discussion of the Vichian tree of knowledge, especially in Section 5, I have deliberately mixed my own interpretation of Vico's viewpoint—an interpretation based on the principles of the *New Science* and on Vico's outline of the "tree" of "poetic wisdom"—with inferences I have drawn from that viewpoint, often adding modern terms and concepts. My purpose in doing so has been to pave the way for a brief description, in Sections 9 and 10 below, of an updated Vichian tree of knowledge—my own, because I am not aware of the existence of any other. Where the interpretation ended and the "extrapolation" began is difficult for me to say because my judgment in this matter tends to be affected by my own "tree," which seems to me to embody all the features I have attributed to Vico's. In any case, it is not essential here to draw a sharp line between interpretation and extrapolation, because my primary purpose in this essay is to single out the character and potentialities of a Vichian—rather than Vico's—solution

---

[49] On Cassirer as compared with, and in relation to, Vico, see the extensive, illuminating discussion by Verene, "Vico's Science of Imaginative Universals and the Philosophy of Symbolic Forms," pp. 311–317.

to the problem of the "unity of knowledge." As to the derivation of corollaries from the *New Science*, let us remember, with Professor Fisch, that "Vico disclaims any pretension of completeness" and that "just as Euclid's Elements as a system is susceptible of indefinite further development without addition to or change in the definitions, axioms or postulates, so Vico's new science is susceptible of indefinite further development without change in its principles, whether in the narrower or in the wider sense."[50]

9. In view of the fact that some vital information on the Vichian tree of knowledge has already been given indirectly in these pages, and that what I am interested in here is to explain the structure and functioning of a Vichian tree of knowledge rather than to elucidate its details, I shall limit myself in this section to a skeletal presentation of my "tree."[51] In the next section I shall explain its basic implications and point out the contemporary significance of a Vichian solution to the problem of the unity of knowledge, with particular reference to a solution to the baffling and unyielding problem of general education.

(*a*) My tree of knowledge encompasses the whole of culture—past and present—within the boundaries of general culture (see Section 10*h*).

(*b*) The "tree" is composed of philosophical and scientific terms (some borrowed, some specially created) with an integrative connotation, including some names of sciences. The latter appear repeatedly at the upper level of the different branches (see *h* and *i*, below). These philosophical and scientific terms perform simultaneously a historical task (see *d*(ii), below), a genetic-historical task (see *c*, below), and a taxonomic-

---

[50] *NS*, p. xlii.

[51] No attempt has been made here to "update" or modify my tree, designed in 1959 (see n. 21, above), in order to accommodate recent cultural developments (such as, for instance, structuralism, which has spread to so many fields of the humanities and the social sciences). Attempts to update the tree are, of course, always possible. The Vichian tree is "open." However, the purpose of this essay does not make such an effort necessary, and its physical limitations make it impossible.

integrative task. They are in fact arranged by kingdoms, phyla, classes, orders, families, genera, species, and subspecies, rising from the lowest to the highest levels of the chart, according to a plan resembling the basic taxonomic scheme of modern biology. This taxonomy of knowledge does not extend beyond the level of the subspecies, for reasons to be explained in Sections 10*h* and *i*.

(*c*) From the genetic-historical viewpoint (as a taxonomy of knowledge) the "tree" shares the general logical character of the basic taxonomic scheme,[52] resembles the *New Systematics*[53]—in which taxonomy and evolution (i.e., history) are intertwined—and rests on postulates which, *mutatis mutandis* (i.e., using terms of the type indicated in *b*, above, instead of "organic systems," "organisms"), are analogous to some characteristic doctrines of "organismic biology."[54] I allude in particular to the doctrine of *historicity*, according to which organisms and other organic systems possess a historical character. The following features are generally included in organismic biology under the heading of "historical character": (i) All organic systems have histories, and it is part of the duty of the biologist to give a descriptive account of those histories: for example, paleontology describes the successive changes in form of groups of organisms. (ii) The past of an organic system determines, or helps to determine, its present structure and behavior. (iii) Many types of organic change (e.g., regeneration and evolution) are irreversible. (iv) Many organic changes are properly described by the term "development," which includes growth, elaboration, and differentiation. (v) The course of development from germ to adult organism is determined in part by the past history of the ancestors of the organism. It might be pointed out that the taxonomic viewpoint on which my "tree" is based is in full

---

[52] See Morton Berkner, *The Biological Way of Thought* (New York: Columbia University Press, 1954), chap. 4.

[53] *Ibid*.

[54] *Ibid*., chap. 1 and *passim*.

harmony with Vico's equating the "nature" of "institutions" with "their coming into being at certain times and in certain guises . . . [so that] . . . whenever the time and guise are thus and so, such and not otherwise are the institutions that come into being."[55]

(d) The trunk of the tree ("Symbolism") is subdivided into two kingdoms: "Presentational Symbolism" and "Discursive Symbolism" (two concepts borrowed from Susanne Langer's *Philosophy in a New Key*[56]). Presentational symbolism (the right branch issuing from the trunk) in turn subdivides into four phyla: "magic," "myth," "religion," "art." These follow one another from right to left, as four parallel vertical branches of the tree, symbolizing the corresponding stages of the human mind. Discursive symbolism (the left branch issuing from the trunk), not being subdivided, is identical with the fifth phylum, "science" (including, in a broad sense, philosophy), whose subdivisions at all levels follow one another from left to right. This change of direction is intended to symbolize: (i) the continuous intercourse taking place between presentational symbolism, a source of incandescent bundles of ideas, and discursive symbolism, which selects, dissects, and rationally develops some of those ideas; (ii) the history of "science" in its various stages; (iii) the trend of successive world views (see *f*, below) toward a more and more deep and comprehensive grasp of reality.

(e) According to the theory of the "tree," all its phyla are analogously structured. So far in my studies and teaching I have developed only the taxonomies of "science" and of "art" in full, and have sketched that of "religion." My research shows that the taxonomies of those phyla are indeed analogous, in spite of the diversity of the subject matter.[57] For the

---

[55] *NS*, par. 147.

[56] Susanne K. Langer, *Philosophy in a New Key* (New York: New American Library, 1948), pp. 63 ff.

[57] The basic ramifications of the "Tree of Art" are as many as those of the whole "Tree of Knowledge," and identically arranged. My results have thus confirmed

sake of brevity, only one phylum will be described in some detail here, "science."

(f) "Science" subdivides into three classes: Euclidean World View, Non-Euclidean World View, and Organismic-Transactional World View (see Section 3). These symbolize the three different modes of "scientific" thought—born at different times from Greece to the present day, and based on different conceptions of space, time, and causality—that coexist in our time.

Euclidean World View (or World of Common Sense) is an expression intended to denote the general outlook on things, and system of thought, derived from Greek geometry and philosophy—and still with us, often disguised in modern reincarnations—which dominated knowledge, within Western civilization, from Pythagoras until the birth, around 1850, of the Non-Euclidean World View, which now coexists with it. The Euclidean World View class is subdivided into three orders: rationalist philosophy, scientific empiricism, and philosophical empiricism. Rationalist philosophy—which originated with Plato and is still alive in our time—is subdivided, at various taxonomic levels from family to species, into: logic, metaphysics, physics, ethics, education, economics, politics, aesthetics. Scientific empiricism—the hypothetico-deductive science of the physical world, born with Galileo, which implies absolute time, space, and causality—has two families: physics (with its several genera, species, and subspecies) and chemistry. Philosophical empiricism—born with Bacon—is subdivided into two families: epistemology and utilitarian ethics. The latter, in turn, has three genera: ethics (with its several species, among which are economics and politics); psychology (which was born from utilitarian ethics through physiology); and (Darwinian) biology (whose principle of "natural selection" is derived from Malthus's *Essay on Population* and from the theory of economic competition).

Herbert Read's thesis, in *Icon and Idea* (Cambridge: Harvard University Press, 1955), that a new type of art is the first step in each development of human thought.

Non-Euclidean World View is an expression coined to denote a general outlook on things, and a scientific mode, characterized by the rejection of absolutes. First to be rejected was absolute space. Non-Euclidean geometry accomplished this basic feat. Hence the term Non-Euclidean applied to the world view. The Non-Euclidean World View class has two subclasses: Image of Nature and Image of Man. The Image of Nature subclass in turn bifurcates into two superorders: Continuity-Certainty, characterized by the rejection of absolutes in general (pragmatist philosophy) and of absolute space and time in particular (relativity theory), and Discontinuity-Uncertainty, more revolutionary than the former, because it also rejects causality (quantum theory). Among the branches of the Continuity-Certainty superorder, at various taxonomical levels, are: non-Euclidean geometry; non-Euclidean mathematics; logical empiricism; pragmatism; relativity theory. As an example of further taxonomic detail, pragmatist philosophy (an order) is subdivided into such families as epistemology, ethics, aesthetics; ethics (a family) is subdivided into such genera as religion, ethics, education, economics, politics. Among the branches of the Discontinuity-Uncertainty superorder, at various taxonomic levels, are: modern theory of infinity; metamathematics; metaphilosophy; quantum physics; quantum biology. When applied to the Image of Man subclass, the expression Non-Euclidean World View is used metaphorically to indicate its loose, but not unmeaningful, analogy with the rejection of absolutes (in particular "common sense" time, space, and causality) which characterizes the Image of Nature branch; more specifically, it is used to convey the idea that, as relativity theory reaches beyond the common-sense meaning of causality, so psychoanalysis and Gestalt theory reach beyond the commonsense meaning of human thought (by showing that the conscious thoughts man has about himself and others are only a small part of what goes on within his mind). The Image of Man subclass has three ramifications (orders): psychoanalysis; Gestalt theory (subdivided into two families: Gestalt and field); psychoanalysis-Gestalt-field. Among the branches of the psychoanalysis order, at various taxonomic levels, are: psychology (subdivided into psychology proper and anthropology); logic; ethics (sub-divided into religion, ethics, education, economics, politics); aesthetics. The branches into which the Gestalt order sub-divides are almost identical to those of the psychoanalysis order; the field order includes, among its branches, experi-mental social psychology and "group dynamics." The psychoanalysis-Gestalt-field order—which I introduced into the tree for the purpose of indicating the tendency of psychoanalysis, Gestalt, and field studies to overlap and to jointly influence contemporary social science—includes, at var-ious taxonomic levels: modern social science (subdivided into cultural anthropology and social psychology), anatomy and pathology of cultures, and traditional social science (in turn subdivided into sociology, history, political science, econom-ics).

Organismic-Transactional World View is an expression I coined to denote a new outlook on things which had begun to appear at the time when the tree was drafted and which seemed destined to characterize a new stage of knowledge. In particular, the term "organismic" was intended to underline the fact that many sciences today are beset by problems which are indicated by notions such as "wholeness," "organization," "Gestalt," and "field." The term "transactional" indicated the impact on biology, political science, etc., of Dewey's and Bentley's concept of "viewing physical nature and human soci-ety from the transactional as against the interactional or self-actional point of view."[58] Combined in a single expression, "organismic" and "transactional" were presented as compati-ble and analogous concepts, and a substantial unity of the new world view was indicated. Because, in its early stage of de-velopment, the Organismic-Transactional World View ap-

[58] John Dewey and Arthur Bentley, *Knowing and the Known* (Boston: Beacon Press, 1949).

peared characterized more by merely promising, and at times parallel or overlapping, new inquiries, than by well-established disciplines—and because it seemed to shun the traditional concept of disciplines as separate entities—the task of organizing the "organismic-transactional" branch of the tree of knowledge was especially difficult. A tentative solution was reached by grouping the new inquiries under relatively conventional titles, enclosed in quotes. Among the branches, at various levels, of the Organismic-Transactional World View class, the following might be mentioned: "philosophy" (subdivided into philosophical anthropology, genetic epistemology, transactional philosophy, general semantics, general systems research, cybernetics); "mathematics" (subdivided into topology, theory of games, information theory, operations research); "physics-biology-psychology" (subdivided into physics, biology, psychology); and "behavioral science" (subdivided into behavioral sciences, ethics—in turn subdivided into scientific ethics, mental hygiene, psychosomatic medicine—and economics).[59]

(g) All the main branches of the tree (I refer especially to science, but analogous remarks would also apply to magic, myth, religion, and art) reach the top at an even level, as names of sciences, through a varying number of ramifications. The uppermost level thus reached portrays: (i) the latest genetic developments which have occurred in each branch; (ii) the coexistence of various strains of thought within each "science"; and (iii) the history of each basic science (see d(ii)). Thus the top level of the tree has a genetic as well as a taxonomic and historical connotation. The implications of this will be explained in Section 10b.

(h) The names of sciences repeatedly appearing at the top of my tree of knowledge—each time, of course, in a different sector of it—happen to be, *mutatis mutandis*, basically the same as those of Vico's tree of "poetic wisdom" (logic, ethics, economics, politics, physics: see Section 5). This confirms the

[59] The reader is reminded here of what I said in n. 51, above.

soundness of Vico's contention that the basic disciplines arise from men's needs.[60]

(*i*) A typical example of a science repeatedly appearing at the top of the tree is economics. In the Euclidean World View class of the "science" phylum alone[61] it recurs once in the rationalist philosophy order, as a species of its ethics family, and once in the philosophical empiricism order, as a species of the latter's ethics family. To be more precise, in its first appearance economics is subdivided into two subspecies, Platonic economics and Aristotelian economics—two quite different strains of economic thinking, which have made their influence felt in very different ways throughout the centuries.[62] In its second appearance, economics represents the economics (born from utilitarian ethics) of Adam Smith and his followers. (Economics is further encountered in the Non-Euclidean World View and in the Organismic-Transactional World View branches of the tree; but I cannot discuss those appearances here.) On the significance of the repeated appearance of the names of "sciences" at the top of the tree, see Section 10*b*.

(*j*) The above implies, for instance, that any reference to economics in the sense to be attributed to this term when it appears at the top of the philosophical empiricism branch of the tree also embodies a reference to the following ascending genetic-taxonomic ladder: symbolism; discursive symbolism; science; Euclidean world view; philosophical empiricism; utilitarian ethics; ethics; economics. Similarly, any reference to economics in the sense to be attributed to this term when it appears at the top of any other branch also embodies a refer-

[60] See Ernesto Grassi, "The Priority of Common Sense and Imagination: Vico's Philosophical Relevance Today," *Social Research* 43 (Autumn 1976): 553–575; see also n.38 and *NS*, pars. 141–142, 367.

[61] If I were also describing the other phyla, I could mention, for example, Vico's "poetic economy" (*NS*, pars. 520 ff), a subdivision of the "myth" phylum.

[62] The first has been the springboard of a long series of utopian ideas for the socioeconomic reform of society up to our time; the second, reinforced by the thought of Thomas Aquinas, is still the basis of the Catholic-corporative trend of economic thinking (see Ralph H. Bowen, *German Theories of the Corporative State* [New York: McGraw-Hill, 1947]).

ence to an analogous genetic-taxonomic ladder. Furthermore, the above description of the tree implies, for instance, that economics as a species of the ethics genus belonging to the utilitarian ethics family of the philosophical empiricism order: (i) is far closer genetically to the politics species of that genus, family, and order than it is to the politics species of the ethics genus and family of the rationalist philosophy order; (ii) is also far closer genetically to the physics family of the scientific empiricism order than, for instance, to the physics family of the rationalist philosophy order or to the physics family of an order belonging to a phylum different from "science."

(*k*) The general conclusion to be drawn from the above examples is that any name of science or philosophical or scientific term appearing at any level within the tree structure: (i) embodies its own genetic history, and (ii) is linked in various genetic-taxonomic ways to all others.

(*l*) The above briefly explains the structure and functioning of my tree of knowledge—my Vichian solution to the problem of the unity of knowledge. Despite vague resemblances between some features of my tree and Kuhn's theory of "paradigms" (see Section 3), the following differences, among many, should be noted: (a) unlike Kuhn's "paradigms," the intellectual trends represented in my tree as unifying concepts, once born, tend to survive indefinitely (this is made possible by their adapting themselves to ever new circumstances, blending with other trends, or hibernating until a favorable time for revival arrives (see 10*b*); (b) in contrast to the single theory of "paradigms," there are various kinds of unifying concepts in the tree, related to their level in the taxonomic ladder and to a variety of other circumstances.

The Problem of General Education

10. I shall now explain the basic implications of my Vichian tree and point out the contemporary significance of a Vichian

solution to the problem of the unity of knowledge, with particular reference to the baffling and unyielding problem of general education.

(a) "Translocation" within culture. A Vichian tree of knowledge of the type indicated suggests the existence of some analogies between culture as a whole (of a society or of a single individual) and a biological organism such as a plant. Experiments with radioactive tracers on the circulatory systems of plants have demonstrated that substances required in the metabolism of plant cells not only travel up from the roots but also move about in other directions. This ebb and flow is called "translocation."[63] Phenomena analogous to translocation undoubtedly occur within culture, but they are not being accurately studied at present. Cultural translocation is implicitly assumed when a certain discovery is said to have occurred owing to a combination of ideas from various fields.

(b) Survival of leading trends of thought. The fact, mentioned in Section 9g, that all the branches of the tree reach the top, through a varying number of ramifications, indicates that intellectual trends, once born, tend to survive indefinitely—although they may change their outer appearance as fashions change, or blend with other trends so as to become hardly recognizable (see 9l). In other words, what survives indefinitely is mainly the core—the "structure"—of the intellectual trends rather than their outer coating.[64]

(c) Coexistence of intellectual trends varying in age. The above implies that the different strains coexisting within any science have, in a sense, a different age, irrespective of the date of their latest appearance. In this sense the history of culture and the panorama of culture at any given time are identical.

[63] See S. F. and Orlin Biddulph, "The Circulatory System of Plants," *Scientific American* 200 (February 1959): 26, 44–49; and J. W. Mitchell, I. R. Schneider, and H. C. Gauch, "Translocation of Particles within Plants," *Science* 131 (June 24, 1960): 1863–1870.

[64] The idea of such a survival was already present in Vico (see Section 5) and, as Pietro Rossi has pointed out, is found again in Dilthey. See Rossi's preface to Wilhelm Dilthey, *Il secolo XVIII e il mondo storico* (Milan: Edizioni di Comunità, 1967), p. 14.

(d) *Conventional "sciences" as mosaics composed of different strains of thought.* The above implies that what is generally called a "science" (e.g., philosophy, ethics, economics, physics, etc.) is, in fact, a mosaic of parts which vary in age, derive from different strains of thought, and at times have little in common except the name and a vaguely analogous subject matter (see the example in Section 9i).

(e) *Semantics of knowledge.* The above suggests that speaking of a "science" without indicating the strain of it to which one is referring is a semantic error, generating confusion (see 6(i), (ii), (iv), (v)). My Vichian tree demonstrates the need for a semantics of knowledge and lays some foundations for it.

(f) *A common pattern for the history of any science; identity of the history of knowledge and the panorama of knowledge.* Points b, c, and d imply that the strains of any "science" tend to be as many as the leading intellectual trends bequeathed by the history of civilization and that, therefore, the basic pattern of the history of any science is substantially the same. Moreover, they imply that, in a sense, the history of knowledge and the panorama of knowledge at any given time tend to coincide, that is, a panorama of knowledge must also be a history of knowledge.

(g) *A pluralistic unity of knowledge.* The same points suggest that the tree is an "open," growing one, and that the unity of knowledge portrayed by it is, in a sense, pluralistic. Because of its pluralism, the tree stimulates comparisons among various trends of thought, tends to dispel exclusivisms, and fosters the "free market of ideas."[65]

(h) *The tree encompasses and defines general culture.* As indicated in Section 9a, the tree encompasses the whole of culture—within the boundaries of general culture. These boundaries are taxonomically represented by the "sciences"

[65] It might be recalled here that "Vico blessed his good fortune in having no teacher whose words he had sworn by, and he felt most grateful for . . . [having] followed the main course of his studies untroubled by sectarian prejudice" (*The Autobiography of Giambattista Vico*, translated by Max H. Fisch and Thomas G. Bergin [Ithaca: Cornell University Press, 1944], p. 133).

appearing as subspecies at the top of the tree. My brief explanation of the tree in this essay indicates—and a full description of it would demonstrate—that the taxonomically organized concepts composing the tree (of which there are approximately 225, with about 130 at the top) are sufficient to encompass the *essential minimum* and the *attainable maximum* for the purposes of general culture. In this sense the tree can be said to have succeeded—perhaps for the first time—in *precisely defining general culture*. The definition achieved simultaneously specifies the basic *contents* of general culture and its *genetic nature* and *taxonomic organization*.

(*i*) *General tree of knowledge and special trees*. Could the tree be developed beyond the boundaries of general culture? If so, how, and for what purpose? There are two different ways of conceiving such a development. One of them would be simply to extend the taxonomic differentiation from the subspecies level to the variety level and possibly beyond. There would be no theoretical obstacles to a development of this kind, nevertheless the practical obstacles would probably be insurmountable (e.g., there would be a jump at the top of the tree from about 130 subspecies to a few thousands varieties) and the possible gain would be minimal, because the development would occur at a level reached only by specialists already familiar with the subdivisions of their own fields. The other conceivable way of developing the general tree beyond the boundaries of general culture would be to create special genetic-historical-taxonomic trees of individual "sciences," or combinations thereof. These trees could be built either by taxonomically developing special branches of the general tree independently of the rest of it or by combining all "genetic ladders" corresponding to the repeated appearance of a given "science" at the top of the tree (see Section 9*i*) in a single tree. I have developed trees of the first type (e.g., a tree of the Euclidean World View, a tree of Art, etc.) and of the second (e.g., a tree of Economics). Such sectional trees have shown themselves to be useful as teaching aids and (by pointing out unexpected analogies, parallelisms, etc., in the development of culture) as heuristic tools.

(k) *A tree of the protagonists of human knowledge.* If, wherever possible, the name of the founder were added to that of each philosophical or scientific term and/or name of science appearing in the tree (see Section 9b), the latter would also become the first tree attempted so far of the protagonists of human knowledge. A general tree, or special trees (see *i*, above), of this type, would, in my opinion, perform a very useful historical, mnemonic, heuristic, and didactic function.[66]

(l) *Vichian unity of knowledge and the problem of general education.* General culture (the general aspects of all that is known at a given time—including, of course, all knowledge about the past) and general education are, ideally, like the two faces of a coin.[67] Thus a Vichian tree of knowledge, while defining general culture, also embodies a general scheme for a curriculum of general education. Because of the historical-genetic-taxonomic nature of the definition of general culture achieved by the tree, the nature of such a curriculum is also historical-genetic-taxonomic. Furthermore, thanks to its historical-genetic-taxonomic nature, a curriculum of this type succeeds in fulfilling the basic requirements of a contemporary theory of education and in suggesting ways to improve upon it.[68] In

---

[66] Frances Yates (*The Art of Memory*, p. 381) recalls Leibnitz's remark that the *Ars Memoriae* suggests a way of remembering a series of ideas by attaching them to a series of personages, such as patriarchs, apostles, or emperors.

[67] I have elaborated on this point in "General Education: The Mirror of Culture."

[68] I am referring principally to Jerome Bruner's theories, embodied in *The Process of Education* (Cambridge: Harvard University Press, 1960), *On Knowing: Essays for the Left Hand* (Cambridge: Harvard University Press, 1962), *Toward a Theory of Instruction* (Cambridge: Harvard University Press, 1966), and *Studies in Cognitive Growth* (Cambridge: Harvard University Press, 1967). I should also like to mention the leading criteria of the Social Studies Curriculum Program of Educational Services, Inc., of Cambridge, Mass. Some of the courses proposed by that organization, embodying Bruner's suggestions, would have the student relive psychogenetically the necessary succession of stages of the whole of mankind and the parallel development of mental attributes and powers in the growing individual. I also have in mind the work of Jean Piaget, Lawrence Kohlberg, and developmental psychologists in general. See the papers by Sheldon White, Augusto Blasi, George Mora, John Krois, Robert Craig, and Jerome Singer, with their valuable bibliographies, in *Social Research* 43

fact, owing to the historical-genetic-taxonomic nature, organization, and presentation of its elements, this curriculum is: (i)
necessary (i.e., made up of essential elements of general culture, chosen on the basis of objective criteria of relevance
implicit in the historical-genetic-taxonomic scheme of the
tree); (ii) *sufficient* (i.e., "complete," inclusive of all the essential
elements of general culture—see *h*, above); (iii) *balanced* (i.e., giving each of its elements the relevance it deserves, according to
objective—taxonomic—criteria); (iv) *unitary* (because of the
unity of the genetic-taxonomic system on which it is based and
of the "translocation" occurring within the tree—see *a*, above);
(v) *economic* (because its genetic-taxonomic organization allows
dealing with basic integrative concepts common to several
disciplines only once rather than repeatedly, i.e., in connection
with each of them); (vi) *psychogenetic* (because it embodies a
psychogenetic viewpoint, i.e., Vico's idea of a parallelism between the necessary phases of human thought and the development of mental attributes in the growing individual[69]);
(vii) *integrative, and hence most favorable to the transfer of training*
(because of the integrative task performed by the concepts of
which it is made up—see 9*b*);[70] (viii) *teachable to anybody in some
form*—a *"spiral curriculum"* (because it lends itself to being
taught repeatedly at different levels).

In view of the foregoing, I hope that the general scheme for
a curriculum of general education embodied in the tree of

(Winter 1976). The following should also be consulted: Maria Goretti, "Vico's
Pedagogic Thought and That of Today," in Tagliacozzo and White, *Giambattista Vico:
An International Synposium*, pp. 553–575; and Howard Gardner, "Vico's Theories of
Knowledge in the Light of Contemporary Social Science," and George Mora, "Vico
and Piaget," in Tagliacozzo and Verene, *Giambattista Vico's Science of Humanity*, pp.
351–364 and 365–394, respectively.

[69] See n. 68. On Vico's belief in the existence of a psychogenetic law by which the
individual develops through a certain series of necessary phases parallel to a set of
"culture stages" traversed by the whole of mankind, see Vico, *On the Study Methods of
Our Time*, p. xxvii.

[70] Some of the "integrative" concepts making up the tree present analogies with
Bruner's pedagogic "structures." According to Bruner, the teaching and learning of
"structures" is at the core of the problem of the transfer of training. See n. 68.

knowledge will be attentively considered by reformers in education in their attempt to devise better curricula of general education and to enrich humanistically the teaching of any subject. In doing so they would help in the present-day fulfillment of Vico's educational aim: "that all divine and human wisdom should everywhere reign with one spirit and cohere in all its parts, so that the sciences lend each other a helping hand and none is a hindrance to any other."[71]

* An earlier version of this paper was presented at the Second Annual Conference, Middle Atlantic Region, of the Society for General Systems Research in 1973.

Curriculum Implications of the Vichian "Tree of Knowledge": An Appendix to Dr. Tagliacozzo's Paper

Let me begin by saying that I found Dr. Tagliacozzo's paper most interesting and that I agree with his highly stimulating thesis that Vico's *New Science* implies a viewpoint concerning the unity of knowledge that is of great importance for modern educational thought and can be usefully applied to the solution of some of the most pressing pedagogical problems of our time: those concerning the need to establish a properly integrated and balanced curriculum of general education.

Since I discussed Tagliacozzo's thesis rather extensively in a recent article,[1] I shall refrain here from repeating those comments. Obviously, his thesis has a special relevance today, when education is

[71] *The Autobiography of Giambattista Vico*, p. 146. It might also be said that such a curriculum would promote the adoption in our time of the advice Vico gave to students in 1732: "Devote yourselves, during your study time, to nothing but a continuous comparison among all the things you are learning, so as to create such a connection among them as will enable them all to harmonize with each of the disciplines you study. . . . Once the habit of comparing has settled in you, you will also have acquired the ability to compare the sciences, which, like celestial limbs, compose the divine body of knowledge in all its fullness" (Giambattista Vico, *Della mente eroica*, in *Opere*, edited by Fausto Nicolini [Milan: Ricciardi, 1953], pp. 920–921).

[1] Michael Littleford, "Vico's Legacy to Contemporary Education," *The Educational Forum* 36 (March 1972): 393–401.

embedded in trends of thought derived from the world view of the Newtonian science[2] and hence is based on an inadequate conception of the nature of man and his forms of knowledge. It is also well known that modern education is conducted without a philosophical foundation for formulating a comprehensive theory of general education and a satisfactory theory of curriculum derived therefrom. No such foundation has been offered by the diverse "critics" and "reformers" of contemporary education.[3]

[2] This view of the world involves an inherent separation of knowledge from human experience and history and science from human values. Within the Newtonian view, "knowledge" is possible only in the "objective world" of empirical science, a world which exists independently of man's activities and thought processes and whose determinate and predictable structures are neatly reflected in discrete areas of inquiry. Knowledge of the external world is valid to the degree that it corresponds to the preexisting mechanical order, and man can best assure this validity through alert and objective spectatorship.

Separate and distinct from the "primary" reality of science is the "subjective" (and secondary) reality of human consciousness, experience, and values. Since the "subjective" realm remains impenetrable to systematic and reflective modes of knowing, issues which arise in connection with this realm tend to be treated as matters of convention, habit, speculation, or opinion.

The dualistic Newtonian world is essentially static and nondevelopmental. A process of change involving genuine evolutionary transformation is foreign to this world. There is no notion of qualitative change involving fundamental structural reorganization of phenomena. Change does occur, but the process of change is quantitative and linear. The outcome of the process is merely additive, an extension of what already exists.

From such a perspective, education is logically viewed as a means to adjust man to an unchanging, objective reality separate from and external to himself. The means of adjustment involve a direct transmission to a passive learner (spectator) of objective knowledge and skills from separate areas of study which mirror the categories and requirements of the external world.

In addition to everyday practices, a survey of some of the major reform movements in the twentieth century demonstrates the profound influence of mechanistic Newtonian thought in education. During the early twentieth century, for example, the "cult of efficiency," the testing movement, and the vocational education movement emerged as major thrusts in education. Raymond E. Callahan, in his book *Education and the Cult of Efficiency* (Chicago: University of Chicago Press, 1962), presents an excellent historical account of that movement. Arthur G. Wirth, in *Education in the Technological Society: The Vocational Liberal Controversy in the Early Twentieth Century* (Scranton: Intext Educational Publishers, 1972), provides a superb philosophical analysis of the predominantly mechanistic emphasis of the vocational education movement. Contemporary extensions and elaborations of these earlier thrusts are found in the concept of accountability, the stress upon behavioral objectives, behavior modification, and programmed instruction, and the career education movement.

[3] As indicated in footnote 2, many modern reformers and critics have simply reinforced the dominant Newtonian view. Others have suggested that educational

In these brief remarks I shall venture a first response to Tagliacozzo's plea to reformers in education, at the end of his paper, to attentively consider the general scheme suggested by his Vichian tree of knowledge in their attempts to devise better curricula of general education and to enrich humanistically the teaching of any subject.[4]

To begin with, a little research beyond the boundaries of the paper we have just heard reveals that Tagliacozzo has already moved several steps on this road himself. Brief remarks and complete outlines have appeared in his published and unpublished writtings;[5] some aspects of those outlines were developed in his courses on the

theory and practice should refer back to trends of thought which emerged prior to Newtonian science. These reformers believe that modern pedagogy can be improved only through a return to the classical educational tradition which had its beginnings in Greek civilization and which emphasizes the development of man's "rational faculties." For a succinct account of these "conservative" critics and reformers, see Lawrence Cremin, *The Transformation of the School* (New York: Random House, 1964), pp. 338–347.

More frequently, alternatives to the Newtonian view have been based upon a romantic notion of education. The romantic reformers and critics have generally presented a negative and reactive view of education which is the polar opposite of the mechanistic view. In contrast to the mechanistic notion of education as primarily a matter of transmission from without, for example, the romantic alternative is that education is exclusively a matter of natural unfoldment from within. Needless to say, an educational philosophy which places primary emphasis upon the inner world of the individual and largely ignores the environmental context is as dualistic on one side as the mechanistic view is on the other. Hence, the romantic thinkers, while providing much needed criticism of existing practices, offer neither an adequate philosophy of man as a social-historical being nor a satisfactory epistemology. For an excellent account of the philosophical inadequacies of both "romantics" and "mechanists," see Lawrence Kohlberg, "Development as the Aim of Education," *Harvard Educational Review* 42 (November 1972): 449–496.

4 See Giorgio Tagliacozzo, "General Education as Unity of Knowledge: A Theory Based on Vichian Principles," *Social Research* 43 (Winter 1976): 768–796.

5 Tagliacozzo's published writings available to me were: "The Tree of Knowledge," *American Behavioral Scientist* 4 (October 1960): 6–12; "General Education: The Mirror of Culture," *ibid.*, 6 (October 1962): 22–25; "Culture and Education: The Origins," *ibid.*, 6 (April 1963): 8–13; and "Culture and Education: The Founding of the Classical Tradition," *ibid.*, 7 (January 1964): 20–25. The unpublished sources are papers for conferences and reports entitled: (1) "A Historical-Taxonomic Tree of Knowledge" (1958); "Unity of Knowledge, General Systems Research, and General Education" (1959); "Taxonomy of Knowledge: Why? What Kind? How Useful?" (1960); "The New Frontier in General Education" (1961); "A New Approach to Liberal Adult Education" (1962); "Unity of Knowledge and General Education: A Modern Conception, Based on Vico's New Science" (1963). In addition, the author obtained information about Tagliacozzo's work through direct correspondence with him and through perusal of the outlines of his courses as they appeared in the New School's catalogues from 1957 until 1961.

history of human thought at the New School for Social Research. This material seems to indicate a Vichian college curriculum basically made up, in structure and content, as follows:

(1) An introductory course—a schematic survey of the evolution and general structure of knowledge in all its basic modes (world views), presentational as well as discursive.

(2) Seven areas of study—successive elaborations of the introductory course. These would deal respectively with: (a) myth, magic, and religion from prehistory to the present; (b) the development of art and science: their parallels, complementarity and interdependence; (c) the Euclidean World View from its origins through the Renaissance; (d) the Euclidean World View from the birth of modern science to the present; (e) the Non-Euclidean World View: the study of nature; (f) the Non-Euclidean World View: the study of man and society; (g) the Organismic-Transactional World View.

To develop specific curriculum proposals for all levels of general education is beyond the scope of these brief remarks. However, a few words concerning this task seem appropriate and will perhaps contribute to setting the stage for further development of a Vichian conception of general education.

The task of developing complete general education curricula requires that Tagliacozzo's formulation be combined with the work of all the key developmental thinkers—not only Bruner, but also Piaget, Kohlberg, etc.—into an overall Vichian model. Such a model would be based upon the unifying concept that the most adequate approach to educational research and practice, whether related to the individual, the culture or the species, is a developmental one.[6] The comprehensive developmental model would thus provide the basis for the construction of "spiral" curricula of general education which allow each learner to establish a vital and meaningful relationship with the subject matter appropriate to his developmental level.

The idea of spiral curricula implies that the leading ideas or structures from the tree would be dealt with in some form at all levels. The idea also implies that the forms in which major concepts are presented to the learner would at first be relatively concrete and simple and would become progressively more complex, sophisticated, and abstract. In the lower grades, for example, much of the material would be presented in the form of myths, fairy tales, and

[6] See George Mora, "Vico, Piaget, and Genetic Epistemology," in Giorgio Tagliacozzo and Donald P. Verene, eds., *Giambattista Vico's Science of Humanity* (Baltimore: Johns Hopkins University Press, 1976), p. 367.

other types of content which stimulate the intuitive and imaginative powers.[7]

The curriculum at the lower levels would also provide opportunities for the student to be active in the learning process in a concrete sense. Elementary students, for example, might be involved in creating and acting out their own myths and tales. Such an activity could be developed both for the purposes of stimulating the imaginative abilities (and thus laying the basis for the later development of logical structures) and for building an initial understanding of the nature of symbols and the symbolic processes by which human beings develop a view of the world.

Opportunities for concrete experience would also be appropriate at the secondary level, but in more sophisticated forms and requiring more abstract and systematic outcomes. In connection with studying the ideas embodied in philosophical empiricism, for instance, secondary students might be involved in actually conducting research on biological and social phenomena from this perspective. The students might conduct a study of some aspect of their school, community, or natural environment which required them to collect detailed empirical data through observation and to arrive inductively at generalizations about the observed phenomena.[8] Such an activity could also be used for building the developmental foundation necessary for understanding subsequent ideas in the spiral curriculum.

[7] For example, such major concepts and transformations as the whole as greater than the sum of its parts, the unconscious, and the transition from an absolutist (Euclidean) to a nonabsolutist (non-Euclidean) perspective could be introduced through mythical and poetic forms.

This should not be construed to mean that the basic skills areas (reading, writing, and numbers) would be neglected. A neglect of basic skills would be obviously absurd, since these skills developed to high levels are necessary for progression through the spiral curriculum.

It should also be remembered that the tree is based upon the Vichian notion of a parallelism between the stages of development in mankind as a whole and in the individual. The psychogenetic point of view begins with the recognition that the beginning of all knowledge and human consciousness lies in the imaginative and poetic side of the human personality. Presentational modes of thought are prior to and more basic than discursive modes. Hence, presentational symbolism would play a much more important role in a Vichian curriculum than is currently the case. It not only provides the basis of spiral curricula but is an important area of study at all levels.

[8] To be congruent with the tree, such activities of course would never be performed in isolation. The concrete activities would be accompanied by inquiry into such areas as the social and historical conditions within which empiricism arose, its impact upon various areas of knowledge, and its contemporary adherents.

The students' natural history research, for example, might be used as a starting point in helping them understand relativity. Cultural relativism could be introduced through directing the students' research toward the cultural patterns in a community and comparing their work with suitable ethnographic studies. Through appropriate related activities (e.g., dealing with conflicts and contradictory situations which require a relativistic perspective for satisfactory solutions), the understanding of cultural relativity could be broadened to include other forms of relativism. The outcome of this developmental activity for the students would hopefully be a firm grasp of the general principle of "freedom from absolutes"—the leading feature of the Non-Euclidean World View.

Whatever the developmental level, Tagliacozzo's formulation and the Vichian tradition from which it is derived require that the learner have a role appropriate to a philosophy of man which views him as an active creator of knowledge, his human world, and his own nature. More specifically, this philosophy requires that the curriculum be designed and implemented to stimulate individual development through the establishment of a dialogue between the learner and the complex sociohistorical process of which he is a part. Through the ongoing dialogue structured at the various levels according to developmental criteria, the learner can gain a progressive understanding of himself, his society, and their relationship to the modern world as parts of a developmental process involving man's entire history and culture. Such understanding should result in highly developed individuals who live in accordance with such Vichian insights as: (a) human nature is not static, but develops at both the individual and the societal levels; (b) all world views are historically relative and humanly constructed; (c) as human beings, we are capable of a reflective understanding of our own and others' social and historical conditionings (i.e., the processes by which various world views come into being): and (d) the human world is made by human beings and can therefore be remade by them in accordance with "human needs and utilities." Large numbers of such highly developed individuals could contribute to a renewal and revitalization of culture which is sorely needed in this age of technological dominance and alienation.

MICHAEL LITTLEFORD

Comment on the "Vico and Pedagogy" Session

A striking—and by no means unmeaningful—feature of the "Vico and Pedagogy" session of this conference appears to me to be the *complementarity* of the two papers we have heard. Professor Perkinson and Dr. Tagliacozzo have respectively stressed the innovative suggestions stemming from Vico's thought for the reform of the *methods* and of the *curricula* of education—the two basic, complementary (and, of course, interdependent) fields of the pedagogic enterprise. This means that, according to the combined views of the two distinguished speakers, Vico has something important to say in both those fields, that is, on the subject of education as a whole. Perhaps it should be pointed out that very few, if any, of the theoreticians of the *methods* of education (I include among them the best known contemporary developmental psychologists) have dealt extensively or in detail with the overall problem of *curriculum building*, and that the devising of *curricula* has generally taken place empirically rather than as a set of systematic corollaries of pedagogic theory. Vico, on the contrary—as the combined papers of the speakers demonstrate—offers a complete program for reform in education, with suggestions very relevant for contemporary needs.

Professor Perkinson discovers Vico's educational thought to be a mean between the extremes of the activity curriculum and a receptor approach to learning. And he finds a general neglect of content or subject matter in contemporary education. Yet one point I find problematic in his paper is his interpretation of John Dewey. Since his argument does not fundamentally hinge on this interpretation, I will only briefly mention it. Perkinson insists that, since Dewey was an exponent of the activity curriculum, he was not as sensitive to content as he might have been. Dewey senses this problem with his "instrumentalism," and his *Experience and Education*, written in 1938, is largely a reply to his critics. In it Dewey finds subject matter to be one of the necessary aspects used in the employment of the scientific method.

Likewise, there needs to be a distinction made between John Dewey and the Progressivists, even though such thinkers as Joel

Spring and Michael Katz in their revisionist histories of the pragmatic movement neglect this point.

Otherwise, I am in substantial agreement with both papers. In
view of this, I shall add only a few remarks on the corollaries of
Vico's thought for curriculum building—which leads me to a brief
discussion of the Vichian "tree of knowledge."

Most "trees of knowledge" developed by philosophers include only
accounts of particularized, individual strands of knowledge, not the
historical-genetic-semantic aspects and taxonomic organization of
knowledge. These "trees" do not develop a complete guide to general education. The Vichian tree is essential in that through its use
general education is definable. Its contents are knowable in the true
sense of the liberal arts.[1] Likewise, the contents of general education
are knowable due to the taxonomic structure of the tree—going up
the taxonomic structure leads to a precise definition of general
education. Thus it is possible for students to grasp knowledge as a
whole at every level of study.

This taxonomic structure makes precise what formerly was vague,
and it affords an exact idea of what is important in the development
of the curriculum. When aspects of subjects are at the same level,
they are equally important—Euclidean, Non-Euclidean, and Organismic-Transactional World View, for example.

The curricular implications of the "tree of knowledge" are varied,
but one point is clear: the curriculum needs to be encyclopedic, and
broad areas of study need to be investigated at each level. Since
various disciplines are different ways of integrating human experience, this interdisciplinary approach would develop what R.S. Peters
terms a "broad cognitive perspective."[2] As important as the specialization of knowledge is, education and specialization are not
synonymous terms, for education is broader than specialization. The
educated human being can view the world from various perspectives
and can visualize the interrelationship among various strands of
thought. This is the exact perspective provided by Tagliacozzo's
interpretation of the Vichian tree.

Likewise, the Vichian tree affords a unified view of the development of knowledge, for all knowledge has a common historical

---

[1] The traditional concept of the liberal arts is composed of at least two notions—the
unification of human experience and the freeing of the individual to view reality in an
integrated manner.

[2] R. S. Peters, *Ethics and Education* (Glenview, Ill.: Scott, Foresman, 1967), pp. 9–10.

origin, according to Vico.[3] And a more integrated concept of knowledge implies an understanding of the historical development of knowledge. Thus various strains of knowledge and various world views can coexist together. For example, primitive economics, Aristotelian economics, medieval economics, utilitarian economics, and capitalistic economics all have value in that they describe the birth of different economic systems in accordance with different historical circumstances and the corresponding evolution of economic theory. This provides needed rationale toward a "relevant" curriculum, for in order to understand contemporary theory, the student needs to be exposed to the historical development of that theory. The justification of the curriculum is not merely reduced to a "principle of politicalization,"[4] or any other romantic consideration, for the Vichian tree provides objective justification for the contents of a "relevant" curriculum. According to Vico, various forms of knowledge are not independent of each other; knowledge has an essential unity.

The Vichian tree is a method of ordering the various aspects of knowledge, for the concepts at the bottom are more comprehensive than those at the top. This is one reason why all knowledge can be reduced to the same source. The trunk of the tree, symbolism, is more inclusive than the branches, for example. This Vichian tree encourages much interaction among ideas, for the tree is open to conflicting and contemporary developments. Students can then discover the evolution and relativity of all ideas. This Vichian tree portrays an organic unity which is "open to all serious systems of thought and ideas."[5]

Based on Tagliacozzo's interpretation of Vico, Professor Littleford suggests that Vichian ideas can be used in a number of ways. In the first place, she insists that a "spiral" curriculum is logically implied by Vico's pedagogical ideas. This curriculum would allow each student to establish a meaningful relationship with various forms of subject matter. Subject matter would be presented to the student at his or her developmental level. Second, following Piaget, she insists that a "spiral" curriculum has implications for educational delivery systems, for ideas are presented in a progression from the most

[3] See *The New Science of Giambattista Vico*, translated by Thomas G. Bergin and Max H. Fisch (Ithaca: Cornell University Press, 1968), pars. 314, 140, 347.

[4] Frederick C. Neff, "How Relevant is 'Relevance'?" in *Proceedings of the Twenty-Eight Annual Meeting of the Philosophy of Education Society*, March 26–29, 1972, pp. 56–60.

[5] Michael Littleford, "Vico's Legacy to Contemporary Education," *The Educational Forum* 36 (March 1972): 399.

concrete and simple to the more complex and abstract.[6] Third, Littleford suggests that elementary students would actively participate in the learning process. For example, students could be concretely involved in creating and acting out their own myths. Lastly, at the secondary level students could deal with concrete experience in a more abstract manner. Students could conduct various studies or empirical surveys, for example. She even suggests an outline for an introductory college course based upon Tagliacozzo's unpublished writings and the courses he has taught at the New School for Social Research. This course would aid students in understanding the evolution and general structure of knowledge—this would include the development of myth, magic and religion, for example. Thus, based upon her reading of Vico and the work of Professor Tagliacozzo, Dr. Littleford has developed specific strategies for education. And, unlike Professor Perkinson, she tries to understand these Vichian ideas in relation to developmental theory.

Although much more could be said about this very important session of the Vico conference, I would like to end this brief comment with some general remarks on Vico's pedagogical theory. It is obvious, for example, that educators are bewildered by the increasing amount of information amassed each year. Knowledge can become both overspecialized and fragmented. There is a growing need to discover some manner of synthesizing the various elements of the curriculum. This synthesis is afforded by the Vichian tree, for various broad systems of thought can be distinguished from less comprehensive systems of thought. Students would be able to grasp the underlying unity of ideas, and they would be able to more readily remember various facts.

These suggestions lead to the development of an interdisciplinary aspect of education in the "positive" sense of interdisciplinary. Courses could be offered which would study the origins of the various social sciences, for example, and the student would be left with some unifying concepts by which to understand the developments in the various social sciences.

But this Vichian tree is also useful to elementary and secondary teachers, as Professor Littleford pointed out, for these teachers could develop concepts and methods for interrelating various disci-

---

[6] For an excellent criticism of the "spiral" curriculum, see Clive Beck, *Educational Philosophy and Theory* (Boston: Little, Brown, 1974), pp. 142–146. I have also commented on this problem in "Form, Content and Justice in Moral Reasoning," *Educational Theory* 26 (Spring 1976): 154–157.

plines. This could lead, for example, to a better integrative approach to social studies, which at present is rather fragmented. There have been many attempts at interdisciplinary education, and many of these have been marred by the emphasis on specialization by members of the interdisciplinary team.[7] At present, both students and teachers seem to view the various disciplines as separate and isolated from one another. At least the Vichian perspective on the development of the curriculum suggests a viable alternative.

ROBERT PAUL CRAIG

[7] At Wayne State University, Bette LaChapelle and I have developed an interdisciplinary approach to an intern teaching seminar. See Robert Paul Craig and Bette LaChapelle, *Performance Objectives for Intern Teaching with Philosophy Component* (Detroit: Institute for the Research and Development of Competency-Based Teacher Education Programs, 1975).

Vico and the
Future of
Anthropology

BY SIR EDMUND LEACH

Vico is all things to all men. Twenty-seven years ago Franz Neumann, then Professor of Government here in Columbia University, made him a Marxist in the following fashion:

> The subject matter of Vico's book is the totality of material and nonmaterial culture in its historical development. The totality is "the work of man." Vico ended the search for cosmic laws under which social change appeared simply as the result of supernatural forces. The world of society is the world of human wants and needs, of the conflicts between man, nature, and history. Vico undertook to establish the general trends, which he considered as stages of a comprehensive historical process. For Vico, no isolated element can be held responsible for the occurrence of social change; it is the totality of interrelationships between social relations and its superstructures that determines change. The change is one from a lower to a higher form of society, but in the very transition to a higher stage there are unfolded the inherent contradictions of society so that it plunges again into barbarism.[1]

Personally, I feel grave doubts whether Vico would have recognized his philosophy in this description. My own evaluation of Vico is very different, though I start from the same point. Let me remind you that Vico's actual text in translation reads:

> [It is] a truth beyond all question: that the world of civil society has certainly been made by men, and that its principles are

[1] Franz Neumann, "Introduction," in Baron de Montesquieu, *The Spirit of the Laws*, translated by Thomas Nugent (New York: Hafner, 1949), p. xxxviii.

therefore to be found within the modifications of our human mind. Whoever reflects on this cannot but marvel that the philosophers should have bent their energies to the study of the world of nature, which, since God made it, He alone knows, and that they should have neglected the study of the world of nations, or civil world, which, since men had made it, men could come to know.[2]

Vico's view of history was not deterministic.

Vico and Linnaeus

The first version of *The New Science* was published in 1725. But as has often been pointed out, the written style is archaic. Vico's sociological profundities emerge from essays written in the manner of the sixteenth-century humanists who often appeared to be arguing as if all possible learning were to be discovered in the classical literature of ancient Greece and Rome. In this regard, therefore, Vico appears to stand at the end of an epoch rather than at the beginning of a new one.

Rather than suggest an anachronistic comparison between Vico and Marx, I would draw attention to the contrast between Vico and Linnaeus. The first edition of Linnaeus's *System of Nature* appeared in 1735. Man is placed at the head of the universe of created species. Two species of man are recognized—*Homo diurnus*, equivalent to *Homo sapiens*, and *Homo nocturnus*, into which was slotted the orangutan. *Homo sapiens* was subdivided into a variety of geographically localized subspecies which were distinguished by their habits as well as by their physical characteristics, rather as one might distinguish local varieties of a single species of bird. The attributes to which Linnaeus draws attention include the following: *European*—fair, sanguine, brawny; covered with close clothing; governed by laws. *African*—black, phlegmatic, relaxed; an-

---

[2] *The New Science of Giambattista Vico* (hereinafter *NS*), translated by Thomas G. Bergin and Max H. Fisch (Ithaca: Cornell University Press, 1968), par. 331.

noints himself with grease; governed by caprice. *Chinese*—monstrous, macrocephalic; and so on.

Now, it must be admitted that even the most enthusiastic zoological and botanical admirers of Linnaeus were not particularly impressed by his treatment of the species Man. But it is the underlying framework of assumptions which matters here. Linnaeus assumed that all existing species had been as they are now from the beginning. Every species had originated in an act of divine creation, and all the original species taken together, including some that are now extinct, collectively form a great chain of being from the simplest to the most complex. Man's relationship to the great apes was not one of common genealogical origin but of similitude. Man stood at the head of the list, and the great apes were immediately below him.

This general way of looking at the facts in which the continuum of our immediate experience is broken up into a vast number of categories, all of which coexist synchronically as members of an interdependent network but in which the entities themselves are never changed as a consequence of their interactions, is still characteristic of many areas of modern science. Admittedly most contemporary scientists—or at any rate all the more sophisticated ones—are well aware that the stability of species entities, inorganic as well as organic, is illusory. A high proportion of the really major scientific discoveries of the last hundred and fifty years in biology, physics, and chemistry have entailed the realization that entities previously thought to be innately stable—for example, the atoms of very heavy chemical elements—were capable in certain circumstances of spontaneous disintegration. Even so, most scientists operate with the assumption that, in *normal* conditions, entities exist in stable equilibrium. Life would become altogether too complicated if we assumed otherwise.

There is no reason to suppose that Vico would have challenged this proposition. But what he did assert was that when we are concerned with sociological problems we should not use the kinds of stable equilibrium model which appeal to natural scientists. Society is made by man. Man exercises choice. Man can change his mind. And, in the outcome, "the common nature of nations" is that each nation has a life history. Every system of institutions is always in a state of becoming something else.

But when Vico insisted that nations are made by man he emphatically did not mean to imply that they are the rational outcome of the cogitations of legislators. It is rather that the social institutions are a kind of by-product of the "poetic"— that is, nonrational—operations of human minds, and since we may assume that, at a psychological level, all human minds are much the same, human beings ought, in principle, to be able to understand the life history of nations since this life history is brought about by the operations of human minds which are like our own.

All of which is very nice in theory but difficult to handle in practice.

In their theoretical and methodological debates over the past century, the professional practitioners of social and cultural anthropology have seldom, if ever, invoked the names of Vico and Linnaeus. Nevertheless, there is a sense in which the polarity to which I have drawn attention has persisted right through. On the one hand there have been social theorists and anthropologists, concerned with making grand-scale generalizations about the evolutionary history of human society, who have based their position in some kind of assumption about the universal principles governing the operation of human minds. At the other extreme there have been those who shied right away from any generalization about human universals and have concentrated their effort on establishing a worldwide inventory of cultural particulars.

The nineteenth-century evolutionists, including Marxists, fall into the first category, while the culture historians and functionalist social anthropologists fall into the second. On the one hand there are those who expound their anthropological ideas through rational argument and resort to ideal-type models; on the other there are the 100-percent empiricists who stick firmly to the facts of the case.

Since about 1955 the increasing prestige of Professor Lévi-Strauss, coupled with the academic vogue for various styles in neo-Marxism, has tended to swing anthropological fashion away from the empiricist pole toward that of the rationalist model-makers. This certainly means that fashionable contemporary academic social anthropology is closer to Vico than it has been at any time during the past century. But whether it also means that a close reading of Vico can provide an aid and encouragement to the budding modern anthropologist is a moot point. This is what I would now like to consider.

Poetic Wisdom

First inspection is discouraging. For the structuralist addict already fully primed with textual comparisons from Lévi-Strauss, Lacan, and Foucault, there is a great deal in Vico's *New Science* which has a familiar ring. But a good deal of this familiarity depends upon Vico's fondness for verbal punning and the interpretations he puts upon the symbolism of mythology is often far-fetched in the extreme. Certainly to suggest to the anthropological novice that his reading list of references to Lévi-Strauss's *Savage Mind* might be replaced by Vico's Poetic Cosmography would be a case of jumping out of the frying pan into the fire. Contemporary Frenchmen are difficult enough; an eighteenth-century Italian in translation may seem well-nigh impossible.

A major trouble is that Vico's formal academic status was that of Professor of Latin Eloquence at the University of Naples, and he was fascinated by the etymological origins of Latin words. Moreover, in order to exhibit his learning he very often uses these words, not in their ordinary meaning, but in the sense which they might have had if his etymologies were correct—and in fact they are often highly dubious. Vico's English translators have commented upon the appalling difficulties which this kind of thing presents to any would-be editor.

Of course the reader can get a lot of fun out of Vico's elaborate puns so long as he does not take them too seriously. In a chapter entitled "Poetic Morals and the Origins of the Vulgar Virtues Taught by Religion through the Institution of Matrimony,"[3] *consortium, connubium,* and *conjugium* are distinguished by reference to *sors* ("casting lots"), *nubendo* ("to cover"), and *jugalis* ("of the yoke"), from which point we are led by way of an astonishing but characteristic free association concerning the names of Greek and Roman gods and goddesses to suppose that Eros (love) is a pun on Heros (hero), which is a variant of Hera, which links with Hymen, and in a different direction with *hereditas* (inheritance), which is taken elsewhere as the starting point for a discussion of the role of property in the structure of class and marriage!

Now it may well be true that Vico was the first theorist of society to recognize that the structure of metaphysical ideas concerning the role and function of deity, the structure of cultural ideas concerning the relations between the sexes, and the structure of political/economic ideas concerning property ownership and the relationship between social classes may be seen as interdependent transformations one of another. But although this is important for those who are concerned with the history of ideas, it does not necessarily mean that the way Vico presented this novel thesis is still significant. Aspects of Vico's ideas are still around, but after 250 years they are not easy to use in their original shapes.

In point of fact, what I myself find interesting about Vico is not that he was a forerunner of later thinkers. That, after all, is in some sense true of all those who come to be admired by later generations. It is rather that Vico, having had a number

[3] *NS*, pars. 502–519.

of structuralist insights into what he himself called "poetic wisdom" but which we now (following Lévi-Strauss) tend to describe as "mytho-logic" (or *la pensée sauvage*), then proceeded to try to employ this "poetic" (synthetic) manner in order to present his sociological arguments. And he did so of set purpose in preference to using the analytical style of discourse which has commonly been used by all kinds of academic writers, at least over the past three centuries. Vico's employment of this style is only partially successful, but it is, in a certain special sense, "revealing." The modern reader has to devote a very special intellectual effort if he is to get anywhere at all with decoding what Vico intended to say, and this effort is likely to fix Vico's text in the reader's mind even if at the end of it all the reader is still not very sure what it was all about! Moreover, sometimes, perhaps almost by accident, the line of Vico's "poetic" reasoning does turn out to have striking parallels with ethnographic evidence. I shall presently cite one or two selected examples.

All the same, I feel considerable doubt about how far the modern reader is entitled to play around with Vico's original text in order to be able to say, "But this is what he really meant." Vico's written style often suggests parallels with that of a highly calligraphic artist (such as Picasso) who, in a few broad, vivid strokes of his brush, can create the *suggestion* of a picture which the viewer needs then to complete for himself. But the completion can be accomplished in many different ways. So in reading Vico I am often worried by an unanswerable question: Are the lines of free association which his condensed "poetic" statements evoke in *my* mind anywhere near those which he himself would have put into the text if he had expanded it?

My reading of Vico assumes that, overall, he means to argue somewhat in the following fashion:

1. Analytical, philosophical discourse with its specialized vocabulary and its reliance on Aristotelian logic is historically a late development.

2. But abstract thinking in the field of politics and morality began long before the development of any specialized philosophic language.

3. This abstract, "prephilosophic" thinking is what Vico calls "poetic wisdom."

4. He holds, very much in the manner of the contemporary heirs of de Saussure, that the customs and religious beliefs of classical antiquity (or of any preliterate nation) constitute expressions of these abstract ideas, and that their combinations and transformations which serve to establish metaphoric associations and metonymic chains between separable entities are the equivalent of philosophic assertions.

5. Furthermore, Vico seems to be asserting that such customs and beliefs reflect the ideas and aspirations not merely of "nations" but of sectional interests within nations. Thus in an aristocratic commonwealth the interests of the "nobles" (heroes) differ from those of the commoners (plebs), and diversity of custom reflects such conflict of interest.

To present a concrete case where this sort of thing can be said to have direct relevance for modern social anthropology is far from easy. But let me make the attempt. The theme I want to consider is the opposition between *clothed* and *unclothed*, a binary opposition which has universal significance in all human cultures throughout the world. What does Vico make of it?

Needless to say, he does not present his arguments on this subject in an order which an Aristotelian would regard as logical. Just the reverse. However, for the purposes of this paper, let me rearrange the propositions. "The plebeian Venus was depicted as naked, whereas Venus *pronuba* wore the girdle."[4] Earlier, we have been told that Juno, as both wife and sister of Jove, signifies solemn matrimony and is fully clothed, while Venus *pronuba*, here called "the heroic Venus" who is likewise "patron goddess of solemn marriage, covers

---

[4] *NS*, par. 569.

her private parts with a girdle.">[5] We learn that nakedness, which "was later taken as an incentive to lust . . . . had been invented to signify the natural modesty or the punctuality of good faith with which natural obligations were fulfilled among the plebeians. For the plebeians had no part of citizenship in the heroic cities and thus did not contract obligations sanctioned by any bond of civil law to make their fulfilment necessary. Hence to Venus were attributed the Graces, likewise nude."[6] We are then told that the expression *pacta nuda* signifies "simple agreements which involve only natural obligation." These were contrasted with *pacta stipulata*, contractual arrangements later covered by the legal term "vested." Vico then makes the point that this distinction between stipulated and nude contracts derives from a metaphor in which *stipula* stands for the stalk which clothes the grain.

Now the ordinary reader of Vico may think that this is simply a verbal trick whereby Vico has ingeniously managed to extract out of the opposition "naked/clothed," by means of a sequential reference to marriage goddesses, heroic cities, contracts and agriculture, a confirmation of his thesis about "these four causes which, as will be observed throughout this work, are four elements, as it were, of the civil universe; namely, religion, marriage, asylum, and the first agrarian law."[7]

However, as an anthropologist of a particular speciality, I found that this particular Vichian formula gave me something of a shock. The Kachins of North Burma are a people about whom I have written extensively, particularly with regard to their verbal usages and their marriage customs. In one such publication, I pointed out that the relationship between a wife-giving lineage and a wife-taking lineage, which is often one of political domination, can be metaphorically viewed as *clothed* versus *naked*, and that the particular metaphor em-

[5] *NS*, pars. 511–512.
[6] *NS*, par. 569.
[7] *NS*, par. 630.

ployed by the Kachins is the distinction between *mayu*, "the green rice stalk still carrying the ear of grain," and *gu*, "the naked grain of rice after it has been dehusked."[8]

It is of course quite absurd that this virtual *identity* of simile should appear in such widely differing contexts, but it does suggest that Vico came nearer to grasping at universals of poetic logic than one might ordinarily suppose!

Like Lévi-Strauss, Vico sometimes seems to have the knack of getting it right even when he appears to get it wrong: "To the plebeian Venus were attributed the doves, not to signify passionate love but because they are, as Horace describes them, *degeneres*, base birds in comparison with eagles, which Horace calls *feroces*, and thus to signify that the plebeians had private or minor auspices as contrasted with those of the eagles and thunderbolts possessed by the nobles."[9] Vico then repeats, as he had previously asserted,[10] that the "heroic Venus" was associated with swans, which appertain also to Apollo, "and under the auspices of one of which Leda conceives the eggs by Jove."

Now in fact modern scholarship shows that the Hellenistic belief that Aphrodite (Venus) was associated with swans arose from a misinterpretation of a text in Sappho. The swans should be sparrows, birds which were supposed to be particularly addicted to copulation![11] The bird associations of the major Greek deities were fairly stable; in particular, Zeus (Jove) = eagle (but sometimes swan); Apollo = swan. However, it seems that there is a fragment of Hyginus which gives a version of the Leda story, to which Vico here refers, in which Zeus, who turns himself into a swan in order to pursue Nemesis (Leda), is then himself pursued by Aphrodite in the

---

[8] Edmund Leach, "The Language of Kachin Kinship," in Maurice Freedman, ed., *Social Organization: Essays Presented to Raymond Firth* (London: Frank Cass, 1967), pp. 141–142, 148.

[9] *NS*, par. 568.

[10] *NS*, par. 512.

[11] Arthur B. Cook, *Zeus: A Study in Ancient Religion*, 3 vols. (Cambridge: Cambridge University Press, 1914–40), 3: 831, n. 2.

form of an eagle![12] To cap this Pausanias (VIII.17.4) tells us that among the species of eagles to be seen in Greece in his day was a snow white bird known as a swan-eagle!

My conclusion is that Vico's *New Science* cannot be recommended as bedtime reading for the budding anthropologist. Even so, as the latter drowsily falls asleep over the ramifications of reconstructed classical mythology, flashes of astonishing insight may well break through. The entities of Vico's man-made world of society are not analytically distinct fixed objects; they are not species which have existed from the beginning. They are generative ideas; their recombinations and transformations are forever producing new "modifications of our own human mind."

[12] *Ibid.*, 1: 279, n. 4.

The Theoretical and Practical Relevance of Vico's Sociology for Today

BY WERNER STARK

WHEN Giambattista Vico was in his nineteenth year, Sir Isaac Newton published his *Philosophiae naturalis principia mathematica* and thereby created a new intellectual condition, not only in the physical sciences but in the social sciences also. There were many who felt that the laws of gravitation explained the social order as well as the sidereal system: publications like George Berkeley's essay *The Bond of Society* started a fairly broad theoretical tradition which is still with us; witness, for instance, the writings of George Homans. Men were defined as animate atoms possessed, like the stars of heaven, of powers of attraction and repulsion, and society was interpreted as an equilibrium system, just like the order which keeps the heavenly bodies in their appointed trajectories. This mechanicism had a very strong appeal because it seemed to tally, to some extent at any rate, with the objective facts of the day. The seventeenth century saw the capitalist system come to birth, and capitalism is a market society. But at a market independent individuals—man atoms, buyers and sellers—meet, and their interests clash. They will go through a test of strength, and only when they have fought each other to a standstill—in other words, when push and pull have produced an equilibrium—will the agreed price emerge as an element of order and social integration. It shows the greatness of Giambattista Vico that he did not fall for this fashionable sociology.

He saw what hardly anybody else realized at the time, namely, that even an economic order will emerge from the contests of the market only if there is established, in the society concerned, a legal order, an order of pacification, and that the emergence and existence of that legal order cannot possibly be explained along mechanistic lines.

But Vico was more than just an early critic of sociological mechanism. Most of those who rejected and still reject mechanism have thrown themselves into the arms of the corresponding opposite philosophy, the philosophy of organicism. Thus the mechanism of the Enlightenment was followed by the organicism of the Romantics. Vico understood the fatal weakness of this alternative also. He realized that organicism is just as erroneous as mechanism, if for a different reason. It exaggerates the integration of the social whole, just as mechanism exaggerates the independence of the individual parts. Social analysis, so Vico taught with all desirable clarity, must not start from any natural science, be it biology or be it physics. It must start from *man*.[1]

Now if man is considered from the sociological point of view, it appears that he is asocial and social at the same time: he is asocial as far as his physical nature is concerned; he can come to be social because he has a mental, a properly human, nature as well.[2] If man were only body, Vico believed, there would be chaos, a war of all against all. There is a purple passage in *De uno principio* where he comes close to Hobbes's forbidding picture of the state of nature; indeed, the famous phrase *homo homini lupus* is literally echoed. Without a legal order, Vico writes, man would be lazy and criminal. He would be bestial in his sexual relationships and live by robbery. He would not know the difference between right and wrong.[3] If

---

[1] See especially *De universi juris uno principio et fine uno*, in Giambattista Vico, *Il diritto universale*, edited by Fausto Nicolini, 3 vols. (Bari: Laterza, 1936), 1: 34.

[2] *Ibid.*, p. 36, and *The New Science of Giambattista Vico* (hereinafter *NS*), translated by Thomas G. Bergin and Max H. Fisch (Ithaca: Cornell University Press, 1968), par. 1098.

[3] *De uno principio,* p. 102; cf. also pp. 41–42 and *NS,* pars. 336, 1100.

man is in fact otherwise, if he is law-abiding and kind, this is due to his second nature, to his mental nature, which is from the beginning potentially a moral nature. It carries in itself the seed of custom. Custom—what the French call *moeurs* and the Germans *Sitte*, terms which encompass mores as well as manners—makes man a creature of society, a neighbor, a collaborator, and not only a competitor. It humanizes the animal man.[4]

Vico, as can be seen, asserts what Berkeley, in *The Bond of Society*, expressly denies, namely, that the reciprocal attraction of men for each other and the integration of the social system is the result of education and law. He thereby ranges himself by the side of such sociologists as Emile Durkheim, Max Weber, and Talcott Parsons, and his theoretical relevance for today consists above all in this, that he is the very archetype of a cultural sociologist. If the *Scienza nuova* is read as a whole, the thesis which stands out most strongly and most convincingly is the assertion of the creativity of man. But by man we must mean, in the context of Vico's sociology, not the individual but the collectivity. In an age in which it was almost a mania to find behind every phenomenon an individual originator, in which for instance the foundation of Cambridge University was artificially traced back to a mythical prince Cantaber, as if an institution could not possibly *grow*, Vico asserted that the cooperation of men, the anonymous forces of society, were a fund of life which could and did bring forth social and cultural institutions without number, and the most essential ones to boot. Seen in this light, the chapter in the *Scienza nuova* on the "Discovery of the True Homer" is not what it is sometimes asserted to be, an excursus, but the very substance of the argument. But the greatest achievement of the collective forces is not this or that imaginative universal like the one known as Homer; it is custom, the integration of social life.

----

[4] *NS*, par. 309; cf. also pars. 343, 525.

It is not an exaggeration to say that Vico revealed the secret of social life—the fact that there are hidden yet real forces which create society (human and not physical or physiological forces), and that society is in this way a self-created entity.[5]

It is obvious that, on Vico's convictions, the social bond can only continue to hold if, and as long as, the mental and moral culture of men has the ascendancy over their physical—that is to say, animal—nature, and that can never be guaranteed. The core of Vico's social theory is therefore, quite logically, social control. All societies have, and must have, effective social control;[6] societies are different from each other because their systems of social control are different. At first, in the age of the gods, social control is achieved through psychological means, through the sentiment of fear; later, in the age of the heroes, it is achieved through the agency of certain human agents, the *patres*, who organize social life and watch over its peace and order; finally, in the age of men, it is brought about through the mutual supervision of neighbors: social pressure does not come from above, as in the second age, but is exerted sideways, as it were, from citizen to citizen. What strikes the sociologist on contemplating this historical scheme is the sharpness of the contrast between the succeeding social systems which Vico sketches. A comparison between the Vichian and the later Comtean law of the three stages is highly revealing. For Comte it is always a certain basic philosophy that rules; its content alters, but it is invariably this one element that dominates. According to Vico, very different factors are in command. He has for every type of society an entirely different social theory and that for the best of reasons: because they are in fact so different in their basic constitutions.

Perhaps we can see all this most clearly if we characterize Vico's three social analyses by comparing them to later theoretical positions which they anticipate or approach. In

---

[5] *NS*, pars. 349, 388.
[6] See again *De uno principio*, p. 102, and *NS*, par. 1100.

the age of the gods, what Jung has called the collective unconscious is decisive. It is filled by shame and fear—shame of animality and fear of its consequences—and it produces, with the help of the imaginative faculty, the great archetype of the sky-god, protector of morality and avenger of evildoing.[7] For the age of the heroes we have an explanation à la Marx. Domination is in the hands of an upper class which creates the great institution of the state and thereby erects a framework of safety for the benefit of all, but which also arrogates to itself great privileges which are then resented and attacked by the plebs and finally brought down. In the age of men, power is spread evenly through society. Men settle down into a condition of decency and benignity because they have learnt that this is best for everybody and all. The theory in the background here is, as can be seen, an equilibrium theory. Vico actually draws close to Berkeley and, what is much more interesting, to Rousseau. We see this best in paragraph 951 of the *New Science*. In free popular states, Vico says there, wealth is divided into as many minute parts as there are citizens. This is precisely Rosseau's vision of an egalitarian commonwealth of cottages; this is precisely the practical ideal of the American and French revolutions: that all should count for one and nobody for more than one. Vico knew the essence of this social experiment even before it had started to get under way.

I have pointed out that the mechanistic or equilibrium theory of social integration as propounded by Berkeley and Rousseau is wrong because it takes for granted what can never be taken for granted, namely, the preexistence and continuation of law and order. Vico was greater than they because he knew that law and order are in deep jeopardy where the unity of society is based only on a libertarian and egalitarian democracy. True, that social democracy, that replacement of the cruel domination of overlords by the mutual supervision of

---

[7] *NS*, pars. 338–340.

free men, is the ideal social constitution.[8] It brings out the best in men, their rationality, which includes not only the power to think clearly but also the inclination to act benignly, but it carries no safeguards for the future. Where social control is in the hands of everybody, it is at the same time in the hands of nobody. It must sooner or later be weakened and go into a decline.

Vico's analysis of the dynamics of the age of man, which lays bare an indwelling tendency toward involution, not toward evolution, is of particular interest to us today because it deals with our own situation, the situation of and in the societies which have sprung from the American and French revolutions: it is an entirely realistic analysis, too realistic for comfort. It contains a number of very subtle points which do not seem to have been sufficiently appreciated as yet. In egalitarian and rationalistic societies, Vico says (to give but one example of his splendid intuitions), custom decays and conscious or deliberate legislation takes its place. We all know that this is so. But made laws can never be as effective as grown custom.[9] They are not so effective, we can say in our modern lingo, because they do not have their last roots in the collective unconscious, because they stem only from the intellect, which is admirable in itself and yet, by comparison, shallow. Vico approaches closely to the position later classically developed by Edmund Burke. Burke's saying that the individual is foolish, but the race is wise, expresses one of Vico's deepest convictions. "Men individually are swayed by their private interests," he says in the *New Science*, "but collectively they seek justice."[10] The more, therefore, the individual is liberated, the weaker becomes justice, and the more problematic the whole social fabric. "In the free commonwealths all look out of their own private interests." Vico declares, and thereby, he adds, they act

[8] *NS*, par. 973.
[9] *De uno principio*, pp. 132–136.
[10] *NS*, par. 1041.

"at the risk of ruin to their nations."[11] Decay begins not only
when the government is paralyzed and the crime rate soars;
it begins already when the enjoyment of luxury is closer to the
hearts of men than the fulfilment of of duty. (This is what Pascal
has called, treading in the footsteps of Saint Augustine, le désordre
du coeur, a curse-laden inversion of the order of values.) It is
then that the apparently free man turns into a slave, namely, a
slave of his own lower or animal nature. A new barbarism is
then at hand.[12] Where each man is thinking only of his private
interests, Vico writes, people become like the beasts, and the
worst of all tyrannies threatens: the tyranny of unchecked liberty,
which is in essence, and in practice, anarchy.[13]

The timeliness of these remarks for our own age, which is
too cowardly to call crimes crimes, as if they were not moral
failures but merely diseases, is manifest, and one who has to
discuss not only the theoretical but also the practical relevance
of Vico's sociology for today must not shirk the unpleasant
duty of drawing attention to these forbidding aspects of the
great Neapolitan's philosophy. Of course, the question remains open as to whether the understanding of the cause of
social decay revealed to us in De uno principio and in the Scienza
nuova, does not also indicate its cure, whether men could not,
for instance, arrest decay by an intensified education in sociality of the oncoming generation and so reverse the trend before it is too late, before mankind is plunged into a new
barbarism. Hegel and Marx claimed that their analyses also
yielded recipes, that they not only illuminated the pathways of
the past but also showed up the roads yet to be traveled. So
far as I know, Vico made no such claim for himself. He left it
to us to consider what his sociological theory means for social

[11] NS, par. 1008; cf. also par. 341.
[12] De uno principio, pp. 157–159.
[13] NS, pars. 1106, 1102.

policy and practice. A great theme is thus indicated for us to think about, and I am sure there is none greater. In the final analysis the *one* concern of Giambattista Vico is also the *one* concern of us all: the eternal and the future fate of the human race.

Vico and
Historical
Sociology

BY WERNER J. CAHNMAN

In *The Gay Science*, Nietzsche says: "Lightning and thunder take time, the light of the stars takes time to get to us, deeds take time to be seen and heard."[1] The 250th anniversary of Giambattista Vico's *New Science* recalls that statement. To be sure, Italian scholarship was always aware of Vico.[2] Outside of Italy, Vico's reputation exists since Herder, Goethe, Victor Cousin, De Maistre, and earlier, most conspicuously in the wake of Michelet's book-length evaluation,[3] but it has been a reputation more generic than precise, more in the way of obeisance to a far-away name than in terms of an awareness of utilizable knowledge. Especially, it is only now that Vico's seminal importance for historical sociology clearly comes to the fore.

By "historical sociology," I do not mean the "new history" that was *en vogue* in the nineteenth century, that is, a compara-

[1] Friedrich Nietzsche, *The Gay Science,* in *The Portable Nietzsche,* edited by Walter Kaufmann (New York: Viking Press, 1968), p. 95.

[2] Much of the pertinent literature is cited in Giorgio Tagliacozzo and Hayden V. White, eds., *Giambattista Vico: An International Symposium* (Baltimore: Johns Hopkins Press, 1969), and in the bibliography in Leon Pompa, *Vico: A Study of the New Science* (New York: Cambridge University Press, 1975).

[3] On Herder, see Tagliacozzo and White, *Giambattista Vico: An International Sym-possium,* pp. 93 ff; on Victor Cousin, *ibid.,* p. 104; Goethe's comment on Vico—with reference to Filangieri—is in *Italiänische Reise,* March 5, 1787; on De Maistre, see Elio Gianturco, *Joseph De Maistre and Giambattista Vico: Italian Roots of De Maistre's Political Culture* (Washington, D.C., 1937); Jules Michelet's extensive treatment is in his *Oeuvres complètes,* edited by Paul Viallaneix, 5 vols. (Paris: Flammarion, 1971–75), vol. 1; cf Alain Pons, "Vico and French Thought," in Tagliacozzo and White, *Giambattista Vico: An International Symposium,* pp. 165–186.

tive account of phenomena that are logically connected but have no continuing identity in time and space. In a paper, "Historical Sociology: What It Is and What It Is Not," I emphasized that historical sociology, as presently constituted, intends to render a conceptualized account of societal processes as they actually occur, meaning that the occurrences are considered as ends in themselves, though illuminated by theory.[4] Speaking methodologically, the implication is that historical sociology cannot be "scientific" in the sense in which a mathematical statement is scientific because it cannot abstract from the dynamic and dialectic quality of man. Yet historical sociology represents valid knowledge, perhaps knowledge of decisive validity in the social sciences. In this regard, Vico will turn out to be a powerful guide.[5]

Religion and Government

Vico was as much in opposition to major trends in the philosophical thinking of his time as historical sociology today is in opposition to major trends in contemporary sociology. However, there are affinities between the various approaches which are easily overlooked in the din of battle. To be sure, Vico objected to the Cartesian assumption of mathematical certitude as the only permissible certitude in the pursuit of knowledge.[6] Vico especially objected to the disregard of history on the ground that it was lacking mathematical certitude.

[4] Werner J. Cahnman, "Historical Sociology: What It Is and What It Is Not," in Baidya N. Varma, ed., *The New Social Sciences* (Westport, Conn.: Greenwood Press, 1976), pp. 107–122. Historical sociology is presented in a comprehensive overview in Werner J. Cahnman and Alvin Boskoff, *Sociology and History: Theory and Research* (New York: Free Press, 1964), with comments on Vico on pp. 48–50.

[5] Michelet, *Oeuvres complètes*, 1: 9, speaks about Vico as the initiator of the "philosophy of history." I believe that "historical sociology" would be a more adequate designation.

[6] On Vico and Descartes, see Yvon Belaval, "Vico and Anti-Cartesianism," in Tagliacozzo and White, *Giambattista Vico: An International Symposium*, pp. 77–92; cf. the chapter on Vico in Bruce Mazlish, *The Riddle of History: The Great Speculators from Vico to Freud* (New York: Harper & Row, 1966), pp. 11–58.

The geometrical method of Descartes appeared to Vico as tantamount to "disregarding the nature of man, which is uncertain because of man's freedom."[7] That is the position taken by historical sociology. Yet, as we move from Descartes to Hobbes, the vista widens. Hobbes connected mechanics and geometry with the science of government. In line with Descartes, Hobbes asserted that we have certitude only with regard to objects which we "make ourselves." Consequently, he continued, as we have knowledge about the geometrical figures whose lines we draw, so we have knowledge about right and wrong, fairness and injury, because we have "made" the laws and agreements on which they are based.[8] Vico contrasts his view of a science of man to Hobbes's materialistic and individualistic (Vico calls it "Epicurean") approach, but it is doubtful whether he knew Hobbes firsthand or from any more reliable source than the writings of the Kiel professor Georg Pasch, who was an opponent of Hobbes.[9] The intention of Hobbes in analyzing the "state of nature" was not to trace the origin of society in the dim ages of the past, as Vico assumed, but to conduct a Galilean thought experiment. Imagine, Hobbes argued, how men would behave if they were "but even now sprung out of the earth, and suddenly, like mushrooms, come to full maturity without all kind of en-

[7] Giambattista Vico, *De nostri temporis studiorum ratione* (Naples, 1709), quoted in Michelet, *Oeuvres complètes*, 1: 354. The entire sentence is as follows: "The Cartesians investigate the nature of objects on account of the prospect of certainty which they contain; they disregard the nature of man which is uncertain because of man's freedom" (my translation).

[8] Ferdinand Tönnies, *Thomas Hobbes: Leben und Lehre*, edited by Karl-Heinz Ilting (Stuttgart: Frommann, 1971), p. 113.

[9] Georg Pasch, *De curiosis hujus seculi inventis* (1695) and *Brevis introductio in rem literariam, pertinentem ad doctrinam moralem* (1706). Georg Pasch (1661–1707) was a professor of moral philosophy, logic, and metaphysics, then of practical theology, at the University of Kiel. For the assumption that Vico knew Hobbes chiefly through Pasch, see Giambattista Vico, *Die Neue Wissenschaft*, translated by Erich Auerbach (Munich: Allgemeine Verlagsanstalt, 1924), p. 89. One must note that the English works of Hobbes in the Molesworth edition comprise 11 volumes, the *Opera philosophica quae latine scripsit omnia*, likewise in the Molesworth edition, only 5 volumes.

gagement to each other."[10] In these circumstances, which would result in a "war of each against all," men would have to construct an alternative to the state of nature by subjecting themselves to moral rules and by authorizing, as individuals, some man or group of men to be their sovereign representative and to guarantee the peace. The construction is ingenious, although, as Tönnies has observed, it covers only *Gesellschaft*, where unity arises from individuality and not from what comes earlier, logically as well as historically, namely, *Gemeinschaft*, where individuality arises from the matrix of unity.[11] Viewed in this way, the Hobbesian approach is preliminary to Vico's argument.

Vico provides the historical dimension to the Hobbesian construction, including the complementation by Tönnies, although, without being aware of it, Vico shares with Hobbes, at least to a degree, the individualistic departure. Originally, Vico imagines—and the term "imagination" is crucial, as we shall see—wild men, with bestial natures, to have roamed the earth in the pursuit of their desires, until they were tamed, "tied," as it were, not by the state but by religion. They were subdued by the clap of thunder and the stroke of lightning, terrifying manifestations of the uproar of nature which they understood to indicate divine displeasure with their bestial conduct. Their bestiality consisted not only in their killing each other, chiefly in competition for women, but also in the raping and the abuse of women, the neglect of their offspring, and the abandonment of the dead. To abolish these horrifying crimes, the family was first constituted in the caves where the thunderstruck fugitives had come to dwell. Thus custom brought order into chaos and *Gemeinschaft* was initiated by the compulsion of religious awe, long before a condition of

[10] Thomas Hobbes, *The English Works*, edited by Sir William Molesworth, 11 vols. (London: Bohn, 1839–45), 2: 108–109.

[11] Ferdinand Tönnies, "A Prelude to Sociology," in *Ferdinand Tönnies on Sociology: Pure, Applied, and Empirical*, edited by Werner J. Cahnman and Rudolf Heberle (Chicago: University of Chicago Press, 1971), pp. 75–86.

Gesellschaft prompted the establishment of governmental authority. Thus Vico's historical construction of the societal order complements, but does not invalidate, the Hobbesian statement. The authority of the Hobbesian "mortal God" in the place of, but not replacing, the Vichian immortal God remains the centerpiece. Not unlike Hobbes, Vico emphasizes that law first establishes responsibility toward the gods and the community established by the gods and only subsequently responsibility toward one's fellow man. Surely, following Vico, the sociology of religion and the sociology of the family, which arises from the sociology of religion, take first place in the scheme of historical sociology. But the institution of the burial of the dead, according to Vico, and hence the initiation of permanent settlements in the vicinity of the graveyards of revered ancestors, completes the establishment of society. The next step is the city, that is, the rise of civilization.[12] In that sense, Fustel de Coulanges' *La cité antique* appears to be the crowning effort in a Vichian historical sociology.[13] In the city, clans dwell together and must adhere to a common loyalty, if disintegration is to be avoided. With the emergence of the city, then, the idea of society is fulfilled and, at the same time, it runs up against a dead end.

The Methodological Concept of Poetry

To the theoretical concept of religion is added the methodological concept of poetry. Poetry in Vico's sense is not an

[12] *The New Science of Giambattista Vico* (hereinafter *NS*), translated by Thomas G. Bergin and Max H. Fisch (Ithaca: Cornell University Press, 1968); I have also consulted the German translation by Erich Auerbach and the Italian original of *Principi di scienza nuova* (Naples, 1744). Cf. at this point Pompa, *Vico: A Study of the New Science* chap. 3. Concerning the rise of civilization, see Cahnman and Boskoff, *Sociology and History*, pp. 537–559.

[13] N. D. Fustel de Coulanges, *The Ancient City* (Garden City, N.Y.: Doubleday Anchor, 1956). It is unlikely that Fustel de Coulanges was not aware of Michelet's volume on Vico and hence the Vichian flavor of his famous book is not without substantial foundation. Inasmuch as Émile Durkheim was a student of Fustel d Coulanges, *Les formes élémentaires de la vie religieuse* can claim at least a remote Vichian ancestry.

esoteric form of art; it is the language of ancient man. What elevated speech and song wish to express is mythology and, by means of mythology, *vera narratio*, that is, history. The poetry of the ancients is not a sophisticated account *post festum* or an allegory, but the depiction of the world in corporeal images rather than its description in thought. There is no sharp break between mythology and poetry. Mythology, expressed through poetry, records the actions of men whereby, as in the songs of Homer, a person may stand for a collectivity, a clan, a city, a generation. The poetic characters are imaginative genera or symbolic expressions, replacing the mute language of signs and physical objects which guided the entrance of bestial man into the social world. In poetry, peoples speak as in a single voice. Systematic thought, philosophy, and individuality come later, when collectivities are dissolved and a widely used "vulgar" language is practiced, in which the laws of a diversified society are written. Yet language preserves the memory of origins and popular usage retains poetic images. Vico quotes examples that may not always be correct yet illustrate the historical methodology he is using. So logic comes from *logos*, as he explains in the beginning of the chapter on "Poetic Logic," and the proper meaning of *logos* is *fabula*, which in Greek is *mythos*, whence is derived the Latin word *mutus*, mute.[14] Vico further points out that the equivalent to *logos* in Hebrew—*davar*—means "word" as well as "deed." Thus the birth of poetry from sign language is indicated and, further, because poetry is song, the birth of religious imagery, as in Greek tragedy, from "the spirit of music," in the meaning with which we are familiar from Nietzsche's Basel dissertation.[15] Or *nomos* means pasturage because landed estate was allocated by heroic kings to subjected clans, with mutual obligations as a

---

[14] *NS*, par. 85, The Hebrew word *davar* means: word, speech, thing, matter, deed. The comparison of the terms *logos* and *davar* would seem to indicate the comparability of the substantial traditions of the Greeks and the Hebrews—Vico's theory of the uniqueness of the spiritual history of the Hebrews notwithstanding.

[15] Cf. Friedrich Nietzsche, *The Birth of Tragedy and the Genealogy of Morals*, translated by Francis Golffing (Garden City, N.Y.: Doubleday Anchor, 1956).

corollary.[16] Examples for the corporeal metaphors we use are head for top, mouth for opening, heart for center; we refer to the vein of a rock, the whistling of the wind, the murmuring of the waves.[17] The methodology referred to here entails a "philologic" in Franz Rosenzweig's sense—rather than a plain logic—an approach which is customary in Hebrew scholarship. Also, Buber's understanding of what he calls "saga" as "the predominant method of preserving the memory of what happens"—in his case the story of Moses and Sinai—is relevant as an extension of the Vichian approach.[18] In the language of sociology, one might say: if people define a situation as real, it is real not only in its consequences, as W. I. Thomas maintained; it also is a record of what is remembered as real, that is, as historically effective. Conventional sociology tends to disregard these guideposts; but historical sociology is aware of the continuities in the human condition. Ethnohistory points in the same direction but has not yet led to a closer integration of Biblical, classical, and mainstream historical research with anthropological and sociological studies.[19] Vico is a guide here, especially because his interest is focused not so much on the past *per se*, but on a comparative approach. The continuities which are implied in that approach point to the mainsprings of human nature which are overlaid but not eradicated and which we must become aware of at a moment in history when one epoch comes to an end and another epoch is about to begin.

Ideal Eternal History

With the preceding statement, we have arrived at the guiding principle of Vichian thought, the concept of the "ideal

---

[16] *NS*, par. 607.

[17] *NS*, par. 405.

[18] Martin Buber, *Moses* (Oxford: Phaidon, 1946), p. 15.

[19] Cf. Robert M. Carmack, "Ethnohistory: A Review of Its Development, Definitions, Methods, and Aims," *Annual Review of Anthropology* 1 (1972): 227–246, esp. pp. 236, 238.

eternal history," but a number of provisos must be entered.[20] Historical sociology, following Vico, does not envisage identical repetitions, but a sequence with modifications, like Christianity in the Middle Ages. Further, Vico has been compared to Hegel, with whom he shares a dialectical approach, but the Hegelian "synthesis" is lacking in the sequence of *corsi* and *ricorsi* and, consequently, the teleological prospect of moving ever higher along the spiral of history, which is present in Hegel, is foreign to Vico. For Vico, history is providentially guided, in rise as well as in decline. It should also be noted that the trichotomy of a religious, heroic, and civic age, which is encountered in one or the other variation not only by Vico and Hegel but also by Adam Ferguson, Auguste Comte, Lewis Morgan and others, is modeled after the concept of the Holy Trinity. There are other holy numbers in the traditions of the peoples, so that one is inclined to assume that the threefold cleavage of reality amounts to a cultural compulsion in the civilization of the Occident. One can find five or seven subdivisions with equal assurance. Perhaps a dichotomy, spanning life from birth to death and from evolution to dissolution, hence indicating limiting points rather than subdivisions, is more in line with the structure of reality. Nevertheless, the scheme of the "ideal eternal history" is acceptable to the sociologist, if only as a working hypothesis. Sociologists do not presume to know what providence has in mind for us, but they look for patterns in events and processes and they use comparison over time and space to ascertain them. Vico is a master in this regard. In order to construct what one may call a culture case study of Greek and Roman antiquity, Vico consults the literary sources that were available to him—not only historians, jurists, and philosophers, but, apart from Homer, also individual poets, like Horace, Virgil, Lucretius, and others. From the point of view of the historical sociologist, the conclusion is that art and literature are neither a play of

---

[20] *NS*, Book IV, "The Course the Nations Run."

fancy nor a literal description of reality but an enhancement of reality in such a way that its essential features come into view. I shall return to the theme of history as a thing of art.

Vico offers a historical theory of stratification which differs from the race relations cycle of Robert E. Park by its very historicity and from the conquest theories of Ibn Khaldun and Gumplowicz because of an ingenious complementation. In the view of Gumplowicz, the strong subdue the weak and put them into service; according to Ibn Khaldun, the tribesmen overwhelm the cities and make them tributary; with Vico, however, the ferocious vagrants of old, embroiled in a "war of each against all," threw themselves at the mercy of the settlers, who received them as dependents, clients, and serfs.[21] Conquest, then, while not excluded, is not a necessary condition of submission. Indeed, following Vico's axiom 79, there is a sequence: the protected associates in the first stage become the plebeians in the urban stage and the subjected provincials in the imperial stage. What happens is that the fugitives from violence become *famuli* who attach themselves to the *fama* (glory, reputation) of the heroes and are accepted as members of their families; they are forerunners of the serfs subdued by conquest.[22] Only a family has a god present in the hearth fire and hence enjoys independent status; one can understand, therefore, that the Roman plebeians, in pursuance of the Law of the Twelve Tables, demanded *connubia patrum*, that is, solemn nuptials, sanctioned by *auspicia*, with equality before God and man and the rights of citizenship as a consequence.[23] Thus the concept of hierarchy, that is, the gradation of duties and privileges, which was the initial principle of the social order, gave way to an egalitarian system; and stratification according to the economic categories of property, income, and conspicuous consumption became the criterion of the division of classes in society. In the course of time, even property

[21] *NS*, par. 258.
[22] *NS*, par. 555.
[23] *NS*, par. 598.

qualifications were, and are, thrown aside. Thus what Vico calls an "age of men" is ushered in, where solidarity has given way to tolerance and public institutions are used for the satisfaction of private appetites. Individualism rules supreme until breakdown within or conquest from without brings about a reversion to a new barbarism. Such conditions prevailed in the waning centuries of antiquity and, if indications are not deceptive, confront us today.[24] Thus, to confirm the above assumption, the Vichian trichotomy is reduced to a dichotomy, both in terms of a societal construct and in terms of the sequence of ages.[25] The "ideal eternal history" thereby is transformed from a theory of successive stages into a unified theoretical system, without losing its historicity.

Methodological Conclusion

Returning to methodology, one must recall at this point the Vichian statement that we know history because we "make it ourselves." But, in actual fact, we do not "make" history in the way we make laws, norms, and rules of conduct, as Hobbes has asserted. We act in history, deliberately or rashly, but, to paraphrase Shakespeare, "there's a divinity that shapes our ends . . . when deep plots do fail." In other words, there are aborted effects and unintended consequences of our actions which cannot be said to have been made by the actors. Conversely, if we knew the course of the "ideal eternal history," we might gain a measure of understanding as far as the structure of the past is concerned, but we would still be on our own in making the decisions of the day. With all that, we would not be enabled to "make" and therefore to understand the deci-

[24] Cf. NS, par. 241: "Men first feel necessity, then look for utility, next attend to comfort, still later amuse themselves with pleasure, thence grow dissolute in luxury, and finally go mad and waste their substance." I leave it open whether Vico refers here to a fivefold sequence of subdivisions or to a continuum from necessity to waste.

[25] Tönnies, like Vico, sees the Middle Ages and the newer centuries as a civilizational unit, moving from a prevalence of *Gemeinschaft* to a preponderance of *Gesellschaft;* cf. *Ferdinand Tönnies on Sociology,* pp. 288, 318.

sions of bestial man, trying to escape the fears and oppressions of aboriginal existence, or the decisions of the patricians and plebeians in ancient Rome. We cannot even be sure that we understand the thoughts of a professor in Naples. At best, we can make a mental experiment, in a variation of Max Weber's suggestion, to make us believe that we are in the other fellow's place and that we know how he felt. It is the contention of this paper that in historical studies science is not enough and that we know little of the thoughts and decisions of the generations, except by the power of a trained imagination. By "being trained," I mean going to the available sources and considering all possible causes, as Vico has done; by imagination, I mean being able to see sources and causes in combination and to recognize what is essential.[26] It follows that historical sociology, as all achievement in historical studies, is an art in addition to being a science. An art requires the free exercise of craftsmanship, beyond the repetitious use of methodological devices. What is further needed is an ounce of luck or, as in the case of Vico, the spark of genius.

[26] Vico calls the faculty of uniting what is separated *ingenium*; cf. *De antiquissima Italorum sapientia* (Naples, 1710), quoted in Michelet, *Oeuvres complètes*, 1: 411.

On the History of the Human Senses in Vico and Marx

BY JOHN O'NEILL

My task is to think together Vico and Marx as historians and poets of the human senses—despite an earlier report which failed to find any real family between Vico and Marx.[1] This is an essay, then, which challenges the patented determination of history to reassemble first and last things in the uninhabited orders of science. If today we can think together Vico and Marx it is because we are open to a more self-conscious practice of science, less inclined now to forget its ties with our vulgar wisdom of origins and ends. Thus we can think together Vico and Marx because each reverberates in the other "in deeseperation of deispiration at the diasporation of his diesperation."[2] For neither Marx nor Vico ever thought history outside of time's body,[3] which is the institution of those fantastic universals "found of the round of the sound of the lound" of the age of men, gathering thunder, acorns, animals, and speech in order to clothe man's bodily beginnings in civil beauty and divine piety.

Here we may reflect how much it took for the men of the gentile world to be tamed from their feral native liberty through a long period of cyclopean family discipline to the point of obeying naturally the laws in the civil states which were to come

---

[1] Eugene Kamenka, "Vico and Marxism," in Giorgio Tagliacozzo and Hayden V. White, eds., *Giambattista Vico: An International Symposium* (Baltimore: Johns Hopkins Press, 1969), pp. 137–143.

[2] James Joyce, *Finnegans Wake* (New York: Viking Press, 1939), p. 257.

[3] John O'Neill, "Time's Body," in his *Making Sense Together: An Introduction to Wild Sociology* (New York: Harper & Row, 1974), pp. 28–38.

later. Hence there remained the eternal property that happier than the commonwealth conceived by Plato are those where the fathers teach only religion and where they are admired by their sons as their sages, revered as their priests, and feared as their kings. Such and so much divine force was needed to reduce these giants, as savage as they were crude, to human deities. Since they were unable to express this force abstractly, they represented it in concrete physical form as a cord, called *chorda* in Greek and in Latin at first *fides*, whose original and proper meaning appears in the phrase *fides deorum*, force of the gods. From this cord (for the lyre must have begun with the monochord) they fashioned the lyre of Orpheus, to the accompaniment of which, singing to them the force of the gods in the auspices, he tamed the beasts of Greece to humanity. And Amphion raised the walls of Thebes with stones that moved themselves. These were the stones which Deucalion and Pyrrha, standing before the temple of Themis (that is, in fear of divine justice) with veiled heads (the modesty of marriage), found lying before their feet (for men were at first stupid, and *lapis*, stone, remained Latin for a stupid person) and threw over their shoulders (introducing family institutions by means of household discipline), thus making men of them. . . .[4]

Vico and Marx are the twice-born scientists of man. This is not because our history survives through sheer repetition or dizzy spells. It is because human history is never displayed before itself and rather folds upon us in our living and dying so that Vico is no more before Marx than we are after Marx. Thus in thinking together Vico and Marx it is also ourselves that we recollect. "Teems of times and happy returns. The seim anew. Ordovico or viricordo. Anna was, Livia is, Plurabelle's to be. Northmen's thing made southfolk's place but howmulty plurators made eachone in person? Latin me that my trinity scholard, out of eure sanscreed into oure eryan."[5] For it is in the spirit of man to remember man in his spirits, and kindly to discover man's history like the beat of his own heart. All history is therefore the history of our species-being (*Gattungswesen*), of the generation of men whose hearts

[4] *The New Science of Giambattista Vico* (hereinafter *NS*), translated by Thomas G. Bergin and Max H. Fisch (Ithaca: Cornell University Press, 1968), par. 523.

[5] Joyce, *Finnegans Wake*, p. 215.

and minds are schooled in that household of being which we have not to assemble through science because it arises above all from our living together whose vulgar wisdom is the limit of all our sciences.

> As for the other part of household discipline, the education of bodies, the fathers with their frightful religions, their cyclopean authority, and their sacred ablutions began to educe, or bring forth, from the giant bodies of their sons the proper human form. . . . And herein is providence above all to be admired, for it is ordained that until such times as domestic education should supervene, the lost men should become giants in order that in their feral wanderings they might endure with their robust constitutions the inclemency of the heavens and the seasons, and that they might with their disproportionate strength penetrate the great forest of the earth (which must have been very dense as a result of the recent flood), so that, fleeing from wild beasts and pursuing reluctant women and thus becoming lost from each other, they might be scattered through it in search of food and water until it should be found in due time fully populated; while after they began to remain in one place with their women, first in caves, then in huts near perennial springs and in the fields which, brought under cultivation, gave them sustenance, providence ordained that, from the causes we are now setting forth, they should shrink to the present stature of mankind.[6]

It is not because Vico and Marx were economists that we must think them together. It is because we cannot think economic life itself apart from its poetry first grasped by Vico and made by Marx the incarnate principle of all human labor, joy, and suffering. The fundamental thesis of *poetic economics* is that man is a work of his own senses and intellect and that these are never so alien to him, even in their remote beginnings, as not to build upon them our very humanity. Thus the human body is the ground of all those institutions of sense and intellect which enter into the gradual making of the history through which we hold together mankind in the face of all its sufferings and losses.

[6] *NS*, par. 524.

Private property is only the sensuous expression of the fact that man is both objective to himself and even more becomes a hostile and inhuman object to himself, that the expression of his life entails its externalization, its realization becomes the loss of its reality, an alien reality. Similarly the positive supersession of private property, that is, the sensuous appropriation by and for man of human essence and human life, of objective man and his works, should not be conceived of only as direct and exclusive enjoyment, as possession and having. Man appropriates his universal being in a universal manner, as a whole man. Each of his relationships to the world—seeing, hearing, smell, tasting, feeling, thinking, contemplating, willing, acting, loving—in short all the organs whose form is a communal one, are in their objective action, or their relation to the object, the appropriation of human reality, their relation to the object, is the confirmation of human reality. It is therefore as manifold as the determinations and activities of human nature. It is human effectiveness and suffering, for suffering, understood in the human sense, is an enjoyment of the self for man.[7]

Poetic economics is therefore never a simple science of needs and utilities but rather belongs to a general theory of human education. Poetic economics is a general science of those divine and human artifacts that men have made in order to make themselves human. Utilitarian economics is merely a science of our first body, our organic body whose emblem is nature. But nature is not outside of man any more than man is outside of nature. Marxist economics is therefore not merely a science of domination, since it cannot be blind to the human costs of man's lordship of nature.[8] Nature is our own doing, neither more hostile nor less kindly than we make it appear in our own institutions.

The human significance of nature is only available to social man; for only to social man is nature available as a bond with other men, as the basis for his own existence for others and theirs for him, and as the vital element in human reality; only to

[7] Karl Marx, "Economic and Philosophic Manuscripts," in his *Early Texts*, translated and edited by David McLellan (Oxford: Basil Blackwell, 1971), p. 151.

[8] John O'Neill, "Hegel and Marx on History as Human History," in Jean Hyppolite, *Studies on Marx and Hegel*, edited and translated by John O'Neill (New York: Harper & Row, 1973), pp. xi–xx.

social man is nature the foundation of his own human existence. Only as such has his natural existence become a human existence and nature itself become human. Thus society completes the essential unity of man and nature, it is the genuine resurrection of nature, the accomplished naturalism of man and the accomplished humanism of nature.[9]

Poetic economics is not hasty with science's separation of man from his elemental needs; it is properly a science of expression which preserves the metaphysical resonance of human religion, politics, economics, and art. Poetic economics therefore does not regard religion as an illusion, as an uncertain way of seeing what science can teach us for sure. Indeed, religion, myth and magic are not the simple expression of man's failure to see things. Rather, they *are* man's vision of the failure of things where men are set against themselves in oppression and exploitation. Thus poetic economics is inspired by the dream of man's wholeness, the dream of love's body, that is, the incarnate union of all men in Marx's day around a round day:

> For as soon as the distribution of labour comes into being, each man has a particular, exclusive sphere of activity, which is forced upon him and from which he cannot escape. He is a hunter, a fisherman, a shepherd, or a critical critic, and must remain so if he does not want to lose his means of livelihood; while in communist society, where nobody has one exclusive sphere of activity, but each can become accomplished in any branch he wishes, society regulates the general production and thus makes it possible for me to do one thing today and another tomorrow, to hunt in the morning, fish in the afternoon, rear cattle in the evening, criticize after dinner, just as I have a mind, without ever becoming hunter, fisherman, shepherd or critic.[10]

Poetic economics rejects the mathematical division of sense and intellect, of nature and society and of town and countryside which have separated the men of the forests from the

[9] Marx, "Economic and Philosophic Manuscripts," p. 150.
[10] Karl Marx and Frederick Engels, *The German Ideology*, Parts I and III, edited and with an introduction by R. Pascal (New York: International Publishers, 1969), p. 22.

dark men of today's factories who labor in the unseasonable accumulation of science and capital. As Vico appealed to our wild and savage nature in order to renew science, so Marx in turn called upon a heroic class of men in whom human nature has been brutalized in order to save our very humanity.

Marxist economics, like Vico's poetic economics, is a general science of the institutions of the human senses as the instruments of a general reality or a universal field of synergy whereby each of us contributes to all of mankind and none of us begins without that anonymous legacy of the human body and the vulgar wisdom of civic life. Therefore socialist society cannot be the product of Marxist economics insofar as Marxism remains a science of domination, forgetful of the poetic foundations of economics.[11] Mathematical economics is merely a science of man's first body which rules inorganic nature and men's exploitative relationships. Thus in industrial societies the productive process tends to integrate man's *organic body* within industry's higher mechanical and physico-chemical processes. At this level the *productive body* is separated from our first organic body through the superfoetation of its needs and its expanding alienation from *love's body* is accomplished by the rationalization of its sensory and intellect processes in the service of commercial life.[12] Poetic economics is therefore not a science of the productive body simply because in the modern world production intensifies labor in pursuit of levels of consumption beyond the sensible and libidinal limits of man's integral body. By the same process the industrial system integrates the world's body into its economy of desires which destroy those elemental times and places that are not simply the dwelling places of unhistorical men but the very sources of our humanity.

[11] John O'Neill, "For Marx against Althusser," *The Human Context* 6 (Summer 1974): 385–398.
[12] John O'Neill, "Authority, Knowledge and the Body Politic," in his *Sociology as a Skin Trade: Essays Towards a Reflexive Sociology* (New York: Harper & Row, 1972), pp. 68–80.

Vico's poetic economics renews science by calling to mind the question underlying all science, namely, how it is men have made themselves human. It is with the same underlying question that Marx recalls the vast alienation of man's labor and intellect which supplies the engines of production and consumption in the modern world. Marx's call for revolution reverberates the memory of a prehistorical unity of sense and society.[13] It resurrects the world's body in the reawakening of history's dream of a time before the separation of sense and intellect, of a place where man's promise and potentiality had not been broken and betrayed.

> Communism as completed naturalism is humanism and as completed humanism is naturalism. It is the genuine solution of the antagonism between man and nature and between man and man. It is the true solution of the struggle between essence and existence, between objectification and self-affirmation, between freedom and necessity, between individual and species. It is the solution to the riddle of history and knows itself to be this solution.[14]

Poetic economics brings forth the education of man's body and spirit. Vico's philological method loves man in his speech and gathers his humanity from poetry. In the same way Marx's method is materialist or sensuous and invokes the unity of man and nature in the history of social development. Now Vico reminds us that the new science of man is not to be practiced without piety, which is the love men of today owe to what their ancestors have yielded to them through the sense and nonsense of history's suffering. Therefore piety must likewise rule Marxist humanism in order that its new men not live in forgetfulness of those whose labor and intellect were wasted before and during the revolution. For surely a great

---

[13] I am not, of course, arguing that there is no need for an analytic element in Marxist thought. My argument is that Marxism becomes a science because it is first of all a humanist project in the light of which it must critically evaluate its specific praxes. Cf. John O'Neill, "On Theory and Criticism in Marx," in his *Sociology as a Skin Trade*, pp. 237–263.

[14] Marx, "Economic and Philosophic Manuscripts," p. 148.

sadness weighs upon communist society mindful of the past's injustice and its unrewarded suffering. Marxist humanism therefore is only truly secular in the remembrance *per omnia saecula saeculorum* of the generations of human labor and suffering that have made possible the very vision of socialist revolution.

A Klee painting named "Angelus Novus" shows an angel looking as though he is about to move away from something he is fixedly contemplating. His eyes are staring, his mouth is open, his wings are spread. This is how one pictures the angel of history. His face is turned towards the past. Where we perceive a chain of events, he sees one single catastrophe which keeps piling wreckage upon wreckage and hurls it in front of his feet. The angel would like to stay, awaken the dead, and make whole what has been smashed. But a storm is blowing from Paradise; it has got caught in his wings with such violence that the angel can no longer close them. This storm irresistibly propels him into the future to which his back is turned, while the pile of debris before him grows skyward. This storm is what we call progress.[15]

In thinking together Vico and Marx, we make of the world's body a reminder that we are never our own creature and are always in flight from ourselves. We are no closer to self-knowledge for living today than our fellow men who once lived in forests and caves, calling down upon themselves their own gods. Like time's body we separate from ourselves from moment to moment in thought and speech, in labor and in prayer. The unity of mankind is therefore at any time and in any place a monument we raise in our own honor to record the history of the world's labor still struggling to bring forth the poetry of man.[16]

[15] Walter Benjamin, "Theses on the Philosophy of History," in his *Illuminations*, edited and with an introduction by Hannah Arendt (New York: Harcourt, Brace & World, 1968), pp. 259–260.

[16] John O'Neill, "Critique and Remembrance," in John O'Neill, ed., *On Critical Theory* (New York: Seabury Press, 1976), pp. 1–12.

Vico and Critical Theory

BY JOSEPH MAIER

Why do men in one epoch worship the sun while in another they consider it sacrilegious or superstitious to do so? Does each age have its own "truth" just as each class has its own "truth," not only in art, poetry, and politics but in every field of human endeavor? Does the value-charged nature of history or the undeniable influence of personal bias and social conditioning in much social science writing encourage caprice and impose logical limitations upon objectivity? Do the existential and sociological roots of human knowledge preclude the possibility of warranted explanation in the human studies?

Under the terms "myth" and "ideology" I shall in the following consider Vico's views and those of the Frankfurt School on the role of men's beliefs and interests in the formation of their outlooks and suggest how they are related to the attainment of knowledge. It is my contention that Vico was more nearly right in holding that knowledge no less than belief springs from myth and ideology; that language, man's prime instrument of reason, reflects his myth-making no less than his rationalizing tendency; and that, as the symbolization of two different *modes* of thought, it reveals itself in discursive logic as well as in creative imagination.[1] That much of the discussion takes the form of a critique of Critical Theory is meant as a tribute to the power of thought of the Frankfurt School and the importance of the issues which it has raised. One of its members, Max Horkheimer, I had the good fortune to count as my special teacher and fatherly friend. It is in the first place

[1] Cf. Ernst Cassirer, *Language and Myth* (New York: Dover, 1946), pp. 1–23, and *An Essay on Man* (Garden City, N.Y.: Doubleday Anchor, 1953), pp. 97–142.

with his thought, and in the second place, however sketchily, with the work of T. W. Adorno, Herbert Marcuse, and Jürgen Habermas (who belongs to a later generation of Frankfurt School writers) that I propose to deal here.

Horkheimer on Vico

There is good reason for believing that the principals of the Frankfurt School all knew and admired the *New Science*. It was Max Horkheimer alone, however, who actually wrote something on Vico, and he did so on two occasions. In his *Origins of the Bourgeois Philosophy of History*, published in 1930, he devoted an entire chapter to "the first real philosopher of history of the modern era."[2] A few years later, in a brief essay on "The Problem of Prediction in the Social Sciences," he praised Vico for his stress on human action as a precondition for understanding history.[3]

What Horkheimer specifically admired in the author of the *New Science* was: his discovery of "laws" of social development and his discernment of a coherence in the entire historical process; his treatment of Providence in a manner analogous to Hegel's "cunning of reason," with the difference, to be sure, that while Hegel's work was "more grandiose and encompassing," Vico's was ever so "much more empirical" and less intent on demonstrating the manifestations of "the divine in this world"; his recognition that the course of ideas was determined by the course of things and that the sciences were not exercises of abstract reason but arose out of social needs; his understanding of the material roots of culture and his realization that manners and laws were not imposed from the outside but were the results of social conflicts; his critique of

---

[2] Max Horkheimer, *Anfänge der bürgerlichen Geschichtsphilosophie* (Frankfurt: Fischer Bücherei, 1971), p. 70.

[3] Max Horkheimer, "Zum Problem der Voraussage in den Sozialwissenschaften," *Zeitschrift für Sozialforschung* 2 (1933).

Cartesian dualism and the contemporary emphasis on mathematics as "the only genuine knowledge" and "true manifestation of man's essence"; his awareness of the historical significance of myth and religion, which the French Enlightenment had cavalierly dismissed as priestly fraud and tricks instead of viewing the entire superstructure as reflective of the class struggle at the base; even his cyclical view of history, to the extent that it admitted of the ever present possibility of a relapse into barbarism and was thus a more realistic standpoint than the simplistic belief in progress; finally, his argument that history was open to human understanding in a manner that nature was not, because men make history.

Many of the same points are made by Jürgen Habermas in a much shorter discussion of Vico in his *Theorie und Praxis*.[4] And while there is no direct mention of Vico in any of the writings of T. W. Adorno and Herbert Marcuse, their emphatic preoccupation with the roles of fantasy and poetry, with the inner link between dialectical thought and the effort of avant-garde literature, with "the search for an 'authentic language'—the language of negation as the Great Refusal to accept the rules of a game in which the dice are loaded"[5]—might lead one to conclude that it was not entirely by chance that Marcuse called his own type of theory (that existentializes Marx and Freud) "a new science."[6] Whatever the possibilities of recognizing a portion of Vico in Adorno, Marcuse, and Habermas, Horkheimer's express evaluation of the *New Science* is easily seen as following the familiar line of interpretation established by such writers as Sorel and Croce, on the one hand, and Paul Lafargue and Georg Lukacs, on the other. For Marxist writers

[4] Jürgen Habermas, *Theorie und Praxis* (Frankfurt: Suhrkamp, 1972), pp. 271–279. Cf. Fulvio Tessitore, "Jürgen Habermas su Vico," and Eugenio Garin, "Max Horkheimer su Vico," *Bollettino del centro di studi vichiani* 4 (1974).

[5] Herbert Marcuse, *Reason and Revolution* (Boston: Beacon Press, 1968), p. x.

[6] Herbert Marcuse, "Beiträge zu einer Phänomenologie des historischen Materialismus," *Philosophische Hefte*, July 1928, p. 52. Cf. Angela Jacobelli, "The Role of the Intellectual in Giambattista Vico," in Giorgio Tagliacozzo and Donald P. Verene, eds., *Giambattista Vico's Science of Humanity* (Baltimore: Johns Hopkins University Press, 1976), p. 419.

generally, Vico, whose work first appeared thirteen years before Montesquieu's *L'Esprit des lois*, nineteen years before Voltaire's *Essay*, and 119 years before Schelling's *Philosophy of Mythology and Revelation*, was an important forerunner of Marxism. He anticipated, Horkheimer emphasized, not only fundamental ideas of Herder and Hegel, Dilthey and Spengler, but also the more particular discoveries of Lévy-Bruhl and the sociology of knowledge.[7]

However, for all the credit Horkheimer was willing to grant Vico for "discoveries as yet not fully exhausted by science," to essay a serious scholarly analysis of Vico's contribution to science was not one of his objectives. And where he did venture to do so, he went astray. He said, for example, that "Vico was the first consciously and explicitly to recognize the similarity of the early peoples in history with the contemporary primitives, and the likeness in the mentality of primitives and children, thus the correspondence of human ontogenesis and phylogenesis." To this we must counter, first, that it is questionable whether the "important discovery" of the "prelogical thought" of primitives past and present was Vico's rather than Lévy-Bruhl's, and second, that it is in any case contradicted by anthropological and ethnological evidence. Horkheimer's principal interest in Vico was not scholarly or scientific but what he might himself denounce as "ideological." That is to say, he turned to Vico not in order to write a more up-to-date and more valid appreciation of the *New Science*, such as might be warranted by the discovery of new or more relevant facts and insights as judged by contemporary canons of scientific inquiry, but to see whether he offered anything in the way of "useful means" in the present struggle for "the establishment of a just order of life."[9]

---

[7] Cf. Eugene Kamenka, "Vico and Marxism," and Werner Stark, "Vico's Sociology of Knowledge," in Giorgio Tagliacozzo and Hayden V. White, eds., *Giambattista Vico: An International Symposium* (Baltimore: Johns Hopkins Press, 1969), pp. 137–143 and 297–307.

[8] Horkheimer, *Anfänge der bürgerlichen Geschichtsphilosophie*, p. 78.

[9] *Ibid.*, pp. 83, 73.

Machiavelli's psychological view of history, Hobbes's theory of natural law, and especially Vico's doctrine of myth, the *Glanzstück* of the *New Science*, were important to Horkheimer not as matters for investigation yielding propositions and doctrines of greater probability but as "mirrors of political conditions" and "ideological forms of consciousness." In fact, Horkheimer's flat statement that Critical Theory "claims no specific authority or justification other than its interest in the abolition of social injustice"[10] raises more questions about the very problems on which he wanted to enlighten us—the sociology of knowledge and the roles of ideology and myth in the social life of men.

In an important essay on " 'Myth' and 'Ideology' in Modern Usage," Ben Halpern has explained how these closely related conceptions have come to enjoy a wide and accordingly very loose usage in our time.[11] These terms, he shows, have come to carry primarily a negative connotation approximating "deceit" or "self-deceit" or, at any rate, to signify an "interested" or "subjective" approach to "reality," an attitude going off at a tangent to "truth." But if we examine the work on myth by Ernst Cassirer, Susanne K. Langer, Sir James Frazer, Bronislaw Malinowski, or M. I. Finley, on the one hand, and the work on ideology by Ernst Troeltsch, Max Weber, Karl Mannheim, Talcott Parsons, or Robert K. Merton, on the other, we may sum up in Ben Halpern's rough formulas:

(1) The study of myth is a study of the origin of beliefs out of

[10] Alfred Schmidt, *Zur Idee der kritischen Theorie* (Munich: Carl Hanser Verlag, 1974), title page. Cf. the highly provocative review essay by Heinz Lubasz on Martin Jay's *The Dialectical Imagination* in *History and Theory* 14 (1975) on the ambivalence toward radicalism in the position of a certain type of middle-class left intellectual which at once reflects his social situation and points to a central problem in Marxism, an "ambivalence which the Frankfurt School embodies and its so-called Critical Theory systematizes." See also Joseph Maier, "Contributions to a Critique of Critical Theory," in Bainya N. Varma, ed., *The New Social Sciences* (Westport, Conn.: Greenwood Press, 1976), pp. 73–99.

[11] Ben Halpern, " 'Myth' and 'Ideology' in Modern Usage," *History and Theory* 1 (1961): 129 ff.

historic experience. The study of ideology is a study of the molding of beliefs by social situations.

(2) The social function of myth is to bind together social groups as wholes or, in other words, to establish a social consensus. The social function of ideology is to segregate and serve special interests within societies in the competition of debate.[12]

The greatness of Hobbes, according to Horkheimer, lay in the fact that his natural-law doctrine raised the question of how the false traditional moral, metaphysical, and religious ideas he criticized came to be held in the first place. "Thereby, he posed, in principle, the problem of ideology which has come to be properly tackled only in the post-Hegelian period," said Horkheimer.[13] According to Hobbes, the powers-that-be needed those false beliefs to maintain their dominion, and even the rising bourgeoisie, with which Machiavelli, Spinoza, and Hobbes identified themselves, could never entirely do without them.

The error of these thinkers, Horkheimer declared, was not so much in what they said about the necessity of ideology as in the unqualified generalization of their doctrines and the universal validity claimed for them. There was great sophistication, he suggested, in Hobbes's awareness of the interconnectedness of ideas, including mathematics, and political realities. He quoted Hobbes as saying: "For I doubt not, but if it had been a thing contrary to any man's right of dominion, or to the interest of men that have dominion, *that the three angles of a triangle, should be equal to two angles of a square*; that doctrine should have been, if not disputed, yet by the burning of all books of geometry, suppressed, as far as he whom it concerned was able."[14] There was even greater sophistication, Horkheimer insisted, in Vico's doctrine of myth as a mirror of political realities in that the tricks and frauds Hobbes had attributed to the ruling classes to maintain themselves in

---

[12] *Ibid*., p. 137.
[13] Horkheimer, *Anfänge der bürgerlichen Geschichtsphilosophie*, p. 45.
[14] *Ibid*., p. 46.

power were now seen to have been historically necessary, to have had a developmental function, the manifestation of reason in the guise of unreason, as it were.

Myth and Reality

Whatever the usefulness as means of political argument of Horkheimer's concept of ideology and his interpretations of Hobbes and Vico, there are grave factual and dialectical difficulties in his several claims and suggestions. Take the case of Hobbes. It is certainly true, as Horkheimer says, that no inquiry takes place in an intellectual vacuum. Every investigator's work is controlled by the dominant problems and conceptions of his culture. But it does not follow from this that the conscious and unconscious value commitments allied with the socioeconomic status of the investigator will inevitably compel his acceptance of one conclusion rather than another. It is precisely because he was aware of this that Hobbes cautioned that "ignorance of remote causes" disposed men to attribute all events to "the causes immediate and instrumental," such as "any man's right of dominion" or "the interest of men that have dominion."

In the sentences immediately preceding those quoted by Horkheimer, Hobbes called attention to the ever-present inclination of men to appeal "from custom to reason, and from reason to custom, as it serves their turn; receding from custom when their interest requires it, and setting themselves against reason, as oft as reason is against them: which is the cause, that the doctrine of right and wrong, is perpetually disputed, both by the pen and the sword: whereas the doctrine of lines, and figures, is not so; because men care not, in that subject, what be truth, as a thing that crosses no man's ambition, profit or lust."[15] Even as he had written many years earlier that in

---

[15] Thomas Hobbes, *The English Works*, edited by Sir William Molesworth, 11 vols. (London: John Bohn, 1839–45), 3: 91.

the two kinds of learning, mathematical and dogmatical, the former was free of controversies and dispute because there was no opposition between truth and the interests of men; in the latter, however, there was "nothing not disputable, because it compareth men, and meddleth with their right and profit; in which, as oft as reason is against a man, so oft will a man be against reason."[16] Biased thinking was a constant challenge to the critical philosopher. While difficult, it was nevertheless possible to identify and to correct bias. Hobbes dedicated his entire philosophical enterprise to obtaining conclusions in better agreement with the evidence, a task he considered far from hopeless.

Or return to the case of Vico. Horkheimer praised him for revealing what was "hidden," that is, the connection between mythology and metaphysics, the "spiritual" sphere, on the one hand, and the "historical reality" of social conditions, on the other. Thus he quoted Vico as saying that Socrates had come to adumbrate intelligible genera and Plato to raise himself to the meditation of the highest intelligible ideas "from observing that the enactment of laws by Athenian citizens involved their coming to agreement in an idea of an equal utility common to all of them severally,"[17] even as he quoted Vico as writing that Aristotle's new concept of justice, indeed all "these principles of metaphysics, logic, and morals issued from the marketplace of Athens."[18] But what sort of connection, causal or logical or both, did Vico actually assert here? Vico's statement on Socrates and Plato begins with the words "Now, because laws certainly came first and philosophies later,"[19] while his discussion of Aristotle ends with the conclusion that, "when our human reason was fully developed, it reached its end in the true in the ideas themselves with regard to what is just, as

[16] Thomas Hobbes, *The Elements of Law*, edited by Ferdinand Tönnies (Cambridge: Cambridge University Press, 1928), p. xvii.
[17] Horkheimer, *Anfänge der bürgerlichen Geschichtsphilosophie*, p. 80.
[18] *Ibid*.
[19] *The New Science of Giambattista Vico* (hereinafter *NS*), translated by Thomas G. Bergin and Max H. Fisch (Ithaca: Cornell University Press, 1968), par. 1040.

determined by reason from the detailed circumstances of the facts."[20] There is no confusion in Vico of source and outcome, no suggestion that the content and form of Aristotle's aesthetic, metaphysical, or moral statements were logically or otherwise determined by his social perspective as a believer in slavery or any other aspects of the economic system of the polis.

To explain an individual's or a people's myriad activities, attitudes, habits, values, skills, and categories under the heading of "myth" or "ideology" may suggest a unity or wholeness of sorts, a conceptualization of what exists empirically, but it does not represent any kind of empirical reality. It may also lead to a blurring of the distinction between the temporal and the causal, the comparative and the universal, of which Horkheimer was no less guilty than Karl Mannheim.[21] There is no factual evidence to support the suggestion that the social perspective of a student of human affairs not only causally affects his inquiry but logically determines his standards of validity and the meaning of his statements. As Ernest Nagel has pointed out: "If, as no one seems to doubt, the truth of the statement that two horses can in general pull a greater load than either horse alone is logically independent of the social status of the one who asserts it, what inherent social circumstance precludes such independence for the statement that two laborers can in general dig a ditch of given dimensions more quickly than either laborer working alone?"[22]

Here is where Max Weber has shown greater insight in recognizing the conceptual nature of all social categories. His basic tool of historical analysis was a series of *Idealtypen* built upon elementary mechanisms of (rational and affective)

---

[20] *NS*, par. 1045.

[21] Cf. Martin Jay, *The Dialectical Imagination* (Boston: Little, Brown, 1973), p. 63; Sidney Hook, *Reason, Social Myth and Democracy* (New York: Harper Torchbooks, 1966), pp. 34–40; Gordon Leff, *History and Social Theory* (Garden City, N.Y.: Doubleday Anchor, 1971), pp. 141–217.

[22] Ernest Nagel, "The Logic of Historical Analysis," in Hans Meyerhoff, ed., *The Philosophy of History in Our Time* (Garden City, N.Y.: Doubleday Anchor, 1959), p. 214.

value-oriented action.[23] Vico, I submit, has done something analogous. In presenting "an ideal eternal history traversed in time by the history of every nation," and in offering the myths of theological and heroic poetry as the key by which the history of a people's language, customs, laws, and institutions may be understood, he has, indeed, provided an important tool for comparative study that may still serve and stimulate the historian and historically oriented sociologist.

Grossly oversimplifying, we may now state the conclusion of our reflections on Vico and Critical Theory. Vico was certainly more objective in his treatment of fact than would appear from Horkheimer's praise of him as a debunking student of myth and ideology. He took seriously Spinoza's injunction not to ridicule human actions, or to weep over them or hate them, but to understand them. His scientific humanism guarded him against the excesses of optimism and pessimism of Critical Theory in its early and late phases respectively. History does not ineluctably move, as Horkheimer and Adorno believed, either in the direction of bliss and salvation or in the opposite direction of hell and damnation. Man has at all times been a thinking, willing, and feeling creature, and his history has always moved between reason and unreason. Horkheimer's statement that "the fascist order is the reason in which reason reveals itself as irrational,"[24] or Adorno's rhetorical sallies against the "irrational rationality" of bourgeois thought and reality,[25] would have struck no responsive chord in Vico. Nor was myth to him reason in disguise of either unreason or diminished reason. It was precisely the nonrational character of myth that enabled it to perform an essential function for the society (*any* society) and the personality. It would never be

[23] Cf. *From Max Weber*, edited by Hans H. Gerth and C. Wright Mills (New York: Oxford University Press, 1958), p. 55, on Weber's construction of history as the "antinomic balance of charismatic movements (leaders and ideas) with rational routinization (enduring institutions and material interests)" as well as their elaborate discussion of the sociology of ideas and interests, pp. 61–65.

[24] Quoted in Jay, *The Dialectical Imagination*, p. 121.

[25] Theodor W. Adorno, *Negative Dialektik* (Frankfurt: Suhrkamp, 1966), pp. 30 ff.

entirely overcome. Neither would it serve as an exclusive guide.

By the same token, we may learn from Vico that there is a limit in the extent to which a society can be guided by sheer rationality. In commenting on Vico's statement about men making their history, Horkheimer said that prediction in the social sciences was difficult, if not impossible, because we live in an unfree society. It will be different in a "rational", society where men will *truly* make their own history and be guided by reason alone.[26] But in that ideal society where, in Lenin's famous phrase (which renders not only Marx's but Horkheimer's, Adorno's, and Marcuse's thought very precisely), the administration of society will become so simplified that every cook will be qualified to take over its machinery, the whole business of politics and of prediction could be of interest only to a cook, or at best to those "mediocre minds" whom Nietzsche thought best qualified for taking care of public affairs.[27]

Though Vico speaks of a possible "relapse" into barbarism, I do not believe he envisioned such a development. To him, the return to a new barbarism serves but to cure man from the overcivilized barbarism of reflection. It is true, in his later writings Horkheimer argued that it was premature to say that men actually made their history. If anything, the trend in modern life was away from the conscious, rational determination of historical events rather than toward it. History, therefore, could not simply be "understood," as he claimed Dilthey or Vico had hoped, but had to be "explained."[28]

If we adopt Vico's point of view, the problem with Critical Theory, whether in regard to its earlier optimistic vision of "a rational society" or in relation to its later pessimistic projection of the "wholly administered world," would lie in Hork-

[26] Horkheimer, "Zum Problem der Voraussage."
[27] Cf. Hannah Arendt, *Between Past and Future* (New York: Viking Press, 1968), p. 19.
[28] Cf. Jay, *The Dialectical Imagination*, p. 49.

heimer's, Adorno's, and Marcuse's commitment to the same eschatological interpretation of history. They discern a rhythm and plot which empirical inquirers fail to detect. While insisting that Providence was the first principle for the understanding of history, Vico never distorted sociopolitical history by an eschatological viewpoint. His development is one without fulfillment. The *corso* is followed by a *ricorso*. There is no denouement and no consummation. There are limits to secularization. If a population becomes too sophisticated and individualistic in its values, if there is nothing sacred to it any longer, it is less likely to stick together. The resulting social disorder may give rise to new religious sects that preach a return to pristine values and promise salvation.

In Vico's view, both progress and degeneration occur in the course of human development, and neither is of infinite extent. That would make his view of history more realistic than Critical Theory's conception of "a rational society," a social system and a new era, wherein both myth and ideology would cease to be relevant. For this refers to a condition in which history itself appears to be abolished.[29]

---

[29] Cf. Halpern, " 'Myth' and 'Ideology' in Modern Usage," p. 149.

"Natural History" and Social Evolution: Reflections on *Vico's Corsi e Ricorsi*

BY FRED R. DALLMAYR

T HE present commemoration of Vico's *New Science* finds a world vastly more receptive to his ideas than at the time of its first publication in 1725.[1] Generations of scholars have unraveled the seminal contributions of the study to a large number of contemporary disciplines, including psychology, philology, pedagogy, and linguistics. Important as these diverse contributions may be, they are overshadowed by the central thrust of the *New Science*: the effort to shed light on, and give a coherent account of, human history and the stages of social development. Given this focus, the study is bound to speak with particular urgency to a time like ours when, despite a disarray of goals and direction signals, social development on a global scale is the order of the day. In Vico's time and for several centuries afterward, European or "Western" society seemed to enjoy a monopoly of evolution and a privileged access to the "meaning" of history; but this monopoly has been shattered by events in our age. Actually, as has frequently been noted, our global context today is neither monolithic nor neatly polarized, but comprised of at least three different

[1] In a letter to a friend, written after the first publication in Naples, Vico noted that it seemed to him "as if in this city I had sent my work into the desert" (Giambattista Vico, *Opere*, edited by Fausto Nicolini [Naples: Ricciardi, 1953], p. 117).

"worlds": Western countries, Eastern communist societies, and the group of "newly emerging" or developing nations. Numerically preponderant but politically and economically disadvantaged, the latter world is in particularly desperate need of secure guideposts—which are in short supply. Relying on its own accomplishments, the West offers as yardsticks technological complexity and steering capacity—variations on the neo-Darwinian theme of "natural selection." Communism in the East holds out the promise of a "classless" society, whose precise connotations are obscure and elusive.[2]

Like a Baroque edifice, Vico's *New Science* is a complex, multifaceted opus offering different points of access; a central Ariadne thread, however, can be found in the *verum-factum* principle, according to which genuine understanding of a subject matter presupposes authorship. What encourages Vico in his venture to construct a "new science" of history is precisely the assumption that, in contrast to nature, "the world of civil society has certainly been made by men, and that its principles are therefore to be found within the modifications of our own human mind."[3] At a first glance, the notion of authorship seems immediately plausible—at least to a modern Western reader. On closer inspection, however, the *verum-factum* principle turns into a source of perplexing issues and quandaries. Not surprisingly, Vico scholars have been sharply divided over the significance of the principle. Steeped in the legacy of Hegelian idealism, Benedetto Croce extolled Vico as a precursor of *Geisteswissenschaften* and as an advocate of historical development seen as a "history of freedom." In Croce's interpretation, the social and historical world is a product of human action and creativity; and since "man" (construed not as single individual but as universal subject) is the exclusive author, historical and social knowledge approximates perfect

---

[2] Compare, e.g., Irving L. Horowitz, *Three Worlds of Development: The Theory and Practice of International Stratification* (New York: Oxford University Press, 1966).

[3] *The New Science of Giambattista Vico* (hereinafter *NS*), translated by Thomas G. Bergin and Max H. Fisch (Ithaca: Cornell University Press, 1968), par. 331.

self-knowledge: "Here is a real world; and of this world man is truly the god." Seen from this vantage point, Vico's conception of history is incipiently (or in its "real tendency") a theory of human progress, but fails to take this step due to a traditional reliance on divine providence.[4]

The stress on human creativity has not gone unopposed. Among others, Karl Löwith challenged Croce's "philosophical liberalism" and his neglect of both providence and natural necessity, pointing to passages in the *New Science* which depict human authorship as neither capricious nor entirely intentional. Perhaps due to his own semi-Stoic leanings, Löwith actually placed his accent chiefly on Vico's notion of *corsi e ricorsi* viewed as a natural cycle of events (although he stopped short of embracing a naturalist or positivist interpretation). Arguing that providence was "immanent" in nature and "closer to fate than to free choice and action," he rejected not only the notion of progress but also that of a "plenitude" of time—thereby jeopardizing both Vico's vision of a fully humanized or "civil world" and his treatment of *ricorso* as a (moral and juridical) "appeal."[5] The issue between Löwith and Croce has not been resolved and is likely to occupy scholars for some time to come. In the following pages I want to draw attention to historical perspectives developed by the founders of the so-called Frankfurt School, as part of their endeavor to fashion a "critical" version of dialectical materialism. As it seems to me, arguments advanced by Horkheimer and Adorno—especially the latter's conception of "natural history"—capture some of the vital insights of Vico's *New Science* (although no effort will be made to demonstrate in every instance a direct lineage or historical influence).

[4] Benedetto Croce, *The Philosophy of Giambattista Vico*, translated by Robert G. Collingwood (London: Howard Latimer, 1913), pp. 28, 115 ff.

[5] See Karl Löwith, *Meaning in History* (Chicago: University of Chicago Press, 1949), pp. 126, 132; also Jürgen Habermas, "Karl Löwiths stoischer Rückzug vom historischen Bewusstsein," in his *Theorie und Praxis: Sozialphilosophische Studien* (Neuwied: Luchterhand, 1963), pp. 352–370.

The Origins of Modern Philosophy of History

Frankfurt theorists have always been preoccupied with historical development and its interpretation. One of Horkheimer's first monographs—published in 1930—examined the "origins" or beginnings of the modern philosophy of history during the Renaissance and early Enlightenment period. The study culminated in a careful and sympathetic analysis of Vico's *New Science*. According to Horkheimer, the modern age has been marked since its inception by the rupture and steadily widening rift between man and nature. Two distinct (but closely correlated) responses have been engendered by this experience. One alternative has been to accept the rift and to turn it into a launching pad for human mastery and control; the other response has been to camouflage the breach by leveling man into an objectified (or reified) universe. Modern science and technology, as founded in the time of Galileo and Bacon, has been wedded mainly to the first alternative: the transformation of the natural world into an arsenal for human manipulation and exploitation. The manipulative thrust, in Horkheimer's view, was not strictly limited to nature, but could also be found in the social and historical arena; Machiavelli's political "instrumentalism" was a manifestation of the striving for mastery deriving from the rift between human designs and nature. The second response—espoused by naturalist thinkers like Spinoza and Hobbes—obliterated the distinction by treating man simply as a link in the natural chain of causation. In terms of historical perspectives, the view bypassed human aspirations in favor of the "eternal return of the present" or the natural cycle of events.

The last chapter of the study was devoted to Vico—described by a competent observer as "one of Horkheimer's early intellectual heroes."[6] In the context of the early En-

[6] See Martin Jay, *The Dialectical Imagination: A History of the Frankfurt School and the Institute of Social Research, 1923–1950* (Boston: Little, Brown, 1973), p. 49.

lightenment era, the chief merit of the *New Science* was found in the simultaneous avoidance of the mastery conception and of a simplistic naturalism—and ultimately in the ability to perceive the intimate, dialectical relationship between man and nature. Vico's attack on Cartesian metaphysics and epistemology was prompted, in large measure, by its glorification of detached, scientific rationality—a rationality devoid of substantive content and liable to be used for purely utilitarian, manipulative tasks. While opposing rationalistic conceit, the *New Science* did not simply negate human reason and intentionality nor submerge man's role in the blind forces of natural causation; despite the emphasis on *corsi e ricorsi* or the rise and fall of civilizations, human activity was treated as key to the interpretation of social development. In Horkheimer's view, the stress on human activity or *praxis* was a crucial contribution foreshadowing insights of dialectical materialism. Instead of denoting a strategy of instrumental domination, Vico's conception linked human endeavors with nature and cultural traditions. From earliest times, man had to resort to concerted activity or labor in order to secure the means of survival; the outcome of his efforts, however, depended not only on his selfish motivations but on the bounty of nature and on the institutional and cultural setting conditioning work. By embedding action in the complex nexus of forces and relations of production, Horkheimer suggested, Vico had anticipated Marx's insight that history is commonly made "behind the backs and without the awareness of individual agents."[7]

---

[7] Max Horkheimer, *Anfänge der burgerlichen Geschichtsphilosophie* (Stuttgart: Kohlhammer, 1930), p. 99. Countering fatalistic pessimism, however, he added (p. 111): "In contrast to Spengler Vico maintains the philosophical conviction that despite the return of old forms of life—despite mankind's lapse into barbarism at the end of a historical cycle—the establishment of the 'good life' or 'good society' is a perennial task." Summarizing Horkheimer's argument, Jay writes: "Vico had understood that *praxis* and domination were not the same. Although he separated man and nature, he did so in a way that avoided placing one above the other. By insisting on the subjectivity of man, he preserved the potentiality of the subjectivity of nature" (Jay, *The Dialectical Imagination*, p. 258).

In subsequent writings, Horkheimer did not directly invoke, or make extensive reference to, the *New Science*; but Vico's influence did not come to an end. Actually, an argument can be made that, over the years, the affinity between the two thinkers grew stronger or more intimate. The cited monograph still contained traces of a man-centered optimism which Vico would hardly have shared. Although shunning the pitfalls of individualism, Horkheimer at the time still tended to view history narrowly as a product of human initiative—an initiative ascribed to leading social classes acting on behalf of mankind construed (in Hegelian terms) as a "universal" subject. Likewise the identification of human *praxis* with labor placed a heavy accent on man's struggle with nature and thus, directly or indirectly, paid tribute to the notion of human mastery or control. The rapidly darkening horizon in Europe, leading to the Nazi takeover and his emigration in 1933, steadily eroded Horkheimer's attachment to Marxist orthodoxy and his trust in human enterprise as motor of social development. His close association with Adorno—following the relocation of the Frankfurt Institute in New York—further strengthened his aversion to the conception of a man-made, linear progress and his appreciation of the multidimensionality of history. A major outcome of these experiences, in the domain of historical exegesis, was the collaborative venture entitled *Dialectic of Enlightenment*, jointly written with Adorno during the war years and first published in 1947.

Dialectic of Enlightenment

As employed in the study, the term "enlightenment" was not restricted to the age of Diderot and Voltaire but covered the entire period of Western rationalism and "scientific" inquiry from earliest times. Contrary to a widespread belief sponsored by its proponents, enlightenment in the authors' view was not simply a process of growing intellectual emancipation but a complex movement involving a counterpoint of advance and regress. The central question motivating the study was why—given the growth of knowledge and material productivity—"mankind, instead of entering into a truly human condition, is sinking into a new kind of barbarism." Although the *New Science* was not specifically cited, the query carried distinct echoes of the "barbarism of reflection" which Vico treated as harbinger of a potential new *ricorso* of civilization. According to Horkheimer and Adorno, our contemporary period was marked by a peculiar mixture of intellectual sophistication and purposive myopia or ignorance. The rising standard of living even among the lower classes, the study noted, was accompanied by a "glittering display of intellect." While its true concern was the "negation of reification," reason or intellect was bound to decay "where it congeals into a cultural commodity which is distributed for purposes of consumption. The flood of detailed information and candy-floss entertainment promotes simultaneously human cleverness and stultification." Despite its grim diagnosis, the purpose of the study was not simply to indict knowledge but to find in reason both the source and a possible antidote for the "self-destruction of enlightenment":

> We are wholly convinced—and therein lies our *petitio principii*—that social freedom is inseparable from enlightened thought. Yet, we believe to have recognized just as clearly that this type of thought, no less than the concrete historical forms or social institutions linked with it, contains the seeds of the very reversal which is happening today. Unless willing to ponder this regressive element, enlightenment seals its own fate.[8]

---

[8] Max Horkheimer and Theodor W. Adorno, *Dialectic of Enlightenment*, translated by John Cumming (New York: Herder & Herder, 1972), pp. xi, xiii, xv. (In this and subsequent citations I have partially altered the translation for purposes of clarity.) Turning against critics of modern culture like Huxley, Jaspers or Ortega y Gasset, the study added (p. xv): "Enlightenment must reflect upon itself, if men are not to be wholly betrayed. What is at issue is not the conservation of the past, but the redemption of the hopes of the past. Today, however, the past persists as destruction of the past."

The mainspring of Western rationalism, and also the motive of the present reversal, was found by the authors in its ambition to terminate man's bondage to nature and to primitive superstition. "The basic program of enlightenment," the study noted, "was the disenchantment of the world, the dissolution of myths and the substitution of knowledge for fancy." From the beginning, the effort of demystification and the attack on prejudice were pervaded by a "patriarchal" impulse, the impulse to govern: "Having vanquished superstition, human reason shall rule over a disenchanted nature." In order to gain ascendancy, reason is bent on simplifying the universe, on subsuming all particular details under abstract categories or systematic schemes—and ideally under handy mathematical formulas: "In advance, enlightenment recognizes as reality or event only what can be grasped in unity; its ideal is the system from which everything is deduced. . . . Number became the canon of enlightenment." The central ambition of rational or scientific analysis is to discover the internal mechanism of phenomena or occurrences—a discovery which, by permitting experimental reconstruction or replication, enhances the range of human control. "Enlightenment," one reads, "behaves toward things as a dictator behaves toward men: he only knows them as objects of manipulation. The man of science knows things insofar as he can make or produce them, thus chaining their reality to his own ends. The transformation reveals the nature of things as always the same: an occasion for domination." In this manner abstract logic and detached analysis reveal their instrumental, utilitarian thrust: "The universality of categories as developed by discursive logic—emblem of domination in the conceptual sphere—is erected on the basis of actual domination. The dissolution of the heritage of magic and of ancient diffuse notions by conceptual unity heralds a way of life shaped by freemen accustomed to rule."[9]

[9] *Ibid.*, pp. 3–4, 7, 9, 14.

According to Horkheimer and Adorno, the escape from nature promised by rationalism was entirely misleading and deceptive. In combating superstition, scientific reason tries to extricate itself from blind determinism; however, by focusing attention on causal mechanisms or permanent laws of nature, science still pays tribute to cyclical recurrence or the "eternal return of the present." "The doctrine of the equivalence of action and reaction," the study observed,

> maintains the power of repetition over life long after men had renounced the illusory hope to identify themselves through repetition with the repeated reality and thus to escape its dominion. The more remote the distance into which magical illusion recedes, the more relentlessly repetition (restyled as lawfulness) chains man to that natural cycle whose reification into a law of nature was supposed to secure his emancipation.

As a result of its universalism and seeming detachment, enlightenment fell prey to the very ritual whose spell it tried to break: "The principle of immanence—the explanation of every event as repetition—which enlightenment pits against mythical fancy, is the principle of myth itself." Mythology, in the authors' view, was marked by the nexus of guilt and punishment, fate and retribution—a nexus perpetuated by rationalism: "In myths every event must atone for having happened. The same occurs in enlightenment: every particular phenomenon is annihilated as soon as it is noted." Facts, moreover, are not only obliterated in their particularity, but also affirmed and worshipped as elements of a universal scheme: "In its figures mythology reflected the essence of existing reality—cycle, fate, mundane dominion—as truth devoid of hope. Both the vitality of mythical images and the clarity of scientific formulas testify to the permanence of facticity, proclaiming it as the very meaning which it occludes."[10]

From this perspective, the source of the present reversal became evident: in functioning as instrument of human domination, reason remained a victim and unwitting vehicle of natural constraints. "In the comprehensive sense of progressive thought," the study argued, "enlightenment has always aimed at liberating men from fear and establishing their mastery; but the fully enlightened world radiates triumphant disaster. . . . Every attempt to terminate natural constraints by rupturing nature only intensifies bondage. Such is the course of European civilization."[11] Reduced to a target of instrumental control, nature retaliates not only through counterforce but also by truncating human sense experience or sensibility toward nature—a paralysis affecting human understanding as well: "The unification of intellectual functions for the sake of gaining control over the senses—reflection's abdication in the interest of conceptual uniformity—entails the impoverishment of thought and experience alike; both are impaired by their mutual segregation." In depicting the human and social costs of rationalism, Horkheimer and Adorno used language whose grimness evoked Vico's portrayal of civilization during the stage of final decay:

> The more complex and refined the social, economic and scientific apparatus to whose service the production system has long accustomed the human body, the more perfunctory the experiences of which it is capable. The elimination of qualitative traits and their conversion into functions spreads from science via rationalized modes of labor to the experiential world of nations—which once again tends to be assimilated to that of dinosaurs. The pathology of the masses today is their inability to hear new sounds with their own ears, to touch the untouched with their own hands—a new kind of stupor far out-distancing defunct mythologies. By means of an encompassing society regulating all relations and emotions, men are reduced again to the

---

[11] *Ibid.*, pp. 3, 13. Compare in this context also the statement (p. 32): "The essence of enlightenment is the alternative which is inescapably domination. Men have always had to choose between their subjection to nature or nature's subjection to human control. With the spreading of the bourgeois market economy, the dark horizon of myth is illumined by the sun of calculating reason beneath whose icy rays the seed of the new barbarism grows to fruition. Under the pressure of domination human labor has always tended to break away from myth—into whose spell it constantly returned under the impulse of domination."

level from which social evolution and human emancipation de-
parted: the level of species creatures, identical with each other
in the atomistic but dictatorial collectivity.[12]

Although somber in tone, the study did not counsel despair;
as presented by Horkheimer and Adorno, the "dialectic of
enlightenment" involved neither linear progress nor unmiti-
gated regression but a confluence of the two: "The curse of
relentless progress is relentless regression." According to the
authors, human thought was irremediably lodged in the tension between image and sign, concrete perception and
concept—unable to find rest in either of the polar alternatives.
Inescapably, thought counteracts the unreflected presence of
nature, only to fall prey to the dialectic of domination:
"Natural bondage derives from the subjugation of nature
without which mind cannot exist." In exerting its analytical
capacity, reason opens up the breach between man and nature, subject and object, which, permitting instrumental mastery, cannot simply be healed by mystical visions or synthetic
formulas: "Concepts are tools ideally suited to that aspect of
things amenable to control. Thought becomes illusory when
seeking to conceal its divisive function, detachment and objec-
tifying impact: all mystical reunion is deception." Only by
clinging to its own dialectic—especially to the power of concrete negation—can thought hope to overcome its conceit and
to dissolve the spell of self-induced bondage:

[12] *Ibid.*, p. 36. Vico's portrayal is as follows: "But if the peoples are rotting in that
ultimate civil disease . . . , then providence for their extreme ill has its extreme
remedy at hand. For such peoples, like so many beasts, have fallen into the custom of
each man thinking only of his own private interests and have reached the extreme of
delicacy, or better of pride, in which like wild animals they bristle and lash out at the
slightest displeasure. Thus no matter how great the throng and press of their bodies,
they live like wild beasts in a deep solitude of spirit and will, scarcely any two being
able to agree since each follows his own pleasure or caprice. By reason of all this,
providence decrees that, through obstinate factions and desperate civil wars, they
shall turn their cities into forests and the forests into dens and lairs of men. In this
way, through long centuries of barbarism, rust will consume the misbegotten subtleties of malicious wits that have turned them into beasts made more inhuman by the
barbarism of reflection than the first men had been made by the barbarism of sense"
(*NS*, par. 1106).

The battle against prejudice has always meant not only expansion but also exposure of domination. Enlightenment is more than enlightenment—nature which becomes accessible in its alienation. . . . By acknowledging itself as domination and retreating into nature, mind soberly abandons the claim to mastery subjecting it to nature. Although compelled to flee from necessity and unable to renounce progress and civilization without forsaking knowledge itself, mankind at least does no longer mistake its ramparts against necessity—the institutions and practices of domination which have always rebounded from nature on society—as synonyms of human emancipation.[13]

Negative Dialectics

As previously indicated, *Dialectic of Enlightenment* was the fruit of close intellectual collaboration; yet, both with regard to style and substance, it is not difficult to detect the influence of Adorno's subtle bent of mind. The intimate nexus of rational emancipation and natural constraints, as sketched in the study, was reminiscent of one of Adorno's central and favorite conceptions, that of "natural history"—a conception which simultaneously portrayed history as an adjunct of nature and nature as a temporal-historical (and ultimately perishable) domain. The notion had first been delineated in one of Adorno's early essays written before his emigration from Germany;[14] but subsequent writings repeatedly returned to the theme, disclosing new dimensions and implications. From the beginning, the notion was meant as contribution to the long-standing controversy regarding the meaning of history and its interpretation. As formulated by Adorno, "natural history" challenged the identification of historical study with

[13] Horkheimer and Adorno, *Dialectic of Enlightenment*, pp. 17–18, 36, 39–40. Compare also the statement (p. 42): "As organ of adaptation or as a mere factory of instruments, enlightenment is as destructive as its romantic enemies have always charged. It comes into its own only by cancelling this consensus and by daring to renounce the false premise: the principle of blind domination."

[14] See Theodor W. Adorno, "Die Idee der Naturgeschichte" (1932), in *Philosophische Frühschriften*, edited by Rolf Tiedemann (Frankfurt: Suhrkamp, 1973), pp. 350–365.

Geisteswissenschaft—a type of inquiry relying exclusively on cultural-hermeneutical exegesis or on the rediscovery of the purposes and intentional designs underlying human actions in the past. Simultaneously, by ascribing a temporal-historical dimension to nature, the conception took a stand against positivist objectivism and reification. A subterranean motif in numerous publications, the notion received detailed attention in Adorno's last major philosophical work, his *Negative Dialectics* of 1966.

The discussion of the theme in that study occurred in a chapter, entitled "World Spirit and Natural History," devoted to a critical assessment of Hegel's philosophy of history. Although appreciating the dialectical complexity of Hegel's thought, Adorno challenged both the idealist stress on human culture and the subsumption of particular events under a predetermined pattern of development. In focusing on national cultures as agents of change, Hegelian philosophy—despite its antiindividualism and antisubjectivism—identified historical purpose with the intentions of collective (potentially "universal") subjects. Apart from the pitfalls of cultural bias, the focus on mind—viewed as collective mind—tended to pit human intentionality against nature, thus enmeshing historical progress in the dialectic of mastery and domination. The glorification of universal reason as epitomized in the "world spirit"—Adorno noted—was synonymous with a glorification of rational control over amorphous nature and over the contingency of particular events. "The apotheosis of universality," he wrote, "is a concession of failure. By banishing particular details, universality reveals itself as particular domination. In its triumph general reason discloses its intrinsic restrictions: instead of simply signifying unity within diversity, it involves a streamlining of reality, a unity superimposed on something. . . . Unity equals division." The conflict between universality and particularity derived ultimately from reason's exclusive thrust toward self-knowledge and self-identification: "Enthroned above the otherness of the world, triumphant reason necessarily constricts itself. The principle of pure identity is in itself contradictory—as it perpetuates non-identity in suppressed and mutilated form."[15]

Seen from this perspective, Hegel's historical conception manifested a dialectic unintended (or not fully apprehended) by its author: rational emancipation and the progressive march of reason had as its counterpoint man's growing ensnarlment in natural constraints. According to Adorno, Hegel's vision of universal history was spurious if treated as blueprint of growing moral perfection; yet its accent on uniformity was not entirely misguided. In his words:

> There is no point in denying the unity cementing the discontinuous and dispersed fragments of history—the unity of progressive domination extending from nature to society and finally to man's psyche. No universal history leads from barbarism to humanism; but there is one leading from the slingshot to the megaton bomb, terminating in the total threat of organized mankind against living creatures—at a point of total discontinuity.

From the vantage point of the world spirit, Adorno added, historical progress paradoxically annulled itself; submerged in the dialectic of domination, reason fell prey to the cycle of nature and the "eternal return of the present." In Hegel's conception, the study commented, "domination is absolutized and projected onto the essence of reality identified with spirit. History, however, as a scheme of events totally explained, acquires the aura of timeless permanence. In the midst of history, Hegel sides with an unchanging immutability—the identical core of a process presumed rational in its totality."

15 Theodor W. Adorno, *Negative Dialectics,* translated by E. B. Ashtotn (New York: Seabury Press, 1973), pp. 317–318. (In this and subsequent citations I have partially altered the translation for purposes of clarity.) Compare also the comment (p. 320): "Worthy object of definition, the world spirit should be defined as permanent catastrophe. Under the sway of the all-powerful principle of identity, everything that eludes identity and the scheming designs of instrumental rationality turns into a source of fright—in retribution for the calamity inflicted by identity on the non-identical world. History permits hardly another type of philosophical interpretation—without succumbing to idealist mystification."

Historical progress and cyclical permanence presupposed each other; their confluence testified to the fact that "wedded to identity, mind converges with the spell of blind nature by denying it."[16]

In lieu of the march of the world spirit, *Negative Dialectics* counseled the perspective of "natural history"—a term initially fashioned by Marx and later refined by Lukács and Benjamin. Under the heading of a "second nature" denoting the fabric of quasi-natural laws governing social life, the perspective preserved Hegel's insight into the "objectivity" of historical experience—but with a critical bent: "The thesis that society is subject to natural laws is ideology if treated as an immutable dictate of nature; however, it contains a real kernel to the extent that it points to the hidden motor of unconscious society." Contrary to the naturalism and scientism of Marxist orthodoxy, Marx—in Adorno's view—stressed natural constraints only as a challenge for human aspirations: "Human history, involving the progressive mastery of nature, continues the unconscious process of nature: devouring and being devoured. Ironically Marx was a Social Darwinist: what Social Darwinists extolled as proper guidelines for human action, was to him a negative foil suggesting the possibility of transformation." That the naturalist thesis could not be uncritically accepted was corroborated by the "strongest theme in Marxist theory, that of the finitude or changeability of natural laws: at the threshold of the realm of freedom they would cease to apply." The notion of a "realm of freedom," however, was not synonymous with the simple rejection of nature or its subjugation to the mastery of reason, a strategy perpetuating the enmity between man and nature; nor could access to the realm be gained through spurious fusion or synthetic formulas. "Once established," Adorno noted,

the boundary between nature and culture can be blurred but not erased by reflection. Without reflection, to be sure, the

16 *Ibid.*, pp. 320, 356–357.

distinction would reduce historical movement to a mere adjunct, while enshrining unchanging permanence as essence. It would be up to thought, instead, to see all nature (and its equivalents) as history and all history as nature.[17]

Like the founders of the School, members of the younger generation of Frankfurt theorists betray an intense concern with historical development and its interpretation; in particular, the writings of Jürgen Habermas give evidence of the continued effort to disentangle the developmental patterns implicit in dialectical materialism. Yet, despite the continuity of preoccupation, it is possible to detect a shift of accent in recent formulations: a tendency to abandon the complexity of the founders' perspective in favor of a more linear, one-dimensional conception of social evolution. Habermas's *Legitimation Crisis*—whose English version appeared in 1975—finds a central lever of development in the progressive "appropriation" of the resources of external and "internal nature" through productive enterprise and socialization, a process involving at its advanced stages rational testing of knowledge claims and discursive justification of behavior. The same study sketches a developmental "logic" of social norms leading from unreflected habits over conventional rules to the level of "communicative ethics" predicated on rationally validated and universally shared principles of conduct. Expanding on these notions, Habermas in a recent manuscript on historical materialism portrays social evolution as a sequential pattern of institutionalized modes of learning and communicative interaction, a sequence manifesting a steady growth in objectively valid knowledge and in moral-practical maturity.[18]

Although remarkable for analytical rigor and attention to empirical detail, Habermas's arguments court the danger of an idealist contraction of history. His conception of com-

---

[17] *Ibid.*, pp. 355–356, 359.

[18] See Jürgen Habermas, *Legitimation Crisis*, translated by Thomas McCarthy (Boston: Beacon Press, 1975), pp. 8–12, 87–92; also *Zur Rekonstruktion des historischen Materialismus* (Frankfurt: Suhrkamp, 1976), esp. pp. 141–199.

municative ethics—and especially the stress on universal consensus—tends to truncate the dialectic of "universals" and "particulars" in favor of abstract general principles devoid of experiential content. More importantly, the focus on "appropriation" and rational validation conjures up the specter of human mastery familiar from the "enlightenment" tradition; despite the rejection of the Hegelian world-spirit, the crucial role assigned to normative-social interaction is liable to transform history into a product of subjectivity and a topic of *Geisteswissenschaften*. To counteract rationalist leanings of this kind, it may be well to remember both the teachings of Habermas's predecessors and of Vico's *New Science*. As I have tried to indicate, Adorno's notion of "natural history" reminds us of the regression implicit in human or social progress while simultaneously alerting us to the human aspirations submerged in cyclical recurrence and quasi-natural constraints. A notion of this type also helps to place into relief the significance of human praxis in Vico's *corsi e ricorsi*. "It is true," the *New Science* observes,

> that men have themselves made this world of nations . . .; but this world without doubt has issued from a mind often diverse, at times quite contrary, and always superior to the particular ends that men had proposed themselves; which narrow ends, made means to serve wider ends, it has always employed to preserve the human race upon this earth.[19]

---

[19] *NS*, par. 1108. In another context (par. 405) Vico points to the "axiom" of his study "that man in his ignorance makes himself the rule of the universe," adding: "As rational metaphysics teaches that man becomes all things by understanding them (*homo intelligendo fit omnia*), this imaginative metaphysics shows that man becomes all things by *not* understanding them (*homo non intelligendo fit omnia*); and perhaps the latter proposition is truer than the former, for when man understands he extends his mind and takes in the things, but when he does not understand he makes things out of himself and becomes them by transforming himself into them."

Vico and Comparative Historical Civilizational Sociology

Wherever Vico looked he saw *meanings* gathered in histories—embedded in custom, in lore, in poetry, in myth, in religion, in science, and most of all in the laws of all peoples of whom he had any knowledge.[1] His passion to extend the understanding of men's ways and all the laws of the nations asserts itself strongly in all his writings, including some which continue to cry out for fuller treatment than they have so far received.[2]

Werner Cahnman and Werner Stark are, therefore, both right in proposing for their variant reasons that today's historical and cultural sociologists will feel an affinity for Vico. Strong sociological accents abound in Vico's cultural-historical studies, especially those bearing on classical antiquities. Formulations having the ring of renowned contemporary hypotheses occur a surprising number of times in the course of his attempted reconstructions of the tangled relations of the religious practices, myths, literatures, and laws of varied peoples.[3]

What type of sociology may Vico be said to have been adumbrating? Here I would add a qualification to a thoughtful remark by Cahnman. Vico was, indeed, moving toward a sort of historical sociology, but it is a sort I would prefer to describe as a *"comparative cultural-historical"* sociology—in *civilizational* perspective.[4] The

[1] Max Fisch, in his introduction to *The New Science of Giambattista Vico* (hereinafter *NS*), translated by Thomas G. Bergin and Max H. Fisch (Ithaca: Cornell University Press, 1968), suggests the themes cited above. See also Isaiah Berlin, *Vico and Herder* (New York: Viking Press, 1976).

[2] One writer goes so far as to insist that we need to perform "a kind of 'Copernican' turning, a reorientation of our categories. It is necessary to assume that the North Star of our research, the cynosure of our attention, is no longer the *Scienza nuova*, but *Il diritto universale*" (Elio Gianturco, "Vico's Significance in the History of Legal Thought," in Giorgio Tagliacozzo and Hayden V. White, eds., *Giambàttista Vico: An International Symposium* [Baltimore: Johns Hopkins Press, 1969], p. 328).

[3] Cf. the illustration offered below under notes 19 and 20.

[4] Characterizations and illustrations of a related—but not identical—perspective will be found in Benjamin Nelson, "Max Weber's 'Author's Introduction (1920)': A Master Clue to his Main Aims," *Sociological Inquiry* 44 (1974): 269–278; "On Orient and Occident in Max Weber," *Social Research* 43 (Spring 1976): 114–129; "Max Weber as a Pioneer of Civilizational Analysis," *Comparative Civilizations Bulletin* 16 (Winter 1976): 4–16.

sociology toward which Vico tended could also be described as having a "differential" accent since he was ever eager to understand the *differences* as well as the similarities in the patterns and paces of social and cultural processes and structures *across histories*.

In approaching these perspectives Vico may be supposed by some to have strangely been moving in the sphere which Max Weber was to make his own. Indeed, a number of the ablest contemporary students of Vico have claimed to find notable similarities between Vico and Max Weber.[5] I am obliged to express reservations about emphases implicit in some of these statements. True, one can find some sort of analogy between Vico's notion of "ideal eternal history"[6] and Max Weber's notion of the "ideal types"; yet Weber's ways of putting questions to the data do not truly allow some of the main constructions which Vico and some of his modern interpreters place upon the notion of an "ideal eternal history."[7]

Although, like Vico, Weber struggled to be able to speak on civilizational issues out of "universal historical" frames, he explicitly set himself against having "a philosophy of world history."[8] Weber shied away from formulations involving universal statements about

---

[5] Thus H. Stuart Hughes writes: "Vico's influence [on Weber] comes mediated through a writer of the intervening century, such as Marx or Dilthey. Yet, for Sorel and Weber alike, a similar Vichian principle of historical understanding applied. The devices that . . . Weber described as ideal types were artificial mental constructions—self-induced modifications of the mind—that enabled the historian or the social theorist to penetrate the new data of his craft which had previously remained opaque" (H. Stuart Hughes, "Vico and Contemporary Social Theory and Social History," in Tagliacozzo and White, *Giambattista Vico: An International Symposium*, pp. 309–319, esp. 321).

[6] For Vico's notion of "ideal eternal history," see esp. the careful writings of Leon Pompa, "Vico's Science," *History and Theory* 10 (1971): 49–83, and *Vico: A Study of the New Science* (New York: Cambridge University Press, 1975).

[7] For helpful comments on Weber's ascetic cautions in the use of the "ideal type," see Günther Roth's introduction to the first volume of his edition and translation (with Claus Wittich) of Weber's *Economy and Society*, 3 vols. (Totowa, N.J.: Bedminster Press, 1968), pp. xxxviii, xliv–lii, 18–21. See also Wolfgang Mommsen, *The Age of Bureaucracy* (Oxford: Basil Blackwell, 1974), esp. chap. 1, "The Universal Historian and the Social Scientist"; cf. his *Max Weber: Gesellschaft, Politik und Geschichte* (Frankfurt: Suhrkamp, 1974), pp. 224–232. Weber's explosive thrusts against Spengler offer an interesting sidelight on this question. See Max Weber, *Werk und Person*, edited by Eduard Baumgarten (Tübingen: Mohr, 1964), pp. 554–555; cf. Marianne Weber, *Max Weber*, translated by H. Zohn (New York: Wiley-Interscience, 1974), esp. pp. 674–675.

[8] I adapt this phrase and one other in this paragraph from Hayden White's essay, "What Is Living and What Is Dead in Croce's Criticism of Vico?", in Tagliacozzo and White, *Giambattista Vico: An International Symposium*, pp. 379–391, esp. at 389.

the careers and cycles of civilizational entities and elements. A Vichian theory of *ricorsi* "as a model for *all* civilizational growth" was surely not for him.[9] Instead, throughout his life Weber carried on arduous and carefully designed comparative-historical "experiments" whose hard-earned results found their way into the cautiously framed hypotheses of the two main bodies of his collected work, the *Gesammelte Aufsätze zur Religionssoziologie* (Collected Essays in the Sociology of Religion) and *Wirtschaft und Gesellschaft* (Economy and Society).[10]

One has to add, moreover, that Weber may not be the modern sociologist whom Vico most resembles. I am not surprised that any extended mentions or discussions of Vico have so far not been found in the writings of Weber.[11] There is more occasion for wonder that, as H. Stuart Hughes reports, references to Vico will not be found either in Spengler or Toynbee and that Toynbee's notion of comparative history was established independently of Vico.[12]

This issue involves Weber's central thrusts and commitments.[13] Throughout his life Weber stubbornly insisted on investigating all historical structures from the point of view of a distinctive analytic which he had been elaborating.[14]

It hardly seems likely that Weber could have accepted the view so strongly emphasized in the following oft-quoted lines by Vico:

The decisive sort of proof in our Science is this: that, since these institutions have been established by divine providence, the course of the institutions of the nations had to be, must now be and will have to be such as our Science demonstrates, even if infinite worlds were born from time to time through eternity, which is certainly not the case.

Our science therefore comes to describe *an ideal eternal history traversed in time by the history of every nation in its rise, development, maturity, decline and fall*. Indeed, we make bold to affirm that he who meditates this science narrates to himself this ideal eternal

[9] Apparently, Croce criticized Vico here, but his reasons seem different from those which Weber might have had; for Vico's views, cf. White, "What Is Living and What Is Dead in Croce's Criticism of Vico?"

[10] See Benjamin Nelson, "On Orient and Occident in Max Weber," esp. pp. 116–120.

[11] H. Stuart Hughes, "Vico and Contemporary Social Theory and Social History," p. 321.

[12] *Ibid.*, p. 320.

[13] Nelson, "Max Weber's 'Author's Introduction (1920)'," pp. 271–273.

[14] Nelson, "On Orient and Occident in Max Weber" pp. 115–116.

history so far as he himself makes it for himself by that proof "it had, has and will have to be."[15]

Actually a sociologist whom Vico resembles in spirit more than he does Weber is Emile Durkheim.[16] In truth, Vico's sensibility in many regards is quite close to that of Durkheim's followers, the Durkheimians, especially Marcel Mauss, Durkheim's nephew, collaborator, and spiritual heir.[17] It is the Durkheimians who exhibit Vico's immense excitement about understanding the transformations in the textures and structures of human existence, experience, and expression.[18] Like Vico, the Durkheimians seek to re-present the morphological metamorphoses and the changing collective representations

[15] *NS*, pars. 348–349; my italics.

[16] David Bidney's interesting remarks in Tagliacozzo and White, *Giambattista Vico: An International Symposium*, p. 270, deserve special attention here. Indeed, he credits Vico with "anticipating Emile Durkheim's sociological method in *The Elementary Forms of Religious Life*." Professor Cahnman links Vico to Fustel de Coulanges, one of Durkheim's teachers and spiritual mentors; cf. esp. Fustel's classic, *The Ancient City*. Fustel is invoked several times in Durkheim's important introduction in the first volume of the *Année sociologique* as one who saw the necessity for new fusions of history and sociology; see Kurt H. Wolff, ed., *Essays on Sociology and Philosophy* (New York: Harper Torchbooks, 1964), pp. 342–343. Helpful introductions to Durkheim's life and thought will be found in: Steven Lukes, *Emile Durkheim: His Life and Work* (New York: Harper & Row, 1973); *Emile Durkheim: Selected Writings*, edited by Anthony Giddens (Cambridge: Cambridge University Press, 1972); Talcott Parsons, *The Structure of Social Action* (New York: Free Press, 1968), vol. 1, chaps. 8–12.

[17] Unhappily, too few American writers have troubled to explore the exceptional works of Mauss and the Durkheimians. See, however, Claude Lévi-Strauss, "French Sociology," in Georges Gurvitch and Wilbert E. Moore, eds., *Twentieth-Century Sociology* (New York: Philosophical Library, 1945); also, Paul Honigsheim, "The Influence of Durkheim and His School on the Study of Religion," in Wolff, *Essays on Sociology and Philosophy*, pp. 233–247. Mauss's works are now collected in *Sociologie et anthropologie*, edited by Claude Lévi-Strauss (Paris: Presses universitaires de France, 1950) and *Marcel Mauss: Oeuvres*, edited by V. Karady, 3 vols. (Paris: Éditions de minuit, 1968). Enzo Paci's interesting passing reference to the work of Mauss has a different focus from the one adopted here. Paci singles out Mauss's much-cited studies "Sur le don" and "Les techniques du corps" but omits references to Mauss's essays on the Person, the essay on *Primitive Classification* done with Durkheim, the *General Theory of Magic* (with Henri Hubert), and some others. He also links Mauss too closely to Piaget and fails to mention Durkheim's seminal *Elementary Forms of the Religious Life*; see Enzo Paci, "Vico, Structuralism and the Phenomenological Encyclopedia of the Sciences," in Tagliacozzo and White, *Giambattista Vico: An International Symposium*, esp. p. 506.

[18] Part of this story, which largely remains to be told, will be found in Lévi-Strauss's discussion of the Durkheimians in Gurvitch and Moore, *Twentieth-Century Sociology*; cf. H. Stuart Hughes's remarks about the relation of Marc Bloch, Lucien Febvre, and the *Annales* school to Michelet and Vico in Tagliacozzo and White, *Giambattista Vico: An International Symposium*, pp. 322–325.

of peoples coping with all the complex predicaments of their lives, including the structures of their coexistence, their conflicts, and their different "totalizations."[19] Again it was Durkheim and the Durkheimians who struggled to grasp the engenderings and expansions of abstract universalities in religion, law, philosophy, science out of critical challenges in the central milieus of the primordial collective experiences. The passionate interest of both the Durkheimians and Vico in issues of this range is readily discovered in their writings.[20]

[19] Too many previous writers have regarded Durkheim from perspectives too narrow to allow for an adequate grasp of the extent to which he may have resembled Vico. One central clue to the clarification of this issue lies in the appreciation of their common views on the sociohistorical origins of the wider universalities, e.g., those of Greek philosophy, Roman law, and Christian theology. In this connection Vico perceives that: "The founders of Roman law, at a time when they could not understand intelligible universals, fashioned imaginative universals. And just as the poets later by art brought personages and masks onto the stage, so these men by nature had previously brought the aforesaid names and persons into the forum" (NS, par. 1033).

[20] The most concentrated discussions in which Vico seems to anticipate the Durkheimian group will be found in NS, pars. 1033–1043. Insights into Vico's seemingly Durkheimian modes of analyzing relate to the following points among others: (1) the relation between "imaginative universals" and the "intelligible universals" among the founders of Roman law; (2) the metamorphoses of the masks (personae) and the notions of personage and person; (3) the passages from the "poetic jurisprudence" of antiquity to the later more formal and systematic structure of concepts; (4) Vico's view of ancient Roman law as "a serious poem, represented by the Romans in the Forum" and the derivation of the law of persons from the masks (personae) in these dramatic fables; (5) Vico's sense of the ways in which "the intellect was brought into play in the great assemblies and universal legal concepts abstracted by the intellect were thenceforward said to have their being in the understanding of the law; (6) Vico's account of the construction of the indivisibility of rights; (7) his sense of the relation of philosophy of law and the development of abstract universals; (8) the significance of forensic contexts and consequent comings to agreement in the adumbration by Socrates of "intelligible genera or abstract universals by induction"; (9) the influence on Plato and Aristotle of Greek political assemblies and public life.

Vico's foremost sociological and sociohistorical hypotheses on this score are offered at par. 1043: "From all the above we conclude that these principles of metaphysics, logic, and morals issued from the market place of Athens. From Solon's advice to the Athenians, 'know thyself,' came forth the popular commonwealths; from the popular commonwealths the laws; and from the laws emerged philosophy; and Solon, who had been wise in vulgar wisdom, came to be held wise in esoteric wisdom. . . ." The wider civilizational bearings of the types of sociological hypotheses illustrated above are discussed in two of my own essays: "Civilizational Complexes and Intercivilizational Encounters," Sociological Analysis 34 (1973): 79–105; "Sciences and Civilizations, 'East' and 'West': Joseph Needham and Max Weber," Boston Studies in the Philosophy of Science 11 (1974): 445–493.

Vico could readily have accepted a good part of the emphases of the main works of Durkheim: the *Division of Labor, Suicide*, and especially *The Elementary Forms of the Religious Life*; he would, indeed, have felt even more warmly about the famed essays which Durkheim and Mauss did together—especially *Primitive Classification* (1903)[21] and the still neglected "Note on the Notion of Civilization."[22]

Vico would surely have subscribed to the spirit of Marcel Mauss's remarkable paper, "A Category of the Human Spirit, That of the Ego or Person."[23] Indeed, that paper sets forth the program of the Durkheim School in terms which Vico would doubtless have accepted as a desired realization of comparative historical interests in the semantics of categorial structures.[24] Mauss's essay on "The Nation," powerfully illustrating the surprising emergence and the metamorphoses of Nation and State, would also have received a warm welcome from Vico.[25]

In the same way, Vico would have hailed the powerful writings of Marcel Granet on festivals, rituals, dance, forms of communion, and communication in China;[26] Louis Dumont's splendid studies in

[21] *Primitive Classification*, translated and edited with an introduction by Rodney Needham (Chicago: University of Chicago Press, 1963).

[22] "Note on the Notion of Civilization," translated with an introduction by Benjamin Nelson, *Social Research* 38 (Winter 1971): 808–815.

[23] See now L. Krader's translation of this too long neglected study in *Psychoanalytic Review* 55 (1968): 457–481. Vico offers a brief discussion of *persona* in *NS*, pars. 1034, 1037, which makes an exceptionally interesting comparison with Mauss (esp. at pp. 471 ff).

[24] Mauss writes: "We [the members of the French School of sociology] apply ourselves above all to the social history of the categories of the human spirit. We attempt to explain them one by one, beginning quite simply and provisionally with the list of the Aristotelian categories. We describe their particular civilizations, and, by this comparison, we endeavor to find in them the changing nature, and thus their reasons for being as they are. It is in this way that, in developing the notion of *mana*, [Henri] Hubert and I thought to find not only the archaic foundation of magic, but also the very general and probably very primitive form of the notion of cause; it is thus that Hubert described certain characteristics of the notion of time; that our lamented colleague, friend, and student, S. Czarnowski, began—but did not complete, alas!—his theory of the 'breaking up of extension,' in other words, of one of the traits, of certain aspects of the notion of space; it is thus that my uncle and teacher, Durkheim, took up the notion of the *whole*, after having taken up with me the notion of kind" (*ibid.*, pp. 457–458).

[25] See Mauss, "La Nation," in *Oeuvres*, 3: 573–625.

[26] See Marion Levy, Jr., "Marcel Granet," in *International Encyclopedia of the Social Sciences* (New York: Macmillan, 1968), 6: 241–243; Granet's works include: *La pensée chinoise* (Paris: La Renaissance du Livre, 1934); *Études sociologiques de la Chine* (Paris: Presses universitaires de France, 1953); *Chinese Civilization* (London: Routledge, 1957).

Hindu sociology[27] and especially his striking statement, "The Individual as an Impediment to Sociological Comparison and Indian History."[28]

A last historical sociologist with whom Vico would bear close comparison is Henry Sumner Maine, surely no less a contributor than Vico to the comparative historical study of law and jurisprudence in civilizational perspective.[29]

A detailed and precise comparison of Vico and Maine will one day document the striking convergences of the two men at the very foundations of their structures as well as in the details of their historical accounts of the Roman legal institutions. At this time, however, it may be more helpful to concentrate on their central approaches in political philosophy.

A fresh reading of Maine in this perspective will help us appreciate the full meaning of Vico's turning away from Descartes, Hobbes, and others committed to what Vico called "intellectualism" and what many today prefer to call Enlightenment uniformitarian rationalism.[30]

Maine, like Vico, recognized the indispensable aid made available through comparative historical jurisprudence in opposing a rationalist account of the origins of political society and culture. Maine directed his shafts against Locke, Bentham, John Austin, and Rousseau as Vico attacked Descartes, Hobbes, Grotius, Pufendorf, and others.

Both related to critical points in the development of jurispru-

---

[27] *Journal of Asian Studies* 35 (August 1976) carries a symposium on Dumont's work. Dumont's writings are listed therein at pp. 647–650.

[28] See Louis Dumont, *Religion, Politics and History in India: Collected Papers in Indian Sociology* (The Hague & Paris: Mouton, 1971), chap. 7, pp. 133–150.

[29] John Fiske offers an exceptionally interesting testimonial on the affinities of Vico and Maine in the following remark set down during his reading of the copy of the *New Science* which Charles Eliot Norton had lent him: " 'Mortgages' and 'Remainders' are pleasanter to peruse. And still it [*The New Science*] has many capital ideas—some of them quite Maine-y-Cornewall Lewisy—enough to keep me from throwing down the book, even while I curse at its clumsy phraseology" (*The Autobiography of Giambattista Vico*, translated by Max H. Fisch and Thomas G. Bergin [Ithaca: Cornell University Press, 1944], p. 102). Maine's importance is also stressed strongly by Elio Gianturco, who describes the year 1861, the date of publication of Maine's classic *Ancient Law*, as an *annus mirabilis* (Gianturco, "Vico's Significance in the History of Legal Thought," p. 328). A helpful introduction to the work of Maine from the perspectives of the present essay will be found in a doctoral dissertation in sociology done by Donald Nielsen at the Graduate Faculty of the New School for Social Research in 1972.

[30] Cf. Benjamin Nelson, "*De Profundis* . . . ," *Sociological Analysis* 35 (Summer 1974): 129–142.

dence, international law, and the theory of society; both took sharp exception to the uniformitarian elements in the assumptions of the theorists of natural rights, natural law, and social contract.[31]

It may still be too early to answer a number of questions which the foregoing evidence will doubtless suggest to the participants in the present symposium. However, it may help to add a closing reflection: One may surely say that Vico was in many profound respects a forerunner of a comparative history and sociology in civilizational perspective. Nonetheless, his horizons need to be seen as understandably different from those of such men as Maine, Durkheim, Mauss, and Weber. These later thinkers confronted a vastly more complex and global reality of pulsating structures—new as well as old—of economies, societies, polities, civilizational communities and intercivilizational encounters. Vico's thought in this sphere was in the main concentrated on the earlier histories and cultures of the West, and his work also continued to the end to include strong stress upon the prescriptive application of juridical frames of reference which, as Werner Stark has emphasized, ultimately trace back to the tradition illustrated by Plato in his *Laws*.[32]

BENJAMIN NELSON

Vico and "History"*

It seems to me that an important aspect of Vico's significance in the intellectual history of Western civilization lies in the fact that he wrote at a particularly important juncture in this intellectual history. This was a time at which the first primary crystallization of thought in the field of physical science had been completed or was nearing completion and that parallel developments in other scientific fields were at the very most in their infancy or had hardly been heard from at all.

---

[31] Cf. Benjamin Nelson, "Communities, Societies, Civilizations," in M. Stanley, ed., *Social Development* (New York: Free Press, 1972), esp. at pp. 111–112.

[32] This stress is particularly strong in Vico's so-called "Practic of the New Science," which is now available in a translation by Thomas G. Bergin and Max H. Fisch in Giorgio Tagliacozzo and Donald P. Verene, eds., *Giambattista Vico's Science of Humanity* (Baltimore: Johns Hopkins University Press, 1976), pp. 451–454.

As is the case with many other parts of human culture and more generally human action, the intellectual world has been subject to a long-standing and complex process of differentiation. A particularly important phase of this process began in the Renaissance when a new order of attention came to be paid to the secular environment and affairs of man. The focus of the Renaissance, of course, occurred in Vico's own Italy with a great efflorescence of art and of early modern science (symbolized by the figure of Galileo). As Werner Stark pointed out in his paper, Newton's *Principia*, the culminating formulation of the new science of mechanics, was published when Vico was nineteen. I wonder how greatly he was influenced by this particular book, but he was an Italian of the late Renaissance and surely was greatly influenced by the achievements in physical science which culminated with Newton.

It was central to the viewpoint of Vico, however, that the new physical science was not simply a matter of the impress on human thinking of the sheer facticity of the physical world, but was a human achievement. It seems to me that Vico's significance can be viewed in the context of his very early attempt, as several of the authors have noted, to see the human situation "whole" and particularly to see it from the point of view of the whole individual human person. From this point of view, the fact that Vico used the word science in the title of his most important work seems to me to be of great significance. It is clearly to be translated as "the new science." This at least can connote man's endeavor to develop an intellectual or cognitive picture of his situation and his work. The significance of Vico, from this point of view, consists in the broader setting in which he attempted to place the physical science achievements which were approaching culmination in his time.

The cultural foundations of many of the disciplines other than physical science were laid during the period following Vico's work. We need only recall that the outlines of modern chemistry, especially by Lavoisier, crystallized before the end of the eighteenth century. And the eighteenth century saw the beginnings of modern biological science, a crucial step of course going back to the seventeenth century and the discoveries of Harvey; Linnaeus was an eighteenth-century figure. These developments reached a first great culmination in the work of Darwin, shortly after the middle of the nineteenth century.

The eighteenth century after Vico also saw certain of the fundamental beginnings of social science, building on philosophical foundations which had been laid down particularly in the work of

Hobbes and Locke in the previous century. The eighteenth century saw the emergence of the physiocratic school of economic thought which was followed by that of the so-called "classical economics" centering in Great Britain. The first great figure of the latter development was Adam Smith, whose great work *The Wealth of Nations* was published in the fabulous year 1776. The more technical theory, however, was a nineteenth-century accomplishment in which the names of David Ricardo and John Stuart Mill stand out most prominently.

The classical economics, along with certain other developments such as association psychology and some very important developments of political thought, laid the foundation for a twentieth-century efflorescence of a new body of social science. The term of the generation which worked and thought in these areas near the end of the nineteenth century and in the very early years of the twentieth have had, I think, a special impact on our thinking and our world view. The science of economics was fundamentally reconstructed in the work of such figures as Alfred Marshall and Leon Walras, that of psychology saw the new behavioristic movement of such figures as Clark Hall and the psychoanalytic psychology of Sigmund Freud; these were followed in the next generation by the notable contributions to understanding of cognitive processes by Jean Piaget. On the more sociological side the great figures of Emile Durkheim and Max Weber stand out.

Perhaps a metaphor may be permitted. The development of physical science which was followed by chemical, biological, and social science played a kind of paternal role in the intellectual history from the earlier eighteenth century to the mid and late twentieth century. There was, however, at the same time, an ancient tradition which crystallized in the Renaissance period of what was later called humanistic studies. If physical science, grounded in the philosophy of René Descartes, can be considered to have played the paternal role in modern scientific development, I think it may be appropriately suggested that humanistic studies have played the "maternal" role. They have been the source out of which encouragements to broadening of the scope of the original physical-science synthesis have been derived; thus they have played a kind of "womblike" function. After all, human culture and knowledge have been created only by human action. It is in no simple sense a mere reflection of the "out there" facticity of external nature. This realization was particularly strong in Vico's work.

It is from this point of view that I venture to speak of history in the present context. Ever since the emergence of written language in the ancient civilizations, the availability of a written record has greatly heightened human self-consciousness about the past. From this point of view, only literate peoples have a history which can be documented on a level transcending oral tradition alone. The availability of history in this sense certainly underlies the development of concern with the historical record and with historical perspective. Expansion of the range of intellectual concern clearly has developed not only in the historical direction but also in a comparative one.

The use of universalizing conceptualization may, in our own cultural tradition, be said above all to center in the tradition of physical science and its philosophical underpinnings. Perhaps the temporal dimension is particularly focused in the human experience of continuity with a past and change from the conditions of that past. That is to say, in history. I think, therefore, that there is a good case to be made for the view that history has been the "mother" of one of the major aspects of modern intellectual traditions. It is above all this aspect which is only understandable in view of the fact that living human beings, anchored in particular times and places, have been the agents of developing our thought, our perception, our feelings about the world in which we live.

In this brief comment, I have stressed the intellectual aspect of the development at a particularly crucial early stage during which Vico lived. I think that the main precipitant of the processes with which I have been concerned will be found in the record of human thinking and of the cognitive precipitate of our experience.

The cognitive aspect, however, has never been and I presume will never be wholly dominant over the phenomena we call human experience. In one respect, a particularly notable contribution to the symposium on Vico was that of John O'Neill on the history of the human senses in Vico and Marx. Marx certainly played an important role in the development of thinking about man and society in the nineteenth century. Mr. O'Neill, however, particularly stresses what he calls the "poetic economics" of Marx. (He characterizes "poetic economics" as a matter of inspiration of human sentiment rather than as a strictly cognitive understanding of human problems.) I might differ from Mr. O'Neill on certain problems regarding the historic significance of Marx and Marxian economics, but I think we cannot afford to neglect the fact that the cognitive enterprise of human culture must be put in a matrix which involves what O'Neill calls "poetry" as well as knowledge. How far this also applies to Vico, I am not altogether certain.

TALCOTT PARSONS

---

* I am writing this brief comment after, not before, the conference which took place in New York at the end of January, 1976. I was scheduled to act as chairman of the meeting on the afternoon of January 31 (the second session on Vico and Sociology), but was unfortunately prevented from being present by an unexpected illness, fortunately proving to be temporary. I have therefore had to rely on the written papers of the participants in that session and the one held on the morning of the same day, without benefit of hearing the actual discussions.

On the
Heroic Mind / BY GIAMBATTISTA VICO

Translators' Note: We have used as our principal text *G. B. Vico: Opere*, edited by Fausto Nicolini, vol. 7: *Scritti vari e pagine sparse* in Scrittori d'Italia, 174 (Bari, 1940), pp. 3–20, with the emendations included in the Appendix to vol. 8 in the same series, Scrittori d'Italia, 183 (1941), pp. 265–266: hereafter, *Nicolini*. A second text available to us for comparison was *Giambattista Vico: Opere*, edited by Francesco Sav. Pomodoro, vol. 1 (Naples, 1858), pp. 260–269: hereafter, *Pomodoro*. Where, using this, we detected one or two additional typographical errors in *Nicolini*, or in a few cases preferred the reading in *Pomodoro*, this is indicated in the footnotes. We are indebted to Nicolini not merely for the above but for his translation into Italian of "De mente heroica" in *Giambattista Vico: Opere*, edited by Fausto Nicolini, in La letteratura italiana: storia e testi, vol. 43 (Milan-Naples, 1953), pp. 909–926.

On the Heroic Mind: An Oration
Given at the Royal Academy of Naples
October 20, 1732

To His Excellency, Count Aloys Thomas von Harrach, Viceroy of the Kingdom of Naples, a man most vigilant, virtuous and honorable, who instructed four nobly born sons in the illustrious arts of peace and war through the example of his ancestors and above all his own, this oration, which guides by precept the young, desirous of learning, to the acquisition of heroic wisdom, is dedicated by the Royal Academy of Naples in witness of its obedience and its gratitude for the many and great services he bestowed upon it.

My young listeners, you of such hopeful promise: for some considerable time now, this royal University has witnessed a lapse in that most profitable custom by which the academic

year was annually inaugurated by a solemn oration delivered
to you students with all due formality. And the appointed day
having come round once more, our recently invested honorable Prefect of Studies, a man of very great learning in all fields
and lavish in regard to the fullest possible provision of educational advantages for you, has seen fit to reinstate the old
custom. As for myself—I who have carried out the duties of
Professor of Eloquence in this very place for over thirty-three
years and am almost wasted away by the rigors of intellectual
work—I take it to be my task to bring before you a theme
which is wholly new. That theme shall not be youthfully
tricked out with lovelocks of apothegms and curled ringlets of
speech; no, it must be replete to the fullest possible extent
with the weight and gravity inherent in its own subject matter,
with the greatest fruitfulness for yourselves. This theme by its
own nature overflows with greatness, with splendor, with sublimity, and in speaking of it,

> I'd rather, I,
> Be like a whetstone, that an edge can put
> On steel, though itself be dull and cannot cut . . .[1]

Since you are roused by such promises and are ready to listen
with attentive welcome to something which concerns yourselves, I will, in the very first exordium of this oration, declare
it to you.

Noble students, you are to bend your best efforts toward
your studies, not surely with such an end in view as the
gaining of riches, in which the low money-grubbing crowd
would easily beat you out; nor for high office and influence,
in which you would be far outdone by the military and by
courtiers; and still less for that which leads philosophers on,
namely, the love of learning itself, enthralled by which almost

---

[1] Vico quotes Horace, *A.P.*, 304–305. Translation by Ben Jonson, *Horace, of the Art of Poetrie.*

all of them pass their whole lives withdrawn from the public light in order to get the full enjoyment from the tranquil working of their minds and nothing else. Something far more exalted than this is expected of you. "Well, but what is it?" one of you may say, marveling; "Are you asking of us something surpassing the human condition itself?" I do indeed so reckon it; but although surpassing, yet befitting that nature of yours.

I repeat: it is expected of you that you exert yourselves in your studies in order to manifest the heroic mind you possess and to lay foundations of learning and wisdom for the blessedness of the human race; by this course of action, not only will riches and wealth, even while you disdain them, accrue to you, but also honor and power will come looking for you, though you care for none of these things. When I speak of your manifesting the heroic mind through studies, I am not choosing those words lightly. If heroes are those who, as poets say or as they invent, were wont to boast of their divine lineage from "all-judging Jove," this much is certain: the human mind, independent of any fiction and fables, does have a divine origin which needs only schooling and breadth of knowledge to unfurl itself. So you see, I do ask of you things greatly surpassing the human: the near-divine nature of your minds—that is what I am challenging you to reveal.

"Hero" is defined by philosophers as one who seeks ever the sublime. Sublimity is, according to these same philosophers, the following, of the utmost greatness and worth: first, above nature, God Himself; next, within nature, this whole frame of marvels spread out before us, in which nothing exceeds man in greatness and nothing is of more worth than man's well-being, to which single goal each and every single hero presses on, in singleness of heart. By the report of just such good deeds spread far and wide amongst humankind—that voice crying abroad through all nations and peoples which Cicero elegantly calls by the name of "glory"—the hero generates for himself an immortal name. Therefore from the very start you must direct your studies toward Almighty God; and next, for the sake of His glory Who commands us to care for the whole human race, toward the well-being of all mankind. To it then, my young auditors, born in your turn for the greatest and best! Heroic in mind, turn your heart and will, brimming over with God, to the pursuit of your studies, and then, purged and purified of all earthly desires, put to the test, by the giant strides you will make, that divine truth: "The fear of the Lord is the beginning of wisdom."

For the mind, which takes pleasure in the divine, the infinite, the eternal, cannot *not* tackle the sublime, not attempt the monumental, not accomplish the outstanding. This is in no way a rash point of view: witness men of piety (I think of Cardinal Caesar Baronius and many others) who, when they turned their minds to scholarship, burned the midnight oil to such good purpose, a certain divine grace aiding, that they produced works one may marvel at, for their solidity as much as for their originality and learning.

While with heroic mind you are making your bow to wisdom on this first threshold, survey with swelling hearts the scene exhibited here before your eyes. Seated on your right, these reverend senior members of the university, marked out by their titles and insignia of honor, represent that public education which His Imperial Majesty Charles VI of Austria, King of the Spains, has provided in this place for your instruction. Just as in the school of courage he has prepared for himself in field and battle line military leaders of utmost valor for the protection of the Holy Roman Empire and its appanages, so too in the school of wisdom may he produce the like from among you in this sheltered spot to bless those same dominions. To this he invites you, both by the numerous privileges in law accorded you, and by the outstanding honors bestowed principally on your[2] account upon the official ranks here before you—you the co-equal hope of the commonwealth, the second especial preoccupation of our supreme

---

[2] *Nicolini* has "tua"; *Pomodoro*, correctly, "vestra."

ruler. His imperial administrator, His Excellency Count Aloys
Thomas von Harrach, who with supreme courage and wisdom
auspiciously presides as Viceroy over this Kingdom of Naples,
so zealously fosters this our seat of learning, and befriends it
so generously that in the space of three years (before this it
would have taken a century) he has nominated to the Em-
peror no less than five professors from this assembly for
investiture as royal bishops. Consider, and again I say consider, what models of learning they must be. Each and every
one of them has stored up in his memory by the command of
each over his own discipline the principal writers in every field
of learning, in all periods of history and all the literate cultures of mankind, so as to have them ready to hand for your
benefit. Furthermore, where they see this to be needful and
profitable, they present them to you with explanations, correc-
tions, and commentary of their own. Each one had to pass the
test of giving a formal lecture to the members of his own
faculty which had to be prepared within very narrow limits of
time, and only after that examination were they elected to this
their present rank of professor. What honor, what reverence
you ought to pay them, you can realize by this fact: look at the
Ministers of State, so many and so noble, seated on their left.
By occupying that exalted station they acknowledge that they
have to thank this university for the wisdom by virtue of which
they have been called to the highest honors in the state. Let
such all-sufficing proofs of achievement here before you con-
jure up a largeness of spirit in yourselves. Show forth that
loveliest mark of magnanimity: the being docile in the best
sense, biddable, grateful to these truly erudite professors of
yours as they chasten you, instruct you, set you to rights.
Their desire is that your estate be a shining ornament to this
city of ours, resplendent not only in Italy but, one may say,
throughout Europe. From patriotism, then, they devote themselves to you so that they may initiate you into every form of
learning, the general or encyclopedic, the esoteric or acroama-

tic. This in very truth is the promise contained in the phrase, "a university education."

It is absolutely clear that from these your preceptors you are to master all the branches of knowledge. Crippled and tottering—such is the education of those who throw all their weight into the study of just one particular and specialized discipline. The various disciplines are of the same nature as the virtues. Socrates used to maintain in his teachings that the virtues and the disciplines were one and the same, and totally denied that any one of them was ever genuine unless all the others were present also. So? A look of trouble on your faces? By what I have just said have I dashed your spirits? If so, you are doing a grave injustice to the divine wellsprings of your minds. Do not breed within you any indolent wishes about learning dropping down from heaven into your bosoms while you slumber. Stir yourselves up with a productive desire for wisdom. By your unceasing and undaunted labors, make trial of what you can do, put to the test how much you are capable of. Ply your gifts and energies in all possible directions. Stir your minds up, enkindle the divinity that fills you. If you take this course of action (poets come to it by nature, as it happens) you too will engender God-inspired marvels of your own, and surprise yourselves in the doing of it. What I am saying is weightily and clearly confirmed by Italian literati who in a forceful phrase, pertinent to our present subject of discussion, call a university a *Sapientia*.

Sapientia . . . Wisdom . . . Plato defines it as purge, curative, completion of the inner man. The man within, however, consists of both mind and soul, each part depraved through and through by original sin; the mind, created for truth, seething with errors and false opinions, the soul, born for virtue, racked by vices and pernicious desires. For this very reason, your university education has the following purpose and it is right that you should keep it fully in view: you have come together here, ailing as you are in mind and soul, for the treatment, the healing, the perfecting of your better nature. I do not want any idle scoffer making silly faces behind his hand at what I am saying. In confirmation of this I can adduce all those learned authors who, by a term consciously transposed from bodies to minds, call universities by the name of "public gymnasia." Hospitals as such were unknown to the ancients, and just as the powers of the body were reinvigorated, strengthened, and multiplied by gymnastics carried on in the public baths, so too today the powers of the mind in universities. Once you have thought this over, you will perceive the immense benefit arising from your studies, namely, that you pay close attention to your university work in order that you may resolve not just to appear learned but truly to be so, because you will wish to be healed, restored, made perfect by wisdom. In all other gifts stemming from nature or good fortune, men are content with the semblance of their desires. Only in this one regard, namely, health, all cannot help desiring the very thing itself.

Once you have this goal in view—it is the true goal of wisdom—there follows a demand: those other far lesser things such as wealth and public renown must fall away from your minds. Even if you lay up riches and accumulate honors, you will not cease to push on—on and on—as you grow in learning. All dishonesty will be far removed from your minds, all puffery and play-acting, since your desire is set on true erudition, not on the mere semblance of it. Untouched by any feeling of jealousy toward others, you in your turn will be unaffected by any jealousy directed at yourselves, that feeling which consumes and tortures those avid of gain, ambitious of high place. What in their case is envy will amongst you turn into honorable rivalry. Since this goal we spoke of is a blessing open to everyone, beyond envy as are all divine things because they are infinite, you will yearn for your own δμοιοθειότητα[3]—that "image and likeness of god" in mind and equally in soul, immune from any contagion of the flesh.

---

3 *Nicolini,* mistakenly: δμοιθειότητα.

To proceed: those who are content with an inadequate stock of learning make such accusations as "inappropriate" or "off the mark" against the whole system of teaching in this university, where not only do individuals teach different things (or if they teach the same things, they do so by different proofs and different methods) but also they seem to teach in flat contradiction to one another. It is an awkward system, we admit; the best and most desirable plan should be uniform throughout. But such an apparently good method is nullified by three noble requirements essential to education: new discoveries, new truths revealed, new efforts better focused. Consequently, our method, which they find fault with, proves to be the best and this for the three related advantages, by no means negligible ones, it brings with it:

First, no one of you will have to swear an oath of fealty to any professor, as happens so often in the sectarianisms of the schools.

Next, you will not get totally absorbed, as can happen in private institutions, by any single period of human knowledge, the study of which is so transient that it no sooner arises than collapses, no sooner comes to the full than it is already obsolete; whereas learned laboring, which produces immortal works, has its being in eternity.

Lastly—and this touches our discussion most nearly—you will fully realize what each discipline imparts to the others (for each has some good in it) and what all contribute to that sum total itself, wisdom in its entirety, toward the laying-hold of which, noble young men, I admonish and exhort you with all the insistence and seriousness I can muster.

For this reason above all, attend the lectures of professors in all disciplines, with that aim in view which we have already set down: that their teachings may cure, heal, perfect all your faculties both of mind and soul. Thus metaphysics will free the intellect from the prison of the senses; logic will free the reasoning power from false opinions; ethics the will from corrupt desires. Rhetoric exists to ensure that the tongue does not betray nor fail the mind, nor the mind its theme; poetics to calm the uncontrolled turbulence of the imagination; geometry to hold in check innate errors; physics, in truth, to rouse you from the blank amazement with which nature and her marvels has transfixed you.

And still we are not at the greatest degree of good with which wisdom is dowered. With high expectation set before yourselves far more glorious things.

By the study of the languages which our Christian religion cultivates as her own, hold converse with the best-known nations of universal history: with the Hebrews in the most ancient tongue of all; with the Greeks, in the most elegant; with the Romans, in the most majestic. Seeing that languages are the natural vehicle, so to speak, of customs, through the Oriental languages which are necessary for the comprehension of the sacred tongue—Chaldean above all—let the Assyrians inspire you with magnificence in Babylon, greatest city of all; the Greeks with Attic elegance of life at Athens; the Romans with loftiness of spirit at Rome. Be present in mind, by your reading of histories, in the greatest empires which ever flourished on the face of the earth. In order to strengthen your prudence as citizens by examples, ponder the origins of peoples and races, how they grow, reach their highest point, fall away, and perish; how outrageous Fortune in her arrogance lords it over human affairs, and how, beyond Fortune, Wisdom maintains her steadfast and unshakable kingdom. But, by heaven, for a delight inexpressible, since most proper to man's nature with its strong bent toward unity, read the poets! Observe their cast of characters, people from all walks of life, in the ethical, the domestic, the political realm, sharply delineated according to the pure ideal type, and by that very fact most real. Compared with these ideal types, men in everyday life will seem rather to be the unreal characters, for where men are not consistent their lives do not cohere. So consider, with a certain godlike mind, human nature as portrayed in the fables of great poets: even in its wickedness it is most beautiful, because always self-consistent, always true to itself, harmonious in all its parts, even as the aberrant prodigies and malignant plagues[4] of nature are perceived by Almighty God as good and beautiful in the eternal order of His Providence. Once you have read great poets and thrilled with delight, read now, to be caught up in an admiration every whit as great, the sublime orators, whose art is marvelous in its adaptation to our flawed human nature: appealing to the passions originating in the body, they twist men's minds around, no matter how settled, into wishing the direct opposite. In this, moreover, Almighty God excels and He alone, but by His own vastly different ways of triumphant grace, Who draws the minds of men to Himself by heavenly delight, no matter how pinned down they are by earthly passions.

From these matters we may proceed to the sublime themes of nature. With geography as guide on that long march, make the circle of the whole range of lands and seas with the sun. Trace out, with astronomy's observations, the swooping tracks of the comets, those sightless couriers of the air. Let cosmography set you down at that spot where "the final ramparts of the universe go up in flames."[5] Further yet, let metaphysics, outpassing nature, lead you forth into those blessed and infinite fields of eternity. Once there, insofar as this is permitted to our finite minds, behold among the Divine Ideas those countless forms already created and those which could come to creation if (as is actually not the case) this world would endure forever.

Make your way in this fashion through all three worlds, of things human, things natural, things eternal, and by learning and scholarship cultivate the godhead, so to speak, inherent in your minds. For in truth these sublime cogitations assuredly enjoin a hope that you will fashion for yourselves souls so lofty and upstanding that you will hold as infinitely beneath you all

---

4 We have accepted *Pomodoro's* "errantia" and "malignas" for *Nicolini's* "errantis" and "malignae."

5 Lucretius 1. 73.

delights of the senses, all riches and wealth, positions of power and honor, and spurn them all.

Concerning the choice of authors,[6] the wise administrators of this royal Academy have amply provided for your welfare in their program. According to that maxim of Quintilian's: "When it comes to teaching, the best authors ought to be singled out," you may, by attending the lectures dealing with these, succeed in acquiring the whole body of knowledge. I cite as example, in theology, the sacred books of the Old and New Testament, of which the Catholic Church offers the authoritative and correct interpretation. Her unbroken tradition, going back all the way to the time of the Apostles, has with solemn fidelity preserved that text in enduring archives of ecclesiastical history. Turning to jurisprudence: the *Corpus juris* of Justinian, most trustworthy witness of Roman antiquities, storehouse of Latin eloquence, most carefully stocked and preserved, the inviolable treasury of human laws. In medicine: Hippocrates above all, who earned the undying praise: "Never deceiving, by none deceived." In philosophy: Aristotle for the main, and where he is found wanting, other philosophers of outstanding reputation. And in the rest of the disciplines, other authors of equally distinguished rank.

To further your reading of these authors, the most exalted in all recorded history, the eminently learned professors here will instruct you by their commentaries, pointing out with their finger, as it were, the reasons why those authors excelled, each in his own branch of learning. This type of commentary will beguile you, from the beginning of your studies, into thumbing and poring over the best authors day and night. Further, it will stimulate you to shape in your minds more perfectly that Idea to which in all fields of knowledge men of genius are conformed. Hence, from being examples for you to follow, they will become exemplifications of that Idea. Thus, in going back to their original archetypes, you

---

[6] We have taken *Pomodoro's* "de Scriptorum delectu" for *Nicolini's* "descriptorum delectu."

could very well rival these men of genius and even outstrip them. In this way and in this alone are the arts and sciences refined, increased, brought to completion. And there is no excuse for those who wear out their entire scholarly careers in reading second-rate authors, not to mention those even worse—authors scarcely recommended to them in this university's program of studies.

All the while that you are under instruction, concentrate solely on collating everything you learn so that the whole may hang together and all be in accord within any one discipline. For this task your guide will be the very nature of the human mind which rejoices in the highest degree in that which forms a unity, comes together, falls into its proper place; as witness the Latin, which seems to have derived *scientia*—that pregnant noun—from the same root that *scitus* comes from, meaning the same thing as "beautiful." It follows that just as beauty is the due proportion of the members, first each to each and secondly as a whole, in any outstandingly lovely body, so knowledge should be considered as neither more nor less than the beauty of the human mind, and once men have been captivated by this, they assuredly do not heed bodily forms, how radiant soever. So far are they from being disturbed by such things!

Once that habit of comparison has been established, you will acquire the capacity to compare the sciences themselves each with each, which go to make up, as celestial members, the divine body, so to speak, of wisdom as a whole. According to Pythagoras, this is what human reason is: the bringing together and comparison of intellectual entities, a process which he either explained or obfuscated by using numbers as an example of it. In this way you will bring all of human reason to its perfection, after the likeness of a most pure and clear-shining light, its rays directed wherever you turn the mind's eye, so that what they call "the universe of knowledge" and all its parts are seen to come together, answer one another, and stand as one, in any single thought you may be having, and, as

it were, in any one point. And there you have it: the crowning
exemplar of the man of unalloyed wisdom!

To what particular discipline above all others will you apply
yourselves (for in order to be useful to your country you must
pursue one in particular)? Your innate ability will teach you
what that discipline is by the delight you feel in learning it as
over against others. Nature, which Almighty God gives you as
your guardian for this purpose, uses that yardstick so that you
may recognize where[7] your willing and ready Minerva waits.
Although nature is the safest guide, I who now urge you on to
the greatest and best do not consider that to be the most
illuminating way. For often a man has capacities for the highest and best hidden within him and so deep asleep as to be
almost completely or indeed completely unperceived by their
possessor. Cimon the Athenian (you all know the story), a dull
inert man, was desperately in love with a young girl; when she
announced in jest—as if this would be an impossibility for
him— that she would love him if he became an officer in the
army, the man enlisted, and ended up a very famous general
in the field. Socrates was born with a marked propensity for
wrongdoing, but, once converted to the pursuit of wisdom by
a divine impulse, he came to be known as the one who first
called down philosophy from heaven, and earned the title
"father of all philosophers." Let us set recent examples
alongside those of past ages, eminent men who in the doing of
something discovered, through the discernment of others, astonishing capabilities hitherto unknown to themselves. Cardinal Jules Mazarin comes on the scene on his own account as a
courtier of private means, a soldier in the ranks and a legal
practitioner. However, on one occasion after another there
arose matters of state which were assigned to him wholly
unexpectedly by persons of the highest degree, and he became an extremely able statesman, privy to the secret counsels
of Louis XIV, King of France, and dying only after a long

[7] *Pomodoro's* "ubi," for *Nicolini's* "ibi."

term of power—a very rare instance of great good fortune. Francesco Guicciardini practiced law in the Roman courts, until the popes of his time, against any desire or wishes of his, made him governor over a number of cities in the papal jurisdiction. When Charles VIII in the French wars threw all Italy into turmoil, Guicciardini on the orders of the papacy negotiated a number of very crucial affairs arising out of the war. And this was the reason why he turned his energies to chronicling the Italy of his time, becoming easily the greatest of all historians writing in the Italian language. In view of all this, let the eyes of your mind rove widely, exercise your talents full circle, pry out your veiled and hidden capacities, that you may recognize your unknown and perhaps superior talents.

After you have traversed the whole circle of knowledge, you must pursue whatever discipline you have chosen with a more exalted spirit even than that shown by learned men themselves. (Let me set out my general meaning with a few examples.) Do not practice medicine merely in order to work successful cures; nor jurisprudence in order to offer sage legal opinion; nor theology simply in order to watch over correct doctrine in sacred matters. Rather, following the precedent given you in lectures and readings, you must employ in your homework the same grandeur of spirit, the same sublime mastery. And so this kind of reading and listening to those undying works of the chief authors will build up in you a nature accustomed to excellence, which will of its own accord lead you on to employ those very authors as ever-present judges in your private studies. Put this question over and over again to your innermost selves: Supposing you are in medicine (I am going back to the examples already given)—"What if Hippocrates himself were to hear what I am thinking and writing?" If in law—"What if Cujas heard this?" In theology—"What if Melchior Cano heard it?" For whoever sets up as his critics authors who have lasted throughout the ages cannot but produce works which will also be admired by subsequent generations. By these giant strides which you take along the main road to wisdom, you will easily make such progress that not one single one of you will say, "I wander along the byroads of the Muses,"[8] and you will bring to completion challenging tasks attempted but not carried through by men of great capabilities and learning, or else you will undertake things never yet attempted. You doctors (I am going to wind up my theme by using my previous examples) must lay down further aphorisms, using medical reports and case histories collected from every quarter—a distinction which up till now was vested for two thousand years and more in Hippocrates alone. You lawyers must embrace the whole of jurisprudence, working through inferences in case law, by rulings upon legal terms, in which branch of learning Aemilius Papinian was considered past master, and Jacques Cujas rose to preeminence above all others in an age teeming with learned interpreters of the law. (I might mention that on this task as a whole Antoine Favre made a beginning in his *Jurisprudentia papinianaea*, a man great not only in regard to his age but also in his knowledge of the law; he did not, however, live to complete it, whether discouraged by the difficulty as he went along, or surprised by death, who knows.) You theologians must establish a system of moral philosophy based on Christian doctrine—Cardinal Sforza Pallavicino put his hand to it in a courageous attempt, Pascal published his *Pensées* so full of insight but fragmentary, Malebranche failed in the very attempt. Read the great Verulam's *De augmentis scientiarum*—a book worth its weight in gold and, apart from a few passages, ever to be looked up to and borne in mind—and ponder how much of the world of learning does remain to be set to rights, filled in, disclosed.

Whatever you do, do not be taken in unawares by that opinion, springing either from envy or cowardice, which says that for this most blessed century of ours everything that could ever have been achieved in the world of learning has

---

[8] Lucretius 1. 926.

already reached its conclusion, its culmination, and perfection, so that nothing remains therein to be desired. It is a false opinion, stemming from scholards with petty minds. For this world is still young. To go back no further than the last seven centuries, four of which were overrun by barbarism, how many new inventions there have been, how many new sciences and arts discovered! The mariner's compass, ships propelled by sail alone, the telescope, the barometer of Torricelli, Boyle's air pump, the circulation of the blood, the microscope, the alembic of the Arabs, Arabic numerals, indefinite classes of magnitudes, gunpowder, cannon, cupolas in churches, movable type, rag paper, clockwork—each one a striking achievement and all of them unknown to antiquity. Hence there have come novelties in ships and navigation (and thereby a new world discovered and geography how marvelously expanded!), new observations in astronomy, new methods of timekeeping, new cosmographical systems, innovations in mechanics, physics, medicine, a new anatomy, new chemical remedies (which Galen so greatly desired), a new method of geometry (and arithmetic markedly speeded up), new arts of war, a new architecture, such an availability of books that they are as common as dirt now, such abundance of them that they grow wearisome. How is it that the nature of human genius is so suddenly exhausted that we must give up hope of any other equally goodly inventions?

Do not be discouraged, noble hearers: countless possibilities still remain, perhaps even greater and more excellent than those we have just enumerated. In the teeming bosom of nature and the busy marketplace of the arts, great things are there, laid out for all to see, destined for the good of humanity and overlooked until now simply because the heroic mind had not turned its attention that way. Great Alexander when he came to Egypt took in with one magnificent glance the isthmus dividing the Red Sea from the Mediterranean, where the Nile runs into the Mediterranean and Africa and Asia meet. He thought it a worthy site where a city might be

founded bearing his name, Alexandria, which straightway became the most frequented merchant city of Africa and Asia
and Europe, of the entire Mediterranean Sea, of the Ocean
and the Indies. The sublime Galileo first observed the planet
Venus "distinct with its duplicate horn"[9] and discovered marvels in cosmology. The towering Descartes observed the trajectory of a stone thrown from a sling, and thought up a new
physics. Christopher Columbus felt a wind from the Western
Ocean blowing in his face, and in the light of Aristotle's
hypothesis that winds arise from land masses, he guessed at
other lands beyond the high seas and discovered the New
World. The great Grotius paid serious attention to that one
remark of Livy's: "Peace and war have each their own laws,"
and produced admirable volumes entitled *De jure belli et pacis*
which, with certain passages excised, deserve to be called
"peerless." With such shining instances, examples so distinguished, before you, apply yourselves, young men born to
great and good things, to your studies, with heroic mind and
coequal greatness of soul. Cultivate knowledge as a whole.
Celebrate the near-divine nature of your minds. Take fire
from the god who fills you. Attend your lectures, read, study
long hours, with lofty spirit. Undergo herculean trials, which,
once passed, vindicate with perfect justice your divine descent
from true Jove, Him the greatest and best. Prove yourselves to
be heroes by enriching the human race with further giant
benefits. Riches and wealth, honor and power in this your
country will with little trouble follow upon these noblest of
services rendered to the human race. And even if these re-
wards fail to materialize, you are not going to be deterred.
Like Seneca you will receive them with equanimity, that is to
say, without exaltation, should they come; and, without dejec-
tion, if they take their leave, you will ascribe their loss to

---

9 To avoid giving the reader a sense of anachronism—this is, of course, from
"Ulalume" by Edgar Allan Poe.

Fortune's witless frenzy. And you will be satisfied with this divine and imperishable reward: that Almighty God Who as I said at the beginning enjoins upon us solicitude for the whole of humankind has chosen some of you[10] in particular for the revelation of His glory upon this earth.

TRANSLATED BY ELIZABETH SEWELL
AND ANTHONY C. SIRIGNANO

---

[10] *Nicolini* reads, mistakenly, "per quas"; *Pomodoro*, rightly, "per quos."

Notes on Contributors

Silvano Arieti
is Professor of Clinical Psychiatry at the New York Medical College. His most recent book is *Creativity: The Magic Synthesis* (1976).

Augusto Blasi
is Assistant Professor of Psychology, Boston University.

Werner J. Cahnman
is Professor Emeritus of Sociology, Rutgers University. He is the author of *Ferdinand Toennies: A New Evaluation* (1973).

Robert Paul Craig
is Assistant Professor of Philosophy and Education, St. Mary's College. He is editor of *Issues in Philosophy and Education* (1973).

Fred R. Dallmayr
is Professor and Chairman of the Department of Political Science at Purdue University. He is editor of *Materialenband zu Habermas' Erkenntnis und Interesse* (1974).

Amedeo Giorgi
is Professor of Psychology at Duquesne University. He is the author of *Psychology as a Human Science* (1970).

John Michael Krois
is Visiting Assistant Professor at the Technische Universität Braunschweig.

Sir Edmund Leach
is Provost of King's College, Cambridge. He is the author, among other works, of *Claude Lévi-Strauss* (1970).

Michael Littleford
is Associate Professor in Foundations of Education at Auburn University.

Joseph Maier
is Professor of Sociology at Rutgers University. His most recent work is *The Future of Democracy in Latin America* (1975).

Rollo May
is a psychoanalyst, writer, and lecturer. His most recent book is *The Courage to Create* (1975).

Michael Mooney
is Special Assistant to the Executive Vice President for Academic Affairs, Columbia University, and Associate Director, Institute for Vico Studies, New York.

George Mora
is Medical Director of the Astor Home and Clinics for Children, Rhinebeck, N.Y., and Research Associate in the Department of the History of Science and Medicine at Yale University. He is the co-editor of *Psychiatry and Its History* (1970).

Benjamin Nelson
is Professor of Sociology and History in the Graduate Faculty of the New School for Social Research. He is the author of *The Idea of Usury: From Tribal Brotherhood to Universal Otherhood* (2nd ed., 1969).

John O'Neill
is Professor of Sociology at York University. His most recent book is *Making Sense Together* (1974).

Talcott Parsons
is Professor of Sociology at Harvard University. His books include *The Structure of Social Action* (1949), *The Social System* (1951), and *The System of Modern Societies* (1971).

Henry J. Perkinson
is Professor of Educational History at New York University. His most recent book is *200 Years of American Educational Thought* (1976).

Elizabeth Sewell
is Joe Rosenthal Professor of Humanities at the University of North Carolina at Greensboro. Her most recent book is *Signs and Cities* (1968).

Jerome L. Singer
is Professor of Psychology at Yale University. His most recent book is *The Inner World of Daydreaming* (1975).

Anthony C. Sirignano
is working on a doctoral dissertation on Aristotle's *Politics* at Princeton University.

Werner Stark
is Professor Emeritus of Sociology at Fordham University. His most recent book is *The Sociology of Religion: A Study of Christendom* (1972).

Giorgio Tagliacozzo
is Director of the Institute for Vico Studies in New York. He is editor with Donald Phillip Verene of *Giambattista Vico's Science of Humanity* (1976).

Molly Black Verene
compiled "Critical Writings on Vico in English" in *Giambattista Vico's Science of Humanity*.

Sheldon H. White
is Professor of Psychology at Harvard University. His most recent book is *Human Development in Today's World* (1976).

NAME INDEX

(Page numbers in *italics* refer to footnotes)